BYZANTIUM AND THE EARLY ISLAM

This book presents an inquiry into a fundamental historical problem in early Byzantine history: why the Byzantine Empire failed to contain emergent Islam in the new religion's initial years, and in particular how and why the Byzantines first lost Syria, Palestine, Mesopotamia, and Armenia before a partial recovery.

Using Greek and Arabic as well as other primary sources (including coinage) in the light of recent advances in late Roman, early Islamic, and Byzantine studies, Professor Kaegi assesses imperial conditions on the eve of the appearance of Islam, including ethnic stereotypes, military and religious miscalculations, dangerous strains and inertia in obsolescent fiscal, military, and political institutions and attitudes, as well as some principal military campaigns and battles. He places local officials' and civilians' collaboration with the Muslims in a longer late Roman context, and shows that it was neither unique to the seventh century nor was it primarily the result of Christian doctrinal disputes. Byzantine stabilization and resilience appeared in intellectual rationalizations of defeat and in institutional transformations and readjustments: demarcation of new borders, improvisations in new military commands and controls to prevent or discourage local collaboration with the Muslims, and new fiscal measures, all intended to prevent further disintegration of the empire.

BYZANTIUM
AND THE EARLY ISLAMIC CONQUESTS

WALTER E. KAEGI
Professor of History, University of Chicago

CAMBRIDGE
UNIVERSITY PRESS

Published by the Press Syndicate of the University of Cambridge
The Pitt Building, Trumpington Street, Cambridge CB2 1RP
40 West 20th Street, New York, NY 10011–4211, USA
10 Stamford Road, Oakleigh, Melbourne 3166, Australia

First published 1992
Reprinted 1993
First paperback edition 1995

Printed in Great Britain at the University Press, Cambridge

A catalogue record for this book is available from the British Library

Library of Congress cataloguing in publication data

Kaegi, Water, Emil.
Byzantium and the early Islamic conquests / Walter E. Kaegi.
p. cm.
Includes bibliographical references and index.
ISBN 0 521 41172 6
1. Byzantine Empire – History – 527–1081. 2. Islamic Empire – History – 622–661. I. Title
DF553.K34 1991
949.5 – dc20 91–14801 CIP

ISBN 0 521 41172 6 hardback
ISBN 0 521 48455 3 paperback

To Louise, Fritz, and Christian

CONTENTS

ILLUSTRATIONS

MAPS

PLATES

Contemporary allusions on Byzantine coins, Muslim imitations of Byzantine coins and reformed coinage: nos. 1–5 are on Plate I; nos. 6–10 are on Plate II. *pages 208–9*

PREFACE

I began to investigate this topic in the middle of the 1970s, after giving a lecture on it in the University of Chicago Islamic Civilization course, and a paper at the First Annual Byzantine Studies Conference at the Cleveland Museum in October, 1975. I have subsequently explored some of my conclusions in other courses at the University of Chicago, at the Byzantine Studies Conference, and in conversations and consultations with undergraduate and graduate students.

I wish to acknowledge the financial assistance of a number of institutions that have helped me to complete *Byzantium and the Early Islamic Conquests*: the American Council of Learned Societies for a Fellowship (which was supported by funding from the National Endowment for the Humanities) that I used in Paris in 1978–9; the Division of Social Sciences of the University of Chicago for almost annual Divisional Research grants during the course of this project; the Penrose Fund of the American Philosophical Society for grants in 1979 and 1985; the American Research Center in Egypt for a grant that I used in Cairo in the summer of 1979; the Center for Byzantine Studies, Dumbarton Oaks Research Library of Harvard University for a Fellowship for Autumn, 1980; the Council for the International Exchange of Scholars for a Fulbright Fellowship to Syria and Jordan during the summer of 1984; and the School of Historical Studies, the Institute for Advanced Study, for a Membership in 1984–5. I wish to express my gratitude for the award of a Fulbright grant in Islamic Civilization for Iraq during the summer of 1988 and for Fellowships from the National Endowment for the Humanities and the John Simon Guggenheim Memorial Foundation in 1988–9 and 1990–1 respectively.

I also wish to thank the Joseph Regenstein Library of the University of Chicago, the Library of the Sorbonne, the Byzantine libraries of the Collège de France and the Seminar of Byzantine and Near Eastern Christian History of the Université de Paris I, Panthéon-Sorbonne, the Firestone Library of Princeton University, Widener Library of Harvard, the Institut d'Etudes Arabes in Damascus, the American Research Center in Egypt, and the American Center for Oriental Research in Amman. These facilities were invaluable.

Many scholars assisted me in countless ways. I owe a great debt to the ground-breaking researches, learning, and hospitality of Irfan Shahid and my colleague Fred M. Donner. Helpful advice and criticisms have come from R. W. Thomson, Michael Bates, Lawrence I. Conrad, Donald Whitcomb, Yūsuf Ghawanmā, Fawzi Zayadine, Ahmad Shboul, William Metcalf, Robert Edwards, Jaroslav Stetkevych, and J. M. Fiey. Nadine Posner generously shared her impressive dissertation with me, while Dr. Robert Schick gave me much archaeological, epigraphic, and critical advice. David Olster and Brannon Wheeler discussed ideas. Hélène Ahrweiler, Adnan Bakhit, Glen W. Bowersock, Gilbert Dagron, Alain Ducellier, Herbert Hunger, David Jacoby, and Paul Walker enabled me to present my researches and conclusions for critical evaluation by many scholars. I particularly thank Professor A. A. Duri, Faculty of Arts, University of Jordan, for reading the manuscript and giving me valuable critical comments.

I also wish to thank the Faculty of Letters, University of Baghdad, the Directors and staff of the Iraqi Museum, and the Mosul Museum for their generous hospitality and assistance to my researches. My graduate students and the staff of the Map Room of the University of Chicago Joseph Regenstein Library gave me invaluable assistance. Dr. Thomas Weber, Director of the German Protestant Institute for Archaeology in Amman assisted my travels and research in Jordan. I am grateful to the many other scholars and local authorities in Iraq, Israel, Jordan, and Syria who facilitated my travels and researches in their respective countries.

I also wish to acknowledge my gratitude to the American Numismatic Society, the Trustees of the British Museum, and the Trustees of Harvard University, Dumbarton Oaks, for permission to use photographs of coins from their respective collections.

I am very grateful for the assistance of William Davies, Senior Editor at Cambridge University Press. I also thank Lyn Chatterton and Margaret Deith for their critical skills and their efforts in producing and editing this book. To all the above I give my deepest thanks. Finally, I thank my wife Louise for her indispensable editorial advice, patience, and encouragement during the long course of this project.

I use standard transliteration of Arabic and Greek words, except for those words and names that familiar usage in English has made most recognizable in their traditional spelling. Translations are my own except where otherwise acknowledged.

I thank Professor H. A. R. Gibb, who introduced me to Islamic Civilization and examined me on it in part of my Ph.D. oral general examinations at Harvard.

ABBREVIATIONS

AABSC	*Abstracts, Annual Byzantine Studies Conference*
AB	*Analecta Bollandiana*
ADAJ	*Annual of the Department of Antiquities of Jordan*
ANSMN	*Museum Notes, American Numismatic Society*
BAR	*British Archaeological Reports*
BASOR	*Bulletin of the American Schools of Oriental Research*
BCH	*Bulletin de Correspondance Hellénique*
BGA	*Bibliotheca Geographorum Arabicorum*
1983 Bilād al-Shām Proceedings	*Proceedings of the Symposium on Bilād al Shām during the Byzantine Period* (1983 conference papers published in 1986), ed. by Muhammad Adnan Bakhit and Muhammad Asfour. Amman: University of Jordan and Yarmuk University, 1986.
1985 Bilād al-Shām Proceedings	*Proceedings of the Second Symposium on the History of Bilād al Shām during the Early Islamic Period up to 40 AH/640 AD. The Fourth International Conference on the History of Bilād al Shām* (1985 conference papers published in 1987), ed. by Muhammad Adnan Bakhit. Amman: University of Jordan and Yarmuk University, 1987.
1987 Bilād al-Shām Proceedings	*Proceedings of the Third Symposium, Fourth International Conference on the History of Bilād al-Shām during the Umayyad Period* (1987 conference papers published in 1989), English section, vol. 2, ed. by Muhammad Adnan Bakhit and Robert Schick. Amman: University of Jordan and Yarmuk University, 1989.
BMGS	*Byzantine and Modern Greek Studies*
BSOAS	*Bulletin of the School of Oriental and African Studies*, University of London
ByzF	*Byzantinische Forschungen*
Byzsl	*Byzantinoslavica*
ByzStratos	Stratos, Zia, ed., Βυζάντιον. Ἀφιέρωμα στὸν Ἀνδρέα Στράτο. *Byzance. Hommage à Andreas Stratos. Byzantium. Tribute to Andreas Stratos.* 2 vols. Athens 1986.
BZ	*Byzantinische Zeitschrift*

CBHB	*Corpus Bruxellense Historiae Byzantinae*
CC	*Corpus Christianorum*
CFHB	*Corpus Fontium Historiae Byzantinae*
CJC	*Corpus Juris Civilis*
CMH	*Cambridge Medieval History*
CSCO, SS	*Corpus Scriptorum Christianorum Orientalium, Scriptores Syri*
CSEL	*Corpus Scriptorum Ecclesiasticorum Latinorum*
CSHB	*Corpus Scriptorum Historiae Byzantinae*
CT	*Codex Theodosianus*
DMA	*Dictionary of the Middle Ages*
DOCat	Grierson, P., *Catalogue of the Byzantine Coins in the Dumbarton Oaks Collection and in the Whittemore Collection*
DOP	*Dumbarton Oaks Papers*
DRBE	Freeman, Philip and David Kennedy, eds., *The Defence of the Roman and Byzantine East*
EHR	*English Historical Review*
EI[1]	*Encyclopedia of Islam*, first edition
EI[2]	*Encyclopedia of Islam*, second edition
EJ	*Encyclopedia Judaica*
EO	*Echos d'Orient*
HSCP	*Harvard Studies in Classical Philology*
IEJ	*Israel Exploration Journal*
JAOS	*Journal of the American Oriental Society*
JÖB	*Jahrbuch der Österreichischen Byzantinistik*
JESHO	*Journal of the Economic and Social History of the Orient*
JRS	*Journal of Roman Studies*
JSAI	*Jerusalem Studies in Arabic and Islam*
Just. Nov.	Justinian I, *Novellae*, vol. 3, Th. Mommsen, ed. *Corpus Juris Civilis*
LA	*Liber Annuus Studium Biblicum Franciscanum*
MGH	*Monumenta Germaniae Historica*
NC	*Numismatic Chronicle*
ND	*Notitia Dignitatum*
OCP	*Orientalia Christiana Periodica*
PEF Palestine	*Palestine from the Surveys Conducted for the Committee of the Palestine Exploration Fund.* Compiled by George Armstrong and revised by Charles. W. Wilson and Maj. C. R. Conder. London: Stanford's, 1900
PG	Migne, *Patrologia Graeca*

PL	Migne, *Patrologia Latina*
PLRE	*Prosopographia of the Later Roman Empire*
PO	*Patrologia Orientalis*
RbK	*Reallexikon zur byzantinischen Kunst*
RE	*Paulys Realencyclopaedie der classischen Altertumswissenschaft*
REArm	*Revue des Etudes Arméniennes*
REB	*Revue des Etudes Byzantines*
ROC	*Revue de l'Orient Chrétien*
ROL	*Revue de l'Orient Latin*
Σύμμεικτα	Σύμμεικτα, Ἐθνικὸν Κέντρον Βυζαντινῶν Σπουδῶν (Athens)
TAPA	*Transactions of the American Philological Association*
Theoph., *Chron.*	Theophanes, *Chronographia*, ed. by De Boor
TM	*Travaux et Mémoires*, Paris
VV	*Vizantiiski Vremennik*
ZDMG	*Zeitschrift der deutschen Morgenländischen Gesellschaft*
ZDPV	*Zeitschrift des Deutschen Palästinas-Vereins*
ZRVI	*Zbornik, Radova Vizantološki Institut, Srpska Akad. Nauk.*, Belgrade

Chapter 1

THE PROBLEM OF BYZANTIUM AND THE EARLY ISLAMIC CONQUESTS

CHALLENGES IN THE SOURCES AND METHODOLOGY: INTRODUCTORY REMARKS

> The Roman emperors and Augusti were always of the same opinion, which I am telling you, not only those who stayed in Rome, but also those who stayed in Byzantium [Constantinople], including Constantine the Great, Julian, Jovian, and Theodosius. Sometimes they stayed in the east, and sometimes in the west, but they stayed in Byzantium [Constantinople] very little. At that time all the provinces were tranquil including all of Europe and Africa, and the best part of Asia as far as Euphratesia, and the lands of Adiabene, Armenia, Syria, Phoenicia, Palestine, and Egypt, and even the great and much-prized Babylon were subject to the Romans. But from the time great torpor fell on men, rather like an epidemic, nothing good has happened to the Roman Empire.[1]

Such was a late eleventh-century Byzantine retrospective diagnosis of the causes for the loss of so many former territories of the Roman Empire. The author, Kekaumenos, simply attributed the downfall of the empire to the proclivity of emperors to avoid leaving the capital for the provinces. This is an inquiry into only a part of the same phenomenon that vexed Kekaumenos: the character and causes of the Byzantine loss of Palestine, Syria, and Byzantine Mesopotamia to the Muslims in the 630s and 640s and the immediate consequences of these developments for the Byzantine Empire, especially Anatolia, for its armies, and for its worldview. The answer, of course, cannot be as easy or tendentious as was that of Kekaumenos, who did not even mention Islam as a possible cause. For some scholars of Islamic history, this subject may appear to be ill conceived, because for them there is no reason why the Muslims should not have defeated and supplanted Byzantium. No adequate Byzantine historical research exists on these

[1] Kekaumenos, *Soveti'i i Razzkaz'i Kekavmena*, ed. and trans. by G. G. Litavrin (Moscow: Nauka, 1972) 298.

problems, certainly none that includes the use of untranslated Arabic sources.

The subject of this inquiry is the initial military collapse and subsequent Byzantine search for a viable strategy against the Muslims. With great difficulty and after experimentation with various strategies and tactics, the Byzantines, unlike the Sassanian Persians, finally managed to regroup and began to stabilize a viable military front against the Muslims. The chronological termini are somewhat restricted: most events fall between 628, the date of the Byzantine Emperor Heraclius' peace arrangements with the Sassanians, and the middle of the 640s, when the Muslims had accomplished their conquests not only of Palestine and Syria but also of Egypt and Byzantine Mesopotamia. The broader historical background, of course, includes the history of Roman and early Byzantine relations with the Arabs, the Christological controversies, the conditions, grievances, and perspectives of the non-Greek populations of the above areas as well as Armenia, the economy of the empire, and its wars with Sassanian Persia in the sixth and especially in the early seventh centuries, between 602 and 628.

This study has been given relatively narrow chronological termini in order to attempt an inquiry into the actual Byzantine efforts to defend Palestine, Syria, and Byzantine Mesopotamia against the Muslims and the nature, causes, and consequences of that failure and the subsequent Byzantine success in persevering – although with grave difficulty – in Asia Minor. It is wrong to ignore both the historical background to the Muslims' invasions and their sequel. The actual conquests deserve reexamination for what they may reveal about the nature of Byzantine institutions and warfare at that time and about the reasons for the empire's failure to develop an adequate response to the early challenges, or stated in another way, the transformation of late Roman military, political, and social institutions and conditions into middle Byzantine, Islamic, and even medieval ones.

SOURCES AND SOURCE PROBLEMS

This study rests upon earlier scholars' painstaking criticism of sources, both Arabic and non-Arabic. Much scholarly attention has been given to the obscurities and contradictions in the Arabic sources. Much of that criticism is justifiable, yet non-Arabic sources tend to be short and have their own problems.[2] The date and the identity of the Armenian historian Sebēos are controversial, as are his sources, some of which appear to be Syriac.[3] He

[2] Most notably, the terse information in the Greek chronicles of Theophanes and Nicephorus, and those written in Syriac.

[3] Sebēos, *Histoire d'Héraclius*, trans. by F. Macler (Paris 1904). R. W. Thomson and Nina Garsoian have discovered many errors in the old Macler translation; there is a new critical

claims to draw on information from prisoners (probably Armenian, but possibly including other ethnic groups) who had fought the Muslims.[4] It is possible that he or his source did converse with Armenian soldiers who had fought in Byzantine Syria or in Persia against the Muslims. The eighth-century Armenian historian Ghevond also used Syriac sources for his earliest passages on the seventh century.[5] The references to seventh-century history in the *History of Taron* by Pseudo-Yovhannes Mamikonian are very suspicious.[6]

The extant Byzantine historical narratives and chronicles concerning the reign of Heraclius (610–41) are few in number and date from later centuries. Most important are the brief history of Nicephorus, from the late eighth century, and the chronicle traditionally identified as that of Theophanes, from the second decade of the ninth century. The important question of their sources and their use of sources is unresolved.[7] The Byzantine tradition contains bias and cannot serve as an objective standard against which all Muslim accounts may be confidently checked. Its contents require critical scrutiny too.

The few shreds of information about the Byzantine Emperor Heraclius' (610–41) role in the defense of Syria were not mere *topoi*, but it is worth considering what the rhetorical tradition had laid down as normal for the literary treatment of an emperor, namely, inclusion of praise of the emperor for avoiding the ambushes of the enemy while contriving those of his own for the enemy. Those who constructed their histories of Heraclius' reign may have been influenced, consciously or unconsciously, by an earlier rhetorical

edition of the Armenian text: *Pamut'iwn Sebeosi*, ed. by G. V. Abgarian (Yerevan: Acad. Arm. SSR, 1979), and a translation by Robert Bedrosian, *Sebēos' History* (New York: Sources of the Armenian Tradition, 1985). See: Mesrob K. Krikorian, "Sebēos, Historian of the Seventh Century," and Zaven Arzoumanian, "A Critique of Sebēos and his History of Heraclius, a Seventh-Century Document," in: *Classical Armenian Culture: Influences and Creativity*, ed. by Thomas J. Samuelian (University of Pennsylvania Armenian Texts and Studies, 4 [Philadelphia: Scholars Press, 1982]) 52–67, 68–78.

4 Sebēos, *Hist.* c. 30 (102 Macler); cf. Heinrich Hübschmann, *Zur Geschichte Armeniens und der ersten Kriege der Araber* (Leipzig 1875) 18, n.3.

5 Ghevond or Levontius, *History of Lewond the Eminent Vardapet of the Armenians*, trans. and comment. by Zaven Arzoumanian (Wynnewood, PA 1982).

6 Levon Avdoyan, "Pseudo-Yovhannēs Mamikonean's 'History of Taron': Historical Investigation, Critical Translation, and Historical and Textual Commentaries" (unpub. Ph.D. diss., Columbia University, 1985) c. lvii, pp. 212–20, 49–55.

7 Suda = Suidas, s.v., "Traianos," ed. by A. Adler (Leipzig 1935) 4: 582. Theophanes: A. Proudfoot, "Sources of Theophanes" esp. 426–38; Cyril Mango, "Who Wrote the Chronicle of Theophanes?," *ZRVI* 18 (1978) 9–18; P. Speck, *Das geteilte Dossier* (Bonn 1988) for an elaborate and complex analysis and most bibliography; Telemachos Loungis, "'Η πρώιμη βυζαντινὴ ἱστοριογραφία καὶ τὸ λεγόμενο 'μεγάλο χάσμα'," Σύμμεικτα 4 (Athens 1981) 49–85, makes some useful points. Cyril Mango, Introduction to his edn of Nicephorus, Patriarch of Constantinople, *Short History* (Washington: Dumbarton Oaks, 1990) 8–18.

tradition[8] that the ideal emperor should anticipate and avoid the ambushes of the enemy and instead prepare ones of his own for the enemy. Heraclius conforms to this in the scraps of Byzantine historical tradition: he warns his commanders against the danger of engaging the Arabs in open battle, but his commanders ignore his warning and fall into the very traps that he feared and cautioned against. Yet the existence of such a tradition requires that the investigator be aware of and prepared to evaluate and, if necessary, discount such reports. Such a rhetorical tradition may have goaded and influenced Heraclius himself, as well as his contemporary historians, into warning his commanders and soldiers against the artifices of their enemies.

Some unidentified and probably Syriac Christian historical source or sources provided some important information for the Byzantine historical tradition about the reign of Heraclius, including events such as Byzantine military actions against the initial Muslim invasions. These historical traditions, which originated while the Heraclian dynasty still ruled the Byzantine Empire, had to explain the potentially embarrassing if not disastrous final responsibility of the dynasty's founder, Heraclius, for the catastrophic loss of Egypt, Syria, Palestine, and Byzantine Mesopotamia. The creators of these traditions, or at least some of them, sought to protect the prestige of Heraclius and his dynasty from being sullied by these enormous defeats. All errors appear to fall on someone or something other than Heraclius: a narrow-minded eunuch who irritates Arabs, rebellious Armenian soldiers who proclaim their General Vahān emperor at the battle of the Yarmūk, Heraclius' illness, confused officials who erroneously make truces with the Muslims that Heraclius later rejects, and dust clouds at Yarmūk that hamper the vision of the embattled Byzantine soldiers. No responsibility attaches to Heraclius himself for these actions. A later layer of criticism attributes the defeats to Heraclius' arrogance and divine wrath for his mistaken compromise theological formula of Monotheletism (one will) in the raging Christological controversy over whether Jesus Christ had one or two natures. The historiography of the court of Heraclius systematically distorted the history of the immediately preceding imperial reigns, namely, those of Maurice and Phocas.[9]

The complete truth, of course, will probably never be known, but it is

[8] *Menander Rhetor*, ed. trans., and comment. by D. A. Russell, Nigel Wilson (Oxford: Oxford University Press, 1981) esp. 84–7.

[9] Michael Whitby, *The Emperor Maurice and His Historian* (Oxford: Clarendon, 1988), and David Olster, *The Politics of Usurpation in the Seventh Century: Rhetoric and Revolution in Byzantium* (Hakkert, 1993) on a conscious historiographical skewing of the respective reigns of Maurice, Phocas, and Heraclius to the benefit of the last emperor and his dynasty. W. H. C. Frend, *Rise of the Monophysite Movement* (Cambridge: Cambridge University Press, 1972); Friedhelm Winkelmann, "Die Quellen zur Erforschung des monoenergetisch-monotheletischen Streites," *Klio* 69 (1987) 515–59.

prudent to take a skeptical approach to the Byzantine traditions about the Muslim conquest, because invariably they seem – in a direct or indirect way – to attempt to deflect criticism of the Byzantine debacle from Heraclius to other persons, groups, and things. This is true even though to later generations, after the end of the Heraclian dynasty, Heraclius' religious policy of Monotheletism was abhorrent. The tone had already been set: to save his person from responsibility for the military disasters. Some of this tradition probably is echoed even in the Muslim sources. There are convergences and divergences in the Muslim and Byzantine images of Heraclius. There is no precise way to discount the efforts of the anonymous Heraclian historical tradition to deflect criticism from Heraclius, and to discover how much actual historical distortion resulted. The result may be a disinclination for such sources to say much about any of these most painful events, which it was better to pass over in silence.[10]

Among the few Latin sources of interest are the seventh-century history of Fredegarius and two eighth-century Spanish chronicles, all of which draw on some Byzantine and oriental historical traditions.[11]

PROBLEMS IN NON-HISTORICAL SOURCES

Non-historical sources present a number of challenges. First, the range of this category of Byzantine sources is vast. They can range from papyri to sermons (most notably those of Patriarch Sophronius of Jerusalem and St. Anastasius the Sinaite), poetry (especially that of Sophronius and George of Pisidia), correspondence often of a patristic provenance, apologetical treatises, including anti-Judaica – such as the *Doctrina Iacobi nuper baptizati* – apocalypses, hagiography, military manuals (in particular, the *Strategikon* of Maurice from the beginning of the seventh century), and other non-literary sources such as epigraphy, archaeology, and numismatics. Very competent studies exist for many of them. The authors of the most contemporary sources did not intend for their works to serve as historical accounts.[12]

10 Kaegi, "Initial Byzantine Reactions to the Arab Conquest," *ASRB* (this revised edn preferred).

11 Fredegarius, *Chronicon*, ed. by Bruno Krusch, MGH Scriptores Rerum Merovingicarum, T. 2 (Hanover 1888); and *Continuationes Isidorianae Byzantia Arabica et Hispana*, ed. by T. Mommsen, MGHAA, T. 11, CM2: 334–69; *Crónica mozárabe de 754. Edición crítica y traducción*, ed. by Jose Eduardo López Pereira (Zaragoza 1980); Jose Eduardo López Pereira, *Estudio crítico sobre la crónica mozárabe de 754* (Zaragoza 1980) 35–6, 95–9.

12 *Doctrina Iacobi nuper baptizati*, ed. by N. Bonwetsch, *Abhandlungen der Königlichen Gesellschaft der Wissenschaften zu Göttingen*, Philologisch-Historische Klasse n.s. vol. 12, no. 3 (Berlin 1910). Vincent Déroche, "L'Autenticité de l'"Apologie contre les Juifs' de Léontios de Néapolis," *BCH* 110 (1986) 661, rightly dates it shortly after 634, as does P. Crone, *Hagarism* (Cambridge 1977) 3–4; Sophronius, "Weihnachtspredigt des Sophronios," ed. by H. Usener, *Rheinisches Museum für Philologie* n.s. 41 (1886) 500–16.

None of these sources contains a coherent account of any of the campaigns of the Muslim conquests, but some do contain invaluable details that survive nowhere else. Some of them provide especially welcome information for the investigation of both *histoire événementielle* (roughly translated, "history of events") and the *histoire des mentalités*. In other words, these sources provide information that conforms well with the kinds of history that many historians want to write today, and they even offer some illumination of military events. But they require attentive reading.

The normal methodology for their utilization is, simply put, an old-fashioned patient reading and rereading of the texts for neglected evidence. Winnowing for the few grains of wheat among the chaff requires lots of work,[13] but even that effort and the reexamination of the assumptions, logic, and conclusions of earlier scholars can result in some valuable gleanings.

Another and most important problem with using these sources is not so much an historiographical one or their use of traditions or their possible contamination with Muslim traditions, which usually is not the case. The reality is that these Byzantine authors were not consciously striving to record historical accounts. They lack any coherent chronology. None of them can hope to present a coherent picture of the contemporary Byzantines or Muslims or of the Byzantine or Islamic world. Sermons and correspondence conform to the frames of reference, expectations, and formidable constraints and canons of traditional literary Greek prose style and therefore are restricted in how they refer to Arabs and to Islam.

What these sources can provide is some evidence for the impressions that some Byzantines held about Islam and Arabs, and miscellaneous valuable details, but not necessarily any accurate information or comprehension of the internal history and character of Islamic community and its polity. That is important in itself. Their authors' knowledge of events and conditions within the Arabian peninsula or Sassanian ʿIrāq both before, during, and immediately following the Muslim conquests, regions that they had never visited firsthand, is hopelessly vague and muddled. They likewise show no accurate detailed knowledge of Muslim religious thought and should not normally be used as authorities for it. That is a vain search. No single one of such texts will conveniently provide the scholar with a lot of evidence, and whatever they do offer requires cautious and prudent assessment.

There are additional methodological problems. It is hazardous to project back information on techniques of Muslim warfare and ways to combat Muslims from later Byzantine and Muslim military manuals to the era of the earliest conquests, from which no Byzantine military manual survives.[14]

[13] Jones, *LRE* vi.

[14] *Das Heerwesen der Muhammadener*, ed. by F. Wüstenfeld (Göttingen 1880).

With respect to testing the validity of evidence or traditions in Islamic sources the most valuable comparative studies may not be specific comparison with certain Byzantine sources, literary or non-literary. More relevant and more reliable are comparisons with the patiently constructed cumulative evidence about late Antiquity in the Middle East that a range of modern archaeologists, historians, sigillographers, and epigraphers have constructed. That body of evidence does not rest on any single fragile historical source or tradition. When Muslim sources refer accurately and consistently to late Roman, i.e., early Byzantine, place-names, official nomenclature, military units, and religious and secular leaders, other uncorroborated information in those texts also deserves very serious attention.

Enough scholarly investigation has taken place to create some awareness of the risks and limitations in trying to draw historical allusions out of hagiographic texts and patristic dialogues. Religious sources such as the Pseudo-Methodius apocalypse and the *Doctrina Iacobi nuper baptizati* (*c.* 634) contain valuable contemporary material in an incidental and naive context, but they must be treated with caution. Some very worthwhile information also exists in such texts as the *Vita* and *Miracula* (Θαύματα, "Miracles") of St. Anastasius the Persian (d. 628), and *The Passion of the Sixty Martyrs of Gaza* (probably written soon after 635).[15] These sources contain important information about Palestine immediately prior to and contemporary with the Muslim invasions. They contain enough incidental details for specialists to appreciate just how firmly they reflect contemporary Byzantine realities. But they provide no coherent description of events. Only disconnected scraps of information survive, yet such sources help us to understand contemporary conditions. There are no seventh-century or eighth-century Byzantine geographical and travel texts about the Islamic world, and for that matter, none survive from the immediately following several centuries. No Byzantine travelers left accounts about the early Islamic world.

The corpus of writings attributed to St. Anastasius the Sinaite, who was a monk on Mt. Sinai, who visited Egypt and Syria and probably died after 700,

[15] *Die Apokalypse des Ps.-Methodios* and *Die dritte und vierte Redaktion des Ps.-Methodios*, both ed. by Anastasios Lolos (Meisenheim am Glan: Verlag Anton Hain, 1976, 1978). Translations of Syriac: P. J. Alexander, *The Byzantine Apocalyptic Tradition* (Berkeley 1985) 36–51; critical edn, trans., and comment. by Francisco Javier Martinez, "Eastern Christian Apocalyptic in the Early Muslim Period" (Washington, DC: Catholic University of America, 1985); Harald Suermann, *Die geschichtstheologische Reaktion auf die einfallenden Muslime in der edessenischen Apokalyptik des 7. Jahrhunderts* (Frankfurt, Bern, New York: Peter Lang, 1985). Cf. David Olster, *Roman Defeat, Christian Response, and the Literary Construction of the Jew* (Philadelphia: University of Pennsylvania Press, 1994). I look forward to the researches of Bernard Flusin on St. Anastasius the Persian.

provide the earliest surviving explicit references in Greek to some Byzantine–Muslim battles and illuminate some details of the conquests and contemporary conditions and moods.

ARABIC HISTORIOGRAPHY

This investigation contributes no new material on the complex issues of criticism of Arabic sources, and the sources of those sources, except the perspectives of a Byzantinist, in the light of the latest interpretations of Byzantine and late Roman history. Excellent historical research and writing was characteristic of Aḥmad b. Yaḥyā al-Balādhurī (d. 892), who wrote the *Kitāb Futūḥ al-Buldān* or "Book of Conquests of the Countries [Lands]," a rich compilation of early traditions, many of which are conflicting, about the conquests, classified by region. Balādhurī also compiled his *Ansāb al-Ashrāf* ("The Genealogies of the Notables"), which concentrates on personalities but includes some references to events that are not found in his *Futūḥ*. Although far from perfect, Balādhurī does cite differing authorities for many of his traditions and points out some of their divergences. A number of the passages in his *Futūḥ* indicate that he had access to some early traditions that very probably derive ultimately from Greek or Syrian Christian sources, more likely oral rather than written ones. Some reflect an awareness of conditions existing at the time of the conquests. Yet he has also preserved many traditions that are suspicious, ones that sometimes reflect later juridical, religious, and fiscal reasoning and motivations and categories that cannot have been meaningful at the time of the original Muslim conquests. Some of Balādhurī's information is unique, while other pieces of it require careful critical control by comparison and weighing in the light of other sources, traditions, and historical information.[16]

Two of the best known and most reliable Arabic chronological histories of the conquests are those of al-Ṭabarī (AD 839–923) and al-Ya'qūbī (d. end of ninth or early tenth century).[17] al-Ya'qūbī wrote both a history, *Ta'rīkh*, and a surviving geographical treatise entitled *Kitāb al-Buldān*, or "Description of Lands." Their handling of Muslim traditions also has been and continues to

[16] Balādhurī, *Kitāb Futūḥ al-Buldān*, ed. by M. J. De Goeje (Leiden: Brill, 1866; repr.), henceforth cited as Balādhurī.

[17] Edition: Abū Ja'far Muḥammad b. Jarīr al-Ṭabarī, *Ta'rīkh al-rusūl wa l'mulūk* (*Annales*), ed. by M. J. De Goeje *et al.*, 15 vols. (Leiden: Brill, 1879–1901; repr. 1964); basic is Franz Rosenthal, *The History of al-Ṭabarī*, 1: *General Introduction* (Albany: State University of New York Press, 1989) 5–134, see translations in this and succeeding vols. Also, Aḥmad b. Abī Ya'qūb al-Ya'qūbī, *Ta'rīkh*, ed. by M. Th. Houtsma, 2 vols. (Leiden: Brill, 1883). Literature: L. I. Conrad, s.v., "Ya'qūbī, al-," *DMA* 12 (1989) 717–18.

be the subject of much scholarly debate. al-Ya'qūbī also wrote a now lost description of Byzantium. Both knew and recounted some essential features of late Roman, early Byzantine, and Sassanian Persian history. The scholarly investigation of their sources and associated historiographical problems has become increasingly sophisticated. Both contain much material of value, yet both histories require prudent assessment. One cannot speak of them alone, because one must also consider precisely which sources they are using in recounting specific events and information.

Another important source is the lengthy *Kitāb al-futūḥ* ("Book of Conquests") of Abū Muḥammad Aḥmad b. A'tham al-Kūfī, who was writing his work *c.* AD 819. It contains some useful traditions, but other sections of it contain fanciful and apologetical passages without any ring of authenticity or credibility. The *History* of Ibn Khayyāṭ al-'Uṣfurī is a relatively early historical compendium, which records some useful material. Ibn Sallām's *Kitāb al-amwāl* ("Book of the Treasuries" or "Book of Finances") includes some early traditions and, moreover, was written by an author who was descended on one side from a Greek. He may have had access to unique Byzantine or other Christian materials. Ibn Sa'd's *Kitāb al-Ṭabaqāt* ("Book of Classes") is a valuable ninth-century biographical encyclopedia full of many early historical traditions. Relatively early is a reference work of al-Ya'qūb b. Sufyān al-Fasawī, who died in 890, yet its scattered reliable traditions cannot provide the framework for understanding the conquests.[18]

All of these histories require careful sifting, as do their Byzantine counterparts. But the Muslim sources are much lengthier. It is impossible to reconstruct the conquests and Byzantine collapse from the sparse Byzantine sources. To complicate matters more, the principal Byzantine historical sources appear to be dependent in part on some common Muslim or Oriental sources. They are not entirely free-standing sources. Realization of this makes the interpretation and weighing of the reliability of respective Byzantine and Arabic sources even more delicate and difficult.

Leone Caetani,[19] M. J. De Goeje, Miednikov, and Julius Wellhausen

[18] Abū Muḥammad Aḥmad b. A'tham al-Kūfī, *Kitāb al-futūḥ* ("Book of Conquests"), ed. by M. 'Abdul Mu'id Khan, 8 vols. (Hyderabad 1968–75), but note wholly anachronistic reference to Malik al-Rūsiya in 1:265; Muḥammad Ibn Sa'd, *Kitāb al-Ṭabaqāt al-kabīr*, ed. by Eduard Sachau, *et al.*, 9 vols. (Leiden: Brill, 1904–40), henceforth cited as *Ṭabaqāt*; Ibn Khayyāṭ al-'Uṣfurī, *Ta'rīkh*, ed. by Akram Ḍiyā' al-'Umarī, 2 vols. (Baghdad: al-Najaf, 1967); Abū 'Ubayd al-Qāsim b. Sallām, *Kitāb al-amwāl*, ed. by Muḥammad Khalīl Harās (Beirut: Dār al-Kuttub al-'Almiyya, 1986); al-Fasawī [incorrectly listed as al-Basawī in the published book], *Kitāb al-ma'rifa wa'l ta'rīkh*, ed. by A. D. al-'Umarī, 3 vols. (Baghdad 1974–6).

[19] L. Caetani, *AI*. M. J. De Goeje, *Mémoire sur la conquête de la Syrie*, no. 2 in: *Mémoires d'histoire et de géographie orientales*, 2nd edn (Leiden: E. J. Brill, 1900), cited as *Mémoire*[2].

rigorously criticized the Arabic sources.[20] Noth more or less refutes the concept of Wellhausen and De Goeje that one "school" of Arabic historiography – particularly that of al-Wāqidī – was more reliable than another; he sees them all as products of similar methods, with similar problems.[21] A. A. Duri and Fred M. Donner contributed to the solution of this scholarly problem.[22] I neither accept *in toto* nor engage in radical rejection of all early Muslim traditions. Where they appear to conform to and offer the best explanations in the light of late Roman and Byzantine conditions, not merely Byzantine historical traditions, they deserve serious consideration. The most reliable traditions appear to be those of al-Wāqidī, Ibn Isḥāq, and 'Ikrima, while those of Sayf b. 'Umar and Ibn A'tham al-Kūfī are less reliable but sometimes indispensable.[23]

Some of the traditions in al-Azdī al-Baṣrī's *Ta'rīkh futūḥ al-Shām* ("History of the Conquest of Syria") are not as improbable as the young De Goeje argued in 1864.[24] 'Abd al-Mun'im b. 'Abd Allāh b. 'Āmir claims to have reedited this source on the basis of a recently discovered Damascus manuscript in 1970. Although L. I. Conrad has discovered some very serious problems with 'Āmir's edition, he nevertheless dates Azdī's authorship to the second century AH and provides convincing evidence for the value of Azdī's information.[25] Caetani even later conceded that Azdī's original text contains

20 N. A. Miednikov, *Palestina ot zavoevaniia eia arabami do krestov'ich pochodov po arabskim istochnikam.* 2 T. in 4 vols. (St. Petersburg 1897, 1907); J. Wellhausen, *Skizzen und Vorarbeiten*, vol. 6 (Berlin: Reimer, 1899).

21 Albrecht Noth, "Die literarisch überlieferten Verträge der Eroberungszeit als historische Quellen für die Behandlung der unterworfenen Nicht-Muslims durch ihre neuen muslimischen Oberherren," *Studien zum Minderheitenproblem im Islam*, 1: *Bonner Orientalische Studien* n.s. 27/1 (1973) 282–314; Noth, *Quellenkritische Studien zu Themen, Formen, und Tendenzen frühislamischer Geschichtsüberlieferung* (Bonn: Selbstverlag der Orientalischen Seminars der Universität Bonn, 1973).

22 A. A. Duri, *The Rise of Historical Writing among the Arabs*, trans. by Lawrence I. Conrad (Princeton: Princeton University Press, 1983); Fred M. Donner, *The Early Islamic Conquests* (Princeton: Princeton University Press, 1981), and "The Problem of Early Arabic Historiography in Syria," *1985 Bilād al-Shām Proceedings* 1: 1–27.

23 F. Rosenthal, *A History of Muslim Historiography*, 2nd edn (Leiden: Brill, 1968) esp. 30–197. F. Sezgin, *Gesch. des arabischen Schrifttums* (Leiden: Brill, 1967) 1: 303–38; C. Brockelmann, *Geschichte der arabischen Literatur*, vols. 1–2, and suppls. 1–3 (Leiden 1943–9); M. G. Morony, *Iraq after the Muslim Conquest* (Princeton 1984) 537–75; Morony, "Sources for the First Century of Islam," *Middle East Studies Association Bulletin* 12, no. 3 (1978) 19–28; Marsden Jones, "The *Maghāzī* Literature," in: *Arabic Literature to the End of the Umayyad Period. The Cambridge History of Arabic Literature* (Cambridge: Cambridge University Press, 1983) 344–51. I offer only limited reference to transmitters of Muslim traditions preserved in Arabic texts.

24 M. J. De Goeje, *Mémoire sur le Foutouh's-Scham attribué à Abou Ismail al Baçri. Mémoires d'histoire et de géographie orientales*, no. 2 (Leiden: E. J. Brill, 1864), henceforth cited as *Mémoire*[1].

25 al-Azdī al-Baṣrī, *Ta'rīkh futūḥ al-Shām*, 'Āmir edn (Cairo 1970); older edn: William Nassau Lees, *The Fotooh al-Sham, Being an Account of the Moslim Conquests in Syria, with a Few Notes* (Bibliotheca Indica, 84, 85, Calcutta 1854–7); Lawrence I. Conrad, "Al-Azdī's

some information that appears to be authentic and is not found elsewhere.[26] Attribution of his information on the indiscipline and disorderly conduct of the Byzantine troops immediately before the battle of the Yarmūk to a tribesman from the Arab tribe of the Tanūkh (*rajul min Tanūkh*) shows that Azdī used some source or tradition that ultimately emanates from the seventh century. The tribe of Tanūkh did remain loyal to Byzantium until the military situation in Syria became hopeless.[27] This ascription of information to someone from this specific tribe conforms to what is otherwise known about the historical situation in the late 630s, including tribal allegiances.

The *Ta'rīkh futūḥ al-Shām* reports a speech in which Heraclius reminded his listeners, who were inhabitants of Syria, of the recent Byzantine victory over the Persian King Chosroes II, "the Magi," and "over the Turk who does not know God,"[28] which is an allusion to the Khazars, which only a source with genuine familiarity with details of the history of Heraclius' relations with Khazars would make; no one could have fabricated such an allusion in the era of the Crusades, the period in which De Goeje supposed that this *Ta'rīkh futūḥ al-Shām* was composed.[29] It is not a literal transcription of what Heraclius said, but it does indicate that the author, or one of his sources, possessed some very specific and accurate information concerning the reign of Heraclius. Moreover, Sebēos and Ghevond include passages in their histories that bear some similarity to al-Azdī's account of the speech of Heraclius, and Azdī's description of that speech is similar to Ibn A'tham al-Kūfī's fragmentary report of Heraclius' communication made in Palestine, which he also reportedly sent to Damascus, Ḥimṣ, Ḥalab/Aleppo, and Antioch.[30] The authors all appear to have drawn on some common source or sources for limited sections of their narratives, perhaps through a common Syriac tradition. al-Azdī's information that Ma'āb was the first city in Syria to fall to the Muslims is repeated in one tradition reported by al-Ṭabarī, but even more important, it is partly corroborated by Sebēos.[31]

The *Ta'rīkh futūḥ al-Shām* of al-Azdī al-Baṣrī requires a critical reading, but its account should not be rejected out of hand. It credibly relates that Heraclius suddenly created emergency military authorities over specific cities

History of the Arab Conquests in Bilād-al-Shām: Some Historiographical Observations," *1985 Bilād al-Shām Proceedings* 1: 28–62.

26 Caetani, *AI* 2: 1149; 3: 205–10, 578–83.

27 Azdī 175. Tanūkh: al-Ṭabarī 2081; I. Shahid, *BAFOC* 455–9.

28 Azdī 28.

29 W. Pohl, *Die Awaren* (Munich: Beck, 1988); P. Golden, *Khazar Studies*. Bibliotheca Orientalis Hungarica, 25/1–2 (Budapest: Akademiai Kiado, 1980) 1: 34, 36; G. Moravcsik, *Byzantinoturcica*, 2nd edn (Berlin: Akademie Verlag, 1958) 1: 70–6; De Goeje, *Mémoire*[1] 29, 38–9; cf. Pseudo-Methodius 10, in: Martinez, "Eastern Christian Apocalyptic" 139.

30 Sebēos c. 30 (124 Bedrosian, 96 Macler); Azdī 28; Ghevond (29 Arzoumanian); Kūfī 1: 100–1.

31 Sebēos c. 30 (96 Macler, 124 Bedrosian); Azdī 29.

in Syria and Palestine,[32] to encourage the local inhabitants of Palestine and Syria to prepare to defend themselves against the impending Muslim invasions,[33] which conforms to earlier practices[34] as well as Heraclius' experimentation with emergency military commands over formerly civilian governmental responsibilities.[35]

Some of the narratives of individual combats, challenges, and rhetorical exchanges in the *Ta'rīkh futūḥ al-Shām* deserve a very skeptical evaluation, yet there does appear to be an authentic and historical core to the body of the history. al-Azdī identifies the Byzantine commander at the battle of Ajnādayn as "Wardān," which is strikingly similar to the very important reference in a very early (seventh-century) fragmentary notice in a Syriac source, in which he is called "B[R]YRDN" in consonantal spelling.[36] Both could represent a popular Armenian name "Vardan" (a favorite of the Mamikounian family), because Heraclius made frequent use of Armenian commanders in his search for trustworthy officers. While it would be erroneous to accept the testimony of al-Azdī al-Baṣrī's *Ta'rīkh futūḥ al-Shām* blindly, some of his statements have more of a ring of authenticity than scholars have previously assumed.

Muslim sources reveal a very limited comprehension of the nature of the Byzantine Empire. They do, however, show some understanding of ethnic diversities within the Byzantine ranks. Their statistics are unreliable, of course. It is a very fragmentary picture, without coherence or any sophisticated understanding and without explanation and qualification when referring to Byzantine institutions. There is no understanding of the relevance of the contemporary situation in Italy and the Balkans to Syria and Palestine.

The Muslim historians' worldview is necessarily dominated by an Islamic frame of reference into which all events are placed, with an understandable emphasis on personalities and religion. It is necessary to think about the narrative structure and purposes of the Muslim historian. There is no evidence that Muslim historians attempted to use Greek sources, whether directly or in translation, although it is tempting to guess what kinds of sources al-Ya'qūbī, who reports that he wrote a description of Byzantium

32 Azdī 31; al-Ṭabarī (Sayf) i 2104; Ibn al-Athīr 2: 311, 317–18.

33 Azdī 28–9, 31; Kūfī 1: 100–1; cf. al-Ṭabarī i 2086; Ibn al-Athīr (2: 311 Tornberg).

34 W. E. Kaegi, Jr., "Two Studies in the Continuity of Late Roman and Byzantine Military Institutions," *ByzF* 8 (1982) 87–113; R.-J. Lilie, "Die zweihundertjährige Reform. Zu den Anfängen der Themenorganisation," *Byzsl* 45 (1984) 27–39; John Haldon, *Byzantium* 208–51.

35 Theoph., *Chron.*, AM 6126, 6128 (338, 340 De Boor). Kūfī 1: 100–1.

36 Azdī 84. Wardān may be identical with Artabūn in al-Ṭabarī i 2398–400, and Ibn al-Athīr 2: 387. Syriac references to B[R]YRDN: *Chronicon miscellaneum ad annum Domini 724 pertinens*, trans. by J.-B. Chabot (CSCO, Script. Syri, ser. 3, T. 4 [Louvain 1903–5], Versio 114); "Extract from a Chronicle Finished in AD 641," Palmer, *Chronicles*, part 1, text 2: AG 945; cf. Th. Nöldeke, *Die ghassânischen Fürsten* (Berlin: Abhandlungen Preuss, Akad. d. Wiss., 1887) 45 n. 3; Caetani, *AI* 2: 1144–5.

(now lost), once possessed. Except for al-Ya'qūbī, most Muslim historians have little reason to explain much about Byzantium to their readers during the course of their narration of the Islamic conquests of Byzantine territories. It is impossible to understand much about Byzantium, and especially about Byzantine thought, from reading Muslim historians. al-Mas'ūdī (896–956) was, like al-Ya'qūbī, a rare Muslim historian who investigated and described events from Byzantine history, but his information is not detailed on the early conquests. The Muslim historians do not appear to have drawn lessons for the future from any analyses of Byzantine battle tactics or strategy, or even those of their Muslim heroes, during the Islamic conquests.[37]

The extant primary sources either provide only the briefest of references to the Muslim conquests or they organize their materials year by year or, in the case of such Muslim historians as Balādhurī, by region. These structures of organization have their value, and of course without specific chronological references the task of the historian would be even more formidable. But what has been lost in all of these narratives, irrespective of the reliability of the traditions they report, is any understanding of the interrelationship and potential coherence of those events. There is always the danger that coherence can be overemphasized, deceptively smoothing over the irregular historical realities and exceptions. But the disconnected and fragmentary historical approach has tended, unconsciously, to obscure the interconnections between the warfare and diplomacy in Syria and that of Egypt and Byzantine Mesopotamia.

Byzantinists on their part have rarely investigated the Muslim conquests and Byzantine resistance, perhaps assuming that the Orientalists had discovered all that there was to find, or perhaps discouraged by the linguistic problems. The few Byzantinists who have studied Byzantine–Muslim relations have generally commenced their studies in the ninth century (e.g., A. A. Vasiliev and M. Canard), although E. W. Brooks and J. Wellhausen did publish long articles on Byzantine–Muslim warfare that followed the termination of the initial Muslim conquests of Syria and Mesopotamia.[38]

[37] al-Ya'qūbī, *Kitāb al-Buldān*, ed. by M. J. De Goeje, *Bibliotheca Geographorum Arabicorum* (Leiden: E. J. Brill, 1892; repr., 1967) 7: 323; William G. Millward, "A Study of al-Ya'qubi with Special Reference to His Alleged Shi'a Bias" (unpub. Ph.D. diss., Princeton University, 1961) 7, 17–18. Ahmad Shboul, *al-Masudi and His World* (London: Ithaca Press, 1979) 227–83.

[38] A. A. Vasiliev, M. Canard, H. Grégoire, *Byzance et les arabes*, 2 vols. (Brussels 1935–50). E. W. Brooks, "The Arabs in Asia Minor (641–750), from Arabic Sources," *JHS* 18 (1898) 182–208; J. Wellhausen, "Die Kämpfe der Araber mit den Romäern in der Zeit der Umaijiden," *Nachrichten d. Kgl. Ges. d. Wiss.* (Göttingen 1901) 414–47; R-J. Lilie, *Die byzantinische Reaktion auf die Ausbreitung der Araber* (Munich 1976); Hugh Kennedy, "From Polis to Madina: Urban Change in Late Antique and Early Islamic Syria," *Past and Present* 106 (1985) 3–27, and "The Last Century of Byzantine Syria: A Reinterpretation," *ByzF* 10 (1985) 141–84; Demetrios J. Constantelos, "The Moslem Conquests of the Near

However, once again, they were Orientalists, not Byzantinists. Again, this decision about a *terminus a quo* has artificially separated consideration of events in Syria from those in Anatolia. Byzantinists tend not to look at the initial conquests but to begin their studies after the conclusion of the Muslim conquests of Syria, Byzantine Mesopotamia, and Egypt. The links and continuities between the conquest of Syria and the longer-term inconclusive Byzantine–Muslim warfare in Anatolia have not been adequately understood.

HERACLIUS IN THE EYES OF THE MUSLIM SOURCES

Arabic traditions on the actions or motives of Heraclius and the other Byzantine commanders at the time of the Muslim invasions have received little attention because of their contradictory reports, doubts about their trustworthiness, and linguistic difficulties. The perception of Heraclius in the Muslim sources is complex. Muslim sources consistently attribute much more personal responsibility to Heraclius himself for the direction of Byzantine strategy and operations. Byzantinists have generally ignored this point. The Arabic sources attribute to Heraclius more personal responsibility for the control of events than he ever possessed. To them he was the backbone of Byzantine resistance:[39] a sovereign who can summon and direct resources from one part of his empire to another in vast quantities. Yet they say almost nothing about other regions of his empire and show no comprehension of the possible interconnections between events in Syria and Palestine and problems in what was left of Byzantine Italy, the Byzantine Balkans, or even in Constantinople.

The Arabic sources describe Heraclius as a leader who reacted to events, as a leader who certainly was not in control of them, who consulted with his leading commanders,[40] but yielded to pressures from them and his subjects in matters of military policy and operations in Syria.[41] They portray him as a leader with strong passions of anger and doubt. They never claim that he was confident of victory in the entire series of campaigns. That is consistent with their own Islamic frame of reference. They also represent him as impatient and sometimes angry with his commanders and soldiers for their inability to perform satisfactorily against the Muslims despite their own numerical

East as Revealed in the Greek Sources of the Seventh and the Eighth Centuries," *Byzantion* 42 (1972) 325–57.

39 Ibn 'Abd al-Ḥakam, *Futūḥ miṣr*, ed. by C. Torrey (New Haven: Yale, 1922) 76.

40 Heraclius consults others, e.g., Jabala b. al-Ayham, Kūfī 1: 126–32; cf 1: 302–10. Others advise Heraclius: Kūfī 1: 218–21.

41 Heraclius yields to pressures: Azdī 92, 106, 139, 152. Ibn 'Asākir 1: 531–2. Cf. Balādhurī 123; al-Ṭabarī (Sayf) i 2102; Kūfī 1: 218–21; but al-Ṭabarī i 2152.

superiority.[42] Their claims that Heraclius intervened personally from time to time in the conduct of the defense of Syria, and that he became angry at specific decisions of his subordinates and countermanded them, are plausible.[43] Implicit in the Muslim sources is respect for Heraclius as a great but unsuccessful leader. They dissociate his wisdom in military affairs from the errors of his subordinate commanders. These Muslim traditions sometimes converge with what appears to be an Heraclian historiographical tradition of avoiding direct personal criticism of the actions of Heraclius. This is not to say that the Arabic sources leave no independence to the Byzantine commanders, because they do attribute to them some freedom to make military decisions about battle tactics.

Muslim sources, whatever the origin of their approach, and it is hard to know how they could have known much about the intimate details of military planning among the Byzantines, had no reason to protect the prestige of Heraclius and his dynasty if he was really at fault.[44] They did not need to protect the myth of imperial rectitude. Although they state that he tried to obtain information about the Muslims, they do not report any comprehension by Heraclius of the personalities, abilities, and qualities of the Muslim leadership. Christian sources, if Chalcedonian, and especially if deriving from traditions that went back to the period of the Heraclian dynasty, which lasted until 711, except for a brief interregnum of 695–705, did not have that freedom. Although Muslim sources ascribe much of the fault to Heraclius, even they criticize those subordinates and local elites who dissuaded him from correct decisions, e.g., his officers dissuaded him from evacuating Syria earlier or seeking a settlement with the Muslims.[45] They completely ignore ecclesiastical problems as a possible complicating factor for him.

The vision of Heraclius in Arabic sources, with such fanciful details as his crown of gold,[46] may be a literary foil for the purpose of the narrators, namely, to show the inevitability of the Muslim conquests due to God's guidance and support of the Muslims, despite competent Byzantine leadership. Yet some of this favorable Muslim description of the military qualities of Heraclius cannot be explained completely in terms of rhetorical or apologetical exposition, or his faulty interpretation of dreams (that Jews

[42] Azdī 44, 150–1; Ibn 'Asākir 1: 477.

[43] al-Ṭabarī (Sayf) i 2103; al-Ṭabarī (Ibn Isḥāq) i 2349; Theoph. *Chron.*, AM 6126, 6128 (337–8, 340 De Boor).

[44] Unless the Muslims learned of Heraclius' role from Christian Arabs or prisoners who had served in the Byzantine armies, or from captured Byzantines, who were numerous, or from deserters such as the Persian Niketas, son of Shahrbaraz.

[45] Heraclius wants to leave Syria: Kūfī 1: 219–20; Ibn 'Asākir 1: 531; *Histoire Nestorienne/Chronique de Séert* c. 106, ed. by Addai Scher, *PO* 13: 627; al-Ṭabarī (Sayf) i 2102.

[46] Kūfī 1: 126–8, esp. 128.

were the circumcised people who he dreamed would overrun his empire) and consultation of astrological books.[47]

No Arabic source on Heraclius indicates any familiarity with or dependence on Greek sources. There are no quotations of plausible Byzantine documents in the Arabic sources concerning Heraclius. These Arabic sources appear to assume that someone was able to gain direct access to Heraclius and some of his important generals and thus was able to report such conversation and messages. Yet they do not specify the names of palace guards and their titles in such a way that one could confidently consider the possibility of the accuracy of their reports.

The Arabic sources do not condemn Heraclius for his personal absence from the front.[48] After all, the Caliphs Abū Bakr and ʿUmar were also absent from the Muslim front-line command. They do portray Heraclius as anxious about the outcome of the fighting in Syria and as a leader who was attentive to the constant flow of information from couriers, generals, spies, and delegations from towns. They do not claim that Heraclius lacked either money or manpower; in fact, they tend to attribute very adequate resources to him. They report that he paid very substantial sums of money to raise vast numbers of troops from among the Christian Arab tribes, the Armenians, and the Greeks. Their specific statistics are, of course, wildly exaggerated. They do not report dissension within the imperial family about the imperial succession or other issues, and they certainly do not blame internal dissension at court for causing the defeat of his armies against the Muslims. They do report that the Muslims made frequent use of spies or collaborators from among the indigenous population, including "al-Anbāṭ" (not necessarily Arabs but perhaps Monophysite Syrians), and from the Samaritans.[49]

Heraclius appears as a Christian apologist in some Muslim sources. Yet most of their accounts provide a militarily intelligible, if disappointingly brief, picture of Heraclius' military decisions and actions. These are plausible, for the most part, in terms of contemporary seventh-century military logic, even if contradictory. They do not comment in detail on the quality of the commanders whom Heraclius appointed to lead Byzantine troops in Palestine and Syria. They do not question the wisdom of his selections, and they do not indicate that he overlooked any outstanding

[47] Ibn ʿAsākir 1: 473. Wāqidī 3: 1018–19. Fredegarius, *Chron.* 4.65 (153 Krusch).

[48] Heraclius keeps distance from fighting: Balādhurī 113–15, 123; Azdī 29; Ibn ʿAsākir 1: 477, 531–2, 548–51. Ibn al-Athīr (2: 317–18 Tornberg). al-Ṭabarī i 2086, 2103, 2104, 2395. Kūfī 1: 101.

[49] Azdī 150–2, 234–6; Kūfī 1: 175, 218–21, 305. Anbāṭ spies for Muslims: Wāqidī 990; their identity: Gérard Troupeau, "La Connaissance des chrétiens syriaques chez les auteurs arabo-musulmans," *Orientalia Christiana Analecta* 221 (1983) 274–5. Ghassānid and other Arab spies: Wāqidī 1018–19; Ibn ʿAsākir 473; Azdī 39; Kūfī 1: 144. Samaritans: Balādhurī 158.

commander in making his appointments. They do differ in their accounts of Heraclius' itinerary and chronology of activities and whether Muslim troops from Iraq played any role in compelling Heraclius to take certain actions.[50]

The Muslim sources do report that Heraclius' name struck fear into the early Muslims, before the initial battles.[51] None attributes ultimate military goals to Heraclius other than the defense of what was Byzantine.[52] Their accounts are consistent with the Byzantine and Syriac Christian traditions that Heraclius ordered those who could to try to hold on to their posts without engaging in open battle in the field against the Muslims.

OBSTACLES TO MILITARY HISTORIOGRAPHY

The historian of these events and processes also encounters another formidable contemporary hurdle. A substantial number of scholars reject the possibility – or are not interested in, or even believe that historians should not have much interest in – whether there were any military dimensions or military explanations, partial or otherwise, for the Byzantine loss of Palestine, Syria, and Mesopotamia to the Muslims. Such scholars have preconceived convictions or even prejudices that non-military causes and dimensions of seventh-century history are the only ones really worth studying or understanding. They can conceive of only social, economic, religious, experiential or socio-cultural explanations and are unsympathetic to and sometimes even unforgiving of any inquiry into "narrow" military matters, let alone military events in their own right. This prejudice is not peculiar to the seventh century, for it burdens the study of modern history as well as other historical subdisciplines, and represents a narrowness of vision that does injustice to the full spectrum of historical reality.[53]

This inquiry assumes, on the other hand, that although religious experiences and change are indeed critical in the seventh century and well worth study, that nonetheless many of the important events of the early decades of the seventh century had a military dimension. Moreover, scholars have offered conflicting interpretations of seventh-century Byzantine military institutions, which they have regarded as very important in themselves and indeed for the broader understanding of the essential lines of Byzantine history and the essential character of Byzantium. With this background in

[50] J. Wellhausen, *Skizzen und Vorarbeiten* 6: 85–9, criticizes reports of a vast role in Mesopotamia and Syria for troops from Iraq; best on itinerary of Heraclius and Muslims is Caetani, *AI* vols. 2–4.

[51] Wāqidī 760, 990.

[52] Heraclius orders closing of gates: Ibn 'Asākir 1: 474. Cf. *Chron. ad 1234 pertinens* c. 107 (Brooks, CSCO, Script. Syri, ser. 3, T.14, *Versio*, p. 188); Heraclius' warning to Christians to guard cities = Palmer, *Chronicles*, part 2, text 13: c. 48.

[53] W. E. Kaegi, Jr., "The Crisis in Military Historiography," *Armed Forces and Society* 7 (1981) 299–316.

mind, as well as broader trends in military historiography, it is desirable to reconsider critical years of the Muslim conquests and the Byzantine evacuation of Palestine, Syria, and Mesopotamia.

Some may question the appropriateness of the terminology "conquest." In addition to the Muslim sources who speak of the *futūḥ* or "victories," moral or material, by war or peacefully or "conquests," from the root of the verb to be victorious or conquer or open, no less significant a Byzantine source than the early ninth-century chronicler called Theophanes also refers to the ἐπικράτησις or "conquest" by the Arabs. Conquests or victories, therefore, are what historical authorities from separate traditions decided to call these events.[54] There is no sensible reason to avoid such terms or to seek alternative ones. In this era of continuing prejudice against military history and against the possibility of military explanation of historical change it is necessary to explain or to defend the rationale for studying the military dimensions of the Byzantine defenses. There are those who wish to find primarily nonmilitary explanations for the *futūḥ* and ἐπικράτησις, but this can only result in very inadequate and incomplete historical comprehension. Although a military analysis cannot pretend to provide an adequate explanation for all of the major changes that occurred, the military dimensions of the conquests cannot be avoided. The study of war has been greatly neglected in recent years, even though war is an important dimension of history. Military events in Byzantium resulted in some of the most significant historical changes.[55]

THE SIGNIFICANCE OF THE DEFENSE OF EGYPT

The focus of this inquiry is on Palestine, Syria, and Mesopotamia. The loss of Byzantine Egypt was a grievous one for the Byzantines, to be sure. With Egypt Byzantium lost immense tax revenues and population, as well as some critical foodstuffs and other unique products such as papyrus. But from a military perspective, Egypt was untenable for Byzantium after the loss of Palestine and Syria. The loss of those regions made continuing communications, administrative control, and defense of Egypt almost impossibly difficult for Byzantium. Egypt became isolated and Byzantine troops, leaders,

[54] Theoph., *Chron.*, AM 6124 (ed. by C. De Boor [Leipzig 1883] 336); Bernard Lewis, "Usurpers and Tyrants: Notes on Some Islamic Political Terms," *Logos Islamikos. Studia Islamica In Honorem Georgii Michaelis Wickens*, ed. by Roger M. Savory, Dionysius A. Agius (Papers in Mediaeval Studies, 6 [Toronto: Pontifical Institute of Mediaeval Studies, 1984]) 260, on *futūḥ*, in Arabic. Theophanes may have indirectly taken his terminology from an oriental, even ultimately a Muslim, source.

[55] John W. Jandora, "Developments in Islamic Warfare: The Early Islamic Conquests," *Studia Islamica* 64 (1986) 101–13, emphasizes the neglected positive martial qualities of the beduin, including their ability to fight on foot, yet he ignores much primary and secondary source material.

and population in contiguous areas to the west of it, for example in Nubia, could do little to save it, however much some of them may have wished to do so. Its fall was only a matter of time. For that reason, this inquiry does not concentrate on the defense of Egypt and events in Egypt even though its tax revenues, agriculture, and population significantly exceeded those of Palestine, Syria, and upper Mesopotamia. Combat and diplomacy to the east of Egypt largely determined that it would soon fall to the Muslims.[56]

The termination of fighting in Palestine and lower Syria did not mean that the Muslims could overrun Egypt and wreak their will upon it unopposed. Indeed there were battles at 'Ayn Shams or Heliopolis, at Babylon (Old Cairo), at Nikiu and its vicinity, and resistance at Alexandria. But the loss of Palestine and Syria meant in effect the defenders of Byzantine Egypt were attempting to resist the Muslims who by the sheer logic of their central position with its "interior lines" could have known much more than the Byzantines. Continuing Byzantine dominance of the sea was very helpful to the Byzantine defense. It permitted manpower, money, provisions, and, at least as important, command and control to remain in touch with the governmental and military nerve center at Constantinople. But it was a partially crippled defense. Detailed and narrowly focused research is indispensable for the achievement of historical accuracy, but it is also important, perhaps after such detailed empirical researches, to determine whether there may be interrelationships or common patterns. Even though the geographical context of the campaigning in Syria, Palestine, and Byzantine Mesopotamia differed from that of Anatolia, it is essential to understand that Byzantine–Muslim warfare with its practices did not develop *ex nihilo* on the Anatolian plateau. It was a direct continuation and outgrowth of the earlier Byzantine–Muslim warfare. Many consequences flow from this.

Obviously, there must be limits to any historical study. It cannot include everything. The more specific studies that have taken place have made valuable contributions to the study of the conquests and the Byzantine failure to develop an effective defense. There have been some careful empirical studies that have made valuable contributions to the understanding of the conquests and Byzantine failure to develop an effective defense. But it is important to look at the evidence from other perspectives as well.

[56] Walter Kaegi, "Byzantine Egypt during the Arab Invasion of Palestine and Syria: Some Observations," *American Research Center in Egypt Newsletter* 121 (Spring 1983) 11–15; Alfred Butler, *The Arab Conquest of Egypt*, revised by P. M. Fraser (Oxford: Oxford University Press, 1978).

METHODOLOGICAL QUESTIONS AND ASSUMPTIONS

Except for works available in translation, Byzantinists, including A. Stratos, have not read the Arabic sources on the momentous events of the 630s. 'Irfān Shahīd is dramatically but primarily contributing to revolutionizing the historical understanding of Byzantine–Arab relations in the third, fourth, fifth, and sixth centuries, although he provides some invaluable insights on events and developments in the seventh century. The Orientalists and Islamicists who have accomplished by far the most distinguished research on the conquests have not studied Byzantine history in detail, let alone that of the late Roman Empire. Although they have made a positive effort to use all available sources and indeed have often given priority to the testimony of the Christian Oriental and Byzantine sources on the Muslim conquests, they have not fully exploited information about the actual late Roman and early Byzantine historical context in the sources. Such a task is formidable but indispensable.[57]

The relative value of various sources, including the Muslim ones, must receive critical scrutiny. The history of the conquests and the Byzantine defenses cannot be reconstructed from Byzantine and Christian Oriental sources alone.[58] This is, however, not a study of the rise of Islam, although Islamicists have made extremely valuable contributions to the understanding of the historical background. This study started with the premise that it was important to reexamine the value of the known Arabic sources for not only the history of the conquests and Byzantine resistance, but also for their incidental information about the state of seventh-century Byzantine institutions, methods of warfare, personalities, economic conditions, local government, and internal cleavages. Early traditions are reported by al-Ya'qūbī, al-Azdī al-Baṣrī, al-Ṭabarī, Ibn 'Abd al-Ḥakam, Ibn Khayyāṭ al-'Uṣfurī, Ibn A'tham al-Kūfī, al-Aṣma'ī, Balādhurī, and Abū Yūsuf, as well as such later sources as Ibn 'Asākir and Ibn Ḥubaysh.[59] Muslim traditions have potentially major value for Byzantine as well as Islamic history.

The great Orientalists at the end of the nineteenth and the beginning of the twentieth centuries, including Wellhausen, Caetani, and De Goeje, concluded

[57] A. Stratos, Τὸ Βυζάντιον στὸν Ζ' αἰῶνα, 6 vols. (Athens: Estia, 1965–77), which has an English translation, *Byzantium in the Seventh Century*, trans. by M. Ogilvie-Grant *et al.*, 5 vols. (Amsterdam and Las Palmas: Hakkert, 1968–80). The original Greek text will normally be cited in this book: Shahid, *BAFOC, BAFIC*.

[58] I basically agree with F. Donner, *EIC* 142–6. Too optimistic is Era Vranoussi, "Byzantino-arabica," Σύμμεικτα 3 (1979) 1–28. Cf. Michael G. Morony, *Iraq After the Muslim Conquest* 537–654.

[59] Ibn 'Abd al-Ḥakam, *The History of the Conquest of Egypt, North Africa and Spain Known as the Futuḥ Miṣr of Ibn 'Abd al-Ḥakam*, ed. by C. C. Torrey (Yale Oriental Series, Researches, III [New Haven: Yale, 1922]).

that the accounts of Christian Oriental sources normally should be preferred over Muslim ones in evaluating the confusing traditions about the Muslim conquest of Syria because of their greater contemporaneity with events. In general, they preferred the Muslim traditions that traced their transmission to Ibn Isḥāq and Wāqidī. Theodor Nöldeke edited and criticized Syriac sources most intelligently for their relevance in the study of the conquests. His contributions were very fundamental. These Orientalists, however, ignored the account of the *Passion of the Sixty Martyrs of Gaza*, the Life and Miracles of St. Anastasius the Persian, the *Doctrina Iacobi nuper baptizati*, and other patristic sources, such as Sophronius and St. Anastasius the Sinaite, and Maximus the Confessor, who do not provide historical narratives, but do provide sources that are contemporary or relatively contemporary – from the seventh century – to the conquests. Although there are some other relatively neglected Syriac sources no new chronicles have been discovered.[60] The above sources are ones that the Muslim authorities never consulted and in turn these authors never consulted Muslim ones. They are not easy to use or to interpret.

Christian Oriental and Byzantine sources are not faultless, and their accounts are very fragmentary. Although the dates the early Syriac sources provide normally deserve acceptance,[61] it is incorrect to assume that Christian chronicles and historians recorded traditions that were completely independent from those of the Muslims. Although it is impossible to trace the stemmata precisely, there are echoes and commonalities and even perhaps some duplications between the two traditions which probably indicate some cross-influences. Of course, if both traditions are reporting the same true facts through the intermediation of different traditions, there is no reason to be surprised at some similar accounts. Such diverse sources as the Byzantine Greek chronicler traditionally called Theophanes, who mishandled materials and chronology, and the late seventh-century Armenian Sebēos and the Christian Arab Eutychius are all drawing on some traditions that have some parallels or common sources, whether Syriac or Muslim, with some Muslim traditions. Yet there is no absolute copying. There is a need for new methodologies to handle accurately the complex problems of the possible interdependence or mutual contamination of Christian and Muslim sources.

[60] So Professor A. Vööbus informed me before his death. Cf. S. P. Brock, "Syriac Sources for Seventh-Century History," *BMGS* 2 (1976) 17–36; Brock, "Syriac Views on Emergent Islam," in: *Studies on the First Century of Islamic Society*, ed. by G. H. A. Juynboll (Papers on Islamic History, 5 [Carbondale: Southern Illinois University Press, 1982]) 9–22.

[61] Witold Witakowski, *The Syriac Chronicle of Pseudo-Dionysius of Tel-Maḥrē. A Study in the History of Historiography* (Acta Universitatis Upsaliensis. Studia Semitica Upsaliensia, 9 [Uppsala 1987]); Palmer, *Shadow*, General Introduction, and Note on Chronology.

This important task deserves sensitivity, not polemics. Investigation of the sources is never easy and risks being manipulated to prove practically anything that the author wants to prove, but it does need to be tried.

Another group of tests for authenticity of material in the Muslim traditions has hitherto not been applied: their consistency with what is known about late Roman and early Byzantine institutions, warfare, topography, and conditions. Advances in the study of late Antiquity, including archaeological discoveries, help to make this another important standard by which to evaluate the credibility of Muslim traditions. It is also important to weigh Muslim traditions much more carefully in the light of Byzantine history after the Byzantine defeat of the Sassanians in 628 – that is, how intelligible and sensible are certain statements in the light of what would have been rational Byzantine policy? These methods are not infallible. But they have not been adequately applied thus far, and it is important that there be such a critical effort.

This is a critical reading of the evidence, with a conscious effort to evaluate credibility in terms of late Roman and early Byzantine facts. Those Muslim traditions that report material that is consistent with those late Roman facts – and not merely historical or chroniclers' traditions – receive, in the absence of other mitigating criteria, more credibility than those traditions that do not. Such an approach involves, quite frankly, critical historical judgments. It will be the task of other critics to express their opinions on the competence of this reading of the evidence. In this fashion, late Antique historical research may make a significant contribution to the understanding of aspects of the Islamic conquests and some aspects of the reliability of some Muslim historical traditions (although not those concerned with events deep within the Arabian peninsula, where there can be no late Antique frame of reference for comparisons and evaluations). Thus far, Islamicists, who tend to have a limited knowledge of late Antiquity, given their understandable need to master their own methodologies, languages, and auxiliary sciences, have not made much use of late Roman materials as a control for their own researches into Muslim traditions. This does not mean the traditional approach of studying literary traditions and their transmissions but rather the examination and comparison of Muslim materials with known late Roman archaeological, topographical, and institutional evidence.

Islamic historians have been attempting a reestimation of the value of the Iraqi traditions of Sayf b. ʻUmar. One group of scholars argues for a more serious consideration of the material that Sayf has preserved. Their arguments call into question the conclusions and assumptions of Julius Wellhausen and, to a lesser extent, those of his admirer, Leone Caetani. This recent trend of criticism in Islamic historiography deserves careful attention by Byzantine historians as well, even though the results of this new methodology were not specifically intended to have implications for Byzantine history.[62]

A balanced analysis requires the investigation and consultation of all of the relevant sources. The controversial question of the accuracy of the Muslim traditions and allusions to Islamic topics in Christian sources, especially events of the life of the Prophet Muḥammad, are, with other aspects of the Arabian peninsula, outside the scope of this study. Islamic traditions must be sifted for any useful information about the situation of and internal conditions within the Byzantine Empire in the early seventh century, but especially in the 630s, for which there is so little Byzantine testimony. Patristic and hagiographic sources provide little information about the military history of the last dozen years of the reign of Heraclius (610–41), but they do preserve some valuable details about Byzantine institutions, conditions, and the diverse populations of the empire.

Accurate research assumes the use of the relevant source materials as well as a knowledge of the basic modern scholarship in late Antique, Byzantine, and Islamic fields, which necessarily means that this study will be incomplete and imperfect. Even with the kind assistance of so many scholarly colleagues, it is impossible to know all of the conceivably relevant material. Yet this investigation can at least attempt to point out the fundamentals of the problem, with the knowledge that there will be criticism and modification of many specific details. It is important to attempt a synthesis. Older studies for the most part are completely out of date, very incomplete, and even misleading.

Although it was probably unavoidable that earlier Orientalists did not know much about late Roman nomenclature and place-names, today it is imperative that there be a reevaluation of sources and syntheses to insure that older omissions and mistakes do not continue to skew historical interpretation and knowledge. Many interrelationships can be understood today – even though there will probably remain some omissions and errors – and the results should be a fuller and more accurate comprehension of many specific events and broader developments. Earlier generations of scholars permitted enormous strides in historical understanding and could not have been expected to know every detail of another specialty. They did the best that they could within the limits of knowledge and their own capacities and the available free time for research. Many errors have crept into scholarship and have survived because of the failure to perceive interrelationships and

[62] Ella Landau-Tesseron, "Sayf Ibn 'Umar in Medieval and Modern Scholarship," *Der Islam* 67 (1990) 1–26.

identities or because they were misconstrued. These require correction and adjustment of focus.

Although the origins and development of middle Byzantine institutions and society are controversial, and much scholarly effort has been expended in their investigation, there has never been an attempt to analyze the Arabic accounts of the early Muslim conquests for their information, if any, on the nature and character of Byzantine institutions at that critical time. Instead, scholars have repeatedly reexamined the same Byzantine Greek sources, with only limited success. Incidental references in the Arabic sources are not easy to find and to interpret – the effort requires sifting a lot of chaff – but it is important to understand what kind of Byzantine army appears to exist in the descriptions of those sources. The methodology required for investigating this involves very close reading of the Arabic sources for nuggets of information and then attempting to synthesize the cumulative results. This is not a sensational methodology, but it is the appropriate technique to achieve whatever accurate results are possible.

Many poorly founded assumptions impede an accurate historical understanding of the Byzantine efforts to defend the empire's eastern provinces against the Muslims in the 630s. These include Greek unfamiliarity with the terrain in the combat zones; criticism of the local populations for their failure to defend themselves against the Muslims; the decisive destructive role of Christian sectarian strife in paralyzing Byzantine resistance; the Emperor Heraclius' alleged illness and inability to take direct personal command of the armies in the field against the Muslims; Phocas' destructive and fateful overthrow of Emperor Maurice in 602; Emperor Maurice's harmful policy against the hitherto friendly Ghassānid Arabs, and Byzantine disdain for Arab federated troops who would have been able to defeat the Muslims; the debilitating effects of the long Byzantine war with Persia; the numerical superiority of the Muslims; the Muslims' ability to select battlefields on the edge of the desert; Heraclius' and his advisers' underestimation of the danger of the Muslims; the indifference of Heraclius and other Byzantines to the problem of the Arabs early in the course of the invasions; contradictory and religious fervor or lack of it either as a critical factor in stimulating the Arabs or as a mitigating factor that encouraged local popular acquiescence in the former Byzantine provinces to the Muslim conquests. Each of those causes considered separately appears to be plausible, and they all do contain some element of fact. Yet a closer examination reveals that they are inadequate explanations of the Byzantine collapse and the Muslim victories and the institutional changes that followed.

Modern scholarship has greatly advanced historical understanding of the conquests, with greater emphasis on the conquests of Iraq than of the

Mediterranean coast and its hinterland.[63] Yet the chronology of conquests in Syria remains obscure, as do the actions of the Byzantines, which necessarily were not the specific object of any Islamicist's investigation. Although it may have some implications for Islamic studies and for the early history of the caliphate, an additional goal is clarification of obscurities in the history of Byzantium. Arab investigators have not solved all remaining problems[64] or eliminated the need to synthesize late Roman, Byzantine, and Islamic primary sources[65] on the strategy and military operations of the Byzantines, including what Heraclius and his subordinates and immediate successors were attempting to do, and how their political, religious, and institutional policies remained constant or altered during the course of military vicissitudes. This is not easy to do but it is worth the effort to try.

[63] Donner, *EIC*; Michael Morony, *Iraq after the Muslim Conquest*; A. I. Kolesnikov, *Zavoevaniye Irana arabami* (Moscow: Nauka, 1982).

[64] Aḥmad ʻĀdil Kamāl, *Ṭarīq ilā Dimashq* (Beirut: Dār al-Infāsh, 1982), contains unsubstantiated chronology; problems beset it and Muṣṭafā Ṭalās, *Sayf Allāh, Khālid ibn al-Walīd* (Damascus 1978). Both authors provide imaginative reconstructions of events, but they make very little use of non-Arabic sources and their perspectives are narrow.

[65] Completely inadequate are M. Cheïra, *La Lutte entre arabes et byzantins. La Conquête et l'organisation des frontières aux VIIe et VIIIe siècles* (University of Paris doctoral thesis publ. in Alexandria by Société des Publications égyptiennes, 1947); Fatḥī ʻUthmān, *Al-ḥudūd al-Islāmiyya al-Bīzanṭiyya*, 3 vols. (Cairo 1967).

Chapter 2

THE BYZANTINE EMPIRE IN AN ERA OF ACCELERATING CHANGE

THE FINAL DECADES OF BYZANTINE AUTHORITY: AN OVERVIEW

> All Christians praise and give glory and thanks to the One God, greatly rejoicing in His Name. For Chosroes, the haughty enemy of God, has fallen. He has fallen and tumbled into the depths, and his name has been obliterated from the earth. For the impious one who arrogantly and contemptuously spoke injustice against Our Lord Jesus Christ, The True God, and his unblemished Mother our blessed lady the Mother of God and ever Virgin Mary has perished resoundingly. His labor turned against him and his wrongfulness came down on his head.[1]

Emperor Heraclius so announced to his subjects how the Byzantine Empire had finally triumphed over the Sassanian Empire and its monarch, Chosroes II Parviz, in 628 after approximately a quarter-century of intensive warfare that had devastated many provinces of both empires. Emperor Maurice's self-sworn avenger Heraclius had overthrown Phocas in 610, and assumed responsibility as emperor for the defense of the empire and the faith, and the expulsion of the Persians. Although the Persians had overrun Syria and Palestine and threatened to occupy all of Asia Minor and even approached Constantinople, it was Heraclius who, after reconstituting his armies, had brought the war to the heart of the Sassanian Empire in early 628. The overthrow and death of Chosroes ensued.

After imposing peace terms on Persia, essentially the territorial status quo ante, restoring the Byzantine borders of 590 at the Khābūr River, Heraclius, now about fifty-three years of age, returned to Constantinople. The humiliated Sassanian Empire degenerated into civil war and chaos. Heraclius was the first Byzantine soldier-emperor since Theodosius I died in 395. He engaged in successful negotiations in July 629 with Persian General Shahrbaraz to pry the Persian troops out of Egypt and Byzantine western

[1] *Chronicon Paschale*, ed. by L. Dindorf (Bonn: CSHB, 1832) 1: 728.

Asia, to enforce the earlier terms agreed with the successor of Chosroes II, Kawadh-Siroes. In March 630 Heraclius personally accompanied the restoration to Jerusalem of what he and contemporaries believed to have been the relics of the cross that the Persians had removed from Jerusalem in 614. But many other problems remained. Many shattered provinces needed help in reconstruction. The needs were great and the financial resources were limited. Of great importance were troubling ecclesiastical problems, especially the divisive problems of Christology and ecclesiology, which had long wracked Syria, Egypt, and Armenia. Heraclius vainly sought, with the assistance of Patriarch Sergius of Constantinople, to find some satisfactory unifying formula, but religious strife persisted. Nevertheless he persisted in trying to persuade provincials and his beloved Armenians to consent to religious union.[2]

No accurate statistics exist for the population of Syrian, Palestinian, Egyptian, and Mesopotamian cities and villages. It is probable that the population on the eve of the Muslim conquests was much smaller than it had been in the fourth or early sixth centuries. Plague and war presumably were the most important contributors to the demographic shrinkage.[3]

It is conceivable that the population of the Greek East in the second-century Roman principate reached 28 million to 34 million at the maximum, although by AD 630 that total had probably declined by 20 percent to 40 percent, if not more, to between approximately 17 million and 27 million. Estimates of the population of Syria in antiquity vary enormously, from 1,900,000 up to 5 to 6 million, including from 400,000 up to 2 million for Palestine, up to 10 million for what now is Syria, Lebanon, Israel, and Jordan. Those figures, however, apply to what may have been the maximum population of the Greek East in a more populous era, that of the Augustan Principate. Estimates of Anatolia's population in that era range from 5 million to 13 million. In the early seventh century, the population may well

[2] Angelo Pernice, *L'Imperatore Eraclio* (Florence: Galletti and Cocci, 1905); N. H. Baynes, "The Military Operations of Emperor Heraclius," *United Service Magazine* n.s. 46 (1913) 526–33, 659–66; 47 (1913) 30–8, 195–201, 318–24, 401–12, 532–41, 665–79; A. Stratos, Τὸ Βυζάντιον στὸν Ζ' αἰῶνα (Athens: Estia, 1965–9) vols. I–III.

[3] Lawrence I. Conrad, "The Plague in Early Medieval Near East" (unpub. Ph.D. diss. in Near Eastern Studies, Princeton University, 1981) 83–166. The demographic effects of the Persian invasion in Palestine were uneven, but in Anatolia, they were traumatic: C. Foss, "The Persians in Asia Minor and the End of Antiquity," *EHR* 90 (1975) 721–47; Wolfram Brandes, *Die Städte Kleinasiens im 7. und 8. Jahrhundert* (Berlin: Akademie-Verlag, 1989) 44–52. Dissents: James Russell, "Transformations in Early Byzantine Urban Life: The Contribution and Limitations of Archaeological Evidence," *Major Papers, The 17th International Byzantine Congress* (New Rochelle, NY: Caratzas, 1986) 137–54; Frank Trombley, "The Decline of the Seventh-Century Town: The Exception of Euchaita," *Byzantine Studies in Honor of Milton V. Anastos*, ed. by Speros Vryonis, Jr. (Malibu 1985) 65–90; but A. P. Kazhdan, "The Flourishing City of Euchaita?," *AABSC* 14 (1988) 4.

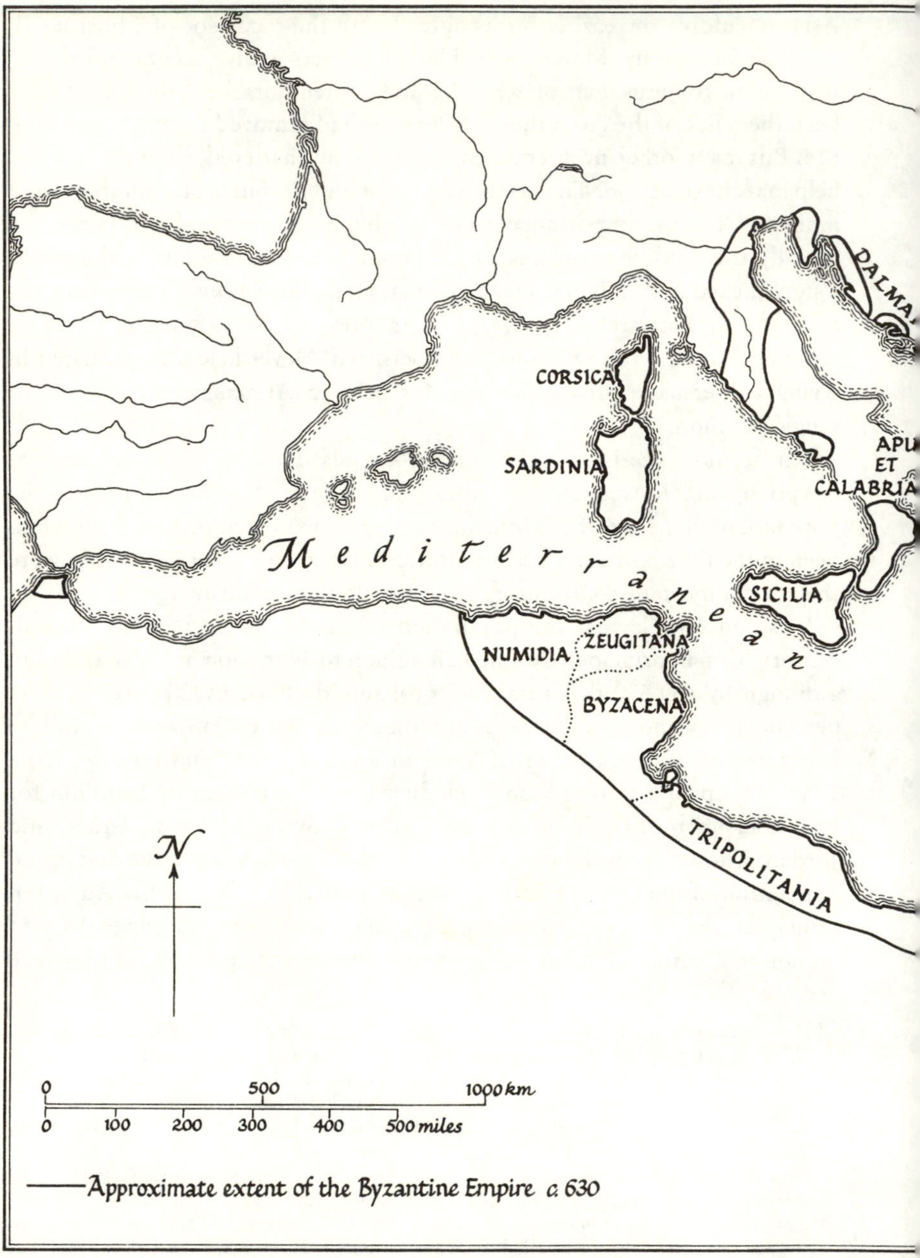
CORSICA
SARDINIA
Mediterranean
SICILIA
APU
ET
CALABRIA
NUMIDIA
ZEUGITANA
BYZACENA
TRIPOLITANIA
N
0
500
1000 km
0
100
200
300
400
500 miles
Approximate extent of the Byzantine Empire c. 630

Map 1. The Byzantine Empire on the eve of the Islamic conquests (after A. H. M. Jones, *Later Roman Empire*, map VI)

have been considerably less numerous, except possibly in Palestine.[4] Estimates for Byzantine Palestine alone run as high as 2·8 million but 1 million is more probable as the maximum for Cisjordanian Palestine.[5] By one estimate, the Byzantine Empire's total population in areas under nominal governmental control (not exactly coterminous with the "Greek East," because the empire [see Map 1] included parts of Latin-speaking Italy, Dalmatia, and North Africa) in AD 600 may have reached close to 17 million: Syria and Palestine 1·9 million [a low estimate], Egypt 3 million, Anatolia 5 million, Byzantine Balkans 2 million, Cyprus 100,000 and the balance in North Africa and Byzantine-controlled areas of Italy. By the late seventh century, after territorial losses to Muslims and Slavs, Bulgars, and Avars, the total population may have fallen to 7 million or less in areas that still remained under imperial control.[6]

Although there was religious dissension, particularly concerning Christology, and both Chalcedonian and Monophysite opposition to the official Heraclian policy of Monotheletism, it is not clear that these divisions were decisive in weakening Byzantine authority. The most disaffected religious minorities were relatively small Jewish and Samaritan communities, although they occupied areas and towns that were important for communications, intelligence gathering, and military strategy (such as Adhriʿāt and Nawā). The population was not homogeneous with respect to religious communion or language, but again, there are no reliable appropriately segmented statistics.[7] There is no evidence for active Monophysite disloyalty between 600 and 638.[8]

The substantial number of pilgrims and travelers, whenever there was a respite in hostilities, probably helped to keep those inhabitants near the roads and in the towns somewhat informed of conditions in remote areas of the

[4] Julius Beloch, *Die Bevölkerung der griechisch-römischen Welt* (Leipzig: Von Duncker und Humblot, 1886) 242–9; F. M. Heichelheim, in Tenney Frank, *Economic Survey of Ancient Rome* (Baltimore: Johns Hopkins, 1938) 4: 158–9. I thank Richard Saller for help on demography.

[5] High estimate: M. Avi-Yonah, s.v. "Palaestina," *RE*, Suppl. 13: 430; cf. Magen Broshi, "The Population of Western Palestine in the Roman-Byzantine Period," *BASOR* 236 (1979) 1–10.

[6] Colin McEvedy, Richard Jones, *Atlas of World Population History* (London: Allen Lane, 1978) esp. 110–12, 115, 135–6, 138–40, 143, 220, 226–7, whose estimates are only indications and cannot be accepted as rigorous figures.

[7] Joshua Starr, "Byzantine Jewry on the Eve of the Arab Conquest," *Journal of the Palestine Oriental Society* 15 (1935) 280–93; A. Sharf, "Byzantine Jewry in the Seventh Century," *BZ* 48 (1955) 103–15; A. J. Butler, *The Arab Conquest of Egypt*, revised by P. M. Fraser (Oxford 1978) lxiv–lxxviii, for bibliography; Lorenzo Perrone, *La chiesa di Palestina e le controversie cristologiche. Dal concilio di Efeso (431) al secondo concilio di Costantinopoli (553)* (Brescia: Paideia Editrice, 1980).

[8] It is, of course, dangerous to argue from silence. Kaegi, *BMU* 64–88, on the situation in the fifth and sixth centuries.

empire. Their expenditures continued to contribute to the local economy. Among these pilgrims were increased numbers of Armenians, who were especially common in Palestine, but also appeared in Syria and Egypt, probably reflecting Heraclius' increased dependence on his fellow countrymen for a supply of reliable officers and officials. In contrast, there is less evidence for the presence of Latin-speaking visitors, except for some pilgrims, probably because of the impoverishment and loss of most Latin-speaking areas of the late Roman Empire.[9]

THE QUICKENING PACE OF CHANGE

The confident and comfortable assertions and assumptions so easy for the ecclesiastical historian Evagrius Scholasticus in the 590s were no longer possible after 602. His boast that "from the time when the renowned Constantine took power, built the city bearing his own name, and dedicated it to Christ, come look with me whether any of the emperors in this city ... either was killed by domestic or foreign foes, or whether a usurper has completely overthrown an emperor,"[10] became obsolete less than a decade after he uttered it.

The overthrow and execution of the Emperor Maurice by the centurion Phocas in 602 is easily the most visible symbol of the new and violent period of the seventh century with its quickening of the pace of change. It would be erroneous to argue that Maurice was an excellent emperor who would have been able to reorganize the eastern provinces and develop satisfactory diplomatic relations with Persia if only he had not met death at the hands of the usurper Phocas. Tempting but false is the formula that "602 equals 622," that it was the overthrow and execution of Maurice that gave historical significance to Muḥammad's *Hijra*, that only the events of 602 made possible the emergence of Islam as a major religion and factor.[11] Many deficiencies in Maurice's policies with the Arabs long before his own overthrow point to his poor political judgment.[12]

Byzantium had not become a geriatric case, although institutional change had been so slow in the late Roman Empire that one scholar described it as "imperceptible."[13] That condition persisted until the beginning of the

9 Increased references to Armenians: Michael E. Stone, "Holy Land Pilgrimage of Armenians Before the Arab Conquest," *Revue Biblique* 93 (1986) 93–110; F. Nau, "Le Texte grec des récits du moine Anastase," *Oriens Christianus* 2 (1902) 81–2, also 78. Note a Musele among the last defenders of Gaza: H. Delehaye, "Passio Sanctorum LX Martyrum," *AB* 23 (1904) 303. 10 Evagrius, *HE* 3.41, ed. by J. Bidez and L. Parmentier (London 1898) 143–4.

11 Paul Goubert, *Byzance avant l'Islam* (Paris 1950) 1: 23–7, 269–72.

12 Kaegi, *BMU* 118–19. Too favorable to Maurice is Michael Whitby, *The Emperor Maurice and His Historian* (Oxford: Clarendon, 1988).

13 A. H. M. Jones, *LRE* vi; Philip Freeman and David Kennedy, eds., *DRBE*, for various contributions; W. E. Kaegi, "Variable Rates of Change in the Seventh Century," in:

seventh century, when the process of change began to accelerate. The Persian invasions that followed under King Chosroes II Parviz exposed, between 603 and 628, the grave vulnerabilities of the Byzantine Empire. The overthrow of Maurice stimulated other attempts at violent rebellion within the Byzantine Empire, including the one under Heraclius that successfully overthrew Phocas, in early October, 610. Heraclius' execution of Phocas brought no stabilization. The virtual collapse of the Byzantine armies between late 610 and 615, the Persian invasion and occupation of Syria, Palestine, and Egypt, and Avaro-Slavic raids and depredations all revealed the extremely perilous condition of the empire,[14] which endured, although frail.

The contemporary Byzantine historian Theophylact Simocatta even expresses a cautious recognition of the desirability of perpetuating the Sassanian Empire, no matter how injurious it had previously been to the Byzantine Empire, for fear that something worse might replace it: "Therefore, even though the Persians were to be deprived of power, their power would immediately transfer to other men. For events will not tolerate lack of leadership, nor such great fortune lack of direction."[15] Again, "...what prosperity would events devolve upon the Romans if the Persians are deprived of power and transmit mastery to another nation?"[16] That attitude might reflect shrewd political realism, but also an almost compulsive Byzantine preference to avoid changing the essential elements of the status quo.

The slow rate of change in so many dimensions between the fourth and early seventh century contributed to the intensity, violence, acceleration, and vast scope of the change that finally hit an unprepared Byzantium in the seventh century. It is less certain whether villagers, townspeople, and rural inhabitants experienced any drastic change in their physical environment and daily lives, if they escaped the destruction of war.[17] A seventh-century Persian envoy had allegedly warned in vain that protracted Byzantine–Persian warfare would reduce both empires "to a wretched and miserable condition," but it is unclear whether contemporaries really believed or foresaw that.[18] The populace responded to news of the changing fortunes of the Byzantine Empire and its armies with violent fluctuations and dramatic

Tradition and Innovation in Late Antiquity, ed. by Frank M. Clover and R. S. Humphreys (Madison: University of Wisconsin Press, 1989) 191–208.

[14] W. E. Kaegi, Jr., "New Evidence on the Early Reign of Heraclius," *ASRB* esp. 319–30; David Olster, *The Politics of Usurpation in the Seventh Century* (Hakkert, 1993); Judith Herrin, *The Formation of Christendom* (Princeton 1987).

[15] Theophylact 4. 13.9 (121 Whitby); Whitby, *The Emperor Maurice and His Historian* esp. 39–51, 309–58.

[16] Theophylact 4.13.13 (122 Whitby).

[17] *Doctrina Iacobi nuper baptizati* (63, 77 Bonwetsch).

[18] Nicephorus, *Short History* 6.42–3 (47 Mango).

swings in moods of despair and joy, which were a symptom of growing volatility, instability, uncertainty, and unrest.[19]

The empire lost its equilibrium when its rigid worldview and religious confidence shattered in 602 and never fully recovered it throughout the ensuing three decades of crisis. Heraclius, after overthrowing and executing Phocas, never had a chance for a respite.[20] The abortive revolt of Phocas' brother Comentiolus in October, 610 enabled the Persians to make their decisive breakthrough on the eastern front in 611 and thus prolonged the crisis. The Muslim invasions followed Heraclius' victory over the Persians too swiftly to permit imperial restabilization. The rapid succession of internal and external crises created insecurity, contradictions, and volatility, which kept Heraclius and his government perpetually off balance. This disorder left its traces in the mood of some of the sources.

THE PERSISTENCE OF THE LATE ROMAN WORLD INTO THE SEVENTH CENTURY

Inconsistencies and contradictions accumulated, inhibited governmental efficiency, and intensified strains. Slow institutional change contrasted with the extreme undulations of popular moods. The institutional mechanisms through which the Byzantines developed their responses to external military challenges in the early decades of the seventh century remained essentially late Roman, modified slightly from their character in the Justinianic era, but strains were appearing.[21]

The titulature of offices and ranks was no exception to the slow rate of change in late Roman institutions. Even more important, Heraclius probably retained or restored parts of the old administrative structure that existed before the hiatus of the Persian occupation in some eastern provinces such as Palestine and Syria. Older provincial nomenclature persisted, as did older nomenclature for some military units like the *equites Illyriciani* and other *numeri*.[22] Byzantine commanders continued to bear traditional late Roman

[19] *Doctrina Iacobi nuper baptizati* (70 Bonwetsch); *Acta M. Anastasii Persae* (12–13 Usener); Pantaleon, "Un discours inédit du moine Pantaléon sur l'élévation de la Croix *BHG* 427 p.," ed. by F. Halkin, *OCP* 52 (1986) 257–70; Mentality of victory and triumph: Michael McCormick, *Eternal Victory, Triumphal Rulership in Late Antiquity, Byzantium, and the Early Medieval West* (Cambridge: Cambridge University Press, 1986), esp. 193–6.

[20] Kaegi, "New Evidence on the Early Reign of Heraclius," *passim*.

[21] Continuity: Georges Tate, "A propos des campagnes de la Syrie du Nord (IIe–VIe siècles). Une tentative d'histoire sérielle," *Géographie historique du monde méditerranéen*, ed. by Hélène Ahrweiler (Paris: Sorbonne, 1988) 207–13.

[22] M. Avi-Yonah, s.v. "Palaestina," *RE*, Suppl. 13 (1974) 321–454. *Le Synekdèmos d'Hiéroklès et l'Opuscule géographique de Georges de Chypre*, ed. and trans. by E. Honigmann (Corpus Bruxellense Historiae Byzantinae, Forma Imperii Byzantini, 1 [Brussels 1939]) 49–50, 66–8, for George of Cyprus, *c.* 600, and pp. 41–4, for the sixth-century *Synekdemos*. F. Abel,

titles and offices: *patricius, drungarius, buccinator, cubicularius, sacellarius,* and *vicarius*, among others.[23] Old recruiting practices continued in parts of the empire,[24] and at least one section of the old imperial post was still operating in October, 610.[25]

The government continued the late Roman practice of concentrating troops in and around towns where warranted, although there had been a tendency already in the late fourth and early fifth centuries in Syria to distribute many of them in the north Syrian countryside to avoid potential friction with townspeople.[26] This rural distribution of troops in northern Syria anticipated what happened when precisely the same troops moved north into Anatolia in the wake of the Muslim conquest of Syria and Byzantine Mesopotamia.

Money was used in Byzantine recruiting in the 620s, but whether that was on an exceptional or regular basis is uncertain. Imperial excubitors were exercising their traditional role of scrutinizing and organizing military

Histoire de la Palestine (Paris: Librairie Lecoffre, 1952) 2: 388–93 on period of Persian invasion and occupation; 2: 393–406 on Muslim invasion and conquest. *Acta M. Anastasii Persae, Thaumata* 14 (26 Usener). Old nomenclature for provinces of Palestine: Balādhurī 109; Kaegi, "Notes on Hagiographic Sources for Some Institutional Changes and Continuities in the Early Seventh Century," *Byzantina* 7 (1975) 59–70; Kaegi, "Some Seventh-Century Sources on Caesarea," *IEJ* 28 (1978) 177–81; repr., *ASRB*.

23 *Patricius*: al-Ṭabarī 2081, 2088, 2108, 2112; see I. Kawar [Shahid], s.v. "Bitrik," *EI*² 1: 1249–50. *cubicularius*: Ibn ʻAsākir 1: 476 Munajjid; al-ʻUṣfurī 1: 87; al-Ṭabarī i 2125, 2126. Zacos/Veglery, *BLS* contains a Βαάνης who is *cubicularius* (no. 566) and another (no. 1086) imperial *chartoularios*. But another seventh-century Baanes has the title on a seal (no. 2831) of στρατηλάτης (*magister militum*?). There is no conclusive identification here. It may be tempting to identify one of these seventh-century seals with the Vahān who commanded at Yarmūk, but that identification cannot be confirmed. *Drungarius*: al-Ṭabarī i 2108, 2127. Azdī 106, 210; *Buccinator* (Ibn al-Qanāṭir): Azdī 210; Theoph., *Chron.*, AM 6146 (345–6 De Boor). *Sakellarios*: Ibn ʻAsākir 1: 531; al-ʻUṣfurī 1: 100; al-Ṭabarī i 2157, 2158, 2347, 2349. *Vicarius*: al-Ṭabarī i 2087; Ibn al-Athīr 2: 311 Tornberg; Theoph. *Chron.*, AM 6123 (335 De Boor).

24 Kaegi, "Two Studies in the Continuity of Late Roman and Byzantine Military Institutions," esp. 90–8. The reservations of J. Haldon in *Byzantine Praetorians* (Bonn 1984) 627–8 deserve rejection because of the improbability of the "scouts" being entrusted with the melting down of the bronze ox of Constantinople at Constantinople, where the *excubitores* normally were located; secondly the occupation of the site of the Forum of the Ox by the *excubitores* in official ceremonies, as cited in the *De Ceremoniis* of Constantine VII Porphyrogenitus, is important additional proof for their participation in the destruction of the bronze ox, which their ceremonial post memorialized. For additional reservations by others, yet unconvincing to me: Nicholas Oikonomides, "Middle-Byzantine Provincial recruits: Salary and Recruits," in: *Gonimos. Neoplatonic and Byzantine Studies Presented to Leendert G. Westerink at 75*, ed. by John Duffy and John Peradutton (Buffalo, NY: Arethusa, 1988) 135 n. 38; Paul Speck, "War Bronze ein knappes Metall?," *Hellenika* 39 (1988) 3–17.

25 *Vie de Théodore de Sykéôn* c. 152.4–9, ed. and trans. by A.-J. Festugière (Subsididia Hagiographica, 48 [Brussels 1970] 1: 121–2).

26 R. M. Price, "The Role of Military Men in Syria and Egypt from Constantine to Theodosius II" (unpub. D. Phil., Oxford, 1974) 375, cf. p. 71; V. Chapot, *La Frontière de l'Euphrate* (Paris 1907).

recruitment, while employing some kind of monetary payment or bounty as an inducement, although it is impossible to state confidently whether this was the case throughout the empire. It was also necessary to provide funds or ration allotments in kind to support expeditionary forces on campaign.[27] Governmental land grants were not yet the instrument for raising and financing such armies.[28] What can be established about the use of money enhances our understanding of Heraclius' relations with the Arabs since it complements other information on the importance of money for the recruitment and the maintenance of Arabs in Byzantine service. It makes more comprehensible the significance of the payment and nonpayment of money for the mobile armies of Arabs and non-Arabs alike whom Heraclius raised to fight the invading Arab tribes from the peninsula. Problems in paying soldiers had long wracked the Byzantine armies and bureaucracy. Now they complicated and hindered the efforts to find and develop a coherent and effective defense of the provinces that the Muslims threatened. The old system was still in place but it was strained to the utmost, and urgent expedients were being taken in the effort to make it still function.

Another indication of financial trouble was Heraclius' appointment of a *sakellarios* (σακελλάριος) or treasurer, whose name was Theodore Trithourios, to command the Byzantine armies in Syria. It underlines the Byzantine government's need to assure its soldiers of its commitment to their regular and full payment of promised funds, although there was a sixth-century precedent. Monetary payments were still crucial in the raising and maintenance of soldiers. There had been problems in assuring the prompt, regular, and full payment of what soldiers expected.[29] The appointment sought to assure tight fiscal control in a situation of potentially risky and even uncontrollable outflows of money for soldiers, some standard of fiscal accountability, and Heraclius' commitment to prompt and full payment of the soldiers for their services, as well as smooth distribution of provisions and fodder to their mounts. Although extant sources do not criticize Heraclius for appointing fiscal bureaucrats to positions of such important responsibility it is questionable whether such bureaucrats were the best

[27] *Parastaseis Syntomoi Chronikai* 42, ed. and trans. by Av. Cameron, J. Herrin, *et al.*, *Constantinople in the Eighth Century* (Leiden: Brill, 1984) 114–17, 228–30; Kaegi, "Two Studies" 90–8, Kaegi, "Late Roman Continuity" 53–61.

[28] Roman soldiers already had begun to possess land in considerable quantities by the third century, although there is a debate whether they simply owned it or personally engaged in the labor of cultivating it: Lothar Wierschowski, *Heer und Wirtschaft. Das römische Heer der Prinzipatenzeit als Wirtschaftsfaktor* (Bonn: Habelt, 1984) 74–88.

[29] Theoph., *Chron.*, AM 6125–6 (337–8 De Boor). Cf. N. Oikonomides, *Les Listes de préséance byzantines des IXe et Xe siècles* (Paris 1972) 312. Narses as *sakellarios*: Procopius, *Bella* 1.15.31, 6.13.16. Yet Oikonomides, "Middle-Byzantine Provincial Recruits: Salary and Recruits" 135.

choices to lead military operations at the time of the empire's greatest external military threat to date. In the immediate wake of the catastrophic Byzantine defeat in Syria, by 640, it will be the *sakellarios* who oversees a general tax reassessment of remaining Byzantine lands, but whether he had gained such a role on the eve of those invasions is uncertain.

Ration allotments of grain, oil, wine, vinegar, and meats, as well as *capitus* or fodder, survived into the seventh century although their ultimate fate in the Byzantine period is obscure.[30] Officials of the praetorian prefecture might determine the need and issue an order, but the unhappy responsibility for procurement and distribution of the rations to the soldiers lay with local provincial and municipal officials. It frequently was converted or commuted into monetary payments in gold or other coin, during and after the fourth century, by a process known as *adaeratio*.[31] The norm for soldiers' revenues was not exclusively monetary payment. Ration allotments in kind continued,[32] as sources from Egypt testify.[33] Nevertheless, there was a continuing role for money in the financing of Heraclius' mobile armies, including those Arabs who were recruited to help to defend Byzantine Palestine and Syria.[34] They needed funds to help defray the costs of their upkeep while under mobilization and on maneuvers during the conduct of military operations.

The precise relationship between Byzantine tax payments in specie and payments in kind is controversial. Large proprietors, in their role as local

[30] See literature in: W. E. Kaegi, "The Annona Militaris in the Early Seventh Century," *Byzantina* 13 (1985) 591–6, and "Variable Rates of Change" 196–200; Haldon, *Byzantium* 179, 223–32; Jean Durliat, *Les Finances publiques de Diocletian aux Carolingians* (Sigmaringen: Jan Thorbecke, 1990) 5–25.

[31] Jones, *LRE* 207–8, 235, 254, 258, 326, 448, 460–1, 566; André Cerati, *Caractère annonaire et assiette de l'impôt foncier au Bas-Empire* (Paris: Librairie générale de droit et de jurisprudence, 1975) 153–89; Philip Mayerson, "The Beersheba Edict," *ZPE* 64 (1986) esp. 142–3. M. Hendy, *Studies in the Byzantine Monetary Economy, c. 300–1450* (Cambridge: Cambridge University Press, 1985) 646, argues that *annonae* and *capitus* "were by the sixth century largely adaerated according to customary rates," see also pp. 647–8, 165–7, 294–5. The drain on cash which Hendy believes, p. 647, to have been so heavy that Emperor Maurice had to try to reduce it, could have been changed in several ways, one of which was simply to resort to less adaeration, and pay the rations in kind. This may not have been the general solution to the cash problem, but in the reign of Heraclius, to judge by Muslim sources, some actual payment in kind of ration allowances took place in some areas. The answer to the cash drain was not wholesale land grants at that time. N. Oikonomides, "Trade and Production in Byzantium from the Sixth to the Ninth Century," *DOP* 40 (1986) 35, n. 12.

[32] Carl H. Becker, *Beiträge zur Geschichte Ägyptens unter dem Islam* (Strasburg 1902) 83–5.

[33] J. Maspero, *Organisation militaire de l'Égypte byzantine* (Paris: Champion, 1912) 112, esp. n. 10; cf. Kosei Morimoto, *The Fiscal Administration of Egypt in the Early Islamic Period* (Kyoto: Dohosha, 1981) 40–113.

[34] Monetary incentives for Byzantine troops: Azdī 152 (100,000 gold pieces); Eutychius, *Ann.* 278–9 (135–7 Breydy edn, 114–15 Breydy trans.); implied in the appointment of Theodore the *sakellarios* or treasurer to command Byzantine troops: Theoph., *Chron.*, AM 6125–6 (337–8 De Boor); Nicephorus, *Hist.* 20 (68–9 Mango). Failure to pay Arab allies of Byzantium their expected stipends: Theoph., *Chron.*, AM 6123 (335–6 De Boor).

officials or *curiales*, participated in and probably profited from converting taxes calculated in gold into compulsory purchases of actual goods for the sake of the Byzantine army.[35] Those conclusions about the fourth through sixth centuries have relevance for the conversion of money taxes into taxes in kind in the early seventh century, including the understanding of the collection and distribution of *adaeratio*, *annonae* (ration allotments), and *coemptio* (compulsory purchases). It is likely that large proprietors in Byzantine Syria were also profiting from distributing stipulated tax payments in kind to soldiers on the eve of the Muslim invasions. This may help us to understand more of their role in the repair of city walls and their role in the defense (and failure to defend) of certain provinces against raids and invasions. Reports of assignments of specific amounts of territory for defense responsibilities to individual families are not evidence for granting these lands to support specific soldiers; thus far there was no creation of any "soldiers' properties" or στρατιωτικὰ κτήματα of the middle Byzantine period, but instead they are symptomatic of the weakening of central governmental power, and a "privatization" of military and civilian responsibilities because of the weakening central power of the government.[36] Privatization was no panacea and was inconsistent with some other governmental policies, such as prohibitions and restrictions on private ownership, sale, and production of weapons.

Ration allotments in kind were not always commuted by *adaeratio* to monetary payment. It was a mechanism by which Heraclius expected to pay and supply the soldiers whom he raised. In the 620s and 630s the Byzantine – and allied Christian Arab – soldiers who concentrated for the defense of Syria expected the localities, their municipal officials, and their inhabitants to furnish them with actual provisions, as did the Muslims to whom the same inhabitants soon capitulated.[37] Naturally, the Muslim recipients of such payments in kind at that early date were soldiers. No thorough alteration of the late Roman fiscal and distribution system had taken place by the early 630s, for even the *optio*, or paymaster, of the traditional payment system still existed in Palestine in approximately 631[38] as a component of the essentially

[35] Jean Durliat, "Moneta e stato nell'impero bizantino," in: *La cultura bizantina. Oggetti e messagio. Moneta ed economia*, ed. by André Guillou (Rome: L'Erma di Bretschneider, 1986) 179–200; Durliat, "Le Salaire de la paix sociale dans les royaumes barbares (Ve–VIe siècles)," and Walter Goffart, "After the Zwettl Conference: Comments on the 'Techniques of Accommodation'," in: Herwig Wolfram and Andreas Schwarcz, eds., *Anerkennung und Integration* 30–2, 35, and 73–6.

[36] Assignment of the defense of the Barbalissos (medieval Bālis region in northern Syria) to two brothers: Balādhurī 150; Ramsay MacMullen, *Corruption and the Decline of Rome* 122–97, on "privatization" of military defenses and the negative consequences.

[37] Syria: Balādhurī 125, 131. Mesopotamia: Balādhurī 125, 152, 173, 178.

[38] *Miracula, Acta M. Anastasii Persae* c. 13 (25 Usener). Cf. *Excavations at Nessana*, vol. III, no. 79, line 59, on p. 230.

late Roman Byzantine army.[39] But the harbinger of change and shakeup was the general reassessment of land by the *sakellarios* Philagrios immediately before Heraclius died in 641.

The payments in kind that the ninth-century Muslim historian Balādhurī mentions in his *Kitāb Futūḥ al-Buldān* at the time of the Muslim conquests survived because they descended from older late Roman fiscal and logistical institutions for the maintenance of the Roman (Byzantine) army.[40] When examined from the perspective of Islamic traditions, these appear to be authentic and represented continuity with late Roman fiscal institutions, for that is why they receive mention in Egypt, Syria, and areas of former Byzantine Mesopotamia.[41] The late Roman system of taxation, distribution of military pay, and supplies was under strain, but it had not yet disappeared in the 630s. The very strains under which the old system labored probably contributed to its demise after the Byzantine withdrawal to Anatolia. The system was not functioning well as the melting of church plate and bronze monuments at Constantinople[42] and Egyptian grievances testify.[43] The existence of payments in kind and older systems of military recruitment does not itself indicate that the entire older system of military and fiscal institutions was still operating, let alone operating smoothly.[44] There was no single coherent system. By the beginning of the seventh century many inconsistent, inefficient, and contradictory practices somehow coexisted.

How much recourse there was in the early seventh century to payments in kind is far from clear. Perhaps the Byzantine government's shortage of money and precious metals contributed to the greater use of this system of payment in kind that still remained nominally the legally authorized system of accounting. Local officials were unready to handle unprecedentedly large

[39] *CT* 7.4.4–11, 7.4.23; *CJ* 12.37.1; Vegetius, *Epitome rei militaris* 3.3. L. Foxhall and H. A. Forbes, "Σιτομετρεῖα: The Role of Grain as a Staple Food in Classical Antiquity," *Chiron* 12 (1982) 41–90.

[40] Vexatious questions about the origins of Islamic taxation: C. Cahen, s.v., "Djizya," "Kharādj" in *EI*² 2: 559–62; 4: 1030–4; Werner Schmucker, *Untersuchungen zu einigen wichtigen bodenrechtlichen Konsequenzen der islamischen Eroberungsbewegung* (Bonn 1972).

[41] A. Noth, "Die literarisch überlieferten Verträge der Eroberungszeit," *Studien zum Minderheitenproblem im Islam* (Bonner Orientalische Studien n.s. 27/1, 1973) 1: 297–301.

[42] *Parastaseis Syntomoi Chronikai* 42 (114–17 Cameron-Herrin); Theoph., *Chron.*, AM 6113 (1: 302–3 De Boor). W. E. Kaegi, "Two Studies" and "Late Roman Continuity in the Financing of Heraclius' Army," *XVI. Internationaler Byzantinistenkongress Akten* II/2 (Vienna 1981 [= *JÖB* 32/2]) 53–61; cf. Nicholas Oikonomides, "Middle Byzantine Provincial Recruits: Salary and Armament," *Gonimos* 135, and Speck, "War Bronze ein knappes Metall?" 3–17.

[43] John, Bishop of Nikiu, *Chronicle* 119.12, trans. by R. H. Charles (Oxford: Oxford University Press, 1916) 190; Antonio Carile, "Giovanni di Nikius, cronista byzantino-copto del VII secolo," *ByzStratos* 2: 353–98.

[44] Kaegi, "Notes on Hagiographic Sources for Some Institutional Changes and Continuities in the Early Seventh Century," *Byzantina* 7 (1975) 61–70.

numbers of Byzantine and allied soldiers and supply them with payments in kind in an area (Syria south of Chalkis, or Qinnasrīn, and in Palestine) where no such large Byzantine armies had previously held exactly comparable positions in the late Roman and early Byzantine periods. Their unpreparedness and lack of cooperation explain the logistical crisis and breakdown that developed into military indiscipline and unrest on the eve of the battle of the Yarmūk in 636, which contributed to the destruction of the cohesion of the Byzantine soldiers and their eventual disintegration as fighting units. Arabs who served in groups as Byzantine allies had been entitled to allotments of rations late in the sixth century.[45]

Financial strain was a reality. Contemporary sources do refer to financial shortages, in particular to the government's difficulty in finding funds to pay troops, irrespective of the ethnic origin of those troops. In the short term, Byzantium was able to raise soldiers to resist the Muslims. But many of the civilian population and their leaders were very unhappy with and unwilling to assume the fiscal burden of supporting those troops even to help defend themselves and their own region.

THE ARMY: ITS SIZE AND EFFECTIVENESS FOR THE DEFENSE OF THE EASTERN BORDERS

The army of Heraclius' empire after demobilization in 629 and 630 was almost certainly smaller than that of Justinian's reign, which the contemporary historian Agathias had speculated in estimating its strength at 150,000.[46] The question is how much smaller were the total disposable Byzantine forces at the beginning of the 630s than they had been late in the reign of Justinian. Perhaps they were smaller by as much as one-third, although it is difficult to conceive how they could have been much less than two-thirds of the late Justinianic armies' size, because of the remaining vast dimensions of the empire.

Heraclius' armies on the eve of the Muslim conquests probably included approximately 10,000 to 20,000 elite mobile praesental expeditionary forces at and near Constantinople.[47] Those troops were capable of fighting in

45 John of Ephesus, *Hist. Eccl.* 3.3, trans. by E. W. Brooks (CSCO, Scriptores Syri [Louvain 1936] 132). On this passage, also: E. Stein, *Studien zur Geschichte des byzantinischen Reiches vornehmlich unter den Kaisern Justinus II. und Tiberius Constantinus* (Stuttgart 1919) 94.

46 Agathias, *Hist.* 5.13.7. Other estimates: Jones, *LRE* 685; Hendy, *Studies* 168–9; Haldon, *Byzantium* 152–3; MacMullen, *Corruption and the Decline of Rome* 173–5.

47 Most of the estimates here are my own. For problems in estimating size of later Byzantine armies: R.-J. Lilie, "Die byzantinischen Staatsfinanzen im 8./9. Jahrhundert," *Byzsl* 48 (1987) 49–55; J. Haldon, *Byzantine Praetorians* 277–82, 546–8, and *Byzantium* 251–3; but

pitched campaigns in the field. These were the best troops who could be sent against the Muslims, or against any other invader. Of varying but usually less reliable quality were other troops: 25,000 mostly mediocre soldiers in Egypt;[48] 5–10,000 in Africa; 5–10,000 in what was left of Byzantine Italy; in the embattled Balkans under the *magister militum per Thraciam* a hypothetical 20,000, of whom probably an inadequate 8,000 to 10,000 or less were available for expeditionary campaigning elsewhere, 5,000 for fleet and island commands; under the *magister militum per Armeniam* hypothetically 12,000, but 5–8,000 or less could be spared from duties in Armenia and the rest of the Caucasus; under the critical *magister militum per Orientem* there were hypothetically 20,000, of whom 1,000 to 2,000 remained in Isauria and Cilicia for constabulary service, 8,000 in upper Mesopotamia, primarily facing the Persians but also to ward off any beduin incursions, 10,000 in Syria, especially northern Syria, of whom surely only 5,000 or less, including friendly but irregular Arab hired guards remained in the three Palestinian provinces and Arabia. The exact military command structure for these troops is unclear and any clarification depends on elucidating how long the system of late Roman *magistri militum* (Masters of the Soldiers) survived. It appears that *magistri militum* still existed on the eve of the Muslim conquests, and more specifically, that the *magister militum per Orientem* or Master of the Soldiers in the East was the military commander who still commanded the Byzantine troops in Syria and Mesopotamia. In addition to these regular troops, although some were essentially performing routine garrison duty, were friendly Arabs, whose numbers could easily match or double or triple, for a very short and specific campaign only, those of the regular Byzantine forces in Syria, Mesopotamia, and Palestine. These are only estimates, not secure figures.

The figures for non-Arab Byzantine soldiers in the Byzantine Empire in *c.* AD 630 would make a total of 113,000 to 130,000 troops at the higher end of a likely range of figures, or 98,000 or even less at the lower end. Fifty thousand or less of these might have been available for all forms of

W. Treadgold, *Byzantine Revival* (Stanford 1988) 353–4 and "On the Value of Inexact Numbers," *Byzsl* 50 (1989) 57–61; R.-J. Lilie, "Stellungnahme zu der Entgegnung W. T. Treadgolds," *Byzsl* 50 (1989) 62–3. Late Roman armies: R. MacMullen, "How Big was the Roman Army?," *Klio* 62 (1980) 451–60, and Jean-Michel Carrié, "L'esercito: trasformazioni ed economie locali," *Società romana e impero tardoantico*, 1: *Istituzioni, ceti, economie*, ed. by Andrea Giardina (Bari: Laterza, 1986) 457–8. William James Hamblin, "The Fatimid Army During the Early Crusades" (unpub. Ph.D. diss., University of Michigan, 1985) 296, estimated that the total Fatimid army in the twelfth century did not exceed 10 to 15,000 men, and its field armies ranged from 5 to 10,000. On praesental forces: John Haldon, *Byzantine Praetorians* esp. 103, 118, who argues that some elements of this force, under the *comes Obsequii*, accompanied Heraclius to Jerusalem (misdated to 629): 173, 176, 178.

48 Jean Maspero, *Organisation militaire de l'Égypte byzantine* 117–18.

deployment against Arabs. Protection of logistical lines and garrison duties probably reduced the maximum potential strength of a regular force to 20,000 or 30,000, in addition to friendly Arab contingents. However, it is possible that the financial strains at the end of the Persian wars led to an even sharper reduction in the total number of effectives, but this is very conjectural. These troops varied greatly in quality. In any case, these totals were insufficient for internal security purposes and for proper defense of the empire's borders after 630. But the logistical problems of supporting even these inadequate numbers of soldiers were formidable.

The relevance of these broader figures for defenses against potential Muslim invasion requires closer scrutiny. Probably only small postings of local regular units existed at scattered points in the three Palestinian provinces, Palestine I, Palestine II, Palestine III, and in Arabia. The largest posting probably was at Caesarea, with maybe 200 or 300 mobile troops available. Small garrisons, composed of Byzantine but in effect long assimilated indigenous troops, many of whom probably carried on some other occupation as well, existed probably of 100 or less to 200 soldiers, at sites on both sides of the Dead Sea and Jordan River valley. The quality of these troops was mediocre but not impossibly bad. Some of them drilled at least occasionally. It was difficult to coordinate these scattered garrisons if some serious external threat appeared. These garrison troops were inexperienced at fighting any open warfare of maneuver and pitched combat. They were best suited for passive, low-intensity stationary guard duty, or for defending well-fortified fixed positions. Individual towns may have held a garrison of the size of a *numerus*, whose numbers likely totalled 100 to 500 soldiers.

The largest garrisons were not in any of the three Palestinian provinces, but in northern Syria and upper Mesopotamia, facing greater traditional threats to security, namely, the Persians. A substantial garrison existed at and near Antioch, probably 1,500 or less, and a much smaller but important garrison at Chalkis (Qinnasrīn) possibly a few hundred. Troops covering the Mesopotamian frontier with Persia may have fluctuated but after demobilization in 629, in peacetime, probably counted several thousand good troops, with additional thousands of troops, and perhaps one thousand or more, established at key points, including Melitēnē, along or near the Armenian frontier. The exact strength of these units is uncertain, but the government probably maintained some strength there to insure enforcement of the peace terms of the recent peace treaty with Persia and the agreement of Arabissos of 629. The threat might come not only from the Persian government, which was weakened by internal strife, but also from dissident Persian forces, irregulars and stragglers, and beduin. Even the Byzantine government's fiscal pressures and the knowledge that Persia was no longer a major threat could not have allowed Heraclius to denude that region of all troops. But some were probably scattered at Callinicum, others at Nisibis and Dara and Edessa, Zeugma, Hierapolis, and Berrhoia. Modest-sized detachments of 100 or so may well have been the emplacements of regular soldiers, supplemented at some sites with encampments of friendly Christian (usually nominally Monophysitic) Arabs.

Local Arab garrisons probably equaled or exceeded the numbers of regular Byzantine soldiers. Likewise there appear to have been modest (hundred or more soldiers) detachments stationed at a few strategic points across the legal border inside Persia, at least at Hīt and Takrīt, on the upper Euphrates and Tigris Rivers respectively. Defenses of areas east of the Jordan and east of the Golan Heights were another matter. The Byzantine army appears to have allowed local sheikhs of a friendly sort to handle security patrols and the guarding of passage through desert and semi-desert peripheral territories.

The mobile effectives among the theoretical 25,000 troops in Egypt were probably small in number, a few thousand, widely scattered and difficult to collect to send to Syria/Palestine, of poor quality, and normally needed for internal security needs in Egypt and Cyrenaica. Even less available were troops stationed west of Egypt, in Numidia, and the Exarchate of Africa, which was exposed to grievous Berber raids. Likewise, the Byzantine government was not defending its Balkan regions well against Avars and Slavs and could temporarily divert Thracian troops, under the command of the *magister militum per Thraciam*, from there to Syria or Egypt only at the risk of experiencing the devastation of those regions and their populations.

The best Byzantine troops, those who were stationed at Constantinople, were located more than 1,600 kilometers from the areas of earliest Muslim penetration.[49] It was possible to shift them to Syria, but it was expensive and time-consuming, requiring several months at least to remove the bulk of them there. Most Byzantine troops who were already stationed in Syria were located in the north, about 800 to 1,200 kilometers away from areas of the earliest major clashes. Time, organization, money, logistical planning, and the risks of offending local population were involved in any shifts. Except for emergency short-term needs, troops other than cavalry could not move much more than 25 to 30 kilometers per day, and even that speed presented problems for transportation of some of their equipment and supplies. After such a lengthy and exhausting trip, moreover, the troops and their animals required some rest and adjustment before being truly ready for serious operations and combat. A basic reality was the government's inability to

[49] See John Haldon, *Byzantine Praetorians* esp. 103, 118.

concentrate all or even most of its potentially available troops for open campaigning or to raise expeditionary armies much larger than 20,000 soldiers, including foot and horse.

The recruitment of additional soldiers required time, money, much training, and could disrupt existing rural social and economic structures. It was easier to raise contingents from the ranks of friendly Arab tribes, who were located more conveniently and who knew the terrain and fighting techniques of the Muslim invaders at least to some extent, than to recruit troops of Greek and Latin stock.[50] Friendly Arab forces may have numbered two to five times the size of the available regular and garrison troops of "Byzantine" (Greek, Armenian, or Latin) stock; by this time very few Germanic recruits were available. Armenians could be and were recruited, but it was hazardous to rely too heavily on them, even though they shared a common Armenian heritage with Emperor Heraclius.

RELEVANCE OF THE RECENT WAR WITH PERSIA

The traditional system of rations allotments in kind probably made it more difficult for the Byzantine troops to pursue the Muslims in open country. The Byzantines were dependent, and their mobility suffered accordingly, because of their logistical system. The logistical problems in Syria in the 630s differed from those they encountered in fighting the Persians in 613 and 614.[51] Likewise, the problem of command, control, and communications in 613 and 614 differed considerably from that of the 630s: Emesa or Ḥimṣ and Damascus had a very different role as bases for the Heraclius' armies in the 630s when planning resistance against the Muslims who were coming from the Arabian peninsula. The praetorian prefecture presumably still survived in some form in the 630s, yet it was unable to cope with issuing orders to recalcitrant local officials for moving and maintaining large numbers of men and animals on the trunk road from the north, from Anatolia and from Melitēnē to Emesa (Ḥimṣ) and Damascus, and even to points further south where the final decisive combat took place.[52]

Symptomatic of difficulties with provisioning and military finance was the refusal of Byzantine authorities to pay both waggoners from the Byzantine

[50] Shahid, *BAFIC* 459–86, on Arab federates of Byzantium in the fifth century.

[51] A. Stratos, "La Première Campagne de l'empereur Héraclius contre les Perses," *JÖB* 28 (1979) 63–74, and *Studies in Seventh-Century Byzantine Political History* (London: Variorum, 1983).

[52] al-Ṭabarī, *Geschichte der Perser und Araber zur Zeit der Sasaniden aus der arabischen Chronik des Ṭabarī*, trans. by Th. Nöldeke (Leiden: Brill, 1879) 297–300, esp. n. 1 on p. 299f. Cf. al-Diyārbakrī, 1: 298; Ibn Kathīr, *Tafsīr al-Qur'ān* (Beirut: Dar al-Andalus, 1983) 5: 344.

expeditionary forces in Ctesiphon, the Persian capital, after the great Byzantine victory in 628 or later, and Arab allies near Gaza a few years later. The waggoners finally secured the reported advice and help of the spirit of St. Anastasius the Persian himself and accordingly managed to go to Constantinople and received their back pay in full. That alternative was not available to the contemporary Arab allies of Byzantium who encountered the refusal of an unidentified Byzantine eunuch to concede them their normal pay. In each of these instances, governmental officials were seeking to ease the government's financial strains by withholding money for military stipends. The difference between the cases, however, is that the refusal to pay waggoners at Ctesiphon involved the refusal to pay for services that the waggoners had already rendered, while the stipends for the Arabs near Gaza may have been for either future or past services.[53]

Byzantine soldiers in the 630s procured their arms from private purchase, or from their officers, or possibly from some of the old *fabricae* or public arms factories that still survived. φαβρικήσιοι or *fabricenses*, or workers in state arms factories, which were a fundamental part of the late Roman military and financial structure (under the *magister officiorum*), were still in existence in the early seventh century in Bithynia and at Seleucia, in northern Syria, but it is unclear whether any of them or their factories functioned elsewhere in Syria at that time or in the 630s.[54] No source reports the existence of earlier attested *fabricae* at Damascus (which had originally been created to produce weapons for use against the Arabs),[55] Edessa, or Emesa[56] in the early seventh century. Motha or Mu'ta east of the Jordan was an important site for the production of excellent swords in the medieval period; indeed, this valuable military resource may have been a motive – in addition to its location astride the principal road north from the Arabian peninsula and the Red Sea – for the early Muslim expedition to it and the battle there.[57] The copper and probably also iron of Petra (or rather of Fenan) were not far

[53] *Miracula, Acta M. Anastasii Persae* c. 3 (21 Usener).

[54] *Vie de Théodore de Sykéôn* c. 159. 45–7 (1: 134–5 Festugière); Zacos/Veglery, *BLS*, no. 1136, vol. 1.2, p. 727, seal from Seleucia, dated to about 617. Background: M. C. Bishop, ed., *The Production and Distribution of Roman Military Equipment* (Oxford: BAR, 1985). See *ND* Or. II.27–8, 32, ed. by O. Seeck (Berlin 1876, repr.) for *fabrica* at Nicomedia. On factories: S. James, "The *fabricae*: State Arms Factories of the Later Roman Empire," in *Military Equipment and the Identity of Roman Soldiers*, ed. by J. C. Coulson (Oxford: BAR, 1988) 257–331.

[55] Joh. Malalas, *Chronicon*, ed. by L. Dindorf (Bonn 1831) 307–8. *ND* Or. II.20 (32 Seeck), *Scutaria et armorum, Damasci*; date of *Notitia Dignitatum*: D. Hoffmann, *Die spätrömische Bewegungsheer* (Düsseldorf: Rheinland-Verlag, 1969) 531. But see: J. C. Mann, "What Was the Notitia Dignitatum For?," *Aspects of the Notitia Dignitatum*, ed. by R. Goodburn and P. Bartholomew (Oxford: BAR Supplementary Ser., 15, 1976) 5–8; Michael Hendy, *Studies in the Byzantine Monetary Economy* 629.

[56] Malalas, *Chron.* (307–8 Dindorf).

[57] Yāqūt/Wüstenfeld 4: 677.

away.[58] Yet the availability of arms production in some of these towns played no known role whatever in the calculations of the Byzantines and Muslims in choosing sites to attack or to defend.

Jerusalem indubitably suffered much at the hands of the Persians when they stormed it in 614. The evidence for physical destruction at the hands of the Persians in other areas of Palestine and Syria is far less well documented. Christian mosaics from the 620s in modern Jordan and Lebanon reconfirm the contention that the Persians, although Zoroastrian, did not systematically destroy churches or prevent Christian worship everywhere in areas that they controlled. Destruction on the initiative of the Persians was probably uneven in Palestine and Syria, in contrast to the contemporary devastation that they definitely wrought in Asia Minor. Persian toleration of Christian cults in some areas of Syria and Arabia allowed another dimension of continuity – religious – to exist in the early seventh century. There was no generalized destruction. This is not to diminish the hardships of some, perhaps many Christians, during Persian occupation. Persian policy may have been to destroy trees and buildings where they encountered stiff military or civilian resistance, as at Adhriʿāt (modern Syrian Derʿa), and to leave areas undisturbed where they met no resistance. The Persians did not destroy everything; they granted pacts to many towns and areas in Syria other than Jerusalem, the devastation of which was exceptional.[59]

The interlude of Persian occupation was not economically or politically favorable to the late Roman provinces of western Asia and Egypt. But although the temporary Persian occupation was disruptive of economic, political, and social life, its long-term consequences were uneven and not generally ruinous. Material conditions were tenuous but not hopeless in the provinces on the eve of the Muslim invasions. The delicate and difficult process of local recovery had begun, although no total restoration of the status of the economy, society, and culture prior to the long wars with Persia was possible.

The Byzantine Empire had undergone a wrenching experience in the long Persian invasions, and physical and economic recovery cannot have been quickly completed after the achievement of peace in 628, with the subsequent Persian evacuation. Yet it is difficult to measure how really exhausted

[58] Andreas Hauptmann, "Die Gewinnung von Kupfer: Ein uralter Industriezweig auf der Ostseite des Wadi Arabah," *Petra: Neue Ausgrabungen und Entdeckungen*, ed. by Manfred Lindner (Munich: Delp Verlag, 1986) 31–43.

[59] Some towns negotiated with Persians and received terms in Palestine, but Jerusalem suffered: Antiochus, *Expugnationis Hiersolymae A.D. 614 Recensiones arabicae* 3.1–3, 5.30–2 (Ar., Textus A: 6-11-12; B: 61–2, 66; C: 113, 118); trans. 4, 8, 42, 45, 75, 79. Michael G. Morony, "Syria Under the Persians 610–629 AD.," *1985 Bilād al-Shām Proceedings* 1: 87–95; Robert Schick, *The Christian Communities of Palestine from Byzantine to Muslim Rule* (Princeton: Darwin, 1993).

Byzantium was from that struggle. The Avaro-Slavic threat had grown enormously in the Balkans, the empire had lost its small hold on the Spanish Mediterranean coast, and its military forces were spread excessively thinly in Africa, where there was a potentially serious danger from Berber and other tribesmen, and there were insufficient resources to recover much of Italy that the Lombards had overrun in the previous three-quarters of a century. Yet it did not appear that imperial institutions were falling into irremediable decay; they were still functioning with some smoothness. The empire was not in a state of collapse at the moment of the first Islamic raids and invasions. Yet it was fiscally, psychologically, and militarily unstable and potentially volatile. Decline and disintegration were not inevitable, but there was a potential for things to go either way, for better or worse. Events overwhelmed a society and government that did not welcome change and wanted to perpetuate its late Roman institutions and mentality and the international status quo into the indefinite future.

Chapter 3

DIFFICULTIES IN DEVISING DEFENSES FOR SYRIA

DISTURBING PRECEDENTS

"All the Romans, both officers and soldiers, were far from entertaining any thought of confronting the enemy or standing in the way of their passage, but manning their strongholds as each one could, they thought it sufficient to preserve them and save themselves."[1] So the historian Procopius of Caesarea described how Byzantine commanders and soldiers in Syria and upper Mesopotamia consciously avoided open resistance to the Persians during their invasion of 540 and instead sought the security of town walls. This Byzantine military conduct in the sixth century was similar to the actions, indeed prophetic of the actions, of Byzantine commanders and officers in the same region who faced Muslim invaders in the seventh century.

The topography of Syria itself varied from empty steppe in the east to the irrigated and populous Orontes valley and the equally populous Mediterranean coastline. Its dimensions stretched from the edge of the Sinai and Arabian peninsulas to the south, to the desert to the east, and to the Euphrates River and foothills of the Taurus to the northeast and northwest (Map 2).[2] Byzantine Syria had experienced Persian invasions of terrifying dimensions in both the fourth and the sixth centuries.[3]

Similar to local garrisons, a number of Syrian and upper Mesopotamian towns had negotiated with the Persians instead of resisting to the end. It was another important precedent for similar action on the part of the town leadership in many centers in Palestine, Syria, and Byzantine Mesopotamia in the face of the Muslim invasions. Already there was a propensity to passive resistance, to seek the security of walled towns instead of trying to establish an effective defensive line in the field, and to seek to purchase peaceful terms

[1] Procopius, *Bella* 2.20.19; the translation is from the H. Dewing Loeb Library edition, vol. 1: 435.

[2] C.-P. Haase, *Untersuchungen zur Landschaftsgeschichte Nordsyriens in der Umayyadenzeit* (diss., Hamburg, pub. Kiel, 1975).

[3] Amm. 18.4.1–19.9.1, 20.6.1–21.13.9.

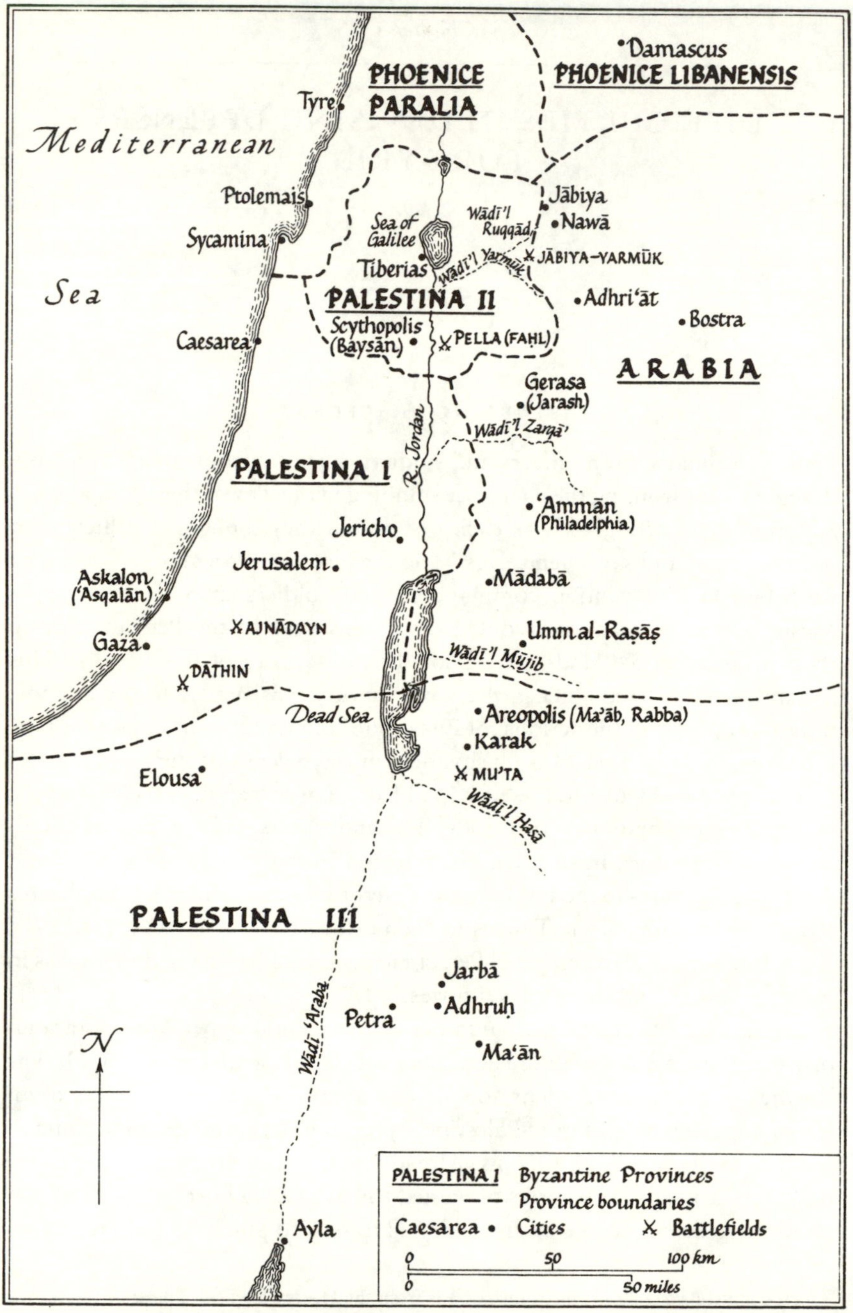

Map 2. Byzantine Palestine and southern Syria, with provincial boundaries and principal wādīs (adapted from F.-M. Abel, *Histoire de la Palestine*, vol. 2, end map)

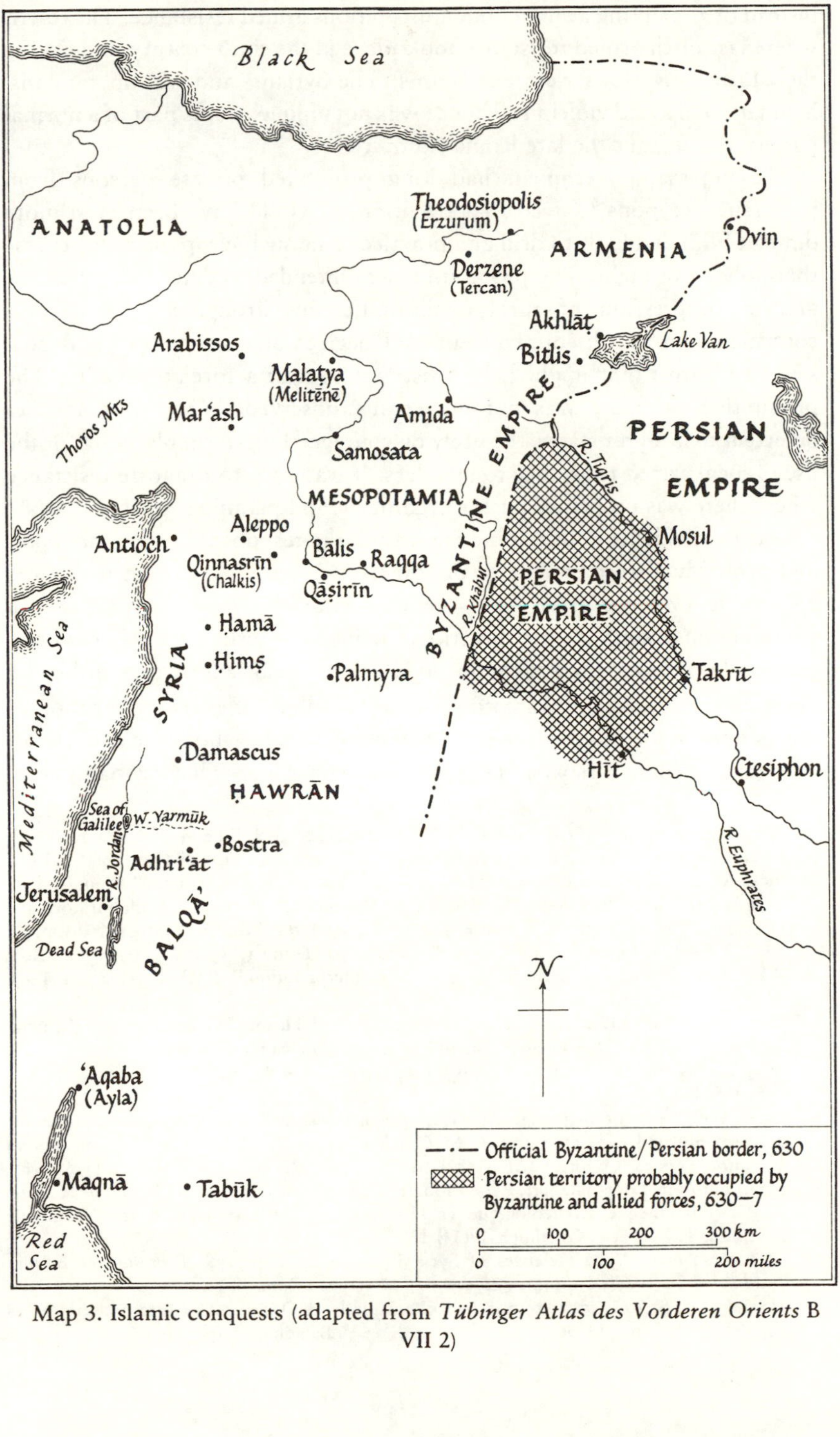

Map 3. Islamic conquests (adapted from *Tübinger Atlas des Vorderen Orients* B VII 2)

instead of attempting a violent but unpropitious armed resistance. The towns where last-ditch armed resistance took place in the sixth century and during the Muslim invasions were exceptions. The Syrians' and Mesopotamians' inclination to avoid violent resistance was not unique. It was part of a normal pattern throughout the late Roman Empire.[4]

The imperial government had long prohibited private persons from possessing weapons.[5] Given that tradition, it would have been even more difficult for individuals to drill and practice using such weapons or to reverse that policy overnight. The prohibition was intended to deter local violence and the oppression of rural communities by strongmen, but it also contributed to the discouragement and neglect of manufacture and possession of arms that might help resistance against a foreign invader. The prohibition probably was not universally observed, but it was another deterrent to local resistance. It surely discouraged long-term planning for the use of local armed resistance to invaders. It was hard to organize resistance where there was no precedent for organizing and planning for it.

Local individuals in Byzantine Syria took the responsibility for the repair and probably also maintenance of some town walls, according to limited epigraphic evidence from the seventh century.[6] This was probably a continuation of sixth-century practices.[7] In fact, the author of the late fourth-century *De rebus bellicis* recommended asking local landowners in border areas to pay the costs of watchtowers.[8] al-Balādhurī offers corroboration of this pattern in mentioning the role of two brothers to whom the defenses of Bālis (ancient Barbalissos) and Qāṣirīn were conceded.[9] They probably were

[4] Negotiated surrenders: Procopius, *Bella* 2.5.12–2.6.25; 2.7.3–9; 2.11.14–2.12.2; 2.13.16–28; G. Downey, "The Persian Campaign in Syria in AD 540," *Speculum* 28 (1953) 340–8. Little local resistance: H. Turtledove, "The Immediate Successors of Justinian" (unpub. diss., UCLA, 1977) 212–20, 238–9, 243, 250; E. A. Thompson, "Barbarian Collaborators and Christians," in: *Romans and Barbarians: The Decline of the Western Empire* (Madison, WI 1982) 239–40; S. Johnson, *Late Roman Fortifications* (Totowa, NJ 1983) 80; H. Kennedy, "The Last Century of Byzantine Syria: A Reinterpretation," *ByzF* 10 (1985) 141–83; A. H. M. Jones, *LRE* 1061–2.

[5] Just. Nov. 85 (AD 539); Priscus, *Hist.*, ed. by L. Dindorf, Historici Graeci Minores (Leipzig: Teubner, 1870) 306; Denis Feissel, Ismail Kaygusuz, "Un mandement impérial du VIe siècle dans une inscription d'Hadrianoupolis d'Honoriade," *TM* 9 (1985) 410–15; Stein, *HBE* 2: 245, 465, 480.

[6] F. M. Abel, "Inscription grecque de Gaza," *Revue Biblique* 40 (1931) 94–5, dated sometime between 614 and 635; cf. Carol A. M. Glucker, *The City of Gaza in the Roman and Byzantine Periods* (Oxford: BAR, 1987) 141. Cf. no. 2828, from Baalbek, *c.* 635/636, for repair of tower: Louis Jalabert, René Mouterde, *Inscriptions grecques et latines de la Syrie*, T. VI (Bibliothèque Archéologique et Historique, Institut français d'Archéologie de Beyrouth. T. 78 [Paris: Geuthner, 1967]) 133.

[7] W. Liebeschuetz, "The Defences of Syria in the Sixth Century," *Beihefte der Bonner Jahrbücher* 38 (1977), 2: *Studien zu den Militärgrenzen Roms* 491–3.

[8] *De rebus bellicis* 20.1, ed. and trans. by Robert I. Ireland (Oxford: BAR International Series 63, 1979) part 2, pp. 19, 36.

[9] Balādhurī 150.

local landowners who were also assuming other responsibilities, such as the collection and distribution of tax revenue. Defences in Syria, it is clear, were not handled exclusively by public authorities. As in other parts of the empire, local landowners legally or illegally controlled private soldiers, ostensibly to restrain brigandage or simply to enforce their own power. Such private soldiers may have been poorly armed but they could have served as a potential reserve pool of men on whom one might draw for resistance to the Muslims. But it is essential to remember that the Byzantine government had been attempting to prevent private individuals from bearing arms. These policies were inconsistent, yet no one remedied the inconsistency. While it would be an exaggeration, indeed inaccurate, to conceive of a total process of "privatization" of Byzantine local defenses in the seventh century, whether in the Levant or elsewhere, the known cases are reminders that some local individuals did draw on their own resources to defend themselves and their fellow inhabitants.[10] Less clear are the social and economic causes and consequences. There was no tradition in Syria or Palestine of arming the broader population in the towns or the countryside for self-defense; that population had no experience in bearing arms. Moreover, the local population, including its elites, was not anticipating any major trouble with Arabs. Local officials were not preparing local civilians to resist any invasions.[11]

The Byzantine Empire of Heraclius could not afford to maintain the dense network of garrisons on which Rome had once depended. The process of the abandonment of the older frontiers was well advanced already by the sixth century. There was insufficient manpower to afford substantial garrisons on any frontier except possibly the Mesopotamian border with Persia.[12]

Religious reasons dictated giving careful attention to the defense of Palestine, including protection of the holy sites and the pilgrims, even though the empire's financial and manpower resources might suffer strain. Insecurity, an alien seizure, or injury now engaged not only earlier strategic and fiscal and security considerations but also in a more direct way the prestige of the government and its ability to defend the faith and land, which was important to the faith and to the faithful.

[10] Ramsay MacMullen, *Corruption and the Decline of Rome* 122–97, on "privatization."

[11] The Muslim incursions surprised Patriarch Sophronius of Jerusalem and others in early 634: *PG* 87:3197D; Christoph von Schönborn, *Sophrone de Jérusalem* (Paris: Editions Beauchesne, 1972) 90.

[12] I thank S. Thomas Parker and Fawzi Zayadine for good advice. Unpersuasive is A. Alt, "Beiträge zur historischen Geographie und Topographie des Negeb, V: Das Ende des Limes Palestinae," *Journal of the Palestine Oriental Society* 18 (1938) 149–60; "Der Limes Palestinae im sechsten und siebenten Jahrhundert nach Chr.," *ZDPV* 63 (1940) 129–42.

BYZANTINE RELIANCE ON ARAB MILITARY ASSISTANCE

The government could not lightly strip its other exposed frontiers of troops to commit to the defense of Syria, Palestine, and Mesopotamia. There was limited elasticity in the assignment of troops other than the elite mobile expeditionary forces at and near Constantinople, and the potential contingents of friendly Arabs who could be raised. The failure of Niketas, cousin of Heraclius, in 613–14 may have taught Byzantine commanders something of the problems involved in moving, coordinating, and supplying reserve troops from Egypt when dispatched to Palestine and Syria and thereby affected Byzantine calculations about coordinating the defenses of Egypt and Palestine in the 630s.[13] It is possible that various Arabs also observed and drew conclusions about those options.

Any effort to train and arm the civilian population of those threatened provinces was a complex and slow affair, which could not meet sudden massive external threats. The government probably did not conceive of a massive militarization of the civilian population of the affected provinces, probably doubting its efficacy or the internal security aspects if it were possible. How well troops could adjust to campaign conditions in Palestine was another matter too. Galilee was one thing, areas east of the Dead Sea presented other challenges of climate and terrain.

The best sources of military manpower for the defense of Syria, Palestine, and Byzantine Mesopotamia in the early seventh century were: (1) Arab beduin on the periphery of the empire, although many Arabs were also settled in the towns and villages, and (2) Heraclius' kinfolk, the Armenians. The Byzantine army was not large in size, and it was poor in discipline, toughness, and combat experience and readiness. More important, its effective mobile striking forces were modest. It could ill afford to commit more than 20,000 of these for major eastern campaigns. Equally uncertain are the numbers of new recruits. Byzantine positions in Africa and Italy were under almost constant threat, so they could serve as no source for soldiers, and actually competed with the eastern frontiers for manpower. They needed reinforcement themselves. There was no alternative, in short, to seeking military manpower for Syria, Palestine, and Mesopotamia from nearby and reliable Armenia and especially from Arab beduin, who had the added advantage of familiarity with the local terrain, climate, and military methods of the empire's potential enemies.[14]

13 Niketas attempted from Egypt to aid defense of Palestine against Persians: John of Barca was sent with troops to aid the defense of Egypt against the Muslims, according to John of Nikiu, *Chron.* c. 111.1–3 (178–9 Charles). Nicephorus, *Hist.* 23 (70–1 Mango).

14 al-Ṭabarī i 2081, i 2347, i 2394; Balādhurī, 135–6, 164, 181–3; Azdī 28, 111, 125, 152, 174–7; Ibn al-Athīr (2: 308, 381 Tornberg). Manpower problem: E. Stein, *Studien* (Stuttgart 1919)

Roman and Byzantine policies toward the Arabs before the 630s remain obscure.[15] The rebellion of the Ghassānids, who had been Byzantine federated allies, after Maurice's very imprudent arrest and exile of their phylarch al-Mundhir in 581 and the termination of their subsidies, and the slaying of Nu'mān III b. al-Mundhir, King of the Lakhmids, in 602, somehow with the connivance if not explicitly on the orders of Chosroes II, had demonstrated the perils of antagonizing hitherto friendly Arab tribal groupings while they had given Arabs relatively recent examples of the perfidy of rulers of empires and additional reason to be wary of their intentions. It was important for Byzantium to retain the friendship of at least some of the tribes. But those events had taken place more than a half-century earlier, and their memory would have existed for some Arabs (perhaps Arabs both inside and outside the Byzantine Empire) and for some Byzantine officials at various levels of authority and rank. Only Monophysite histories mentioned the rebellion of al-Mundhir; court histories such as Theophylact's omitted that embarrassing subject, even though knowledge of it might have helped Heraclius and his advisers make more intelligent decisions.[16]

Whether or not the Byzantines approached the Ghassānids for some kind of restoration of relationships in the reign of Phocas or Heraclius, the fact is that they and their last king, Jabala b. al-Ayham, were foremost among the allied Arab tribes of Byzantium in the early 630s.[17] The Byzantines diversified their relationships with the Arabs by also drawing on other friendly tribes.

117–29; R. MacMullen, "How Big Was the Roman Army?," *Klio* 62 (1980) 451–60; MacMullen, *Corruption* 173–5, 185.

15 Rudolf E. Brünnow, Alfred v. Domaszewski, *Die Provincia Arabia*, 3 vols. (Strasburg 1904–9); G. W. Bowersock, *Roman Arabia* (Cambridge, MA: Harvard, 1983); Irfan Shahid, *BAFOC*, in which is also bibliography of his articles on Ghassānids, also his *BAFIC*, esp. his art. On "Ghassān," *EI*² 2; 1020–21; S. T. Parker, *Romans and Saracens: A History of the Arabian Frontier* (Winona Lake, IN 1986) and Parker, *The Roman Frontier in Central Jordan* (Oxford: BAR International Series 340, 1987); M. Sartre, *Trois études sur l'Arabie romaine et byzantine* (Brussels: Revue d'Etudes Latines, 1982); M. Sartre, *Bostra: Des origines à l'Islam* (Paris: Geuthner, 1985) 99–139; Benjamin Isaac, *Limits of Empire* (Oxford: Clarendon, 1990).

16 John of Ephesus, *HE* 3.3.42 (Brooks, CSCO, Versio 132). Theophylact Simocatta, *Hist.* 2.10.4 (89 De Boor). Background: P. Goubert, *Byzance avant l'Islam* 1: 249–60, "Le Problème ghassanide à la veille de l'Islam," *Actes, VIe Congrès International des Etudes Byzantines* (Paris 1950) 1: 103–18, makes an unconvincing defense of Maurice's Ghassānid policy. I. Shahid's advice was helpful on this problem.

17 al-Ṭabarī i 2081, 2109, 2124–5, 2347; Balādhurī 135–6; Th. Nöldeke, *Die ghassânischen Fürsten* 46–51. Ibn 'Asākir 1: 531; al-Ya'qūbī (2: 160 Houtsma). J. Sauvaget, "Les Ghassānides et Sergiopolis," *Byzantion* 14 (1939) 115–30; H. Gaube, "Arabs in Sixth-Century Syria: Some Archaeological Observations," *British Society for Middle Eastern Studies Bulletin* 8 (1981) 93–8; René Dussaud, *La Pénétration des Arabes en Syrie avant l'Islam* (Paris: Geuthner, 1955); Henri Charles, *Le Christianisme des arabes nomades sur le limes et dans le désert syro-mésopotamien aux alentours de l'Hégire* (Paris: Bibliothèque de l'Ecole des Hautes-Etudes, 1936); J. S. Trimingham, *Christianity among the Arabs in Pre-Islamic Times* (London, New York: Longman, 1979).

The policy was perfectly consistent with Byzantium's preferences and practices in the search for internal and external security in other areas of the empire and in other situations and crises. What precisely the relationships of the Byzantines were with any of these tribes, however, remains, like the number of their effectives, unclear. Arab manpower was often recruited in groups from specific tribes, with such soldiers retaining their tribal affiliations and identity; they were not simply individual recruits.

BYZANTINE AUTHORITY AND THE NOMADS: DIVERGENT VIEWS

Less clear is the relationship between Arab nomads beyond the Byzantine frontier with the settled population on the land and in the towns inside the frontier. In the centuries previous to the Muslim conquest, that relationship had fluctuated between armed conflict and peaceful mutual dependence and support. But the Byzantine army did not maintain costly bases and responsibilities for nothing, especially in an era of great fiscal pressures. Nomadic and sedentary populations were not always in violent conflict on the Transjordanian, Syrian, and Mesopotamian frontiers.

A principal function of the late Roman troops who were stationed there was enforcement of Byzantine authority, the monitoring of tribal movements, and the prevention of nomadic raiding. There unquestionably was at least intermittent interdependence and mutualism. But the empire did not commit hard to obtain, expensive, crack troops to posts there merely to observe pastoral activities. The quality of the elite troops who garrisoned some posts probably deteriorated during the course of their stationing, but their assignment to this region involved major real costs to the government and presumably was not decided lightly. Those expensive troops had military functions. Behind them lay a genuine fear of potential damage to settled areas and their populations and to the integrity of Byzantine authority. One should not assume constant warfare, but those Byzantine troops had genuine military functions. They were not mere symbols. They were expensive commitments of good troops, which the government, if it could, would have gladly moved to some other hard-pressed and exposed frontier. Military force at a considerable financial cost helped to contribute some order to the edge of human habitation.[18]

[18] Relative degree of armed strife on the frontier before the Muslim conquest: E. B. Banning, "Peasants, Pastoralists, and *Pax Romana*: Mutualism in the Highlands of Jordan," *BASOR* 261 (1986) 25–50; E. B. Banning, "*De Bello Paceque*: A Reply to Parker," *BASOR* 265 (1987) 52–4; S. Thomas Parker, "Peasants, Pastoralists, and *Pax Romana*: A Different View," *BASOR* 265 (1987) 35–51; Philip Mayerson, "The Saracens and the Limes," *BASOR* 262 (1986) 35–47; Philip Mayerson, "Saracens and Romans: Micro–Macro Relationships," *BASOR* 274 (1989) 71–9.

The Byzantines also used sedentary Arabs in southern Palestine to protect that region from raids by hostile beduin in the late sixth century.[19] Camps of friendly Arabs on the outer perimeter of the region of important towns had potential military significance for the security of those cities. In seventh-century Byzantine Syria at the time of the Muslim conquest there was a camp, or *ḥāḍir*, of Arabs near Ḥimṣ or Emesa, and other such camps appear to have existed in northern Syria.[20]

It is uncertain how many camps of allied beduin existed near other major Byzantine towns on the edge of the desert at the beginning of the 630s such as the *ḥīra*, that is, an encampment that the Byzantine client Arabs had formerly used as their base for guarding the approaches to Gaza.[21] The Byzantine government obviously had become dependent upon them because they were perceived to be less expensive and more effective and more available than alternative military manpower. Such Arab camps appear to have been a critical element in the defenses of such towns. They helped to substitute for the lack of military training of the townspeople, and they probably were expected to provide information and supply guards for travelers as well as serve as stationary guards of these towns and their neighboring villages and countryside. At one of the earliest Byzantine battles against the invading Muslims, that of Ajnādayn, the Byzantines depended very heavily on local Arabs for provisions.[22]

BYZANTINE COMMUNICATIONS IN THE SYRIAN DESERT AND THE TWILIGHT OF PALMYRA

The *Acta* of St. Anastasius the Persian, which were recorded very soon after 631, mention a route across the Syrian desert from the Sassanian royal palace at Dastagert, which is relatively near the Diyala River at Zindān, ʻIrāq, to Palmyra, in the Syrian desert.[23] It was possible to traverse that route only with the aid of an unidentified Arab *phylarch* [φύλαρχος, head of tribe], but the reference to one indicates that some friendly Byzantine phylarchate with Arabs did exist in that area of the Syrian desert at the very moment of the emergence of Islam. One of the reasons for its existence, as is indicated in the

[19] C. J. Kraemer, *Excavations at Nessana*, 3 vols. (London: British School of Archaeology in Jerusalem, 1950–62); Philip Mayerson, "The Saracens and the Limes," *BASOR* 262 (1986) 35–47.

[20] Balādhurī 144; Shahid, *BAFOC* 401–4; Caetani, *AI* 3: 790–1.

[21] Theoph., *Chron.*, A. M. 6124 (336 De Boor).

[22] Christian Arabs give Byzantines supplies at Ajnādayn: Kūfī 1: 144. Donner, *EIC* 320.

[23] ʼΕπάνοδος τοῦ λειψάνου τοῦ ἁγίου μάρτυρος ʼΑναστασίου ἐκ Περσίδος εἰς τὸ μοναστέριον αὐτοῦ, in: *Acta M. Anastasii Persae*, ed. by H. Usener (Bonn 1894) 13b.31–7. Location of Dastagert in Iraq: F. Sarre, E. Herzfeld, *Archäologische Reise im Euphrat- und Tigris Gebiet* (Berlin: D. Reimer, 1920) 2: 87–9.

evidence in these accounts of miracles, is the Byzantine government's presumed need for friendly Arabs to guard the desert regions and the routes through them.[24] At least some kind of friendly Byzantine relationship with this unidentified phylarch existed in that region after the overthrow of Chosroes II and the imposition of a Byzantine–Persian peace treaty. But some kind of phylarchate had been established or restored in that region after the cessation of hostilities with Persia and after the Persian armies' evacuation of Shyria and Byzantine Mesopotamia. This final Graeco-Roman reference to Palmyra before the Muslim conquests indicates that Palmyra remained a fortified point.

The Arab phylarchate in the Syrian desert was inadequate to the task of containing beduin there. It is possible, of course, that relations between that phylarchate and the Byzantines soured in the decisive but brief period between the transferral of the remains of St. Anastasius the Persian and the beginning of the Muslim conquests. In theory there was no absolute power vacuum, at least not in 631. The size of the armed forces that were at the disposal of that phylarch is unknown, but Palmyra was serving as some kind of terminus for trade, communications, and travel on the very eve of the Muslim invasions. Moreover, the Byzantines were able, probably with the assistance of regional authorities such as this unidentified phylarch, to make use of or possibly even dominate the route between Palmyra and the center of Sassanian Mesopotamia. The implication it left, however, was that travel was still otherwise insecure. It was, in short, very imprudent and dangerous to travel or ship anything via that route without the cooperation of a friendly phylarch.

THE STATE OF STRATEGY AND WARFARE

Blind spots of vulnerability remained in Byzantine strategic and operational frames of reference. Byzantine histories and manuals of warfare contain no special wisdom on how to defend Palestine, Syria, or Byzantine Mesopotamia, or Egypt or what were the best tactics and strategy and forms of military operations to employ in fighting against Arabs. The historian Procopius, who wrote in the middle of the sixth century, claimed that beduin could not storm city walls: "For Saracens are by nature unable to conduct sieges. For even the weakest barrier constructed with mud becomes an obstacle to their attack." The late sixth-century ecclesiastical historian

24 This phylarch [φύλαρχος] was a tribal leader, but not necessarily a formal Byzantine federate, although this is not excluded. The author also refers to "camps" or encampments or stages in using the term παρεμβολαῖς. Basic is I. Shahid, *BAFOC* 496 and *BAFIC* 181–91, 212–13. On φύλαρχος, Shahid, *BAFOC* 514–19.

Evagrius Scholasticus, who, significantly, came from northern Syria, where he had some familiarity with Arabs and problems of local terrain, remarks that the best way to fight the Arabs was to use other Arabs against them.[25]

The late sixth-century historian Menander Protector spoke of the "uncouthness and unreliability" of Arabs, and a few decades later, in the early seventh century, another historian, Theophylact Simocatta, similarly wrote "for the Saracen tribe is known to be most unreliable and fickle, their mind is not steadfast, and their judgment is not firmly grounded in prudence."[26] Problems of Arab raiding in southern Palestine and Byzantine countermeasures were familiar to such local Byzantine authors as Choricius of Gaza[27] and St. Nilus the Sinaite.[28]

The Byzantines may have heard something about Persia's experiences on that eastern border with beduin, but if so, it is unknown. The experiences of Heraclius' father, Heraclius the Elder, as a general on the northern edge of the Mesopotamian plain, in addition to Heraclius' own during his war with the Persians, may have formed the emperor's impressions about the fighting abilities of the Arabs and the best ways to fight them.[29] Equally unknown is how much local commanders communicated to Heraclius and his immediate circle of military and political advisers and decisionmakers about their immediate experiences and perceptions about the fighting ability and threat of the Arabs on the eastern frontier.

Waging war had its challenges in the seventh century. Distances and slow communications contributed to organizational problems of command, control, communications, and intelligence, and in particular, procurement, distribution and maintenance of arms and equipment, provisions, delegation of authority, and the deployment of soldiers and mounts. It was difficult to

[25] Procopius, *De Aed.* 2.9.4–5 (my trans.). This dangerous assumption may have led to serious Byzantine miscalculations in the late 620s and early 630s, including overreliance on walled towns. The repetition of this axiom by Procopius may have reinforced its seeming weight of authority. Evagrius, *HE* 5.20 (216 Bidez-Parmentier).

[26] Menander Protector, frg. 9.1 *Hist.*, trans. by R. C. Blockley (Liverpool: Cairns, 1985) 100–1. Theophylact Simocatta, *Hist.* 3.17.7 (151 De Boor); trans. by Michael and Mary Whitby, *The History of Theophylact Simocatta* (Oxford: Clarendon Press, 1986) 100.

[27] F. Litsas, "Choricius of Gaza: An Approach to His Work: Introduction, Translation, Commentary" (unpub. Ph.D. diss., University of Chicago, 1980).

[28] F. Nau, "Le Texte grec des récits du moine Anastase sur les saints pères du Sinai," *Oriens Christianus* 2 (1902) 65–6; Nilus, *Narrationes*, *PG* 79: 589, 597, 604, 637. Antoninus Placentinus, *Itinerarium* 40. 7, cf. 35–9, ed. by Celestina Milani (Milan: Università Cattolica, 1977) 214, cf. 200–13, for problems in Sinai in late sixth century.

[29] A. Pernice, *L'Imperatore Eraclio* 25–6; N. H. Baynes, "The Military Operations of the Emperor Heraclius," *United Service Magazine* n.s. 46 (1913) 526–33, 659–66; 47 (1913) 30–8, 195–201, 318–24, 401–12, 532–41, 665–78; C. Toumanoff, "The Heraclids and the Arsacids," *REArm* 19 (1985) 431–4. Gustav Rothstein, *Die Dynastie der Lakhmiden in al-Ḥîra; ein Versuch zur arabisch-persischen Geschichte zur Zeit der Sasaniden* (Berlin 1899; repr. Hildesheim: Olms, 1968) 116–19; Irfan Shahid, "Lakhmids," *EI*² 5 (1986) 633–4.

enforce commands, because generals did not always respect other generals' competence and authority. They sometimes even refused to cooperate in the implementation of military operations.

Byzantium usually waged protracted wars on its eastern frontiers, avoiding decisive and potentially bloody battles. The reasons for this dominance of protracted warfare, despite the fact that many of its practitioners were mounted, were complex. But clearly among them was the limited amount of available resources, namely, money, men, and material. The Byzantines accordingly chose to exercise caution and cleverness in warfare more than sheer quantitative strength and raw power. Dissimulation and attrition were preferable to bloody combat on the battlefield with all of the risky potential of the uncontrollable unknown. The norm was a slow and crafty warfare of attrition that required endless patience, dissimulation and false negotiations, timing, cleverness, and seemingly endless maneuvering. The objective was the disruption of the opponent's equilibrium but not necessarily his total physical destruction. Glory and zeal in battle were not necessarily essential for success. Caution, prudence, and a minimum of casualties were more important. They assumed frequent Byzantine numerical inferiority and the need to compensate for this with intelligence and cunning in military planning and operations.[30] The empire's acceptance of a cautious military strategy of risk minimization helped to reduce the chance that some gamble would result in a total military catastrophe or the very dissolution of the empire. There was nothing of the essentially modern strategic concept of the maximum concentration of force but a reluctance to commit all of the forces. Yet the fog of war still created many risks and uncertainties and opportunities for Byzantine commanders to try to employ craftiness.

The *Strategikon* of Maurice, written *c.* 600, embodies contemporary Byzantine military thought.[31] This strategist warns against open battles and advises in favor of cunning, guile, caution, and suspicion in war. Defeat and disruption, not slaughter, of the enemy is the objective to achieve by means

[30] *Anonymous Byzantine Treatise on Strategy* c. 33, ed. and trans. by George Dennis, *Three Byzantine Military Treatises* (Dumbarton Oaks Texts, IX [Washington, DC: Dumbarton Oaks, 1985]) 102–5. Cf. *Menae patricii cum Thoma referendario De scientia politica dialogus...*, ed. by C. M. Mazzucchi (Milan 1982), a contemporary sixth-century source, although it draws on earlier Graeco-Roman texts. Broader context: W. Kaegi, *Some Thoughts on Byzantine Military Strategy* (Hellenic Studies Lecture for Ball State University, published at Brookline, MA, by Hellenic College Press, 1983).

[31] *Das Strategikon des Maurikios*, ed. by G. T. Dennis and Ger. trans. by E. Gamillscheg, *CFHB*, (Vienna 1981); Eng. trans. by G. T. Dennis, *Maurice's Strategikon: Handbook of Byzantine Military Strategy* (Philadelphia: University of Pennsylvania Press, 1984); C. M. Mazzucchi, "ΚΑΤΑΓΡΑΦΑΙ dello 'Strategikon' di Maurizio," *Aevum* 55 (1981) 111–38; J. Witta, "The Ethnika in Byzantine Military Treatises" (unpub. Ph.D. diss., University of Minnesota, 1977); A. Kollautz, "Das Militärwissenschaftliche Werk des sog. Maurikios," *Byzantiaka* 5 (1985) 87–136.

of secrecy, flexibility, and a readiness to use diverse techniques for fighting different types of opponents.[32] He displays a readiness to exploit uncertainties while minimizing one's own casualties, resort to artifices, diplomacy, delay, dissimulation, dissension, corruption, caution, and the indirect approach to warfare. By the seventh century this Byzantine approach to waging war was set. No extant sources indicate what kinds of military treatises or memoranda resulted from Heraclius' wars with the Persians in the seventh century. It is impossible to know how Byzantine tacticians and strategists drew up – if they ever did – assessments of how to wage war in the light of their recent experiences against the Persians. Yet it seems unlikely that they were unaffected by that protracted conflict.

There is no evidence whether Muslims possessed copies of Byzantine manuals of war on the eve of or during the course of their early invasions and conquests of Byzantine territories. It is even less certain whether the Muslims profited from seizing or acquiring any other written Byzantine manuals of war or other more secret written military and political documents and information. The military events of the Muslim conquests did not derive from the writing of any special military manual. Some might well attribute ultimate responsibility to Muḥammad's writing ability, but there was no military treatise, whether anonymous or by a specific author, that inspired or changed military strategy, tactics, or operations for the Byzantines or the Muslims in the middle of the seventh century. Muslim sources imply that espionage was transmitted in the form of verbal reports rather than confidential written documents and reports to Muslim leaders.

LIMITATIONS OF A DEFENSE-IN-DEPTH STRATEGY

There is no simple organizational theory to explain Byzantine strategy, Byzantine defeat, or Muslim strategy and Muslim victories. Likewise, bureaucratic politics cannot explain Byzantine or Muslim strategy during the early Islamic conquests. Byzantine strategy of the 630s and 640s did not emerge from any organizational or bureaucratic matrix. Some bureaucrats were involved in activities on eve of Muslim invasions and in actual operations, such as the *sakellarios* at Yarmūk, but probably not in formulating any strategy.

A broad strategy of mobile defense-in-depth characterized Byzantine military operations and defense efforts in Palestine and Syria. This resulted from the small-scale frequent nomadic raids that did not normally require the mustering and dispatch of large intervention forces for the defense of the

[32] Maurice, *Strategikon* 2.1; 7A pr.; 8.1.7; 8.2.4; 8.2.8; 8.2.47; 8.2. 80–1; 8.2.92.

empire. The empire lacked the proper topography or sufficient manpower to resort to a frontal/forward defense strategy, which would have committed the bulk of troops along the empire's periphery to stop hostile incursions before they resulted in serious damage to the terrain, structures, agriculture, and civilian population of exposed areas.

Such a strategy would have resulted in great risks if the invader somehow broke through the outer perimeter with its garrisons, because there would have been insufficient reserves to shift against the forces of penetration. This strategy of mobile defense-in-depth was consistent with Byzantine avoidance of big pitched battles and risky military engagements. It was coupled to use of timing, delay, and diplomacy to try to check, stave off, or neutralize enemies. The Byzantine strategy on the eve of the Muslim conquests was one of defense-in-depth, even though we do not have the precise figures for size of armies and their precise garrison locations.

Defense-in-depth depended on several other conditions. A strategy of mobile defense-in-depth also placed great need on accurate intelligence to identify where to send central intervention forces. Yet the Byzantines lacked that high quality of timely information about the Muslims and their intentions. It also assumed that the civilian population could avoid much damage by taking cover in secure places, namely, walled towns and rough terrain or terrain with adequate cover for hiding from invaders.

Anyone contemplating a defense against an invasion from the south could envisage using a sequence of defense lines that stretched from south to north in the region east of the Dead Sea: the Wādī'l Ḥasā, the Wādī'l Mūjib or Arnọn River, the Wādī'l Zarqā', and, of course, the River Yarmūk. Topography, length of exposed area, limited manpower, potential and probable mobility of foe all encouraged or required some kind of defense-in-depth instead of a frontal/forward, linear defense along some fixed barrier to foes. It was possible to attempt to create barriers at or near some wādīs, but nothing more was practicable until withdrawal to the Taurus Mountains and their passes. Even there, the basic strategy continued to be experiments with various adaptations of defense-in-depth. Fortresses provided fixed points for defense, in this larger scheme of a mobile defense-in-depth, but Byzantine fortresses were not located in some manner that interlocked them so that no one could take or neutralize them except sequentially one by one. Only modest numbers of light forces, in the hundreds of troops, were stationed at scattered posts in a frontier zone of considerable depth (100+ miles, probably) itself. They were the most that could be afforded given the empire's financial and manpower conditions.

The Byzantines were prepared in Syria and Palestine to confront small-scale penetrations by having mobile garrisons of local troops under *duces*, but local Arab allies did most of the patrolling and fighting. The central intervention forces who were best able to counter rare, large-scale penetrations were located near Constantinople and behind upper Mesopotamian frontiers with Persia, and, to lesser extent, in Byzantine Armenia to contain the enemy's rare major incursions after the peace of 628. It was hoped that there would be no more Persian incursions given the situation of a weakened government there. Muslim strategy and operations were well suited for this defense-in-depth of the Byzantines and took good advantage of it.

Several military experiences of previous decades contributed to the framework of military thought on campaigning and tactics for both antagonists during the Muslim invasions. Most relevant for the warfare of the 630s were experiences in the lengthy war between Byzantium and Persia, which had lasted almost three decades, from about 603 to 628. In that war Byzantium had become familiar with topography and had developed a fundamental understanding of how to wage offensive decisive warfare, which included an appreciation of the critical role of various mountain passes and roads, such as those of the Taurus. Yet already in the middle of the sixth century Procopius of Caesarea had been aware of the protective role of the Taurus Mountains for the security of Anatolia; it did not require experiencing the fighting of the early 600s to learn that.[33]

The Byzantine defense-in-depth basic strategy continued and intensified in the face of defeats in battle. The Byzantines attempted to use assassinations and kidnappings and deception and sowing dissension in enemy ranks to reinforce their enfeebled and broken defense-in-depth. The Byzantines, like any power, developed their own mix of frontal and defense-in-depth forces for strategies to contain opponents. Byzantines placed special reliance on Arab mercenaries of friendly tribes to assume the essential early role of containment in forward or frontal areas of contact with invaders and raiders. Most of their best defense forces were kept far in rear, nowhere near areas of initial Muslim penetration. This strategy of defense-in-depth, because it avoided decisive tests whenever possible, probably, although at great civilian and territorial costs, contributed to the survival of at least one part of the Byzantine Empire.

VOLATILITY AND FLUCTUATING LOYALTIES

Fluctuating and alternating loyalties created another dimension of volatility, risk, and uncertainty in war for Byzantium but one that also offered opportunities for achieving objectives without horrendous losses in battle.

[33] Procopius, *Bella* 1. 10. 1–2; cf. 1. 17. 17.

The propensity to switch sides worked well with the Byzantine resort to cunning in the search for military victory. Desertion and switching sides had played a very important role in the Byzantine–Persian war between 603 and 628.[34] Inducement to desert and treacherous seizure of the enemy leadership typified internal strife early in the seventh century[35] and intensified volatility, instability, and lack of cohesion even though their practitioners sought to create cohesion.

The Byzantine troops stationed on the eastern frontiers had a long heritage of military unrest. Problems of provisioning that seriously irritated civilians and soldiers in the fourth[36] and sixth centuries[37] accompanied the late sixth-century concentration of troops in northern Syria and Mesopotamia.[38] Some of these restive soldiers from upper Mesopotamia probably brought their restlessness and readiness to mutiny along with themselves when they came to help defend Syria and Palestine.

Fears about the cohesion of their own armies and dangers of unrest appear to have acted as a restraint on the employment of Byzantine troops and as a restraint on the freedom of their commanders to undertake certain military operations. The dangers of unrest were quite real. Nervousness about the risk of betrayal heightened tensions within the Byzantine armies, often at critical moments.

Both Byzantine and Muslim armies were vulnerable to volatility. The recent Ridda wars (local resistance movements in the Arabian peninsula that opposed the Islamic government at Medina) had demonstrated the potential fragility of the political loyalties of tribes, although hardly any tribe reverted to polytheism.[39] Byzantine leaders probably distrusted all Arabs and were on the watch for desertion, whether from their own side or from that of the opponents. They may well have hoped, through negotiations and playing for time, to have found ways to induce some Arabs to break away from others, as they and their predecessors had previously experienced. It is doubtful that Heraclius, in the light of such sentiments, ever placed complete reliance even on Christian Arabs for the defense of Syria.[40] The *Miracula* of St. Anastasius the Persian confirm that on the eve of the Muslim invasions there remained

[34] Shahrbaraz: Ibn ʻAbd al-Ḥakam, *Futūḥ miṣr* (35–7 Torrey); Theoph., *Chron.*, A. M. 6118 (323–4 De Boor); cf. Thomas Artsruni, *History of the House of the Artsrunik'* (Detroit: Wayne State, 1985) 162–3; Stratos, Βυζάντιον 2: 635–42; Cyril Mango, "Deux études sur Byzance et la Perse sassanide," *TM* 9 (1985) 105–17. [35] Kaegi, *BMU* 120–49.

[36] G. Downey, "The Economic Crisis at Antioch under Julian the Apostate," *Studies in Roman Economic and Social History in Honor of A. C. Johnson* (Princeton 1951) 312–21. But, J. Liebeschuetz, *Antioch* (Oxford 1972) 80–117.

[37] Joshua the Stylite, *Chronicle*, c. 92–5, ed. and trans. by W. Wright (Cambridge 1882) 71–73. Joh. Ephes. *HE* 3.3.6.28 (252 Brooks); *S. Eutychii Patriarchae Constantinopoli Vita*, *PG* 86: 2344. [38] Kaegi, *BMU* 64–88. [39] Donner, *EIC* 85–9.

[40] Theophylact Simocatta, *Hist.* 3.17.7 (151 De Boor).

a mortal hostility between some Samaritans and Byzantine soldiers, although other Samaritans reportedly fought alongside Byzantines against Muslims when Sergios was defeated near Gaza in 634.[41]

MILITARY LEADERSHIP OF HERACLIUS

Heraclius continued to be an energetic emperor, the embodiment of the empire, at the beginning of and throughout the 630s. It is incorrect to assume that illness had decisively incapacitated him. Although he visited Syria, Palestine, and Byzantine Mesopotamia, he – like other Byzantine emperors – never visited Egypt. However, he had a much better acquaintance with topography, roads and communications, availability of food, climate, and weather conditions in Syria, Palestine, and Byzantine Mesopotamia than had any emperor since the end of the fourth century. He was both the first emperor since Julian the Apostate to use Antioch in Syria as his base of operations[42] and the first emperor to take personal command of armies in the field since Theodosius the Great.[43] Antioch was a good base for monitoring and safeguarding communications between Byzantine troops in Syria and Palestine and those in Anatolia and Byzantine Armenia. His presence there underlined his personal interest in and commitment to a successful defense of these threatened areas. He may also have consulted memoranda or summaries of memoranda of earlier emperors and their military advisers on how to fight various enemies, including the Persians.[44] Heraclius reportedly studied earlier military precedents from antiquity, but those were more relevant for fighting the Persians than Arabs. Thus earlier Roman and Byzantine precedents for concentrating troops at Antioch were probably of little or no relevance, especially because Antioch had previously served as a base of operations against the Persians to the east, not against Arabs coming from the south and southeast.

Heraclius was the only reigning Byzantine emperor to visit Jerusalem. He was familiar with the principal roads to Palestine, the formidable Taurus mountain range, and the roads of northern Syria and Mesopotamia. His cousin Niketas probably gave him first-hand reports on the problems of leading armies from Egypt into Palestine and Syria, problems that Niketas encountered in 610 and 613. Part of the time between 631 and 634 Heraclius

[41] Samaritan poisoning of Byzantine soldier: *Miracula, Acta M. Anastasii Persae* c. 13 (25–6 Usener). But Samaritans (allegedly 5,000) aided Byzantine defense: *Chronicon Anonymum ad annum Christi 1234 pertinens*, trans. by J.-B. Chabot (CSCO, Scriptores Syri, ser. 3, T. 14: 189–90 Versio); Palmer, *Chronicles*, part 2, text 13, sect. 49.

[42] G. Downey, *A History of Antioch in Syria from Seleucus to the Arab Conquest* (Princeton 1961) esp. 380–97.

[43] Kaegi, *BMU* 20–3, 126, 146–8.

[44] Earlier military memoranda: Kaegi, "Constantine's and Julian's Strategies of Strategic Surprise against the Persians," *ASRB*.

was observing the Persian evacuation of Syria and the determination of a new border. He was also restoring holy relics, such as fragments of the cross to Palestine. He was attempting to resolve various ecclesiastical disputes. In the final part of his stay, between 634 and 636, he was seeking to organize an effective defense of Syria against the Muslims. How much reconstruction he supervised is unclear. He probably found Antioch a useful place to stay during part of his time because of its critical importance for safeguarding communications with his native Armenia.

On the eve of the Islamic conquests Heraclius was indisputably at the height of his prestige because of his recent decisive defeat of the Persians, which had resulted in their evacuation of those Byzantine eastern provinces that they had occupied, the determination of an international boundary with Persia on satisfactory terms for Byzantium, his personal accompaniment of the relics of the True Cross to Jerusalem (as the first reigning Byzantine emperor to visit that holy city), his liberal expenditure for the restoration of war-shattered Jerusalem, his repayment of funds borrowed from the churches, especially those of Constantinople, and what appeared to be substantial progress in nudging some recalcitrant Monophysites, including his fellow Armenians, toward acceptance, however grudging, of some compromise formula on Christology.[45] He was mature in his years – in his mid-fifties, having been born around 575 – and very experienced in war. He had apparently overcome the propensity to internal military strife that had plagued the empire at the beginning of the century. He appeared to be in total control of the government at Constantinople, the church, and the far-flung imperial provinces. His ethnic background[46] potentially attracted the confidence and support of that increasingly important component of the empire's military commanders and soldiers far more than had another emperor of probable Armenian origin, Maurice.[47] On the surface, Heraclius appeared to be an emperor who could meet the greatest of challenges. Disquieting problems of his marital life, and related potential friction and

[45] The final sections of Norman Baynes, "The Military Operations of the Emperor Heraclius," *The United Services Magazine* n.s. 47 (1913) 665–79, and esp. 669–75, are weakened by the illness of the author and by inadequate knowledge of place-names. F. Sarre and E. Herzfeld, *Archäologische Reise im Euphrat- und Tigris Gebiet* 2: 87–9, which appeared a few years later, provides much better although neglected topographic details on Heraclius' campaign of 628.

[46] Background: C. Toumanoff, "The Heraclids and the Arsacids," *REArm* 19 (1985) 431–4.

[47] A. Pernice, *L'Imperatore Eraclio* (Florence 1905); G. Ostrogorsky, *History of the Byzantine State* (New Brunswick 1969) 87–92; Stratos, Βυζάντιον 1: 226–456, 2: 491–643; N. H. Baynes, "The Military Operations of the Emperor Heraclius," *United Service Magazine* n.s. 46 (1913) 526–33, 659–66; 47 (1913) 30–5; I. Shahid, "On the Titulature of the Emperor Heraclius," *Byzantion* 51 (1981) 288–96; E. Chrysos, "The Title Βασιλεύς in Early Byzantine International Relations," *DOP* 32 (1978) 29–75; Kaegi, "New Evidence on the Early Reign of Heraclius," *ASRB*.

competition for the imperial succession, his alleged predilection for astrology, and his brusque handling of ecclesiastical dissenters did not appear so serious as to threaten the solidity of his government or his military astuteness. He appeared to be an Augustus and commander who could capably meet any external military challenge to Byzantine control of Syria and upper Mesopotamia.

Heraclius benefited and suffered from his long military experience. He had created a formidable military reputation that should have caused potential opponents to be cautious about initiating military tests with him. On the other hand, he had by the 630s established a long and well-publicized record of how he commanded armies and how he was likely to react in the course of operations and tactical situations. By the time that the Muslim invasions started, it was unlikely that Heraclius would develop any new surprises in his military repertory. He was, in short, a known quantity to his Muslim opponents. By observing and weighing his record, they had a fairly good framework of reference against which to estimate what would be his next moves. This familiarity with Heraclius was probably, on balance, beneficial to the Muslims, who were, on the other hand, far less well known to Heraclius and his advisers, except in so far as the Muslims conformed to earlier Arab patterns of conducting war.

For some, at least in retrospect, there had been fearful portents: "There was an earthquake in Palestine. And a sign called an apparition appeared in the heavens to the south, predicting the Arab conquest. It remained thirty days stretching from south to north, and it was sword-shaped."[48]

[48] Theoph., *Chron.*, A. M. 6124 (336 De Boor); cf. "Extract From the Chronicle of Zuqnīn," Palmer, *Chronicles*, part 1, text 10, AG 937.

THE FIRST MUSLIM PENETRATIONS OF BYZANTINE TERRITORY

THE INVASIONS AND ASSUMPTIONS ON CHRONOLOGY

> Abū 'Ubayda b. Jarrāḥ advanced until he traversed the Wādī'l Qurā and then he approached Ḥijr and it is a place of the Banū Ṣāliḥ ... and it belongs to the Ḥijāz and what is beyond Ḥijr belongs to Syria. And he advanced to Dhāt Manār and then to Zīzā. Then he proceeded to Ma'āb in the territory of 'Ammān. The Romans [Byzantines] sallied forth against them and the Muslims continued routing them until they forced them to enter their town [of Ma'āb] and the Muslims besieged them in it. The people of Ma'āb made peace [*ṣulḥ*] and it was the first city in Syria that made peace with the Muslims.

Such is Azdī's account of the initial permanent Muslim penetration of Byzantine territory by the Muslim commander Abū 'Ubayda b. Jarrāḥ, who followed a traditional trade route from Medina to Syria. His description correlates with the earliest Christian narrative of the Muslim invasions, that of the Armenian Sebēos, as well as with traditions reported by al-Ṭabarī and al-Balādhurī.[1]

Many chronological and historiographical problems complicate investigation of the last moments of Byzantine rule in Palestine and Syria and the final years of the reign of Heraclius. Yet it is possible to find some well-attested events.[2] In February and March 628 Heraclius crushed the Persians, whose sovereign Chosroes II was overthrown and assassinated by his own son Siroes. In July, 629 Heraclius and Persian General Shahrbaraz met at

[1] Azdī 29; Balādhurī 113. al-Ṭabarī i 2108. Sebēos (123–4 Bedrosian, 96 Macler).

[2] This chronology is a synthesis of my own analysis of Byzantine events with my interpretation of principal features of Islamic history. For the latter I owe a great debt to the researches of Leone Caetani, *AI*, and to Fred M. Donner, *EIC*, although my own selection of data may well diverge from theirs. H. Delehaye, "Passio Sanctorum Sexaginta Martyrum," *AB* 23 (1904) 290–1; and J. Pargoire, "Les LX Soldats Martyrs de Gaza," *EO* 8 (1905) 40–3, provide important elements for the reconstruction of a chronology that is not dependent on Muslim or other oriental Christian historical traditions. See André Guillou, "La Prise de Gaza par les Arabes au VIIe siècle," *BCH* 81 (1957) 396–404.

Arabissos, in Cappadocia, and agreed on terms for the withdrawal of Persian troops from occupied Byzantine eastern provinces. In September, 629, Byzantine forces defeated the Muslims at Mu'ta. Several actions distinguished the year 630: on 21 March 630 Heraclius returned the presumed relics of the cross to Jerusalem, while the Muslims sent an expedition to Tabūk (northwest corner of Arabian peninsula, perhaps in October), where the leading official or bishop of Ayla ('Aqaba), and the people of Jarbā' and Adhruḥ made treaty arrangements with Muḥammad, as did the local leader (*'āmil*) of Ma'ān. The Prophet Muḥammad died in 632.

The actual conquest of Syria commenced in late 633 or early 634 when the key town of Areopolis/Ma'āb probably fell to the Muslims, who then penetrated to and clashed with Byzantine forces at 'Ayn Ghamr, in the Ghor or Wādī'l 'Araba. Probably on 4 February, 634, Muslims defeated the Byzantines at Dāthin, near Gaza, and even more decisively on 30 July 634 [Jumādā I, AH 13] at the battle of Ajnādayn. Later in 634 [Dhū'l Qa'da AH 13] there occurred the death of Caliph Abū Bakr and the Muslim victory at Scythopolis/Faḥl. In 635 [Rajab AH 14] the Muslims captured Damascus and Ḥimṣ for the first time. But sometime before August, 636, the Muslims evacuated Ḥimṣ and Damascus in face of a Byzantine counterthrust led by Theodore, brother of Heraclius, and General Vahān. 20 August 636 [AH 15] was the final part of the battle of Jābiya-Yarmūk. In late 636/early 637 the Muslims recaptured Damascus, Ba'labakk, Ḥimṣ (Emesa), and initially occupied Syria almost as far as Qinnasrīn/Chalkis. Sometime in 637 (by autumn at the latest) the Muslims captured and occupied Jerusalem. At the end of June or in early July 637 the Muslims captured Gaza, and in its wake possibly also Ascalon for the first time; and the Byzantine authorities in Egypt purchased an expensive truce, which lasted three years. Sometime in 637 Byzantine and Muslim authorities agreed to a truce at Qinnasrīn/Chalkis after the Muslim defeat (and death) of Byzantine commander Menas. In 638, the Muslims occupied northern Syria, except for upper Mesopotamia, which they granted a one-year truce. At the expiration of that one-year truce, in 639/640, 'Iyāḍ b. Ghanm overran Byzantine Mesopotamia. In 640 the Muslims terminated the conquest of Palestine by storming Caesarea Maritima and effecting their final capture of Ascalon. In December, 639 the Muslims departed from Palestine to invade Egypt in early 640. Probably in 639/640 the Muslims invaded Byzantine Armenia from Mesopotamia under the command of 'Iyāḍ b. Ghanm. Sometime in 640 the Muslim commander Mu'āwiya led a raid into Cilicia and then sacked Euchaita in Anatolia while the Byzantine Generals Dawit' (David) Urṭaya and Titus made an abortive campaign in Mesopotamia. An alleged Byzantine raid towards Ḥimṣ may have taken place. On 11 February 641 Heraclius died. His death was followed by the death of his son, Emperor Constantine III, in April or on 20–24 May 641, which exacerbated the succession quarrel. In late 641 Heraclius' second wife and niece, Martina and her son Heraclonas fell from power, leaving Constans II, the eleven-year-old grandson of Heraclius by Constantine III, as sole Byzantine emperor. Byzantine internal instability continued in early 642 with the abortive revolt of General Valentinus, which was contemporary with the completion of Muslim conquest of Egypt, and the beginning of Muslim invasion of Cyrenaica. These dates provide a frame of reference for discussion of Byzantine efforts at creating an effective defense and their partial collapse. Some of them are more securely fixed than others.[3]

INITIAL CONTACTS AND CLASHES

The Byzantines probably relied on local Arab tribes other than their traditional Arab allies, the Ghassānids, in the region south of the Yarmūk. In several cases local notables of Arab families were the prominent civic leaders, as at Ma'ān. The names of several Arab leaders who fought on the Byzantine side at Mu'ta indicate the coalitions of north Arabian tribes on whom the Byzantines could rely, including the Balī (especially from the sections of B. Irāsha, Quḍā'a), Judhām, Lakhm, B. al-Qayn, and B. Kalb.[4]

Farwa b. 'Amr al-Judhāmī, the governor of Ma'ān, whom the Byzantines allegedly executed for conversion to Islam, was a member of the Judhām tribe.[5] The earliest example of a Byzantine governor who personally

[3] P. Speck, *Das geteilte Dossier* (Bonn 1988) 317–41, 355–77, is ingenious but does not persuade me to change my chronology.

[4] Wāqidī 755–69. Ibn 'Asākir, *TMD* 1: 392, 402–7, 446; Donner, *EIC* 101–10. Also, Moshe Gil, "The Origin of the Jews of Yathrib," *JSAI* 4 (1984) 203–24; S. Thomas Parker, "Retrospective on the Arabian Frontier after a Decade of Research," *DRBE* 633–60; esp. Shahid, *BAFIC* 242–51, 271–89, 507–9.

[5] Ibn Hishām 958; Ibn Sa'd I/2, 18, 31, 83. Donner, *EIC* n. 53, p. 304, wonders whether Farwa may have turned to Muslims during the period of Persian occupation because of the relatively favorable Muslim attitude to Christians, but this is unlikely because Persians appear to have been relatively tolerant to Christians except for the massacre of the inhabitants of Jerusalem after it was stormed in 614. Circumspect Persian policies: A. Pertusi, "La Persia nelle fonti bizantini del secolo VII" 605–28. Completion of dated mosaics from the 620s in areas of Persian occupation implies some Persian circumspection or tolerance to Christians: esp. Noël Duval, Jean-Pierre Caillet, "Khan-Khaldé (ou Khaldé III). Les Fouilles de Roger Saidah," and Jean-Paul Rey-Coquais, "Inscriptions grecques inédites découvertes par Roger Saidah," in: *Archéologie au Levant: Recueil à la mémoire de Roger Saideh* (Collection de la Maison de l'Orient Méditerranéen, no. 12, série archéologique, 9 [Lyon: Maison de l'Homme, 1982]) esp. 360–7, 407–8; Michele Piccirillo, *Chiese e mosaici della Giordania Settentrionale* (Studium Biblicum Franciscanum, Collectio Minor, 30 [Jerusalem: Franciscan Printing Press, 1981]) 73–4, 80–2; Janine Balty, *Mosaïques antiques de Syrie* 148–51 (Brussels: Centre belge de recherches archéologiques à Apamée de Syrie, 1977); Salim 'Abd al-Haqq, "Naẓarāt fī al-Fann al-Suri Qabl al-Islām," *Annales archéologiques de Syrie* 11–12 (1961–2) 61–7; William Waddington, *Inscriptions grecques et latines de la Syrie*, no. 2412 (Rome: Bretschneider, 1968) 550–1.

established relations with the Muslims, Farwa went to the extreme of converting. His was one type of local response to the Muslims, without, of course, permission from higher Byzantine authorities, that the Byzantine leadership wished to prevent. The story may be an invention, but it is possible that a local leader was impressed by the Muslims and tried to make an unauthorized personal response. His story anticipates what other local officials would do in the course of the conquests, and harsh reactions of the imperial government to unauthorized local improvisations.

Muslim traditions report that Muḥammad sent envoys to announce Islam to various contemporary great monarchs, including the Byzantine emperor, whom he sought to contact through the Byzantine governor of the province of Arabia at Bostra. Yet it is doubtful that any kind of authoritative documentation will ever be found. The Byzantine "ruler of the Balqā'" (normally the Transjordanian region between the Wādī'l Zarqā' and the Wādī'l Mūjib, but here possibly the governor of the province of Palaestina Tertia) reportedly intercepted the first Muslim messenger at Mu'ta and had him executed. Such an event is not out of the question, although no definitive answer is possible. Such a messenger would likely have been regarded as insolent and threatening to the prestige of the emperor. The Balqā' is the closest region in the Byzantine Empire to Medina, so it is logical that it would have been the site of the initial contacts and communications.[6]

Muslims may have made some effort to deliver such a letter to Heraclius, but it would have been very difficult for anyone to gain direct access to him or even to have him read the contents of such a letter that was delivered by a third party. Of course, if there ever had been such a letter delivered somehow to Heraclius, Byzantine Christian apologetical considerations would likely have dictated its destruction and the destruction of any records or memory of it or anything that might give comfort to Muslims or, conversely, would give Christians and supporters of the Heraclian dynasty cause for doubt. It is imprudent to attempt to investigate this problem any further; there is no solid group of sources to permit such inquiry to have any hope of positive results. Moreover, there cannot have been any significant effective Byzantine control of the Balqā' immediately prior to the battle of Mu'ta. There may have been local authorities who claimed to act in the name of Heraclius, but in fact they would have been taking action independently of the emperor and without reliable and prompt communication with him or with his immediate subordinates and advisers.

The Muslim traditionist Ibn Sa'd reports that a Muslim messenger

[6] Wāqidī 755. Donner, *EIC* 96–108. Muḥammad's letter to Heraclius: al-Ṭabarī (Ibn Isḥāq) i 1562–8; Ibn Hishām/Wüstenfeld, 971; also, A. Guillaume trans. 654–7. Ibn Sa'd, *Ṭabaqāt* I/2: 16. This tradition fictitious: M. Cheïra, *La Lutte entre arabes et byzantins* 15–18.

delivered a message from Muḥammad to Ḥārith b. Abī Shamir al-Ghassānī, who was waiting to receive Heraclius at the Ghūṭa of Damascus, when he was making his pilgrimage from Ḥimṣ to Jerusalem. The news about Muḥammad allegedly so angered Ḥārith that he threatened that he would travel as far as Medina to eradicate Islam. He was gathering soldiers for such an expedition when Heraclius ordered him to accompany him to Jerusalem.[7] An improbable tradition reports that on hearing of Muḥammad, Heraclius gathered his commanders in a closed building and addressed them from a raised place because he feared his commanders. He allegedly advised them to agree to divide territory with the Muslims.[8] There is no certain way to determine definitively whether these stories are false. There is even a completely fanciful late Byzantine tradition that Muḥammad actually met Heraclius when he was returning from his Persian campaigns and received permission from him to settle at Medina.[9]

There were commercial contacts between the Arabian peninsula and Syria. Travel and communication were not impossible. Religious communities remained in contact with their coreligionists elsewhere, perhaps with delayed communications but nevertheless with some information passed back and forth. It would be foolish to assume absolute ignorance of Syria by some in the Arabian peninsula, or vice versa. Some impressions and perceptions and information about respective military strength and vulnerability accompanied such peaceful contacts. Very few Greeks or Armenians, if any, however, penetrated as far as the Arabian peninsula in the early seventh century, and probably few went south of the Wādī'l Mūjib. That unfamiliarity may have contributed to later Byzantine nervousness about operating there, far away from more familiar territory. There was much more danger of the unknown in that area.

The slaying of Ziyād b. 'Amr Nuqīl, an early convert to Islam, by Christian zealots at the Christian stronghold of al-Mayfa'a/Umm al-Raṣāṣ ("Mefa" of the *Notitia Dignitatum*) east of the Dead Sea involved no official Byzantine troops, but it was a harbinger of important strife between Byzantines and Muslims in the following decade. It had previously been a "fort where soldiers are stationed against the desert." According to Muslim traditions, this slaying took place before the restoration of any Byzantine control to the area.[10] It demonstrates that Islam was penetrating and anticipated, probably

7 Ibn Sa'd, *Ṭabaqāt* I/2: 17. al-Diyārbakrī 1: 298–9.

8 Ṭabarī i 2102; Ibn 'Asākir, *TMD* 1: 439–40, 531.

9 Pseudo-Psellos, *Historia Syntomos* 76, ed. by W. J. Aerts (CFHB [Berlin: De Gruyter, 1990]) 65.

10 The new inscriptions: Michele Piccirillo, "Le iscrizioni di Umm er-Rasas-Kastron Mefaa, in Giordania I (1986–7)," *Liber Annuus Studium Biblicum Franciscanum* 37 (1987) 184–6, 196, 219, photos 3, 8. One of the most important probably dates to AD 718, according to Dr.

more consciously than unconsciously, the weakening of Persian power in areas east of the Dead Sea. Muslim proselytization, in effect, was penetrating a power vacuum before or while the Byzantines were trying to take effective control of the region again after the departure of the Persians. The Muslim sources mention neither Byzantines nor Persians with respect to the incident. At best anyone acting in the name of Byzantine authority at Mayfa'a was acting as a surrogate, and not as commander of any regular Byzantine forces in 628.

Instability and volatility prevailed in areas east of the Dead Sea at the end of the 620s. Umm al-Raṣāṣ was not very far to the north of Areopolis or Mu'ta. The Muslims rapidly developed a threat to Byzantine communications with Palestine and to Byzantine control of Palestine itself in the area east of and below the Dead Sea. The historical record remained almost submerged until recent archaeological discoveries and a careful rereading of Arabic and late Roman sources clarified the identity and significance of Ma'āb/Areopolis as well as Mu'ta.

MU'TA

The battle or skirmish of Mu'ta was the first armed clash between the Muslims and Byzantine military forces, and it occurred during the lifetime of the Prophet Muḥammad. It resulted in a clear Muslim defeat, but it loomed large in later Muslim traditions about the hostile odds that the early Muslims encountered. Muḥammad allegedly sent four commanders against Byzantine Syria, partly in response to the slaying of his messenger and rejection of his message.[11] One tradition claims that inhabitants of the unidentified village of al-Hathab, south of Karak, attacked the Muslims on their way to Mu'ta – a rare report of local resistance.[12] The Byzantine *vicarius* Theodore had his base at the town of Moucheai and learned from a member of the tribe of the Quraysh the time of the intended Muslim attack. As for the identification of Moucheai, a possible corruption of Ma'āb has been suggested, or the town of Mu'ta as opposed to the plain of Mu'ta, but

Robert Schick. Also: *ND* Or. 37.19. Cf. Eusebius, *Das Onomastikon*, ed. by E. Klostermann (GCS III.1 [Leipzig: J. C. Hinrichs, 1904]) 128; Jerome trans., p. 129. al-Bakrī, *Das geographische Wörterbuch*, ed. by F. Wüstenfeld (Göttingen, Paris: Deuerlich'sche Buchhandlung, Maisonneuve, 1877) 569, where its inhabitants slew Ziyād b. ʻAmr Nuqīl, who wished to meet the Prophet Muḥammad. Unpersuasive is Yoel Elitzur, "The Identification of Mefaʻat in View of the Discoveries from Kh. Umm er-Raṣāṣ," *IEJ* 39 (1989) 267–77.

11 Ernst Axel Knauf, "Aspects of Historical Topography Relating to the Battles of Mu'ta and Yarmuk," *1985 Bilād al-Shām Proceedings* 1: 73–6.

12 Ibn ʻAsākir, *TMD* (*al-Ta'rīkh al-Kabīr*), ed. by ʻAbd al-Qadir Badran (Damascus: Rawdat al-Sham, 1911) 1: 397. I owe this reference to R. Schick.

it is spelled differently. The identification is uncertain; plausible is the identification of it as the village of al-Miḥna, which overlooks the plain of Mu'ta, about 19 kilometers south of the Jordanian stronghold of Karak.[13]

The battle of Mu'ta possibly was fought on 10 April (10 Dhū'l Ḥijja) but I Jumādā, AH 8, that is, September 629, is more likely. Mu'ta was no accidental place to meet. Byzantine troops were not stationed there in the late fourth century, according to the *Notitia Dignitatum*. Although archaeology reveals no late Roman or Byzantine military occupation and use of this area in the late sixth or early seventh century, it is a point where Byzantine resistance might have been expected. The troops that the *vicarius* Theodore used against the Muslims were τοὺς στρατιώτας τῶν παραφυλακῶν τῆς ἐρημίας, that is, soldiers of the guards of the desert, who were Arabs themselves.[14]

Tactical details are tantalizing. Khālid b. al-Walīd reportedly employed sophisticated battle order at Mu'ta.[15] It was not a mere clash of armed mobs. Theophanes reports that Theodore received information from one of the Quraysh about the impending time of the Muslim assault. The Muslims attacked while the Byzantine-allied Arabs were worshipping. The phrasing is odd. Theophanes may be drawing on a Muslim source that was speaking of Christian idolatrous sacrifice.[16] Theodore successfully attacked the Muslims in the plain of Mu'ta and slew three of their commanders, although Khālid b. al-Walīd escaped. The reference by Theophanes is the unique explicit testimony in Greek – as opposed to Arabic Muslim traditions – concerning the battle and situation in the region east of the Jordan after the restoration of Byzantine control,[17] although a "second victory" of Heraclius mentioned by the Heraclian court author George of Pisidia in his *Hexaemeron* may refer to the Byzantine victory at Mu'ta.[18]

The battle of Mu'ta took place little more than two months after Heraclius met with the Persian general and later king, Shahrbaraz, in July 629 at

[13] Theoph., *Chron.*, AM 6123 (335 De Boor). Wāqidī 755–65. On Ma'āb, Yāqūt 4: 377, 571. Caetani, *AI* 2: 84–5; De Goeje, *Mémoire*[2] 6–7. On the feast of sacrifice, Caetani, *AI* 2: 85. Ma'āb as destination: Ibn Hishām/Wüstenfeld 793 and in general on Mu'ta, 791–7 Wüstenfield; al-Ṭabarī i 1612. L. I. Conrad, "Theophanes and the Arabic Historical Transmission: Some Indications of Intercultural Transmission," *ByzF* 15 (1990) 22–3.

[14] Late Roman detachment: *ND* Or. 37.14 (81 Seeck). Theoph., *Chron.*, AM 6123 (335 De Boor).

[15] F. Wüstenfeld, "Das Heerwesen der Muhammedaner und die arabische Übersetzung der Taktik des Aelianus," repr. from *Abh. der hist.-philol. Cl.*, *König. Gesell. der Wiss. zu Göttingen*, vol. 26.1 (1880), text 11, trans. 42. But this is a thirteenth-century (eighth-century AH) military manual. Wāqidī 755–69; Ibn 'Asākir, *TMD* 1: 440.

[16] L. I. Conrad, "Theophanes and the Arabic Historical Transmission: Some Indications of Intercultural Transmission" 23–6.

[17] Theoph., *Chron.*, AM. 6123 (335 De Boor).

[18] George of Pisidia, *Hexaemeron* lines 1845–58, in *PG* 92: 1575–6. David Olster, "The Date of George of Pisidia's *Hexaemeron*," *DOP* 45 (1991) 159–72.

Arabissos in Cappadocia to discuss final peace terms.[19] Only then did Shahrbaraz undertake the evacuation of Persian troops from occupied Byzantine territories in Syria, Palestine, Egypt, and Mesopotamia. The battle was part of the Byzantine probing into regions where they had not operated for more than two decades. The Byzantines were attempting to reestablish their authority in areas after the Persian evacuation. The Byzantines were extending south, with the aid of allied tribes, and the Muslims were probing north. They collided at Mu'ta.

Reports of Mu'ta indicate that, irrespective of the chronology, somehow the Byzantines had already resumed control of this relatively distant region that was east of the Jordan. Yet the Byzantine return to the Balqā' would have been only brief – a couple of months at the maximum for direct rather than indirect control – by September 629. There already was some Byzantine commander that far south. The Byzantines also apparently swiftly hired Arabs to help to guard against incursions by other Arabs. Perhaps some local tribes and segments of the local population had nominally declared the sovereignty of the Byzantine Empire and Heraclius in that region, but effective tight control by Heraclius would not have been possible. Others may have acted in the name of Heraclius. It would have been risky, and really inconceivable, for Heraclius to have dispatched significant numbers of troops to the areas east of the Jordan while it was uncertain whether the Persians were really evacuating other more critical occupied areas – whether or not they had effectively occupied the territory that lay east of the Jordan River and Dead Sea. A revived Persian threat, or simple clashes with the Persians in northern Syria and Mesopotamia, would have threatened communications with any Byzantine troops and officials who had extended their presence into Palestine and areas east of the Dead Sea.

Most of the Byzantine soldiers and commanders, unless recruited locally and simply designated as representatives of the authority of the emperor, cannot have had time to familiarize themselves with the local situation there and military needs. Except for local recruits, they cannot have had much local experience, and they would have had little time to build or repair structures, roads, bridges, warehouses, supplies, or watchtowers. They had virtually no time before the Muslims struck at Mu'ta, and their very freshness may have tempted, or contributed to tempting, the Muslim attack, a point that was naturally not made in subsequent Muslim historiography. The Byzantine military presence east of the Dead Sea was very vulnerable so soon after the end of hostilities with the Persians. They would hardly have

19 Stratos, Βυζάντιον 2: 647–85; cf. Paul Speck, *Das geteilte Dossier* 317–41. It was possible for Persian troops to remain on Byzantine soil after Heraclius' victory in Persia itself in early 628.

completed occupying old and probably disused camps and positions. Those with experience from the era before the Persian invasions would have suffered from a fifteen-year absence of Byzantine authority. Under those circumstances, the best that the Byzantines could have done would have been, in so far as budget and numbers of troops permitted, to reoccupy the old Byzantine positions until new surveys and strategic decisions could be made about any changes. That would have been the situation at the time of the battle of Mu'ta, in September, 629.

THE PILGRIMAGE OF HERACLIUS

The dating of Heraclius' visit to Jerusalem to 21 March 630 (or, less likely, 631) is important for the history of his reign, for the history of Jerusalem, and, although this has been neglected, for the history of Byzantine resistance against the Muslims in Palestine and Syria.[20] Heraclius came to Jerusalem, Palestine, and other parts of southern Syria when the Muslim threat was maturing and growing more evident, at a time when it would have been more difficult for at least some report of Muslim expansion to escape his ears, especially when he was making a personal visit to the area that was about to be threatened. Ibn Hishām reports that Heraclius came to Jerusalem by way of Emesa/Ḥimṣ, and indeed it is probable that carpets, scented with aromatic herbs, were strewn on the pathway that he personally trod.[21] Such an act of splendid humility would have impressed itself in the minds of contemporary observers, who preserved it by oral tradition and it thus found its way into Muslim tradition. Any possible planning for an expedition would have possibly created the kinds of rumors about Byzantine concentrations that found their way into al-Wāqidī's *Kitāb al-Maghāzī*. Heraclius' pilgrimage indisputably left a strong imprint on the memory of some Arabs, whose reports found their way into the narratives of some Muslim traditionists.[22]

It is conceivable that Heraclius did learn of religious activities within the Arabian peninsula but rejected the risks of some vague military expedition there and instead ordered that the Ghassānid tribal leadership escort him to Jerusalem. His route to Jerusalem in 630 passed through territories that the

[20] *Acta M. Anastasii Persae* (12 Usener). A. Frolow revised that date to 630, in an important article, "La Vraie Croix et les expéditions d'Héraclius en Perse," *REB* 11 (1953) 88–105. Grumel proposed 21 March 631, a date that has some logic but was persuasively rejected by Cyril Mango, who prefers 630: V. Grumel, "La Reposition de la Vraie Croix à Jérusalem per Héraclius. Le Jour et l'année," *ByzF* 1 (1966) 139–49; Cyril Mango, "Deux études sur Byzance et la Perse sassanide," *TM* 9 (1985) 112–13. P. Speck, *Das geteilte Dossier* (Bonn 1988) 355–77, unconvincingly argues that Heraclius restored the cross to Jerusalem in 628.

[21] Ibn Hishām 1: 192; al-Ṭabarī i 1562.

[22] Wāqidī 760.

Ghassānids normally controlled. His elite praesental army probably accompanied him to Jerusalem.[23] The date of 630 for Heraclius' visit to Jerusalem makes more plausible the reports in Iraqi tradition that Heraclius learned of the threat of a Muslim invasion while he was in Palestine (tradition of Azdī, Ibn A'tham al-Kūfī and Sayf) or Damascus (according to Ibn Sa'd and Eutychius).[24] But even at that date he could scarcely have conceived of the scope of their imminent military campaigns. The clash at Mu'ta is more comprehensible because of the understandable Byzantine desire to secure the area east of the Dead Sea in the second half of 629, in September, before the emperor's personal pilgrimage to Jerusalem the following March. It was necessary to try to avoid any embarrassing beduin raids during that pilgrimage.

Whether or not Heraclius ever delivered a speech of the kind that Azdī reports that he gave in Palestine – certainly there is no Byzantine text that confirms this – it is more possible that he learned something of a threat of Muslim or Arab troubles and threat of invasion, and attempted to make some defensive preparations against it. No contemporary Christian source shows any awareness of a threat of Arab or Muslim invasion or defensive preparations against such an eventuality. Sophronius of Jerusalem in early 634 states that the Muslim incursions hit "unexpectedly."[25] Heraclius cannot have begun his major emergency defense measures for the security of Palestine and Syria in early or middle 630. But he may have made provisional military arrangements at that time and may have become aware of potential problems with Arab tribes east of the Dead Sea and of the 'Araba.

Azdī's Iraqi tradition gives no dates, but implies that Heraclius learned of the imminent Muslim threat while on pilgrimage to Jerusalem and there, as well as at Damascus and Ḥimṣ, began to alert the populace for defense, and finally made his base of operations at Antioch in northern Syria. He did really depart from Jerusalem, after his pilgrimage and restoration of its patriarchate in early 630, and went immediately to Damascus.[26] He probably did not return to Damascus until early 634, where he was, according to Eutychius, when he learned of the defeat of the Byzantines 12 miles from Gaza, at Dāthin. The fact that he apparently made this second trip gave him an even

[23] See remarks of John Haldon, *Byzantine Praetorians* 173–8.

[24] Caetani, *AI* 2. 1: lxvii, erroneously assumed that Heraclius visited Jerusalem in 629 and was restoring the cross there at the time of the battle of Mu'ta, which harmed his understanding of events, their sequence and interrelationships. Heraclius spent the winter of 628–9 at Amida, met with Shahrbaraz at Arabissos in July, 629, returned to Constantinople in September, 629, and brought the fragments of the cross to Jerusalem in March, 630. In 631/2 he participated in the synod at Theodosiopolis, in Armenia. Azdī 28–9.

[25] Sophronius, *PG* 87: 3197D.

[26] That statement of Azdī and Ibn 'Asākir is confirmed by Eutychius and by version "C" of the Antiochus threnody on the Persian capture of Jerusalem in 614.

better military comprehension of the terrain, climate, communications, population, and towns along the trunk road between northern Syria, including the linchpin at Chalkis/Qinnasrīn, as well as Emesa/Ḥimṣ and Damascus. He indeed possessed a far better understanding and familiarity with the area than had any emperor since the third century. His travel in the region would have alerted him to the importance of the Christian Arabs in providing security. In spite of everything, he failed to make efficient defensive preparations against the Muslims, whether by using friendly Christian Arab tribes or raising sufficient Byzantine troops from other areas.

Heraclius' principal concerns, after departing from Jerusalem in 630, were (1) reconstruction of ruined holy sites in Jerusalem, (2) settling problems within the ecclesiastical hierarchy, such as Modestus' episcopacy in Jerusalem, (3) Jewish policy, and (4) especially efforts to heal the Christological controversy concerning the nature of Jesus Christ, by inducing reconciliation, reunification, and theological reformulation, especially to reconcile various Monophysites, including his own fellow Armenians and the Jacobites.

Later in 631 Heraclius' participation in a church council at Hierapolis/Manbij, in northern Syria, and then at a council in Theodosiopolis/Erzurum, in Byzantine Armenia, between February 631 and February 632, indicates that he was not exclusively concerned with any Muslim or Arab menace immediately on departing from his pilgrimage to Jerusalem with the relics of the cross. These two councils of Manbij and Theodosiopolis are sufficiently well authenticated to lead to the conclusion that, if there is substance to the Iraqi tradition, it has conflated and telescoped Heraclius' return from pilgrimage to Jerusalem with events at the end of 633 and early 634, about which there is no secure documentation in the Byzantine sources. By visiting Hierapolis and Theodosiopolis/Erzurum, he remained in areas where military reports from east of the Dead Sea and east of the 'Araba and from Persia could easily have reached him. It would have been relatively easy for military commanders or prominent inhabitants of Syria and Palestine to report their concerns about restive Arab tribes to the southeast.

There is no evidence that Heraclius made a second pilgrimage to Jerusalem. Surely it would have received mention in the sources if it had taken place. At the moment of the major Muslim attacks on the Balqā' and region around Gaza, Heraclius was giving his attention to ecclesiastical and ecclesiological and theological problems. Yet, according to Eutychius, a rather reliable source, Heraclius was at Damascus, which was not far from Jerusalem, where he received news of the battle of Dāthin (4 February 634) which underscored how critical the Muslim threat was (note, for example, the anxious tones of Patriarch Sophronius of Jerusalem – a Damascene by birth, incidentally – in his 634 synodal letter and his Christmas 634 sermon). Yet his travel at least as far as Damascus increases the credibility of the Iraqi tradition and the understandable reasons for the easy confusion of the emperor's 630 pilgrimage route with his military activities of 634.

This does not invalidate the testimony of the Iraqi traditions. It is easy to see how confusion could have developed, especially because Heraclius later used Emesa/Ḥimṣ as an initial base of operations, and probably attempted from it to arouse the people of Palestine and Syria to defend themselves under the authority of the special emergency military regimes and the commanders that he appointed over their cities in the face of the imminent invasion of the Muslims. Granted the Iraqi tradition cannot be accepted at face value, yet this does not mean that all of it is worthless. The challenge is to try to discern what parts have validity, given conflation, confusion in the Iraqi tradition concerning the fact of Heraclius' pilgrimage to Jerusalem, and departure for the north via Damascus, where he did make a halt.

The Iraqi tradition preserves part of a reality. To reject it is to reject Eutychius as well, without whom it is really impossible to reconstruct the events of Heraclius' reign. In sum, Heraclius probably did not return to Jerusalem after his pilgrimage with the fragments of the cross in 630, but he probably came as close as Damascus in early 634. Because he was at Damascus in early 634, he cannot have ignored the Muslim threat. He probably made some arrangements for stiffening resistance while awaiting reinforcements from other parts of his empire.

Azdī does not claim that Heraclius was in Jerusalem when he heard of the Muslim invasions. He claims that he was in "Palestine" (Filasṭīn), whether designating the province of Palaestina I, or even Palaestina II, or in a vaguer generic sense. While it is important whether he was in Palestine or Damascus, the more important point is that in either case he was close enough, as the Iraqi tradition maintains, to have attempted to organize local resistance and to have appointed emergency military commanders over important fortress cities, which were to become the Byzantine strongholds and the critical points for the initial Byzantine defensive strategy.

Shortly after citing Heraclius' speech to the inhabitants of Syria, al-Azdī claims that Heraclius took up residence at the city of Antioch and "appointed as his deputies over the cities of Syria commanders from his army" (*khallafa umarā' min jundihi 'alā madāin al-Shām*). This is a reference to the sudden creation of emergency military authorities over specific cities in Syria and Palestine.[27] There is nothing incredible about this reference. It is consistent with earlier Byzantine experimentation, especially in the sixth century, with emergency military commands over formerly civilian governmental re-

[27] Azdī 31; al-Ṭabarī (Sayf) i 2104; Ibn al-Athīr 2: 311, 317–18.

sponsibilities,[28] and with other contemporary appointments by Heraclius of military commanders to take over formerly civilian governmental positions.[29]

Important corroboration for Azdī comes from Ibn A'tham al-Kūfī, who probably died in AD 926. Ibn A'tham died long before the Crusades, and therefore the contents of his history cannot be contaminated by Crusading literature, which De Goeje thought was a problem in the account of Azdī. Part of Ibn A'tham's initial sections are lost. The extant part of his *Kitāb al-futūḥ* (Book of the Conquests) begins in the middle of a speech or letter of Heraclius, who was apparently (this is evident from next page of his history) in Palestine. He is warning of the coming of the Muslims. His warning in the narrative of Kūfī is similar to the fuller text that Azdī reports. He informs his audience that he is appointing commanders over them and that they should obey these commanders.[30] According to Ibn A'tham al-Kūfī, Heraclius sent this letter to Damascus, Ḥimṣ, and Ḥalab (modern Aleppo, ancient Berrhoia) while he went on to Antioch, where he established himself. This fragmentary section of Ibn A'tham is extremely important for showing the breadth of this tradition about Heraclius in Iraqi traditions. It raises the question, how would traditionists in Kūfa or Baṣra know this and not those from other regions of the Muslim world? It again shows the existence of a Muslim tradition that Heraclius did attempt to warn the inhabitants of major towns of the impending Muslim attack and of the need to defend themselves, their families, their religion, and their property.

De Goeje was definitely wrong in claiming that the Azdī tradition about Heraclius derives from the Crusading era. Conrad has convincingly refuted the totally skeptical conclusions of De Goeje.[31] These traditions about Heraclius were circulating among traditionists in Kūfa already early in the tenth century, as Ibn A'tham shows, but the traditionalist Sayf b. 'Umar, as al-Ṭabarī preserves him, shows some familiarity with this tradition as well. So Azdī's account gains more credibility – not in all details, but in part, because he appears to refer more credibly to Byzantine towns and official titles and conditions than does Ibn A'tham.

[28] W. E. Kaegi, Jr., "Two Studies in the Continuity of Late Roman and Byzantine Military Institutions," *ByzF* 8 (1982) 87–113; R.-J. Lilie, "Die zweihundertjährige Reform. Zu den Anfängen der Themenorganisation," *Byzslav* 45 (1984) 27–39; survey of earlier literature in Haldon, *Byzantium* 190 n. 70.

[29] Theoph., *Chron.*, AM 6126, 6128 (338, 340 De Boor). Michael the Syrian, *Chronique* 11.7, ed. and trans. by J.-B. Chabot (Paris 1901) 2: 424–5. But cf. Narses who was in command of Constantina, Theophylact Simocatta, *Hist.* 3. 1. 1.

[30] Kūfī 1; 100–1; cf. "Extract From the Chronicle of AD 1234." in Palmer, *Chronicles*, part 1, text 13: sect. 48. L. I. Conrad, "Azdī's History" 28–72.

BYZANTINE MILITARY PRESENCE EAST OF THE DEAD SEA

The friendly Arab tribes from whom the Byzantines raised troops against the Muslims included the Bahrā', Kalb, Salīḥ, Tanūkh, Lakhm, Judhām, Ghassānids, and the Banū Irāsha.[32] At Mu'ta the Byzantines used troops raised from the Lakhm, Judhām, B. al-Qayn, Bahrā', and Balī.[33] Their commander was one of the Balī, from the section of B. Irāsha. Another tradition that asserts he was a Ghassānid, Ibn Abī Sabra al-Ghassānī, is a rare indication that Ghassānids operated that far south. It is difficult to reconcile with the other tradition, unless there was no overall Arab commander, just the Byzantine Theodore. The Byzantines do not appear to have used many Greek, Armenian, or other non-Arab soldiers at Mu'ta, even though the overall commander was the *vicarius* Theodore.[34] The numbers that the Byzantines raised are, of course, uncertain, but unlikely to have exceeded 10,000.[35] They had not lost all of their ties with Arab tribes, who may well have resented – violently – the intrusion of other Arab tribes in their region.

No source claims that the Muslim invasions were a complete surprise to the Byzantine leadership, although they astounded the broader Christian public in Syria and Palestine. Even the Byzantine sources, such as Nicephorus, imply that Heraclius was aware of the problem, that that was the reason why he moved to Antioch, because of the Arab threat to the region and the desirability of his being near the scene of conflict, apparently to make better judgments and to be able to react more quickly to crises.[36] The larger question is why, if the Byzantines had the ability to learn about the Muslims and to exploit their vulnerabilities, they did not make better use of it. Perhaps the victory at Mu'ta lulled them into negligence. Or perhaps they simply lacked the ability to draw on adequate resources to meet the challenge.

Muslims were, in the year 629 and the immediately following several years, afraid of the Byzantine ability to raise troops and to strike against them, especially from the area immediately south of the Wādī'l Mūjib. It may well be that the Byzantines had no regular garrisons, as the Romans once had, south of the Wādī'l Mūjib, but the very battle of Mu'ta and the reports, both true and false, of Byzantine concentrations of Arab tribesmen, and possibly

32 Wāqidī 760, 990. Ibn 'Asākir 1: 439–40, 531; Azdī 84–5, 107, but esp. 111. al-Ṭabarī i 2081. Kūfī 1: 230–1. Tribes: Donner, *EIC* 101–10; Shahid, *BAFIC* 507–9.

33 al-Ṭabarī (Ibn Isḥāq) i 1611–12; cf. Wāqidī, 760; Donner, *EIC* 101–10. In general, Mu'ta: Caetani, *AI* 2: 80–9.

34 *TMD* 1: 392. Theoph., *Chron.*, AM 6123 (335 De Boor).

35 The small numbers that Donner, *EIC* 221, cites, such as "perhaps 20,000 to 40,000" at Yarmūk, are more plausible than higher numbers estimated by others, but any number over 20,000 is very doubtful for any battle. Perceptive is Lawrence Conrad, "Seven and the *ṭasbī'*," *JESHO* 31 (1988) 54–5; Lawrence I. Conrad, "Abraha and Muḥammad: Some Observations Apropos of Chronology and Literary *Topoi* in the Early Arabic Historical Tradition," *BSOAS* 50 (1987) 236–40.

36 Nicephorus, *Hist.* 23 (68–9 Mango).

some of their own Byzantine troops, at Ma'āb/Areopolis indicate that the Byzantines were still able to exercise some authority there and draw on their prestige for various purposes. The rumors that the Byzantines – including possibly Heraclius himself – were raising troops and massing them at Ma'āb/Areopolis, indicate that it was still a Byzantine military post of some kind, however skeletal or nonexistent its military personnel were; its possessor could dominate movement from the south or the north.

After the recovery of Syria, and in anticipation of Heraclius' visit to restore the relics of the cross to Jerusalem, it was natural to reassert Byzantine claims in the areas east of the Jordan and the Dead Sea, and for the Byzantine commander to use allied Christian Arab tribes in the implementation of such a policy. Both Mu'ta and the false report of Byzantine forces massing at Ma'āb/Areopolis were reflections of the possibility that in the light of the defeat of the Persians, the Byzantines would restore their authority far to the south in the areas east of the Jordan. Muḥammad's concern about this massing contributed, some scholars sensibly believe, to the decision to send an expedition against Tabūk.[37] It was not yet clear just how far Byzantium would be able to reassert authority in the southern region to the east of the Dead Sea.

The interrelationship of the Byzantine effort to reassert authority after recovery of territory from the Persians and the early military clashes at Mu'ta and Ma'āb are comprehensible in the light of Byzantine calculations of policy and interests after the defeat of the Persians, not simply in terms of Byzantine fears of Islam. The Byzantines probably sent probes and expeditions southwards whether or not there was a new religious threat in the Arabian peninsula. And they would have expected opposition from other tribes to their efforts to recover territory that had been out of control during the Persian occupation of Syria and Palestine.

Byzantine commanders may have considered, and even made preliminary plans for a move in force south of the Arnon River or Wādī'l Mūjib, although this did not materialize in 630. Such a military maneuver would have been an active option as part of the systematic reassertion of Byzantine claims to authority that had been in abeyance since the Persian invasions. They would have relied upon friendly Arab tribes to do this. There is no record of such requests, but it is inconceivable that the lively and thriving Christian communities north of the Wādī'l Mūjib did not seek Byzantine aid against the potential danger of the tribes. The result of such requests and pressures

[37] Wāqidī 760, 990, 1015–18. Donner, *EIC* 107. Important poetic reference to Muslim goal of Ma'āb cited by al-Ṭabarī i 1612, reportedly in connection with Mu'ta campaign underlines contemporary Muslim perceptions of the strategic importance of the old Late Roman and Byzantine base at Ma'āb/Areopolis.

was to increase the likelihood of some kind of clash between Byzantine authorities and tribesmen, whether or not Islam was involved at all.

The initial reports of clashes and threats of concentrations of troops therefore involve the Byzantine attempts to (1) safeguard the flank of Palestine, especially on the eve of Heraclius' visit to Jerusalem, (2) respond to probable demands for protection by townspeople who lived in flourishing communities east of the Jordan and Dead Sea, (3) restore the boundaries of empire to their former limits as far as possible, and possibly also (4) protect pilgrims who were travelling to Jerusalem and other holy sites west of the Jordan or to Mt. Nebo, the only pilgrimage site east of the Jordan, and (5) secure trade routes with nomads and the Red Sea littoral. Probably more important than the last-mentioned economic motives, however, were complaints of merchants and traders who suffered from the insecurity of travel and shipping.[38]

Although there probably were initial Byzantine probes south of the Wādī'l Mūjib, Heraclius obviously never occupied that area in force. It was Heraclius' brother Theodore who reportedly persuaded him to send units there as an initial preventive measure against the impending Muslim threat. There is no evidence that Heraclius ever personally visited the Balqā', even though he passed relatively close to it during his trip to and from Jerusalem.[39] His unfamiliarity with that very different region probably made him even more dependent than usual on information from friendly Arabs. In fact, Arabic sources not implausibly claim that Heraclius did use Arabs to gain information about Muḥammad, Islam, and the Muslims.[40] He reportedly sent troops to occupy the Balqā' and to await more reinforcements that he was sending.[41] He probably already wanted to avoid major battles with the Muslims, fearing their tactics, even though his forces had won a clash at Mu'ta. It was in the course of their probing south to restore Byzantine authority that his forces began to confront and learn of growing Muslim power. The initial Byzantine response appears to have been to pull back and avoid decisive confrontations if possible in open country. Heraclius probably heard of the battle of Mu'ta, at least during the course of his visit to Jerusalem in 630. Yet it is unlikely that he thought it was important. If anything, Mu'ta may have encouraged Byzantine complacency about their ability to contain any Arab menace.

[38] Azdī 43, 92, 106, 107, 149, 151–2, 165.

[39] Ibn 'Asākir 1: 440; Ibn Sa'd, *Ṭabaqāt* II/1: 137, 37 and II/1: 93, 11, Heraclius was reported in the Balqā'. Ibn Hishām 1: 792; Wāqidī 990, he is reported at Ma'āb.

[40] Byzantines use Arab spies; Wāqidī 1018; Ibn 'Asākir 1: 473, 474, 476. Heraclius inquires about Arabs: Ibn Qutayba, *Kitāb al-'Uyūn al-Akhbār* (Cairo 1925) I 126–7.

[41] Ibn 'Asākir 1: 439–40. Wāqidī 760 reports that Heraclius was in the Balqā', but no confirmation exists.

Except for the isolated clash at Mu'ta there is no evidence of any serious Byzantine military presence as far south as the stronghold of Karak (ancient Charac-Moab), let alone to the Wādī'l Ḥasā. Aggressive Byzantine patrols, or those of friendly federated Arab tribesmen, may have reached Karak or south of it, but there was no occupation. Local communities and ecclesiastical groups south of Areopolis may have announced their allegiance to Byzantine authority, but the absence of meaningful Byzantine officialdom and occupation left the local inhabitants to determine the meaning of any such declarations.

Mu'ta became only a temporary reversal for the Muslims. Muḥammad soon dispatched two other expeditionary forces that penetrated the periphery of lands outside of direct Byzantine control, but nevertheless indirectly threatened Byzantine Syria, and more specifically, Transjordanian territory. These were separate expeditions, probably in October, 630, to Tabūk in the northern Ḥijāz and to the oasis of Dūmat al-Jandal, the modern Saudi site of Jawf, which is astride the Wādī'l Sirḥān. Muslims penetrated even further on the edges of Byzantine-controlled territory.

The Bishop (or *ṣāḥib*, governor) of Ayla (al-'Aqaba) Yuḥannā b. Rū'ba reportedly journeyed to Tabūk in 630/1 to arrange with Muḥammad the terms of surrender of Ayla; although the story has not received universal acceptance, there is nothing inherently implausible about a bishop engaging in such negotiations, for others did so in the sixth and seventh centuries. At the same time Tabūk witnessed the related contemporary submissions of the inhabitants of Maqnā, Jarbā', and Adhruḥ.[42] There was no regular Byzantine garrison at Maqnā or Ayla, or Jarbā' and Adroa/Adhruḥ, the other two towns whose populace reportedly submitted in 630/1, but the Byzantines were theoretically able to operate in the Adhruḥ region at the time of the Muslim invasions.[43] A local tradition reports that some Muslims died at Adhruḥ, but literary sources state only that the inhabitants of the town submitted to the Muslims. Adhruḥ dominated the road between the Arabian peninsula and the Balqā' and access to the iron ore from the Wādī Mūsā (Petra) region.[44] Similarly, the *'āmil* or local leader at Ma'ān allegedly made terms with representatives of Muḥammad, but none of these traditions has

[42] Wāqidī 1031 (the identity of Yuḥannā's office is unclear); Yāqūt/Wüstenfeld 1: 422; Balādhurī 59–60; Ibn Sa'd, *Ṭabaqāt* I/2: 28, 37; al-Ṭabarī i 1702; Ibn Hishām 902; Donner, *EIC* 109; Caetani, *AI* 2: 253–6.

[43] J. Sauvaget, "Les Ghassanides et Sergiopolis," *Byzantion* 14 (1939) 125–6, underestimated the ability of the Byzantines to operate and recruit east of the Dead Sea and the Jordan River.

[44] Adhruḥ: Wāqidī 1031, 1032; Caetani, *AI* 2: 255–6; A. Alt, "Aila und Adroa im spätrömischen Grenzschutzsystem," *ZDPV* 59 (1936) 92–111; Alistair Killick, "Udruh and the Southern Frontier," *DRBE* 431–46. Local inhabitants showed me graves which they identified with Muslim martyrs from the time of the conquests.

received universal acceptance. The Byzantine sources offer no clarification about these plausible events, which probably took place after the conclusion of Heraclius' pilgrimage to Jerusalem, when screening Byzantine forces may have been removed or thinned out in the Transjordanian region.

AREOPOLIS

The critical sequence of events began after the death of Muḥammad in 632. It is out of place here to study the important Ridda wars in the Arabian peninsula that followed the death of Muḥammad. The earliest clashes that involve the Byzantine Empire took place east of the Wādī'l 'Araba and of the Dead Sea. Thus Balādhurī reports a tradition that Ma'āb/Areopolis even fell before Bostra, which many assume was the first Syrian city to fall.[45] This is likely to have been the case, but he does not identify the *isnād* (chain of source traditions). It seems logical that this city would fall before Bostra because it is further south, on the line of march from Arabia – unless one assumes an attack from the Wādī'l Sirḥān. There is the problem of the actual direction of Khālid's march from Iraq, but this appears to be connected with reinforcing the Muslims at the time of the battle of Ajnādayn, which was slightly later. Abū 'Ubayda b. al-Jarrāḥ is said to have conquered Ma'āb, according to Balādhurī's unidentified tradition.

The Muslims feared that Heraclius and the Ghassānids had massed Christian tribesmen about 30 kilometers north of Mu'ta at Ma'āb or Areopolis (modern Jordanian Rabba). Although that rumor turned out to be false,[46] it was plausible because that strategically important position south of the Wādī'l Mūjib and approximately 80 kilometers south of modern 'Ammān, was a likely military staging-point for a massive Byzantine strike against Arab tribesmen who were associated with or were themselves Muslims. Areopolis may have possessed some sort of Byzantine garrison, because there was a *fusṭāṭ* or encampment there,[47] which was reminiscent of

45 Balādhurī 113. al-Ṭabarī (Ibn Isḥāq) i 2108. Sebēos (123–4 Bedrosian, 96 Macler). Azdī 28–9.

46 Wāqidī 760, 990, cf. 1015, 1018.

47 Balādhurī 113; al-Ṭabarī i 2108 on Muslims at Ma'āb, including the encampment, but see Sebēos (124 Bedrosian, 96 Macler); Azdī 29. Caetani, *AI* 2: 1147–8, criticizes Pernice, *L'Imperatore Eraclio* (Florence 1905) 321–2. Caetani did not understand – nor did Pernice – the identification of Ma'āb as Areopolis, or the significance of that identification in past Late Roman military history. Pernice wrongly supposed that Rabbath Moab and Ajnādayn were identical, but he was correct in assuming that there was a clash at Rabbath Moab, which is modern Rabba. Identification of Moab as Areopolis: Eusebius, *Das Onomastikon*, ed. by Erich Klostermann (GCS III.1 [Leipzig 1904]) 10, line 17. Jerome's Latin translation is on opposite page, which is p. 11. A. Stratos, Βυζάντιον 2: 63, n. 189, likewise failed to understand the identification of "Rabbath Moab" and its significance.

the local unit that the *Notitia Dignitatum* mentions.[48] It occupied a key point on the road between Syria and the Arabian peninsula (see Map 2).[49]

Balādhurī reports that the Byzantines were massed in Ma'āb. Is this an echo of the false rumor reported by al-Wāqidī in his *Kitāb al-Maghāzī*, that the Byzantines were massing at Ma'āb, or was this a second case, a real one in which there was a Byzantine concentration at Ma'āb? Because Ma'āb was a traditional site for Byzantine troops or late Roman troops these reports are not to be ignored and discarded.[50] It was a logical concentration point in the still essentially late Roman defenses of the edges of Roman Palestine. Other Byzantine narrative histories do not mention Areopolis. The reason for massing Byzantine troops there may not have been the intention to strike against Islam so much as a natural interest in once again extending Byzantine authority to its former limits as part of the reoccupation of areas that had been lost or abandoned during the Persian occupation of Syria and Palestine. The Muslims naturally feared that this was intended against themselves. Their fears may have been well founded. Yet throughout the east, including the Mesopotamian border with Persia, Heraclius and his brother were seeking to settle the old boundaries and establish the exact limits of Byzantine authority.

The number of the troops the Byzantines massed at Areopolis, or their character and quality, is uncertain. The later geographer Yāqūt identifies them simply as *Rūm*, presumably regular Byzantine troops, of some sort of Hellenic affiliation, and Arabs, but he does not explain their proportions. Balādhurī – or his unknown source – does not explain what happened to these massed Byzantine troops after Abū 'Ubayda captured Areopolis, whether they were captured or slain, or withdrew in order or fled in panic. No exact date is given for this event, except that it was said to be before the fall of Bostra, and apparently before the battle of Dāthin, near Gaza, on 4 February, 634. Ma'āb was the ostensible true goal of the Muslims who fought at Mu'ta.[51] al-Ṭabarī also reports that Abū 'Ubayda was opposed at

[48] Former garrison strength: *ND* Or. 30.7.14, 17 (81 Seeck). Albrecht Alt unpersuasively argued to the contrary forty-five years ago and ignored the references to Ma'āb/Areopolis in the Arabic sources. He thought only of Mu'ta, Ayla, and Adroa: Albrecht Alt, "Beiträge zur historischen Geographie und Topographie des Negeb, V: Das Ende des Limes Palestinae," *Journal of the Palestine Oriental Society* 18 (1938) 149–60; cf. Alt, *ZDPV* 1940, *ZDPV* 1942.

[49] I visited modern Rabba and environs (including the village of Yārūt, which has traces of ancient ruins) in the summer of 1984 and again on 22 October 1987. For the walls of Areopolis, see the mosaic reproduction in Piccirillo, "Iscrizioni" 177–239, esp. photo 9.

[50] *ND* Or. 37. 14. 17 (81 Seeck). Whether there was still a unit called *Equites Mauri Illyriciani* in the seventh century is uncertain, but some Illyriciani still existed in Palestine in the early 630s: *Miracula M. Anastasii Persae* c. 14 (26 Usener).

[51] Yāqūt 4: 377, 571; see Caetani, *AI* 2: 84–5, De Goeje, *Mémoire*[2] 6–7. On Rabba/Ma'āb, see R. Brünnow and A. v. Domaszewski, *Provincia Arabia* (Strasburg 1904) 1: 54–9.

a camp, not the city itself, at Ma'āb. They (the Byzantines) fought him, then they asked and received *ṣulḥ*, peace.[52]

Ma'āb thus became the first Byzantine city in Syria to surrender, probably late in 633 or early in 634. Its importance has apparently been distorted by later traditionists' desire to exaggerate the importance of Khālid and Iraq. In any case, there was armed resistance of some kind at the *fusṭāṭ* or *fossatum* at Areopolis, although not in the town itself. It was then soldiers, not townspeople, who resisted. Ethnically those soldiers may have been exclusively or largely Arab, but this is not specified. They may have been regular or irregular soldiers. They offered military resistance at the camp. The term *fusṭāṭ* implies the unidentified old site of late Roman/Byzantine encampment. There was continuity of Byzantine military occupation. This was the sensible place for the conquest to begin, in Syria. That is, the neglect of the late Roman identity of Ma'āb – and its long history of having been a late Roman military post – has contributed to misunderstanding the significance of this conquest and the resistance there. There was, then, Byzantine resistance south of the Wādī'l Mūjib, even though it proved to be unsuccessful. The civilian population does not appear to have suffered. The number of Byzantine and Muslim battle casualties is unknown.[53]

Heraclius learned that the Muslims would attack, so, according to Ibn 'Asākir, he called his commanders together and warned that there would be a Muslim attack within one month.[54] It is in response to his report that his brother Theodore urged him to send *rābiṭa* (troops or possibly βάνδα) to the Balqā' until more could come. Somehow the battle took place while the Muslims and Byzantines were massed at Ma'āb/Areopolis. Sebēos reports that the Muslims attacked the Byzantines by surprise. al-Azdī's and al-Ṭabarī's information that Ma'āb was the first city in Syria to fall to the Muslims is partly corroborated by Sebēos who reports a major battle near Rabbath Moab, which is Ma'āb (classical Areopolis, modern Rabba in Jordan): "They reached Moabite Rabbath, at the borders of Ruben's [land]. The Byzantine army was in Arabia. [The Arabs] fell upon them suddenly, struck them with the sword and put to flight Emperor Heraclius' brother

[52] al-Ṭabarī i 2108. The categories of *ṣulḥan* and *'anwatan* may not be contemporary with the conquests: Albrecht Noth, "Some Remarks on the 'Nationalisation' of Conquered Lands at the Time of the Umayyads," *Land Tenure and Social Transformation in the Middle East*, ed. by Tarif Khalidi (Beirut: American University of Beirut, 1984) 223–8; Noth, "Zum Verhältnis von Kalifaler Zentralgewalt und Provinzen ... die '*Sulḥ*'-"Anwa' Traditionen," *Die Welt des Islams* 14 (1973) 150–62.

[53] al-Ṭabarī i 2108; Azdī 28–9; Sebēos (123–4 Bedrosian, 94, 96 Macler). The more complete account of al-Ṭabarī, albeit short, is decisive and permits making a choice between traditions. The *fusṭāṭ* is unidentified. It may have been part of the site of Areopolis, or the modern town of Qaṣr or the village of Yārūt or some other site. I thank Dr. Fawzi Zayadine for advice.

[54] Ibn 'Asākir 1: 439–40. Cf. Azdī 28–9.

T'ēodos. Then they turned and encamped in Arabia." The brother of Heraclius was Theodore, not Theodosius.[55] There is no doubt that this is not confused with Ajnādayn, because he specifies that the Byzantine army was camped "in Arabia." Theodore, the brother of Heraclius, was said to have been routed with his troops,[56] although he may be confused with Theodore the *vicarius*, who is mentioned as Byzantine commander at the battle of Mu'ta. Areopolis technically was not in the province of Arabia but in Palaestina Tertia. Sebēos claims that after defeating the Byzantines the Muslims returned to Arabia, which may mean that they moved north and then crossed the Arnon River/Wādī'l Mūjib and thereby returned to territory that was within the province of Arabia. This account emphasizes the strategic value of Ma'āb/Areopolis. It was after receiving news of this defeat, with indeterminate casualties, that Heraclius raised still larger numbers of troops.[57] In any case, the Byzantines did not cede the Balqā' by default. They tried, unsuccessfully, to halt the Muslims there.

It was hazardous for the Muslims to undertake major military activities west of the 'Araba, in Palaestina Prima, for example, until the capture of Ma'āb (Areopolis) secured their northern flank. It became possible for actions at 'Ayn Ghamr in the 'Araba to take place, followed by the more sensational clash at Dāthin that first attracted much widespread notice. But these actions all followed that less spectacular securing of the region south of the Wādī'l Mūjib or Arnon River by the occupation of Ma'āb (Areopolis), a traditional Byzantine major muster point. It was military action east of the Jordan–Dead Sea–Wādī'l 'Araba line, including al-Mayfa'a, Ayla, and Ma'āb (Areopolis), which first really tested the relative strength of the Byzantine and Muslim units, and it resulted in the Muslims' acquiring a strategically important springboard as well as assuring their logistical lines.

Byzantine officers may have deliberately floated rumors of massing troops in order to frighten Arab tribesmen on the eve of Heraclius' procession to and return from Jerusalem. The truth may never be known. But there really may have been a temporary show of force and threats of increasing those forces, in advance of and until the end of Heraclius' visit to Jerusalem. The very fact of the need to prepare for that procession probably caused Byzantine military authorities to become apprised of the existence of a potential danger from the Arabian peninsula. Heraclius' visit to Jerusalem would have occasioned security preparations that might have lapsed after his departure from Jerusalem. But his visit to Jerusalem probably made the Byzantines far more

55 Sebēos c. 30 (96 Macler, 124 Bedrosian); also Azdī 29.

56 Sebēos c. 30 (123–4 Bedrosian, 96 Macler). It is true, however, that Theodore, brother of Heraclius, commanded at Ajnādayn, where he was defeated and compelled to flee ignominiously.

57 Ibn 'Asākir 1: 440.

interested than normal in the areas east of the Jordan and Dead Sea. If anything, they had more opportunity than usual to learn of the imminent perils. It is unlikely that they were taken completely by surprise. These temporary Byzantine troop concentrations may have been withdrawn after Heraclius returned from Jerusalem to northern Syria. But his visit may explain why there were at least temporarily some Byzantine troops south of the Wādī'l Ḥasā in 629, and 630, but few or none in 634. Mu'ta was not such a decisive victory that the Byzantines continued to seek another test in the area.

Islamic tribesmen did not simply overrun a static and gravely weakened Byzantine Empire. Instead, their invasions occurred while Byzantium was still in the process of restoring her authority over the full extent of the former eastern borders of her empire. Heraclius was in that region because he was personally involved in overseeing that restoration and reunification. If he had had more time, he might have succeeded. The Muslim invasions caught him and the empire off balance at a very awkward time, and kept them off balance. The exertion of minimal pressure at the critical moment and place was able to bring the Muslims maximal rewards in terms of military victories and territorial conquests, with a minimum of casualties. The Byzantines were just restoring their authority in the Syrian cities and countryside, but that process of restoration and creation of lines of authority and a viable power structure with conscious identification with Byzantium was even more tenuous in the areas east of the Jordan and the Dead Sea when the Muslims began their own probes and raiding, which they very soon greatly intensified.

Chapter 5

EARLY TESTS IN SOUTHERN PALESTINE

THE DEFENSES OF GAZA AND THE BATTLE OF DĀTHIN

The lack of any coherent Byzantine strategy for the defense of Syria quickly became clear after the Muslims penetrated southern Palestine. The Byzantine military, religious, and civilian authorities were not expecting any major Arab invasions and accordingly had made no special preparations to resist or to prepare the local civilians.[1] Whatever Heraclius or his subordinates intended, the reality was just a poorly informed and an *ad hoc* Byzantine military reaction, which resulted in disaster.

Southern Palestine experienced some of the most savage early clashes between Byzantines and Muslims. The unfortunate Byzantine military commander who had responsibility for leading those inept and disastrous defensive operations was Sergios, who, as a *candidatos* (office formerly reserved to a personal bodyguard of the Byzantine emperor, but one that had become more honorific and widely distributed in the seventh century; holders wore special white uniforms), had direct access to Emperor Heraclius.[2] The Sergios of the Greek sources is probably identical with the Byzantine commander B[R]YRDN, which is "Vardan" or "Wardān," from Damascus mentioned in an early Syriac source. He fell in the battle of Dāthin near (12 miles distant from) Gaza, on 4 February 634. It is this commander whose name has inspired Azdī to report a Wardān as Byzantine commander, formerly of Ḥimṣ, at the battle of Ajnādayn.[3] It is unclear why there should

[1] Sophronius, *PG* 87: 3197D, on the unexpected character of the Muslim "uprisings" or incursions.

[2] *Doctrina Iacobi nuper baptizati* 86, lines 13–14. The two mentions of *Kandidatos* (ὁ Κανδιδάτος) in this very contemporary source leave no doubt about his identification. On *candidatos*, Haldon, *Byzantine Praetorians* 129–30, 154–9; R. Guilland, "Etudes sur l'histoire administrative de l'empire byzantin. Le titre de candidat," *Polychronion*, ed. by P. Wirth (Heidelberg 1966) 210–25. Sergios' relationship to Niketas: Nicephorus, *Hist.* (68–9, 186–7 Mango).

[3] Azdī 84, on Wardān; Th. Nöldeke, *Die ghassânischen Fürsten*... 45, n. 3. Like Nöldeke, M. J. De Goeje believed that "Les caractères ... B(r)jrdn doivent contenir le nom du patrice,"

be two different names for the Byzantine commander. The Semitic tradition of the Syriac chronicle may simply be incorrect, yet it is the only source for the date, but it is possible that Sergios originally had an Armenian name, by which he is identified in the Syriac and Arabic tradition. There is no absolutely satisfactory answer. No sigillographic or epigraphic record of any Sergios is extant.[4]

The eighth-century historian Nicephorus and twelfth-century Armenian chronicler Samuel of Ani attribute Arab invasions to the despoiling of Arab merchants by a Sergios attached to Niketas (probably cousin of Heraclius), one possibly different from the commander at Dāthin. Saracens charged this Sergios with persuading Heraclius "not to allow Saracens to trade from the Roman country and send out of the Roman state the thirty pounds of gold which they normally received by way of commercial gain."[5] Although not impossible, Samuel of Ani, who identifies Sergios as a patrician of Damascus and identifies Khālid b. al-Walīd as the avenger of the aggrieved Arabs, may well simply conflate or elaborate on the passage in Nicephorus' *Short History*, or its source. His account requires very cautious and critical handling. But both accounts of economic treachery explain the rage and ferocity of the passions of Arabs against Sergios, whom the enraged Arabs reportedly slew by suffocation in a drying camel stomach.[6] Possible corroboration of the horrible fate of Sergios and the reputation of Arabs for ferocious treatment of certain men who fell into their hands is found in other historical parallels[7] and in the *Doctrina Iacobi nuper baptizati*, which quotes one oath of a contemporary who swears that even if a Saracen threatens to cut him to pieces he will not deny Jesus Christ.[8]

*Mémoire*² 32. A. Palmer, "Extract from a Chronicle Finished in AD 641," *Chronicles*, part 1, text 2: AG 945; *Liber Calipharum*, ed. by J. P. N. Land, Anecdota Syriaca (Leiden 1862) 1: 17 (original), and 1: 116 (erroneous translation); *Chronicon miscellaneum ad annum Domini 724 pertinens*, trans. by J.-B. Chabot (CSCO, Script. Syri, ser. 3, T. 4 [Louvain 1903–5] Versio, 114), who corrects reading of Land; Caetani, *AI* 2: 1144–5. Professors Nina Garsoïan and the late Arthur Vööbus gave me important advice in identifying B[R]YRDN as Wardān. P. Speck, *Das geteilte Dossier* (Bonn 1988) 348–9, also believes that Sergios is identical with the officer mentioned in Syriac sources who fell presumably at Dāthin, but he does not clarify the location.

4 So I learn from Dr. John Nesbitt and Dr. Clayton M. Lehmann, who are respectively studying seals and inscriptions from Caesarea.

5 Nicephorus, *Hist*. 20 (68–71 Mango).

6 Samuel of Ani, *Tables chronologiques*, in: *Collection d'historiens arméniens*, ed. and trans. by Marii Ivanovich Brose [Brosset] (St. Petersburg 1876) 2: 403.

7 His manner of death is not out of the question. Note that the cadaver of Muḥammad b. Abū Bakr was reportedly inserted in the stomach of an ass and then burned, in 658, another nearly contemporary case of disgracing the death of someone who was much reviled (for his role in the murder of Caliph 'Uthmān).

8 Death of Sergios, *Doctrina Iacobi* c. 16 (86, lines 12–15 Bonwetsch). Oath of Justus, for Jacob, that even if Jews and Saracens cut him into pieces piece by piece, he will not deny

The engagement at Dāthin represented Arab resistance to Byzantine attempts to tighten economic and military control of the frontier after reoccupying the coast in the wake of the Persian withdrawal. Unidentified Arabs had become accustomed, during Persian occupation, to engaging in lucrative untaxed or minimally taxed trade in Palestine. They naturally resented being deprived of what they regarded as normal profits. The Byzantines were attempting to impose tighter controls in 632 or 633, just as, in 629 during the process of restoring their authority east of the Dead Sea, they had clashed with other Arabs at Mu'ta. Byzantine and Arab economic interests conflicted.

Theophanes reports that the other cause also combined military and financial grievances:

> There were some nearby Arabs who received small payments from the emperor to guard the entrance of the desert [τούς στρατιώτας τῶν παραφυλακῶν τῆς ἐρημίας]. But in that time some eunuch came to pay the soldiers, and the Arabs, according to custom, came to receive their pay, but the eunuch drove them out, saying that "the ruler scarcely pays the soldiers, how much less these dogs." Aggrieved, the Arabs departed for their fellow tribesmen, they led them to the countryside of Gaza, the entrance being by the side of Mount Sinai.

The anonymous eunuch paid the regular Byzantine soldiers but not the irregular local Arabs who helped to guard the region. The subsidy may have nominally been a payment to protect Byzantine territory from hostile Arab incursions. It may also have been intended more as a bribe – a frequent Byzantine custom on various frontiers – to persuade those Arabs themselves not to raid Byzantine territory. Yet the greatest probability is that it was intended to pay them to guard the edge of inhabited territories against hostile Arabs, because those who received such a subsidy actually possessed an unidentified *ḥīra* or encampment near Gaza, which they presumably used to watch for hostile raiders. Theophanes states that "they came and captured the camp [*ḥīra*] and the whole countryside of Gaza. Scarcely having arrived from Caesarea of Palestine with a few soldiers, Sergios fought a battle and was killed first with three hundred soldiers." It has been difficult to understand the Byzantine texts and their underlying Arabic meanings.[9] The

Jesus Christ, *Doctrina Iacobi* c. 17 (88, lines 5–7, Bonwetsch). The manner of Sergios' recent death may have been an additional cause for such a subject and oath.

[9] First quotation from Theophanes: Theophanes, *Chron.*, AM 6123 (335–6 De Boor); second: AM 6124 (336 De Boor). Location: Yāqūt 2: 514–5. W. E. Kaegi, "New Perspectives on the Last Decades of the Byzantine Era," *1983 Bilād-al-Shām Proceedings* 2: 84–5; L. I. Conrad, "Theophanes and the Arabic Historical Transmission" 30; cf. Philip Mayerson, "The First Muslim Attacks on Southern Palestine (AD 633–4)," *TAPA* 95 (1964) esp. 161–2. Lack of manpower, Sauvaget, "Les Ghassānides et Sergiopolis" 115–30. But A. Alt, "Der Limes

effectiveness of those posts may be debatable. But they had hardly been restored after the Persian evacuation, so they had not been in existence long enough to be evaluated for their military efficiency.

The payment of such a subsidy cannot have lasted very long, because the Byzantines were able to reoccupy the area only in approximately 629; perhaps only token numbers of regular soldiers, with officers, were originally sent. Although Arab tribesmen had previously been used as guides and guards for pilgrims and caravans between Gaza, Elusa, the Sinai, and Egypt, their numbers and details of their subsidy in 633/4 are unknown; perhaps several years' payment was due when the eunuch advised cancellation of the payments.[10]

The Byzantine government's cancellation of payments to the federated Arabs was not unique. There was a sharp retrenchment in military expenditures, including soldiers' pay, all over the empire after Heraclius' victory over the Persians. The contemporary *Miracula* of St. Anastasius the Persian reports that Byzantine officials refused to pay waggoners their stipulated pay of ten silver milliaresia at Ctesiphon, the Persian capital. Only with difficulty, and allegedly with the miraculous aid of St. Anastasius the Persian, were they able to collect their pay by going to Constantinople, where officials finally paid it. It is possible that this nonpayment of silver was their portion of a special distribution of silver confiscated from the Persians at Ctesiphon, not regular pay.[11] This is a plausible detail that has survived in a separate tradition. Thus retrenchment and nonpayment of irregular soldiers was not directed against Arabs alone. It was applied generally, and should be understood in that broader context. Another contemporary, John of Nikiu, also reveals contemporary resentment against the high expenditures for the upkeep of soldiers in Egypt.[12] That this was happening generally did not mollify those Arabs who expected, like the waggoners, their payments, and probably desperately needed them for their essential living expenses. They certainly resented the selective payment of funds to regular soldiers only.

The *ḥīra*, their former encampment, from which the furious Byzantine-allied Arabs had guarded the Gaza region, resembled encampments[13]

Palestinae im sechsten und siebenten Jahrhundert n. Chr.," *ZDPV* 63 (1940) 129–42, argues that much of the old defenses survived.

[10] Mayerson, "First Muslim Attacks" 185–8. W. Goffart, "From Roman Taxation to Mediaeval Seigneurie: Three Notes," *Speculum* 47 (1972) 177–8. Antonini Placentini, *Itinerarium* 40, cf. 35–9, ed. by Celestina Milani (Milan 1977) 214, 200–13.

[11] *Miracula, Acta M. Anastasii Persae* c. 3 (21 Usener). On Heraclius' distribution of silver from a tower at Ctesiphon to his soldiers as booty: Hrabanus Maurus, *PL* 110: 132–3.

[12] John of Nikiu, *Chronicle* 119.12 (190 Charles).

[13] It was not, as De Goeje supposed, a place-name Ḥīra, *Mémoire*[2] 34, nor, as Caetani supposed, a garbled reference to the famous Lakhmid Ḥīra far to the east: *AI* 2: 1143.

scattered near other Syrian cities: Berrhoia (modern Aleppo), Emesa (modern Ḥimṣ), and Chalkis (medieval Qinnasrīn, modern village of al-Is).[14] Theophanes used Christian Arab or Syriac or possibly Muslim sources,[15] and did not know how to translate *ḥīra* into Greek, nor did his own Latin translator. It was natural for the angry Arabs to punish the stingy Byzantines by leading other beduin to capture their former guardpost for Gaza, which had strategic significance.

Ghassānids had already raided Syria extensively in 581, threatening to capture Bostra in angry response to Maurice's arrest and exile of their phylarch al-Mundhir and the cancellation of their stipends.[16] Heraclius and his advisers may have been unaware of that crisis, because it was reported in Monophysite historiography, such as John of Ephesus, but not, for example, in historical or other literature that was generally available at the court of Heraclius.[17] Some individuals might have recalled hearing about the incident and its consequences, but it was too embarrassing and sensitive to report, and now many decades had passed.

Muslim troops under 'Amr b. al-'Āṣ travelled by way of Ayla ('Aqaba), which had already submitted to the Muslims.[18] The texts of treaties and guarantees given by Muḥammad to Ayla, Adhruḥ (Adroa), and Ma'ān may be substantially authentic. They do not define a hermetically sealed frontier but instead assume the possibility of persons passing between Muslim and Byzantine territories without physical harm.[19] The Muslim troops occupied the former *ḥīra* of the dismissed Byzantine Arab guards of the Gaza region near Dāthin and began raiding the area. They had already begun raiding the 'Araba, indeed a skirmish had taken place at 'Ayn Ghamr, in the Ghor.[20]

[14] On the *ḥaẓīra*: Shahid, *BAFOC* 402–7, 426, 428, 469, 471, 481–5, 546, 548. Caetani, *AI* 3: 790–1. Ibn al-'Adīm, *Zubdat al-Ḥalab min Ta'rīkh Ḥalab* 1: 25–6.

[15] Theoph., *Chron.*, AM 6121 (332 De Boor).

[16] P. Goubert, *Byzance avant l'Islam* (Paris 1951) 1: 249–60.

[17] John of Ephesus 3.3.42 (131–2 Chabot trans.). Evagrius Scholasticus, *HE* 6.2 (223 Bidez-Parmentier). H. Turtledove, "The Immediate Successors of Justinian" 310–20; E. Stein, *Studien* (Stuttgart 1919) 40–3, 51.

[18] Muslims go to Ayla. Eutychius. *Ann.* 276 (131 Breydy text, 111 Breydy trans.). Balādhurī 59-60, 108; Caetani, *AI* 2: 253–5. A. Alt, "Aila und Adroa im spätrömischen Grenzschutzsystem," *ZDPV* 59 (1936) 92–111. Ph. Mayerson, "The First Muslim Attacks on Southern Palestine (AD 633–4)," *TAPA* 95 (1964) 169–77.

[19] Study of Ayla treaty, Caetani, *AI* 2: 254–5. Important new excavations at 'Aqaba by Dr. Donald Whitcomb are revealing much about the medieval site.

[20] Skirmish at 'Ayn Ghamr: al-Ṭabarī i 2108, 2125; Balādhurī 108–9. De Goeje, *Mémoire*[2] 35–6. Already in 619 the road beyond Ascalon to the south had been blocked by Arabs, *PL* 74: 121. Michael Breydy, in his German translation of Eutychius, *Ann.* 276 (p. 111, n. 5), erroneously identifies "Tadun" as a place in modern Jordan, although Eutychius expressly identifies it as a village of Gaza. Caetani, *AI* 2: 1138, 1141, has achieved a plausible identification of Dāthin near Gaza. Breydy's identification must be rejected; cf. Yāqūt 2: 514–15.

There is no Byzantine documentation of the loss of Ayla. 'Amr probably crossed to Gaza from the 'Araba, skirting wells and earlier settlements. Yet according to Ibn 'Asākir he did not take along donkeys and sheep, because he presumably planned to live off the land and to increase mobility.[21]

It is questionable whether the Limes Palestinae ever existed in the form that some have claimed; consequently it is inappropriate to hypothesize its abandonment or survival until the 630s.[22] Instead, it is better to assume continuation of some very old troop emplacements in coastal areas, but very heavy reliance on friendly Arabs in encampments on the settled fringes of semi-desert, especially in southern Palestine, the Wādī'l Mūjib region, the Balqā', the Ḥawrān, the Golan, and even in upper Mesopotamia and near the Euphrates on the Syrian bank. Fiscal considerations reinforced a Byzantine wariness about trying to fight Arabs in their own terrain, to result in reliance on Arabs to guard the edges of settled territory against hostile Arabs.

The Byzantine commander (*dux* and *candidatus*) Sergios learned of the Muslim harassment of the Gaza region and assembled what is reliably and reasonably reported as about 300 men at Caesarea to come to the rescue of the Gaza region, as his predecessors had done.[23] Byzantine soldiers were in short supply. It probably took Sergios and his horsemen several days to reach and regroup at the beleaguered region of Gaza, some 76 miles or 125 kilometers south of Caesarea. It is unknown whether there were no other units available south of Caesarea. In any case, Sergios was defeated, apparently on 4 February 634, his men were routed, and he himself was slain. This was the battle of Dāthin.[24] The number of Muslim troops probably far exceeded that of the inadequate contingent of Byzantines; they may have numbered even more than a thousand, perhaps double or triple that. Tactical details of this clash are unclear.

[21] Ibn 'Asākir on 'Amr not taking donkeys, sheep: *TMD* 1: 461; cf. Eutychius, *Ann.* 276 (131 Breydy). Misidentification of Heran (Ἥραν) – which is really *ḥīra* – in Theophanes' narrative completely vitiates any thesis of some kind of a Muslim approach to Gaza by way of the inner Sinai, as argued by Mayerson 161–2.

[22] See G. W. Bowersock, *Roman Arabia* (Cambridge 1983) 103–5. Nomad raids are: D. F. Graf, "The Saracens and the Defense of the Arabian Frontier," *BASOR* 229 (1978) 1–26; Benjamin Isaac, *Limits of Empire* 374–418, criticizes limes theories; cf. S. T. Parker, *Romans and Saracens* (Winona Lake, IN, 1985); Ph. Mayerson, "The Saracens and the Limes," *BASOR* 262 (1986) 35–47.

[23] Cf. Choricius of Gaza, *Or.* 3.10–38, 4. 16–32, on Aratios, Stephanos, and Summus, who stopped nomadic raids, brought peace, and fairly distributed tax assessments; s.v. "Summus," *PLRE* 2: 1038–9.

[24] Nicephorus, *Hist.* 20 (68–71 Mango). Theophanes, *Chron.*, AM 6123 (335–6 De Boor). *Doctrina Iacobi nuper baptizati* c. 16 (86, lines 12–15 Bonwetsch). Date of *Doctrina* estimated to be written soon after 634 in Palestine: P. Crone, M. A. Cook, *Hagarism* (Cambridge: Cambridge University Press, 1977) 3–4. Michael the Syrian, *Chron.* 9.4 (2: 413 Chabot).

The Arab's reputation for fierceness in war probably aided the Muslim conquest, creating an atmosphere of terror. Probably some acts of physical mutilation were a real basis for such stories and fears. Yet cases are rarely documented. Many Byzantines were slain at Dāthin and Ajnādayn, and later at Gaza. Patriarch Sophronius' Christmas sermon gives more indication of fear of the ferocity of the "Saracen" sword.[25] Yet it is essential to understand that the battle of Dāthin took place after clashes, however large or small, at Ma'āb and in the 'Araba. Dāthin extended the successes that Muslims had initially won further east into a very different region.

The defeat at Dāthin left an enormous echo in literature, starting with the *Doctrina Iacobi nuper baptizati*. This news struck hard in the Jewish community at Sycamina, not far from Caesarea, between it and Acre, near modern Haifa.[26] Their reaction was shock and joy that "The *candidatus* is slain!" The fact that Sergios had been such an official (ὁ Κανδιδάτος), with his accessibility to the emperor, associated the imperial majesty with his death. The prestige of Heraclius was stained even more by the violent death of a *candidatus* than by any ordinary military commander. Although more of a disastrous skirmish than a major battle, contemporaries and posterity remembered Dāthin as one of the key defeats of the Byzantines, usually in the same line with references to the battle of the Yarmūk.[27] Its impact was instantaneous.

Eutychius reports that the Byzantine commander at Gaza, whom he does not name, tried to capture 'Amr b. al-Āṣ and other Muslim commanders during a parley about why the Muslims were attacking Palestine. Such a report can be fabulous, but there is some element here of plausibility, because such a practice was typically Byzantine.[28] However ineffective, it was typical of the kinds of stratagems that would have been employed in the pursuit of that goal, to use craft to decapitate the leadership of the Muslims. The Byzantine commander asked why the Muslims had come, and wished to know the identity of their leader. When introduced to 'Amr, he plotted to have him arrested, an event similar (not mentioned by Eutychius) to the arrest of al-Mundhir at a parley in 581, followed by his permanent exile. This indeed may be a common literary theme. There appears to be some common

[25] Weihnachtspredigt des Sophronios," ed. by H. Usener, *Rheinisches Museum* n.s. 41 (1886) 506–7. Sophronius, *Epistola synodica ad Sergium Cp.*, *PG* 87: 3197D.

[26] *Doctrina Iacobi nuper baptizati* c. 16 (86, lines 11–23, Bonwetsch).

[27] Anastasius Sinaita, *Sermo adversus Monotheletas* 3.1.86–92, in: *Anastasii Sinaitae Opera*, ed. by Karl-Heinz Uthemann (CC, Ser. Graeca, 12 [Brepols-Turnhout: Leuven University Press, 1985]) 60. Theoph., *Chron.*, AM 6121, 6123 (332, 335–6 De Boor); Eutychius, *Ann.* (131–2 Breydy text, 111 Breydy trans.), mentions it, apparently conflated with Ajnādayn.

[28] Eutychius, *Ann.* 276 (131–5 Breydy text, 111–13 Breydy trans.). Cf. al-Ṭabarī/Sayf i 2398–400. Ibn 'Asākir 1: 461–2. N. H. Baynes, "The Date of the Avar Surprise," *BZ* 21 (1912) 10–128. Maurikios, *Strategikon* 9.2. 12 (306–7 Dennis-Gamillscheg).

source for this story. al-Ṭabarī, however, reports that there was such a plot by Wardān – yet not at Dāthin, but at Ajnādayn – to seize 'Amr, who escaped.[29] More source critique is necessary. The accounts are plausible. Yet Ibn 'Asākir, who also reports that there were parleys, does not mention any attempt to arrest 'Amr. The warning of 'Amr's multilingual slave Wardān, who understood precisely what the Byzantines intended to do, saved him from captivity, because he explained to the Byzantines that there were others, presumably more leaders, so the Byzantine commander waited to seize them all, thereby allowing 'Amr to escape.[30] It is consistent with Byzantine practice in such situations against barbarians. Oral tradition about the fate of al-Mundhir and possibly other tribal leaders at the hands of the Byzantines may have made the Muslims wary of dealings with the Byzantines, but there is no specific documentation of the existence of such traditions. Yet it had not been much more than a half-century since the arrest and exile of al-Mundhir. The existence of such stories did not leave a favorable memory of Byzantine rule among Christian Arabs, who fell under Muslim control. Yet, it is unclear why the Muslims would have omitted such a report of Byzantine treachery. The report of the contents of the parley with the Byzantine commander in Ibn 'Asākir's *Ta'rīkh Madīnat Dimashq* is reminiscent of the statements in the histories of Sebēos, Azdī, and in turn with that of al-Ṭabarī/Sayf; Sebēos may draw on a common Muslim tradition used, directly or indirectly, by them all.[31]

Gaza did not finally surrender to the Muslims until August or September of 637. At that time 'Amr gave security to its civilian inhabitants, but not to its soldiers. They were removed to Eleutheropolis and then to Jerusalem, where they were executed after refusing to abjure Christianity. At least some of them had wives and children, all of whom were spared. The existence of families with the garrison may indicate, although it is not certain, that the garrison had held the post for a long time. Their execution appears to have been exceptional. It is possible that the severity of their fate, although not inconsistent with Islamic law, which was then only in the process of

[29] al-Ṭabarī (Sayf) i 2398–400.

[30] On Wardān's perception of the words and intentions of the Byzantine commander: Eutychius, *Ann.* (132 Breydy). Capture of al-Mundhir by means of an invitation to a parley: Goubert, *Byzance avant l'Islam* 1: 249–57. Al-Nu'mān was initially unsuccessfully sought to be seized at a meeting, Goubert, *Byzance avant l'Islam* 1: 257–9; John of Ephesus, *HE* 3.3. 42–3, 56 (132–3, 135–6 Brooks, CSCO trans.). Evagrius, *HE* 6.2 (223 Bidez-Parmentier).

[31] Ibn 'Asākir, *TMD* 1: 461–2. Sebēos c. 30 (124–6 Bedrosian, 96–7 Macler). Of course Sebēos states, "We heard this [account] from men [who had returned] from captivity in Xuzhastan Tachkastan, who themselves had been eye-witnesses to the events described and narrated them to us" (131 Bedrosian = 102 Macler), and claims to have gained his information from prisoners, which is plausible. But cf. Heinrich Hübschmann, *Zur Geschichte Armeniens und der ersten Kriege der Araber* (Leipzig 1875) 18, n. 3. Bedrosian does not show awareness of Hübschmann's comments. Azdī 25, 26, 27; al-Ṭabarī (Sayf) i 2398–400.

developing, may have been exacerbated by their prolonged resistance at Gaza. But in particular, although not mentioned by the anonymous author of this martyrology, they may have been executed because of the continuing anger of ʻAmr at Gaza and its officers because of their leader's attempt to murder him and other Muslim envoys during a parley early in the conquests, presumably before the battle of Dāthin in early 634, or if confused, that of Ajnādayn. The unsuccessful tricky negotiations between the commander of the Byzantine troops at Gaza and ʻAmr, as described by Eutychius, may have led to the execution of these Byzantine soldiers in 637.[32] This was a detail that the author of the martyrology would not have wished to mention.

The immediate consequences of the clash at Dāthin were shock among the Byzantines and license for ʻAmr's nomads to raid. It is possible that Gaza paid some tribute to avoid being assaulted at that moment of vulnerability. Yet Gaza was not occupied by the Muslims until September, 637. It continued to have a Byzantine garrison, even though that garrison may have been a small one – only eighty soldiers are mentioned in the *Passio LX Martyrum* as having been captured in 637, although others may have escaped.[33] The countryside around Gaza may have become very insecure. ʻAmr b. al-ʻĀṣ continued to operate in this area, not only at the battle of Ajnādayn later in 634 but also in 637. Presumably ʻAmr continued to exercise authority in the area continuously between 634 and his invasion of Egypt. He also gained control of Eleutheropolis (Bayt Jibrīn). Because of his early establishment of initiative in southern Palestine, in the vicinity of Gaza and Eleutheropolis, ʻAmr was in an excellent position to learn details of the vulnerability of the Byzantines in the Sinai and in Egypt. Moreover, he was the Muslim commander who was situated to take advantage of that Byzantine weakness. He knew more about the conditions in Egypt and how to supply Muslims in southern Palestine and the Gaza area to approach Egypt, and he was the natural commander to undertake such an invasion, whenever it became appropriate to do it.[34]

Agapius of Manbij and Theophanes, who are both Christian, although one is anti-Chalcedonian and one is Chalcedonian, state that a three-year

[32] Commander was that of Gaza: Eutychius, *Ann.* (132 Breydy). Martyrs of Gaza: Delehaye, "Passio sanctorum sextaginta martyrum," *AB* 23 (1904) 289–307; J. Pargoire, "Les LX Martyrs de Gaza," *EO* 8 (1905) 40–3. The remains of the executed garrison were probably buried in a special church, that of the Holy Trinity, at Eleutheropolis (Beth Guvrin or Bayt Jibrīn). See Bellarmino Bagatti, "Il cristianesimo ad Eleuteropoli," *Liber Annuus* 22 (1972) 116; Bagatti, *Antichi villaggi cristiani di Giudea e Neghev* (Studium Biblicum Franciscanum, Collectio Minor, 24 [Jerusalem 1983]) 125. At present, no ruins have been thus far identified.

[33] Delehaye, "Passio sanctorum sextaginta martyrum" 303 and explanations of Pargoire, "Les LX Martyrs de Gaza" 40–3.

[34] Kaegi, "Byzantine Egypt during the Arab Invasion of Palestine and Syria: Some Observations," *American Research Center in Egypt Newsletter* 121 (Spring 1983) 11–15.

peace was made to prevent a Muslim invasion of Egypt.[35] It is plausible that the Byzantines would have attempted to purchase such a peace, for that was a typical Byzantine practice of the seventh as well as earlier and later centuries.[36] Some question whether the Muslims would have been so foolish as to engage in such an agreement, given their growing momentum and strength. The Muslims may well have accepted considerable sums of money to implement such agreements because of the immediate financial gain, of course, but also because it released soldiers and leadership to concentrate on other military sectors, thereby avoiding splitting Muslim soldiers and directions of attack during the critical early moments of the invasions when the maximum concentration of force was desirable and perhaps necessary against the Byzantine forces to the north and/or against the Persians in the east.

Rational calculations may have persuaded Muslim leaders to accept such payments in return for guaranteeing Egypt, and perhaps also Gaza, against assault at that time. In the future, however, they were free to turn against Egypt. But there is no record of a payment to protect Egypt until 637, probably following the fall of Gaza to the Muslims. The Byzantines never peaceably evacuated Gaza, in the manner that they evacuated certain central and northern Syrian cities and Jerusalem itself. There may have been some earlier payments or understandings between the Byzantine authorities at Gaza and 'Amr's Muslims, but there is no precise record of this, except for some Muslim traditions that Gaza made some kind of peace with the Muslims. The Byzantine garrison that the Muslims finally captured at Gaza in 637 apparently had orders to defend it to the last. But there are no reports of fighting or incidents of any kind at Gaza between the battle of Ajnādayn and the fall of Gaza in 637.

More immediately significant than any threat to Egypt, however, was the Byzantine defeat at Dāthin's removal of any serious military barrier to the Muslims' ability to raid southern Palestine at will. A few Byzantine walled towns such as Gaza and Ascalon held out, but Muslim raiding compelled Byzantine military authorities to collect and rush another and more respectable force to stem the raiders in southern Palestine. A more substantial test in battle necessarily followed.

[35] Theoph. *Chron.*, AM 6126 (338 De Goeje). A. J. Butler, *The Arab Conquest of Egypt*. rev. by P. M. Fraser (Oxford 1978) 481–3. See Stratos, *Byzantium in the Seventh Century* 2: 88–90, 214.

[36] Corippus, *In laudem Iustini, pr.* 6–9; 3.230–407, ed. and trans. by Averil Cameron (London: University of London Press, 1976). E. Stein, *Studien* (Stuttgart 1919), in general; E. Stein, *HBE* 2: 486–92; Charles Diehl, *Byzantium: Greatness and Decline* (New Brunswick 1954) esp. 53–9.

AJNĀDAYN

Byzantine sources do not specifically mention a battle of Ajnādayn, perhaps conflating it with Dāthin and with Jābiya-Yarmūk.[37] Some Arabic sources state that Muslim armies concentrated at Ajnādayn, under Khālid b. al-Walīd or, less likely, 'Amr b. al-'Āṣ. Its location has been satisfactorily identified between Ramla and Bayt Jibrīn on the Wādī'l Samt in modern Israel about 9 kilometers northeast of Bet Guvrin.[38] Its probable date was 30 July 634. The earliest extant source is probably the Latin *Chronicle* of Fredegarius, composed *c.* 658/60, who briefly reports concerning the Muslim or "Saracen" invaders that "Heraclius sent soldiers against them in order to resist them. When, however, it came to a battle, the Saracens defeated the Roman soldiers and inflicted a serious defeat on them. In that battle 150,000 Roman soldiers were slain. The booty, however, the Saracens offered through their envoys to Heraclius for repurchase. Heraclius, who wished to take revenge on these Saracens, did not wish to repurchase any of this stolen goods."[39] The Muslim envoys' unsuccessful attempt to sell booty and possibly also prisoners back to Heraclius is not inconceivable. Other sources provide more details. The Byzantines, under Theodore, the brother of Heraclius, and possibly also under Wardān, who according to some

[37] Muslim sources often conflate Dāthin and Yarmūk. Yet Byzantine sources such as Theophanes, *Chron.*, AM 6121 (332 De Boor), and St. Anastasius the Sinaite, *Sermo adversus Monotheletas* 3.1. 86–92 (60 Uthemann), mention Dāthin or "Dathesmon" and Yarmūk as separate battles in recounting lists of Byzantine military disasters at the hands of the Muslims. The references by St. Anastasius the Sinaite here are the earliest surviving references in Greek to the name of the site of the battle of Dāthin (in contrast to still earlier, almost contemporary vague allusion by the author of the *Doctrina Iacobi nuper baptizati* to the defeat and death of the Candidatos Sergios) and to the battle of the Yarmūk, calling it a battle at the Yarmūk.

[38] Ajnādayn is probably located approximately at latitude 31° 41′ N and longitude 34° 57′ E. It is about 37 kilometers southeast of Jerusalem, 9 kilometers northeast of Bet Guvrin (Arabic Bayt Jibrīn), 3 kilometers east of Agur, and 2 kilometers south of Zekharya. See Sheet 11–12, *Israel Series 1:100,000* (Tel Aviv: Survey of Israel, 1981) ("Yerushalayim"), and for an older map, see sites of "Jannaba at Tahta" and "Jannaba al Fawqa" on Sheet 10 "Hebron," in *Survey of Palestine* (1935), at scale 1:100,000. Caetani, *AI* 2: 24–81, summarizes the previous scholarship and provides rather definitive treatment. I thank Professor Mordechai Gichon for giving me a personal tour of that battlefield, in the spring of 1979. H. A. R. Gibb, s.v., "Ajnādayn," *EI*² 1: 208–9.

[39] Fredegarius, *Chron.* 4.66 (153 Krusch) = (55 Wallace-Hadrill). Andreas Kusternig edn and trans., *Quellen zur Geschichte des 7. und 8. Jahrhunderts* (Darmstadt: Wissenschaftliche Buchgesellschaft, 1982) 232–3; cf. 9–13; W. Goffart, "The Fredegar Problem Reconsidered," *Speculum* 38 (1963) 206–41, esp. 218; Alvar Erikson, "The Problem of the Authorship in the Chronicle of Fredgar," *Eranos* 63 (1965) 76. Here Fredegarius is not referring to the battle of the Yarmūk, but to Ajnādayn: Ekkehart Rotter, *Abendland und Sarazenen* (Berlin: de Gruyter, 1986) 152–3; date: p. 149. Fredegarius is using directly or indirectly some oriental source, whether Syriac or Greek, for this is probably too early for direct use of an Arabic source. The other possibility is that this section of Fredegarius' chronicle was interpolated later. I thank Walter Goffart for advice.

traditions was the military governor or *patricius* of Emesa (Ḥimṣ), massed in the hopes of striking decisively at the Muslims in order to drive them out of Palestine. Such action probably made the situation of Muslims far to the north in the areas east of the Dead Sea and Jordan untenable or at least dangerously exposed.

The Wardān of al-Azdī is also called Artabūn, who is probably the same person. This name is not fanciful. It is confirmed by the small scrap of Syriac text which is nearly contemporary with the events. It refers to the *patricius* who fought and fell at the battle as B[R]YRDN, which was wrongly translated as "into the Jordan" or "son of Iardan," but in fact it is an Armenian name Vardan, which has been disguised when transliterated into Syriac. It indicates that a Vardan – presumably an Armenian, possibly from the Mamikonian family – held a military post in Palestine in 634. Also there was another prominent Armenian commander, who was Vahān or Baanes. Heraclius relied heavily on Armenians for his appointees in that period, just as he appointed the Armenian Manuel in Egypt, who also was a military commander imposed in a civilian post. This is a confirmation of some of the details mentioned in Azdī.[40]

Wardān reportedly was *ṣāḥib Ḥimṣ*, military commander of Ḥimṣ, although his precise Latin or Greek title is unknown. It was logical for the commander of Ḥimṣ to become involved at Ajnādayn, because Ḥimṣ/Emesa was a communications nodal point and unquestionably was the major military base of Heraclius in Syria before he withdrew to Antioch. At that particular date the commander of Ḥimṣ was very important, perhaps the first or second most important military command below Heraclius during the course of the Muslim invasions, until Ḥimṣ fell to the Muslims. It is likely that he commanded troops who had come freshly from the north, from Armenia and Constantinople, or from the units who accompanied Heraclius himself at Antioch, although he may also have raised some local Arab tribesmen.[41]

Theodore, the brother of Heraclius, also commanded at Ajnādayn. Heraclius used his brother as a commander just as he had used him as a trusted commander to regain control of Edessa a few years earlier, and just as he used his cousin Niketas in the conquest of Egypt during the rebellion against Emperor Phocas in 610. The confusion in the Muslim sources can come from the existence of several Byzantine commanders, which caused

[40] Cf. note 3, above. A. Kamāl, *Ṭarīq ilā Dimashq*, makes unsubstantiated statements, among other places, esp. on pp. 196–259, in establishing a chronology and itinerary for the Muslim invasions.

[41] al-Ṭabarī i 2125–6. Ibn 'Asākir, *TMD* 1: 447, 480–3; Ibn Khayyāṭ al-'Uṣfurī 1: 87; Balādhurī 113–14; al-Ya'qūbī 2: 134; Azdī 84–9.

some Muslims who encountered or heard of one instead of the other to imagine him to be the supreme commander there. Divided command was not unusual in Byzantine history, even though it may be an imprudent way to organize the chain of military authority. One Byzantine commander was said to fall at Ajnādayn – possibly he was Wardān, or according to some, the *cubicularius*, possibly also serving as *sakellarios*. But the other one, Heraclius' brother Theodore, escaped to fight elsewhere.[42] According to Byzantine sources, Theodore met defeat at the hands of Muslims, then fled to Heraclius at Emesa, who replaced him with Vahān and Theodore Trithurios, the *sakellarios*. Heraclius, angry with his brother Theodore, ordered him sent to Constantinople, where he had his son Constantine (III) imprison him;[43] the exact date is uncertain. Hostilities between him and Martina, Heraclius' controversial second wife (and niece), may have contributed to his fall from favor and disappearance.

Ajnādayn was a real battle in the open, and it made the Byzantines even less eager for combat in the field against Arabs than they had been before. Henceforth there would be fear of open conflict. In principle it took place closer to the Byzantine lines of communication, and so should have favored them somewhat from the beginning. The precise battle tactics of both antagonists are not well understood. Christian Arabs did help to supply the Byzantines.[44] The Byzantines who fled to the protection of other cities in Syria lost all coherence and effectiveness as military units, at least for a while. The Muslims won relative freedom to overrun much of the countryside unopposed, and paralyzed communications between towns, even between Bethlehem and Jerusalem. Insecurity spread throughout most of Palestine, especially the areas away from the coastal towns, where the Byzantines managed to hold out. Civilians and ecclesiastics were shocked because they had not been expecting any such major invasions.[45] Heraclius departed from Ḥimṣ for Antioch when he learned of the outcome of Ajnādayn, which was not close to Ḥimṣ, but the Byzantine defeat unhinged the entire Byzantine position in southern Syria.

THE BYZANTINE STRATEGY OF RELIANCE ON WALLED TOWNS

Byzantine troops who escaped from the debacle at Ajnādayn fled to the security of various cities in Syria. The only coherent defensive line was one that may have been made near the Yarmūk River, but accounts of it become

[42] al-Ṭabarī i 2125–6. Ibn ʿAsākir, *TMD* 1: 447, 480–3; Ibn Khayyāṭ al ʿUṣfurī 1: 87; Balādhurī, 113–14; al-Yaʿqūbī 2: 134.

[43] Theoph., *Chron.*, AM 6125 (337 De Boor); Nicephoros, *Hist.* 20 (68–9 Mango).

[44] Christian Arabs supply Byzantines: Kūfī 1: 144.

[45] Sophronius, *PG* 87: 3197D.

confused with the 636 battle of the Yarmūk. Instead of any natural barrier, cities became the frontier. The problem of the Byzantine soldiers crowding into the cities is not described well in these sources on the 630s, although analogous concentrations in earlier centuries had caused many problems of provisioning and health. None of this was conducive to military morale and discipline.

Many civilians fled from the countryside to the apparent security of walled towns in Palestine and Syria after the battle of Ajnādayn. Insecurity grew for travellers and merchants who engaged in intercity commerce. There was fear, even panic. Indeterminate numbers of people crowded into Jerusalem, Damascus, and Caesarea Maritima.[46] The Christmas sermon of Patriarch Sophronius of Jerusalem, given in 634, is contemporary confirmation of civilian flight to Jerusalem and the blocking of the road to Bethlehem.[47] Flight to the protection of walled cities had happened several times in the eastern provinces during the sixth century, including during the Ghassānid uprising in 581.[48]

The flight of soldiers and rural population to walled towns probably acted as a constraint on Heraclius' military strategy – Byzantine military authorities had to attend to the needs of masses of people who crowded into towns for security. Muslim military operations first concentrated on controlling the countryside, especially in the interior, and only later on capturing and holding towns. Flight of Byzantine troops to towns also made it easier for Muslims to observe the Byzantines. It was more difficult for the Byzantine troops to spring surprises, because their locations were highly visible towns, visible from outside and probably visible to spies and to others who reported about them to the Muslims. Protecting towns during popular crises gave military authorities a pretext for staying inside comfortable quarters in the towns, which offered the officers and soldiers, too, more safety. It became easy to avoid searching out the enemy until more reinforcements came. The nature of open and often dry terrain in Syria reinforced these tendencies to concentrate defense at towns.

A strategy of dependence on walled towns theoretically could be a viable element in an effective strategy of defense-in-depth, although it also brings risks. Success with such a strategy requires mobile forces, preferably deployed between or behind the self-contained strongholds. And there are other

[46] Balādhurī (114 De Goeje). Flight of Byzantine troops to cities: Balādhurī (115, 175, 177 De Goeje); Kūfī 1: 194: Azdī 165.

[47] Sophronius, "Weihnachtspredigt" esp. 506–15 Usener; Azdī 92; Balādhurī 114.

[48] Walled towns, sieges: Procopius, *Bella* 2.5.12–33; 2.6.17–25; 2.7.3–9; 2.11.14–2.12.4; 2.12.31; 2.13.16–29; Joh. Ephes., *HE* 3.3.42–3 (130–3 Chabot). Stein, *HBE* 2; 486–92; H. Turtledove, "Immediate Successors of Justinian" 314–22; Goubert, *Byzance avant l'Islam* 1: 69–70.

requirements: (1) that the strongholds be sufficiently resilient to survive assault without needing the immediate support of mobile forces; (2) that the mobile forces be able to resist or avoid the enemy's concentrated attacks in the field without recourse to the protection of the strongholds; (3) that the attacking forces must seize the strongholds in order to be victorious; (4) that the defense of walled towns be incorporated into a larger viable defensive strategy, such as that of the Byzantines in Italy in the sixth century, during which Ostrogothic troops were lured close to walls of Byzantine-held towns where skilled archers waited to pick them off.[49] Such a strategy offers resilience but risks serious enemy devastation of one's territory, and eventual counteroffensives are mandatory for its success. Strongpoints could serve as supply depots, obstacles, bases for rear-area security and rear-area intelligence, points from which mobile forces could sally against invaders, and bases of temporary refuge for mobile forces. But they could also inhibit the morale and offensive abilities of defending troops.

The whole direction of Byzantine military affairs in Syria and Palestine after Ajnādayn turned to passive defense, avoidance of battle whenever possible and use of walled towns – or natural barriers such as wādīs and river gorges – as bases from which to sally forth occasionally to fight the Muslims. Strategic wisdom, the desire to avoid injury, the crowding of cities, all converged to cause, somehow and perhaps unintentionally, the development of a strategy, based on the defense of walled towns and fixed bases. This restricted the mobility of the Byzantine army and implicitly conceded military initiative to the Muslims. By dispersing the best troops it reduced their concentration of force and weakened their ability to strike at their foes. It created a defensive mentality. It was an understandable but deficient strategy. Its best hope would have been for impatience or disunity to have splintered the invaders and created opportunities for major sallies from Byzantine-occupied towns or for major Byzantine offensives from the north using new, fresh manpower raised outside of Syria. But such calculations, if they ever were serious, rested on too many external variables to assure success. Furthermore, Islam provided a cohesion to the invaders that Byzantines had never previously experienced among Arabs.

Concentration of troops in towns threatened to isolate troops in one town from those in another, leading to isolated, uncoordinated actions. Military efficiency became additionally dependent on the state of repair and the watch of the town walls, and all points of entry and exit, including water and sewer conduits, and on the whims and weaknesses and food supplies of the local population and their elites. Yet these troops were in no shape to resume

[49] Procopius, *Bella* 5.22.2–8, 5.27.6–15.

fighting at once. They needed to recuperate, and the towns were one place to do it, if the protection of those walls did not become too seductive and corruptive of the will to fight.

The walled town strategy began even before the defeats at Dāthin and Ajnādayn, if one believes the implicit chronology of Azdī and Ibn ʻAsākir's sources. Heraclius originally gathered the people of Damascus and told them to shut their gates tightly and to obey the commander that he was appointing over them, and he encouraged people to take an interest in defending themselves.[50] His strategy of holding many walled towns created a negative mentality that could easily become excessively involved with details of inspection and maintenance of walls instead of prime readiness for combat.

A walled-town strategy created situations that were favorable to a warfare of exhaustion and cunning and negotiation. There was no constant warfare, but blockades, exchanges of messages and parleys between commanders, secret communications between town notables and military commanders of the besieging side. This classic strategy of positional warfare emphasized possession of walled towns to control territories and their populations.

Siege warfare during the Muslim conquests included mounted clashes outside of town walls. There were no massive human wave-like assaults on such town walls. Towns were blockaded, and could not receive supplies or communications from outside, except on an irregular basis, when messengers could somehow manage to pass through. No towns were stormed, with the attendant massive civilian casualties and physical damage to property, until late in the conquests when certain points of resistance, such as Caesarea Maritima and one or two towns in Byzantine Mesopotamia, fell in heavy fighting. The civilian population rarely engaged in physical combat from such town walls, although some may have contributed financially to the support of repairs and extraordinary measures to protect individual towns. The logical hope of the defenders was the exhaustion of the Arabs, the protection of the civilians, and above all the eventual arrival of decisive Byzantine military relief in massive numbers from the north (or from other directions, if there were sufficient soldiers there). Such a strategy probably involved the loss of sizable amounts of livestock, primarily sheep. Sheep could not be maintained indefinitely in quarters of restricted size with limited pasture, nor could they all be brought in from the countryside.

Another reason why the Byzantines, including Heraclius, probably decided to rely on walled towns was their own superiority in military engineering, and the presumed Arab weakness in or ignorance of and impatience with

[50] Ibn ʻAsākir, *TMD* 1: 473–4; cf. "Extract From the Chronicle of AD 1234," Palmer, *Chronicles*, part 2, text 13, sect. 48.

siege techniques. An extensive Graeco-Roman strategic literature on siege warfare was potentially another asset of the Byzantines in this conflict, but there is no evidence that they put it to good use, or even that they used it at all. The role of siege machines, including defensive ones, is not clear, although ballistae are mentioned in Mesopotamia. There is some limited evidence that some Muslims did know how to use such machines, or like barbarians on other imperial frontiers, they may have found individuals who would make, maintain, and use such machines for them.[51]

Heraclius was more familiar with the walled towns of Syria and Palestine than any other Byzantine emperor. He had personally visited some of the most prominent, including Jerusalem, Damascus, Ḥimṣ, Antioch, and Edessa. Presumably he had also passed by Chalkis/Qinnasrīn and Aleppo. He knew something of the local terrain, and by that time in his life he had a practiced eye for military topography and for the military potential of regions and sites. He knew the trunk road from the north through Ḥimṣ and Damascus on to Jerusalem. What he did not personally know was the terrain of southern Palestine and the region east of the Dead Sea and the ʿAraba and Ghor. He had some idea of the condition of the principal walled towns. Yet it is uncertain whether he knew anything of the coastal towns' defenses. But he had recently visited and was aware of conditions in some of the most critical areas where there would be decisive combat during the Muslim conquests. He had some idea of the problems of transportation, communications, provisions, water, climate, and strategic significance.

Heraclius had originally heard of the Muslim threat while in Palestine, according to Azdī and other Iraqi traditions. It is not at all impossible that his subordinates passed word to him in Palestine of reports of threatening groupings of Arab tribes. Such information might have been ignored or not released to an emperor when he was in Constantinople, but it would have been much more difficult to hide from an emperor who personally passed through southern Syria to Jerusalem and back. But he was in a position to hear something about the security situation when visiting Palestine, and there would likely have been security precautions and explanations given for why they were necessary. This could have led Heraclius or his advisers to make further inquiry. All of this is conjecture. It is plausible, but nothing more can be said. It is not solid history.

Azdī reports that Heraclius gathered people and made a speech, warning of the impending threat, and stimulating the local inhabitants to defend themselves, their families, their livestock, and their property. It is unclear

[51] Siege machinery in the Ḥijāz during the Prophet's lifetime: Ibn Hishām (Wüstenfeld 869, 872–3) – catapults for use against walled towns. I learned much from a conversation with Professor Kister about this problem.

precisely where he allegedly made this speech in Palestine. He urged the populace to obey the commander whom he was appointing over them.[52] He mentioned recent Byzantine victories over the Persians and the Khazars ("Turks"). He then went to Damascus and did the same while staying there. Both the Christian Arab historian Eutychius and the threnody on the fall of Jerusalem in 614 state (in passages of the same textual origin) that Heraclius did go to Damascus after leaving Jerusalem, although neither of these Christian texts mentions Heraclius speaking or appointing military commanders at Damascus or elsewhere. It is logical that he did appoint military commanders for such cities. It is not known what their precise titles in Greek or Latin were. There is no archaeological, sigillographic, or epigraphic record of any of them, as far as extant evidence shows. Azdī states that from Palestine Heraclius went to Damascus, Ḥimṣ, and then on to Antioch, appointing commanders from his army as his deputies. al-Ṭabarī preserves one tradition from Sayf b. ʻUmar that appears to come from the same tradition as that of Azdī. Both are, of course, Iraqi.[53]

These military commanders presumably possessed emergency military powers for the safeguarding of these cities and their immediate regions. Heraclius had appointed the commanders and thought them to be absolutely reliable individuals who would obey his instructions and coordinate their policies with his absolutely and unhesitatingly. This was a form of emergency militarization of certain towns that were assumed to be critical for the defense of Syria and presumably were key targets of the impending Muslim invasion.

Azdī says nothing about the numbers of soldiers whom these commanders had at their disposition. There may have been billeting problems. Likewise unknown is the size of what garrisons, if any, existed before the Persian invasion. The precise powers that these commanders possessed were implicitly extraordinary. These appointments were *ad hoc* reactions to a specific threat. There is no suggestion that they involved any social significance, other than the interesting and important effort to stir the population from lethargy to defend themselves. There is no talk of any comprehensive social and economic reform. But the Azdī account supports inferences that Heraclius was not lethargic, that he at least tried to alert and prepare the Syrian population, especially at key cities, for imminent danger, which was no surprise. It was foreseen. It is unlikely that after his visit to Palestine he would have been completely oblivious to unrest among Arab tribes. This is especially true if he made his pilgrimage to restore the relics of the cross in 630, by which time word, however confused and inaccurate, had

[52] Azdī 28–9, 34. Ibn ʻAsākir 1: 440, and esp. 473–5. Ibn al-Athīr (2: 414 Tornberg).
[53] Azdī 28–9; al-Ṭabarī i 2104. Cf. Ibn al-Athīr, *Chronicon* (2: 311 Tornberg).

very likely trickled into Palestine and Damascus about stirrings in the Arabian peninsula among various Arab tribes.

The commanders whom Heraclius appointed probably came from areas of the empire outside the ones they were defending. No source identifies any of them as a native of the town or region that he was trying to defend against the Muslims. This fact has a number of implications. Their lack of identity with the area may have impeded their understanding of local terrain, climate, and problems of local provisioning. But above all, it may have impeded the creation of the kinds of bonds of trust and familiarity that might have helped to create an enthusiastic morale and will to resist the invaders.

The apparent lack of local ties on the part of commanders may have encouraged the passivity and noncommittal character of the local population. There was no evident solidarity of local civilians with the Byzantine military leadership. Lack of local ties may have inhibited local communication and mutual understanding between military and civilian leadership and population. It may have caused mistrust. Yet it is not clear that able local military leaders existed on whom Heraclius could have drawn for major commands. No such tradition of military leadership is known to have existed, except among such friendly Arab tribes as the Ghassānids. It is not known to have existed much among the sedentary population, even though some of them may have helped to finance the maintenance or repair of walls. The lack of identification of local population with the military leadership probably contributed to instances of plundering on the part of some Byzantine soldiers. The appointment of such a local military leadership was not a normal practice, however – in fact, there was no precedent for it. But initiating such a practice there might have smoothed and assisted the implementation of Heraclius' strategy of relying on walled towns.

Little epigraphic evidence exists for the repair of city walls in this period, except for Gaza and Ba'labakk in 635/6, where local inhabitants spent something of their own financial resources to try to improve the security of their towns. This limited evidence suggests that there was not total passivity, indifference, or active welcome of the invaders on the part of the local urban population of some major towns. If anything, Heraclius' reported warnings to towns may have induced some to try to do something to defend themselves. The inscriptions are consistent with the policy of privatization or local responsibility for maintenance of fortifications, which had already been the case in Syria in the sixth century.[54] Contemporary mosaics give visual

[54] Gaza: F. M. Abel, "Inscription grecque de Gaza," *Revue Biblique* 40 (1931) 94–6. Baalbek: *Inscriptions grecques et latines de la Syrie* no. 2828. (Bibliothèque Archéologique et Historique, T. 6 [Paris: Geuthner, 1967]) 133. J. H. W. G. Liebeschuetz, "The Defenses of Syria in the Sixth Century," *Beihefte der Bonner Jahrbücher* 38: Studien zur Militärgrenzen Roms 2 (1977) 461–71.

confirmation of the prestige and appearances of security that walls and towers gave to towns.[55]

Some of Azdī's references to Heraclius have been cited as evidence of his implausibility. Yet there is nothing impossible or improbable in what Azdī attributed to Heraclius.[56] However, the question of Azdī's reliability remains. Yet comparison of texts in Theophanes, where Heraclius sends τις στρατηλάτης, "some general" [or possibly, "some *magister militum*"], whose name was Ptolemaios, to replace John Kateas, the *epitropos* or *curator* of Osrhoene, is one example of a military commander replacing a civilian official in the north, several years later, in the face of the impending Muslim invasion, and specifically because the civilian governor had negotiated peace and tribute payments with the Muslims. Theophanes similarly mentions the Armenian Manuel, who boasts that "I am armed" – εἶμι ἔνοπλος – being appointed by Heraclius to replace Cyrus, the governor who also had negotiated peace terms and tribute with the Muslims.[57] Both truces had not been approved by Heraclius. These are not the specific cases that Azdī mentions, of commanders being appointed over Palestine, Damascus, and Ḥimṣ from his army. These are two examples of militarization. But they are analogous to what Azdī was mentioning for the other localities, except that they were not appointed out of displeasure with civilian governors.

The account of Azdī, therefore, does not appear so implausible. Theophanes offers partial confirmation. Ibn al-ʿAdīm in his *Zubdat al-Ḥalab min Taʾrīkh Ḥalab* also reports that Heraclius appointed Menas, who was the highest in rank after him (although his exact title and rank are unknown) over Chalkis/Qinnasrīn, after Heraclius himself had evacuated the area.[58]

One motive of Heraclius in appointing such commanders over cities was possibly to insure that these cities did not surrender or negotiate peace with the Muslims, especially terms that drained funds or tax payments in kind. The empire had already been concerned that Damascus had paid so many years of tax payments to the Persians, which were lost to the Byzantine Empire. The explanation for this policy is not hard to discern. Heraclius did not wish to strengthen his enemy or lose his cities, and above all he did not wish to lose more valuable tax revenues at a time of great fiscal strain on the government. He wished to deter the leadership of local towns from

55 Piccirillo, "Le iscrizioni di Umm er-Rasas-Kastron Mefaa," *Liber Annuus Studium Biblicum Franciscanum* 37 (1987) 185–6, 196, 219. One of the most important mosaics illustrating towns and their walls probably dates to AD 718, according to Dr. Robert Schick.

56 De Goeje, *Mémoire*[1] esp. pp. 29–31.

57 Theoph., *Chron.*, AM 6126, 6128 (338, 340 De Boor).

58 Ibn al-ʿAdīm, *Zubdat al-Ḥalab min Taʾrīkh Ḥalab* 1:25. This is another partial confirmation of Azdī. al-Ṭabarī i 2094.

negotiating unauthorized separate peace with the Muslims, which set dangerous precedents. The cases of early surrenders or negotiations of towns in Transjordania, such as Adhruḥ and Ma'ān and Ayla, may have stimulated him to take specific stern action to try to prevent a repetition of such occurrences in more important and larger cities in Palestine and Syria.

The substance of Azdī's account about Heraclius' creation of military commanders may be true, even though the text of his speech and that of others to him may well be fabulous. There is no evidence about the nature of the substructure of command below the level of military commander in those cities or about the precise relationship of his command to former local civilian authorities. How these improvised emergency military governors were intended to function and how they actually functioned is not known in detail. Likewise, there is no information about the relative efficiency of such government, or problems or friction related to efforts to make it function. Heraclius' appointment of military commanders over towns was an understandable but inefficient improvisation that drained away some good military talent from challenges of combat. It did not happen all at once, but gradually as Heraclius withdrew north.

Damascus, which was one of the cities over which he appointed a special commander, did hold out for a while. The performance of its garrison – in the face of the readiness of Manṣūr, the important local fiscal official at Damascus, and others who had grudges against Heraclius to collaborate – is evidence that a strong-willed commander could stiffen resistance. Damascus, of course, eventually succumbed, and in fact succumbed twice, to the Muslims. But it and Caesarea both held out for quite some time. Prolonged resistance did take place in cities and not at points in the countryside. This does not mean that those in the mountains of Lebanon and elsewhere instantly surrendered to the Muslims. But the difficult places for the Muslims were not in the countryside at first, despite the late seventh-century problem with the Mardaites or al-Jarājima (caliphate of 'Abd al-Malik). To the extent that there was resistance, it centered on the cities. So Heraclius miscalculated, but there was some essence of wisdom in his calculations for using cities as the strongholds for resistance. This may well have been part of a very ancient pattern in that part of the world. It was not a brilliant idea unique to Heraclius. Heraclius and his commanders inaugurated no system of training the urban or rural population to bear arms or operate war machinery in cities, as far as it is known.

It is reasonable to ask whether or not the failure of the Syrian populace to respond resolutely to Heraclius' efforts is in itself not an admission, a sign, that nonmilitary factors really explain the failure of the Byzantine military effort. It would be foolish to deny the potential significance of social, economic, and religious complications for the Byzantine defense. These factors, however, were not new and unique to the early seventh century for the most part. It is true that Jews had special incentives to withhold support from the Byzantines and possibly to give active aid to the Muslims and the recent Persian occupation had demonstrated that survival was possible outside of Byzantine authority. These were new factors. But the lack of military preparedness or training or will to resist on the part of the broader population was not new. It was an old condition, and one that was not confined to Byzantium's eastern provinces, or to those with large numbers of Monophysite Christians.

Patriarch Sophronius speaks fearfully of the bloody Saracen sword, and fear of death that prevented people from traveling.[59] The *Doctrina Iacobi nuper baptizati* also implies that Muslims tried, on threat of death, to make Christians abjure Christianity and accept Islam.[60] The deaths of the Gaza garrison in 637 are consistent with this. These are reminders that the conquests were not peaceful for everyone, that some violence or threat of violence was present at that time. More violence was feared. Yet the known cases of massacre are limited, although mass slaughter of combatants followed some battles. Some civilians were caught and slaughtered in the countryside as well, although these instances appear to have been exceptional.[61] The initial reaction was fear and terror, and uncertainty about the future and where to look for security.

Creation of emergency military commanders did not necessarily solve the problem of authority and implementation of imperial commands in cities. Scraps of references suggest that on the eve of and during the course of the Muslim invasions there was at least occasional friction between military, civilian, and ecclesiastical officials in various provinces, although it is impossible to know how universal the problem was. Such sources include a law of Heraclius dated, significantly, to the year 629, as well as the case of the resentments of Manṣūr of Damascus against Heraclius and the Byzantine military commanders, as well as various instances of friction between military, civilian, and ecclesiastical officials in Egypt. The existence of such problems was consistent with such friction in eastern Mediterranean provinces in the preceding centuries. The lack of adequate documentation, however, makes it impossible to investigate this problem thoroughly. The friction probably detracted from the possibility of creating a coherent, highly motivated, and viable defense based on walled towns.

59 Sophronius, "Weihnachtspredigt" 508.

60 *Doctrina Iacobi nuper baptizati* (88 Bonwetsch).

61 Lawrence I. Conrad, "Abraha and Muḥammad: Some Observations apropos of Chronology and Literary *Topoi* in the Early Arabic Historical Tradition," *BSOAS* 50 (1987) 236–40.

BYZANTINE DEFEATS AND LOSSES IN THE WAKE OF AJNĀDAYN

Bostra (modern Buṣrā, in southern Syria) fell to Khālid b. al-Walīd after he marched from Iraq.[62] However important, his precise and controversial itinerary is not of immediate concern here. Traditions of his itinerary indicate again that the Byzantines, despite cancellation of payments to Arabs near Gaza, did possess the loyalty of some tribes in the Syrian desert and on its fringes. Bostra fell in part because Khālid approached from an unexpected direction, which probably unsettled any plans for its defense. His approach from Iraq created a threat from another direction, thereby disrupting any Byzantine effort to hold the Muslims at Adhri'āt and Bostra, where there were potential choke-points to limit areas of attack. With the surrender of the important provincial town of Bostra, and some neighboring areas in the Ḥawrān, the road was definitely open to approach Damascus. Hence the battle of Marj Rahiṭ, in the plains south of Damascus.[63]

Other Muslims, with 'Amr b. al-Āṣ, had in the meantime captured Scythopolis (Baysān, west of the Jordan River) and Pella (Faḥl, east of the Jordan River) after a battle and flight of the Byzantines. Heraclius, according to Balādhurī, had already moved to Antioch when he sent one of his eunuchs to command Byzantine troops and others, presumably of Arab extraction, from upper Mesopotamia.[64]

HERACLIUS WARNS AGAINST OPEN BATTLE WITH ARABS

Several Christian primary sources assert that Heraclius warned his brother Theodore to beware of the Arabs, that he should avoid battle with them. These diverse sources include the late eighth-century Byzantine chronicle by Nicephorus and the probably eighth-century chronicle tradition that is preserved in the Latin translation of an Arabic continuation (Spanish provenance) of Isidore of Seville's chronicle.[65] It is uncertain precisely when Heraclius allegedly gave this warning, perhaps before the battle of Ajnādayn, where his brother Theodore apparently was commander and met defeat. Ancient military manuals contained much advice on avoidance of battle,

[62] Balādhurī 113. On the controversy concerning the route of Khālid: Donner, *EIC* 119–27. P. Crone, s.v. "Khālid b. al-Walīd," *EI*² 4: 928–9; cf. Caetani, *AI* 2: 1213–20.

[63] Marj Rahiṭ: Balādhurī 112; al-Ṭabarī i 2109–10; De Goeje, *Mémoire*² 39–41; Donner, *EIC* 124–5. Nearby obscure battle of Marj al-Ṣuffar: Balādhurī 118; Donner, *EIC* 130–1; Caetani, *AI* 3: 310–24.

[64] Balādhurī 115, 116, 118, 135, 140.

[65] Nicephorus, *Hist.* 20 (68–71 Mango). *Continuatio [Isidoriana] Hispana*. ed. by T. Mommsen, MGHAA, Chron. Min., 11: 337–8 = *Crónica mozárabe de 754*, ed. by Jose Eduardo López Pereira (Zaragoza 1980) 30–1. Also a hint of Heraclius' warning in Sebēos, *Hist.* c. 30 (96–7 Macler); Ibn 'Asākir 1: 439–40. W. E. Kaegi, "The Strategy of Heraclius," *1985 Bilād al-Shām Proceedings* 1: 104–15.

which the early Byzantine military manuals borrowed and repeated.[66] It is indeed plausible that Heraclius had warned his brother to avoid battle if possible until the most opportune moment. A report that Theodore was contemptuous of the fighting ability of the Arabs deserves skepticism because of the author's Monophysite, namely Jacobite, leanings.[67]

Heraclius apparently wanted his brother Theodore to wait for additional reinforcements and, in general, avoid decisive tests in the open country. This tradition is plausible, although of course, once again, it exonerates Heraclius and implicitly honors him for his wisdom in anticipating the ambushes and snares of the enemy. Uncertainties persist: whether advocacy of caution by Heraclius preceded or followed the Byzantine defeat at Ajnādayn; whether caution about Arab resort to ambushes was a standard reflex reaction by Heraclius, given the long history of Roman and Byzantine problems with Arabs, or whether it was a response to recent Byzantine defeats and a recognition of the actual situation of Byzantine numerical vulnerability at the time. He probably gave his warning after Ajnādayn, but when he gave it to his brother Theodore he was also remembering the traditional military axioms about fighting Arabs. An even more important question is whether this historical tradition is in fact a *topos* in conformity with normal rhetorical handling of the virtues of a reigning emperor, who is supposed to anticipate and overcome ambushes.[68]

66 Sixth-century admonitions of *The Anonymous Byzantine Treatise on Strategy* 33 (102–5 Dennis, *Three Byz. Mil. Treatises*).

67 Michael the Syrian, *Chronique* 11.5 (2: 418 Chabot).

68 *Menander Rhetor*, ed., trans., and comment. by D. A. Russell, Nigel Wilson (Oxford: Clarendon Press, 1981) 84–7.

Chapter 6

PROBLEMS OF COHESION: THE BATTLE OF JĀBIYA-YARMŪK RECONSIDERED

> ... when the cavalry wing is broken, the infantry is outflanked, nor does there remain any means or will to defend itself, and thus having lost courage the infantry throw their arms on the ground and beg for mercy.
>
> Raimondo Montecuccoli, *Memorie* (Colonia, Ferrara, 1704), xxvii, p. 37

JĀBIYA

After their victory at Faḥl (Pella), the Muslims rapidly penetrated north. Damascus surrendered to them. Forces of Abū ʿUbayda pushed on to seize Heraclius' former base of operations at Ḥimṣ, ancient Emesa. Its occupation threatened the rich Biqāʿ valley as well as the heart of Byzantine Syria, the Orontes valley, and opened the way for expansion even further northwards. Muslims did raid into the Biqā'. In early 636 their occupation of Damascus and Ḥimṣ brought matters to a decisive military test. The strong Byzantine response involved the collection and dispatch of the maximum number of available troops under major Byzantine commanders, including the *sacellarius* [certain] and possibly also *cubicularius* Theodore Trithurios and the Armenian General Vahān, to eject the Muslims from their newly won territories.

The climax of the early Muslim invasions of the Byzantine Empire was, according to Muslim and Christian sources, the battle of Jābiya-Yarmūk. It was a battle in the fullest sense of the term, although extant narratives provide a confused description (Map 4).[1] The battle began in the vicinity of Jābiya or Gabitha, which was, with its grazing areas and water, a key site of the most important Byzantine Arab ally, the Ghassānids,[2] about 5 kilometers

[1] P. Speck, *Das geteilte Dossier* (Bonn 1988) 172–81, imaginatively criticizes and reconstructs Theophanes' account, but he does not understand the oriental sources and does not use Caetani, *AI*, or Donner, *EIC*, or other basic modern scholarship on the battle of Jābiya-Yarmūk and related campaigning.

[2] Theoph., *Chron.*, AM 6121 (332 De Boor); Anastasius the Sinaite, *Sermo adversus Monotheletas* 3.1.86–8 (60 Uthemann); Pseudo-Methodius, *Die Apokalypse des Ps.-Methodios* XI. 1, ed. by Athanasios Lolos (Beiträge zur klassischen Philologie, H. 83

↑ *Golan Heights*

to *Kiswe* and
Damascus

ROMAN ROAD

ROMAN ROAD

① ● *Jābiya*

● *Nawā*

ROMAN
BRIDGE

③ *Tall al-Jamū'a*

ROMAN ROAD FROM NAWĀ TO FĪQ AND GALILEE

② ● *Dayr Ayyūb*

④

Wādī'l Ruqqād

Wādī'l 'Allān

Wādī'l Harīr

Fīq ●

④

Yāqūṣa ●

Wādī'l Yarmūk

Wādī'l Yarmūk

BYZANTINE
? ○ CAMP

N

| 0 | 5 | 10 | 15 km |

| 0 | 5 | 10 miles |

Wādī'l Yarmūk

Adhri'āt
(modern *Dar'a*)

The four stages of battle:

① Byzantine advance to Jābiya. Muslims retire.
② Muslims lure Byzantine attack by feigned flight, then counter attack.
③ Muslim cavalry find gap, penetrate Roman road, seize Roman bridge over Wādī'l Ruqqād, thereby trapping Byzantines between three gorges.
④ Muslims overrun Byzantine camp at Yāqūṣa, annihilate Byzantine troops trapped between gorges of wādīs and pursue remnants who escaped.
⇨ Direction of Byzantine movements
➡ Direction of Muslim movements

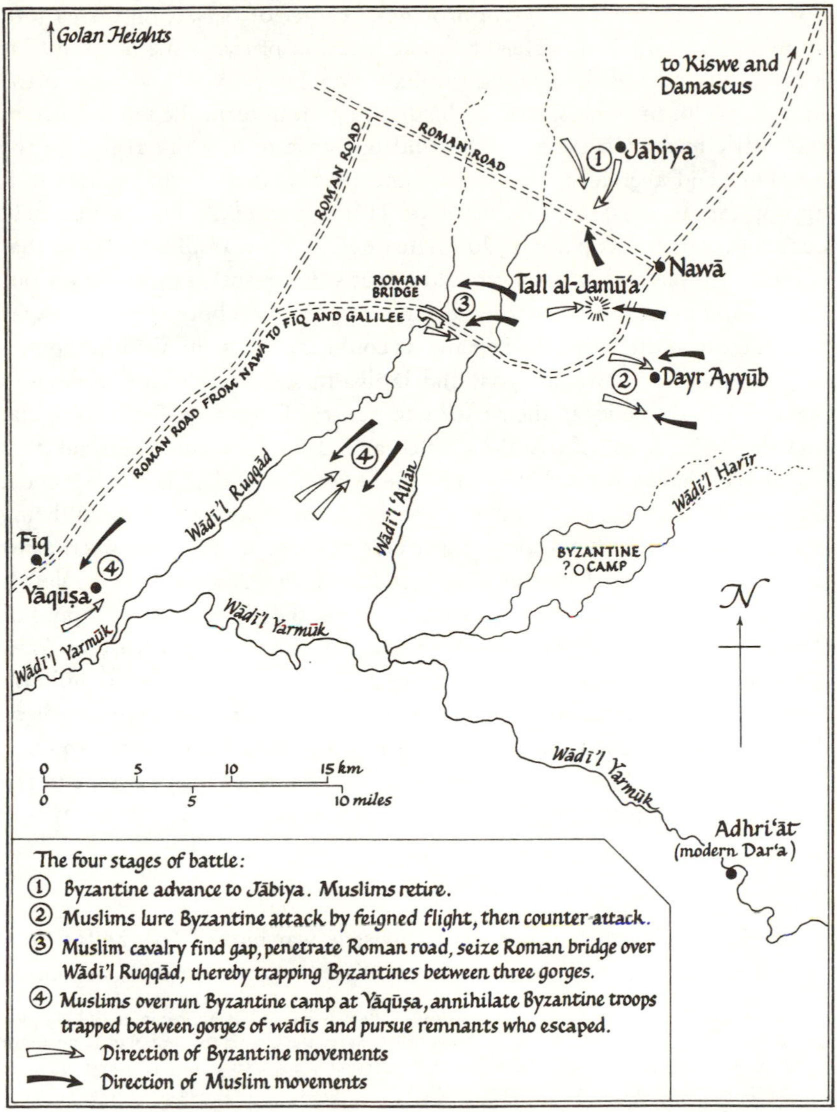

Map 4. The battle of Jābiya-Yarmūk (adapted from Sheet 7, Palestine Exploration Fund, 1898/1907)

[Meisenheim am Glan: Verlag Anton Hain, 1976]) 96–7. Theodor Nöldeke, "Zur Geschichte der Araber im 1. Jahrhundert d. H. aus syrischen Quellen," *ZDMG* 29 (1875) 78–80; Cont. Byz. Arab., MGHAA 11: 337. Michael the Syrian, *Chronique* 11.6 (2: 429 Chabot). See M. J. De Goeje, *Mémoire*[2] 119–20. On Ghassānids in the vicinity: al-Mas'ūdī, *Les Prairies d'or*, ed. and trans. by Barbier de Meynard, Pavet de Courteille (Paris 1864) 3: 220.

northeast of the modern Syrian provincial center of Nawā, on the eastern approaches to the Golan Heights.[3] The location of the battle at Jābiya, at least during part of the fighting (probably the beginning), underscores the importance of the Ghassānids at this battle and, in turn, the importance of this battle to the Ghassānids. They did not wish to lose this region to the Muslims and therefore were important participants in the battle. It is appropriate to speak of "the battle of Jābiya-Yarmūk." The battle's final decisive combat took place on 20 August 636, but it was a battle not of that one day but possibly of a month and a half's duration.[4] It involved various clashes and maneuvering, with attendant casualties on both sides, before its final stage near the Yarmūk River and its confluence with the Wādī'l Ruqqād.

Jilliq (modern Kiswe, in Syria) and Jābiya furnished excellent fodder and water for both armies in their efforts to control Damascus, Transjordania, and the high ground above the Galilee and Lake Tiberias: the Byzantines might well have assumed that they could remain at that location almost indefinitely with sizable numbers of troops and animals without being pressured to move off or disperse for reason of supplies. The area was the key to communications between Damascus and the Arabian peninsula. It threatened the Muslims by dominating Bostra, the old provincial capital of Arabia, as well as the Ḥawrān, by exercising pressure on Christian Arab tribes such as the Ghassānids, and limited the effect of any Muslim hold on Pella (Faḥl) and Scythopolis (Beth Shean, Baysān).[5] The site of the battle of Jābiya-Yarmūk is good country for cavalry maneuvers. Yet there is also some cover for men to hide in, because there are clumps and depressions in the land. More of it may have been wooded in that period than it is today.

THE PRECEDENT AT ADHRI'ĀT

There is a propensity for mortals to envisage war in terms of the last one, including its mistakes, successes, and missed opportunities. The region

[3] Location of Jābiya: Sheet 7, *PEF Palestine*, Jābiya is located at approximately longitude 36 °E and latitude 32° 56′ N, about 3 miles northeast of the district town of Nawā and about 8 miles northeast of the old Roman bridge over the Wādī'l Ruqqād, and about one mile north of Tell Jābiya, which is marked as "Tell ej Jabiyeh" on *PEF Palestine*, Sheet 7. See G. Cornu, *Atlas* 3: 6. I wish to thank Syrian authorities and civilians at Nawā for assisting me in my visit to Jābiya and vicinity in July, 1984.

[4] Date: Palmer, "Record of the Arab Conquest of Syria, AD 637," *Shadow*, part 1,1, line 21; cf. Theodor Nöldeke, "Zur Geschichte der Araber im 1. Jahrhundert d.H. aus syrischen Quellen," *ZDMG* 29 (1875) 78–9; De Goeje, *Mémoire*[2] 108–10; L. Caetani, *AI* 3: 573. But Donner, *EIC* 140–6. I see no reason to reject the dating of Nöldeke and Caetani, assuming that one understands that the military operations of the battle between Jābiya and the Wādī'l Ruqqād probably lasted several days and the given date is that of the climactic final action.

[5] Location: Caetani, *AI* 3: 508–30; John Bagot Glubb, *The Great Arab Conquests* (London: Hodder and Stoughton, 1963) 141–51.

experienced one decisive battle for Palestine in 613–14, and another in the 630s in the battle of Jābiya-Yarmūk. The effort to defend Palestine against the Persians in 613–14 after they broke through Byzantine defenses in the north, even after the loss of Antioch in the north and the severing of communications, caused the Byzantines to attempt a stand against the Persians in a logical area in southern Syria, namely, the vicinity of Adhri'āt and Bostra,[6] which resulted in a Persian victory that the *Sūrat al-Rūm* of the *Qur'ān* memorializes.[7] Its relevance for Byzantine history, especially Byzantine military history, has remained unappreciated. Adhri'āt, which dominates north–south communications east of the Jordan, was the natural place to attempt to halt an invasion of Palestine.[8] It is unclear how many soldiers the Byzantines mustered. Presumably these included friendly Arabs. Byzantines and Arabs thus had an opportunity to see two belligerents engage in decisive battle in the region that was again to experience decisive battle between them in the 630s. Both sides could appreciate the strategic moves, the topography, the range of alternatives available to commanders, thereby learning from the experiences of 613–14. Probably the Arabs learned more, as local observers, either directly or vicariously through reports from other friendly Arabs and from local inhabitants of towns and villages in the vicinity of the maneuvering and fighting, with whom they may have discussed the fighting while engaging in commerce. They understood the terrain and its strategic importance, including how military forces occupying respective positions near the choke point of Adhri'āt could react and make moves. Against this interpretation it is possible to argue that the Byzantines may have had institutional means for remembering such lessons and conveying them to another generation of commanders, while the Arabs did not. Secondly, the Arabs who observed the battle in 613–14 were not those who commanded Muslim armies in the 630s, although they may have been consulted by the latter.

The Byzantines did not occupy the same physical position in the 630s that they had in 613–14. In fact, their logistical and tactical situation was reversed. They were still on the defensive, as in 613–14, but now were facing south, not north. Yet because of earlier experiences, both Byzantines and Arabs could more easily try to place themselves in the position of their opponents because there was a record of what others had done in a comparable position in 613–14. Some of the most important maneuvering and combat in the 630s did not take place in an unfamiliar region; it occurred in a region where there

[6] Kaegi, "The Strategy of Heraclius," *1985 Bilād al-Shām Proceedings* 109.

[7] al-Ṭabarī/Nöldeke 297, 299–300. *Qur'ān, sūra* 30: 1–3. See commentary of Ḥusayn ibn Muḥammad al-Diyārbakrī on this passage, *Ta'rīkh al-khamīs fī aḥwāl anfas nafīs* (repr. Beirut 1970 of 1866 original edn) 1: 298.

[8] John Bagot Glubb, *The Great Arab Conquests* (London: Hodder and Stoughton, 1963) 136, 140–3.

were precedents for strategic and tactical moves. But whether anyone on the Byzantine side had systematically attempted to study these precedents and draw conclusions is uncertain and indeed doubtful.[9]

The region in which the battle of Jābiya-Yarmūk was fought was not, however, ideal for the Byzantines. Adhri'āt and Nawā both contained sizable Jewish communities who were very probably hostile to Heraclius because of his anti-Jewish policies. The Heraclian court historian Theophylact Simocatta expresses contemporary hostility to Jews: "they are a wicked and most untrustworthy race, trouble-loving and tyrannical, utterly forgetful of friendship, jealous and envious, and most implacable in enmity."[10] However much suspicion the Byzantines held for Jews, no source specifically mentions any actions whatever on the part of these Jewish communities at that time.

Indeed, if the Byzantines had been aware of Jewish aid to the Muslims, they probably would have blamed their own debacle on the Jews (of course they might have blamed them, whether or not they had any role). Yet this was a very disaffected group in two of the most critical towns close to the scenes of these battles and astride the communications. The Byzantine armies, then, were operating there in a very hostile environment.

The Jewish Arab tribe of the Banū Naḍīr had been expelled from Madīna and the Arabian peninsula by the Muslims in AH 4 (Rabī al-Awwal), and settled at Adhri'āt, that key nodal point for trade, transportation, and communications, when the area was under Persian occupation. Probably the Persians wanted an ethnic group of loyal tendencies to settle in such a sensitive area. They were, significantly, makers of weapons. They knew and disliked the Muslims, but as Jews they very probably had even stronger dislikes for the policies of Heraclius. Like the Jews of Nawā, they were strategically positioned to observe and make contacts. They presumably retained some contacts with tribesmen in the Arabian peninsula. The Banū Naḍīr had no special affection for the Muslims because of what they had suffered at their hands recently in Medina. They had been expelled and had

[9] M. Avi-Yonah, s.v. "Naveh," *EJ* 12 (1972) 897; F. Buhl-N. Elisséeff, s.v. "Adhri'āt," *EI*² 1: 194; Claudine M. Dauphin, "Jewish and Christian Communities in the Roman and Byzantine Gaulanitis," *Palestine Exploration Quarterly* 114 (1982) 137. Ghassānid location: Nöldeke, *Die ghassanidenischen Fürsten* 46–51; F. E. Peters, "Byzantium and the Arabs of Syria," *Annales Archéologiques Arabes Syriennes* 27–8 (1977–8) 97–113; H. Gaube, "Arabs in Sixth-Century Syria: Some Observations," *British Society for Middle Eastern Studies Bulletin* 8 (1981) 93–8, esp. 96–7, argues Ghassānid extension into Golan was "atypical". But at least two Golan place-names mention the Ghassānids (although it is possible that they derive from later settlers who claimed, rightly or wrongly, descent from the Ghassānids): Tell el Ghassaniye, Mumsiyye el Ghassaniye, in D. Urman, *The Golan: A Profile of a Region during the Roman and Byzantine Periods* (Oxford: BAR, 1985) 68, 192, no. 57, who does not discuss these problems.

[10] Theophylact Simocatta, *Hist.* 5.7.9, trans. by Michael and Mary Whitby (Oxford: Clarendon, 1986) 142.

resettled at Adhriʿāt, perhaps because the Persians had believed that they would be a reliable replacement for the former populations who probably had shown support for the Byzantines. That is why the Persians had ravaged the region before allowing the Banū Naḍīr to settle there. It is probable that the anti-Jewish policies of Heraclius antagonized the Banū Naḍīr even more than did the policies of the Muslims.[11]

Heraclius, allegedly acting in response to the pressure from local clergy and the civilian population, had ordered a massacre of Jews around Jerusalem and in the mountains of Galilee, presumably in 630. Many Jews had fled from this action. There was a special liturgical celebration with fasting by Chalcedonians to expiate the sacrilege of violating the peace pact made by Heraclius with Jews.[12] Every effort is again made in the sources to avoid assigning responsibility to Heraclius. Yet this massacre surely embittered Jewish survivors, who would have looked even more favorably on the Muslims. Christian (presumably Chalcedonian, that is, Melkite) petitioners claimed that they feared that if another enemy people came against them, the Jews might side with them against the Christians as the Jews had done when the Persians came.[13] This may indicate awareness of the imminent threat of the Muslim invasions, although Muslims or Arabs are not specifically mentioned as a threat. It is another index of instability and nervousness in the area at that time. It is another reason why some Jews may have accepted conversion. The fact of a massacre is credible, but the actual number of Jewish victims is unknown, as is the nature and distribution of the surviving Jewish communities. Some Jews had risen violently against Christians at Acre and Tyre, in addition to Jerusalem, during the Persian invasions.[14]

The Persian general who commanded the Persian forces in 613–14 at Adhriʿāt was Shahrbaraz, whose wisdom in the entire campaign was confirmed. He already had conquered much of Byzantine territory, later

[11] Ibn Hishām, *Das Leben Muhammed's nach Muhammed Ibn Ishak bearbeitet von Abd el-Malik Ibn Hischâm*, ed. by Ferdinand Wüstenfeld (Göttingen: Dieterische Universitäts-Buchhandlung, 1859), vol. 1, part 2, p. 657; s.v. "Naḍīr," *EJ* 12 (1972) 754–5. Date: J. M. B. Jones, "The Chronology of the *Maghāzī* – A Textual Survey," *BSOAS* 19 (1957) 268. Eusebius, *Onomasticon*, GCS (Leipzig 1904) 136; Jerome's Latin version on p. 137 of same edn. Examples of Jewish violent action against Christians north of Jerusalem, in Acre and Tyre, during the Persian invasions: Sargis of Aberga, *Controverse Judéo-Chrétienne*, *PO* 13: 84; Eutychius, *Ann.* 270 (1: 121–2 Breydy edn).

[12] *Expugnat. Hierosol. Arab.* 24.10f-n (Garitte Versio 1: 149–50). Eutychius, *Ann.* (Breydy 129 text, 109 trans.).

[13] *Expugnat. Hierosol. Arab.* 24.10f-n (Garitte Versio: 149–50). Eutychius, *Ann.* (128 Breydy text, 108 Breydy trans.); cf. Michel Breydy, *Etudes sur Said ibn Batriq et ses sources* (CSCO vol. 450, *Subsida*, T. 69 [Louvain: E. Peeters, 1983]).

[14] Sargis of Aberga, *Controverse Judéo-Chrétienne*, *PO* 13: 84; Eutychius, *Ann.* 270 (1: 121–2 Breydy edn).

deserted to Heraclius, negotiated terms for Persian troop withdrawal from occupied Byzantine territory in 629, and briefly reigned as Persian king after the death of Kawadh-Siroes.[15] It was his son Niketas, who had fled to the Byzantines after his father was overthrown as king and slain, who was one of the principal Byzantine commanders in much of the fighting against the Muslims in the 630s. Probably Heraclius thought that he shared his late father's military abilities. It is probable that Niketas had heard his father talk about his campaigning in the Adhriʿāt and Bostra regions. It is not known whether he had personally accompanied him on that campaign there. But his father may well have given him advice about how to fight there. In any case, Heraclius and his advisers may have confidently assumed that Niketas possessed excellent personal experience of the local terrain, population, and communications, whether or not he really did.

Although Heraclius probably had passed through or at least near parts of the terrain of the battle of the Yarmūk on his way to and from Jerusalem in 630 or 631, there is no evidence that this fact in any way affected the outcome of the battle. He may have learned of the decision of Byzantine generals Theodore and Vahān to camp in that region without concern. His travel to and from Jerusalem probably would not have involved viewing the wādīs that flow into the Yarmūk or the precipitous banks of the Yarmūk itself.[16] Nothing is known of the quality of Byzantine maps or intelligence concerning the battlefield of Yarmūk.

The earlier battle between Byzantines and Persians at Adhriʿāt in 614 may have influenced the course of battle in 636. The Ghassānids fought on the side of the Byzantines so they would not have been the source of information for the Muslims. The other battle had taken place more than twenty years previously. Muslim traditions preserve the only known record of it, and they may exaggerate its significance. It is improbable that the actual maneuvers of 636 repeated those of 614 – otherwise the Byzantines would surely have known to avoid being trapped as they were in 636.[17] The Muslim leadership in 636 had not been participants in that earlier fighting and, in all probability,

[15] Speck, *Das geteilte Dossier* 317–41, for a different chronology and excessive skepticism about alleged details of the life of Shahrbaraz.

[16] The itinerary of Heraclius is obscure in primary and modern sources. *Expugnat. Hiersol. AD* 614 Arab., 24.12, Version C, ed. and trans. by G. Garitte (CSCO, vol. 347 [Louvain 1974]) 102, translation, 150 Arabic original, indicates Heraclius left Jerusalem by way of Damascus; and it is similar to Eutychius, *Ann.* 271 (127–9 Breydy).

[17] On the earlier battle between Adhriʿāt and Bostra, al-Ṭabarī/Nöldeke, *Geschichte der Perser und Araber zur Zeit der Sasaniden aus der arabischen Chronik des al-Ṭabarī* (Leiden: Brill, 1879) 297, 299–300. Ibn Kathīr, *Tafsīr al-Qurʾān* (Beirut: Dār al-Andalus, 1983) 5: 344. On Niketas: Michael the Syrian, *Chronique* 11.6 (2: 421 Chabot); Nicephorus, *Hist.* 1–2, 5 (38–9, 44–5, Mango). Heraclius arranged the marriage of his son Theodosius to Nike, daughter of Niketas, son of Shahrbaraz, probably in the abortive hope of inducing the conversion of Persia to Christianity: Nicephorus, *Hist.* 17 (64–5, 184 Mango).

would not have possessed much detailed information about it. It was the Byzantines and their Ghassānid allies, if anyone, who should or could have drawn any "lessons" from 614, and their advantage with respect to this did not achieve any positive results at all. It is possible that the previous battle had no particular effect on military operations in 636 or merely underscored the otherwise perceptible strategic value of the territory between Adhri'āt and Bostra. Yet it is injudicious to infer very much from the existence of a battle at Adhri'āt in 614. The Ghassānids were the allies of the Byzantines and would not have deliberately supplied information of a helpful sort to the Muslims. That battle is a noteworthy but not necessarily decisive element in the background of the military operations of 636. It may have no importance beyond emphasizing the continuing strategic importance of the area between Adhri'āt and Bostra.

THE PRINCIPAL EVENTS OF THE BATTLE

In brief, here is an outline of the course of the battle. Having heard of an imminent Byzantine counterthrust, the Muslims first evacuated Ḥimṣ and Damascus. The supreme Byzantine commander was Vahān, but another important commander was the *sakellarios* and probably *magister militum per Orientem* (στρατηγόν τε ἀνατολῆς, Master of the Soldiers in the East), Theodore Trithurios, who came from Emesa on 26 May 636.[18] Other Byzantine commanders included Gargīs, commander of the Armenians, and Jabala b. al-Ayham, king of the Ghassānids. Their Byzantine forces came from Edessa or Antioch, or from both cities. Byzantine forces under Theodore Trithurios advanced through the Biqā' valley and then across the Golan Heights and encamped at and near Jilliq, which is modern Kiswe. Muslim forces withdrew from the Jābiya region to a line between modern Dayr Ayyūb and Adhri'āt (modern Der'a). This move placed the Muslims in a topographically and strategically strong position, from which position they could attempt to block the advancing Byzantines and resist their penetration southwards. The principal commander of Muslim forces was Abū 'Ubayda b. al-Jarrāḥ. The Muslims waited two to three months before the decisive battle took place.

The Byzantines delayed combat, probably in part to allow their soldiers to gain some familiarity with the Muslims and the terrain, and to gain confidence. Other possible motives for their delay were their attempts to subvert the Muslims by diplomacy and intrigue and their desire to gain more intelligence about them. Meanwhile the Byzantine troops clashed with the

[18] Nicephorus, Hist. 20 (68–9 Mango); for the meaning of στρατηγόν τε ἀνατολῆς, see index of C. De Boor, *Hist.*, who identifies the office as *magister militum*, p. 244.

local Syrian population. Tensions rose between them. Manṣūr, the chief Byzantine administrator of Damascus, refused to supply General Vahān with his requested number of provisions, claiming that the requisition was too great for the available resources in Damascus. Manṣūr resented Heraclius and Vahān. He contrived a noisy demonstration that frightened and caused the confusion and flight of some Byzantine soldiers in the night.

There was an initial clash in the vicinity of Jābiya, which compelled the Muslims to retire. Theodore Trithurios' forces were defeated by the Muslims near Jābiya, perhaps on 23 July 636/13 Jumada AH 15. The tradition that discontented Byzantine troops reportedly mutinied and proclaimed Vahān Byzantine emperor is questionable, and may be an example of dynastic disinformation, an attempt to shift the responsibility away from Heraclius to others. It may even be a misunderstanding of an earlier pro-Heraclius tradition that sought to depict the Byzantine troops as rebellious in the sense that they arrogantly refused to obey Heraclius' order to avoid combat with the Muslims, which in time became transformed into a claim that they not only rebelled but proclaimed their commander emperor. Or it may reflect the indubitable disarray within Byzantine ranks and tensions and clashes between the Byzantine soldiers and the local civilian population. But it is possible that the tradition of a disruptive quarrel between the *Buccinator* (al-Qanāṭir) and Gargīs, who refused to obey his command, is a trace of the tradition of the problem. The *Buccinator* commanded the Byzantine right wing. Mu'āz b. Jabal led the Muslim right wing, Qubātha b. Usāma commanded the left, Hāshim b. 'Utba led the infantry and Khālid b. al-Walīd led the cavalry. Four leaders were Khālid, 'Amr b. al-'Āṣ, Yazīd b. Abī Sufyān, and Abū 'Ubayda. This was the first day of battle of three or more days of battle.[19]

The Byzantines moved some of their forces to encamp between the Wādī'l-Ruqqād and the Wādī'l-Ḥarīr. Byzantines suffered some desertions. The Byzantines failed to cover all of the territory between Dayr Ayyūb and their encampment, which allowed Muslims to penetrate and turn the Byzantine left flank with the hope of cutting off their retreat. Negotiations opened between the Byzantines under Vahān and the Muslims. The Muslims consciously prepared a trap for the Byzantines by staging their withdrawal in the direction of Adhri'āt from previously held positions. The Byzantines moved forward to occupy positions that the Muslims had evacuated, without taking adequate notice of the Muslims who were hiding in the clumpy terrain.

[19] Ibn 'Asākir, *TMD* 1: 535, via traditions from Abū 'Alī b. Ṣawwāf, from al-Ḥasan b. 'Alī al-Qaṭṭān, from Ismā'īl b. 'Īsā al 'Aṭṭār, from Abū Ḥudhayfa Isḥāq b. Bishr, and Sa'īd b. 'Abd al-'Azīz; cf. Caetani, *AI* 3: 557–8.

The commander entitled *drungarios* commanded the Byzantine left, while Gargīs of Armenia commanded the Byzantine right wing. The Byzantine left pushed back the Muslim right wing and approached the Muslim camp, which even women defended. Likewise the Byzantine right forced the Muslim left to pull back on the center and the Muslim camp. The Muslims counterattacked. The Byzantines broke ranks, took flight, and were shattered.

Byzantine cavalry became separated from the Byzantine infantry, probably while attempting one of the complicated Byzantine maneuvers identified with the "mixed formation" or "convex formation."[20] One Muslim commander, Khālid b. al-Walīd, noticed this gap in Byzantine forces and managed to interpose his cavalry between Byzantine cavalry and Byzantine infantry, whom his horsemen proceeded to slaughter. A dust storm unsettled the Byzantines and created an opportunity which the Muslims exploited. In the meantime, many Christian Arabs who had been supporting the Byzantines fled.

Muslim cavalry under the command of Khālid b. al-Walīd managed during the evening to capture the only bridge over the Wādī'l Ruqqād.[21] This act effectively isolated much of the Byzantine forces between the steep and dangerous bluffs of the Wādī'l Ruqqād and the Wādī'l 'Allān, both west of the Wādī'l Ḥarīr. Muslims then attacked and stormed the Byzantine camp. The main force of Byzantines was thus cut off by the Muslims and could not extricate itself. The Byzantine camp at Yāqūṣa (perhaps a kilometer east of Fīq, in the Golan Heights, on the southern flank of the Wādī'l Ruqqād) was stormed.[22]

On 20 August the battle reached its climax. Byzantine panic spread as soldiers learned that some Christian Arabs had deserted by simple flight or switching to the Muslim side and that the Muslim capture of their only route of escape, the bridge, had eliminated their options. Some Byzantine forces simply ceased to fight and were slaughtered without resistance by the Muslims the next day. Other Byzantine troops and horse were destroyed when they fell down the sharp slopes into the wādīs while trying to escape. The outcome was the annihilation of most Byzantine forces and hot and thorough pursuit of those who managed to escape.

Various reports circulated on the fate of the Byzantine commanders at the battle. Muslims pursued the Byzantines and then proceeded to besiege Damascus. The news of the outcome of the battle finally reached Heraclius,

[20] Maurice, *Strategikon* 12A.7 (133–6 Dennis trans).

[21] Location of this old Roman bridge, see Sheet 7, from maps in *PEF Palestine*. The approximate latitude is 39° 53′ E and the longitude is 32° 52′ N.

[22] *PEF Palestine*, Sheet 7. Yāqūṣa is located about 12 miles southeast of the old Roman bridge over the Wādī'l Ruqqād.

who was following military events from Antioch, which lay more than 500 kilometers to the north.

BYZANTINE OBJECTIVES

The Byzantines' objective had been to pursue and try to force the Muslims to evacuate Syria. Indeed, they forced the Muslims to evacuate Damascus, and even the region around Jābiya itself. By turning movements whenever possible, they were attempting to seek out and to eject the Muslim armies. For the first time they were trying to follow the withdrawing Muslims as closely as possible, presumably to try to prevent them from establishing new fixed defensive positions. One of their objectives became the Muslim camp, which served as a tempting and successful bait for the Byzantines. The Byzantines tried to maneuver the Muslims out of their positions by threatening their communications, which indeed forced the Muslims to retreat from Jābiya itself to the vicinity of Adhri'āt.

Alleviation of logistical problems, in addition to the important Ghassānids' predilection for their own camping-ground, probably dictated the Byzantine armies' halt at Jābiya and their establishment of camp at Jilliq (Kiswe), which was not very far away. The troops and their mounts were less of a burden to feed there. The troops also controlled very strategically important ground for defense and offense and for communications. That again probably explains the reason for the previous combat with the Persians there in 614. The Byzantines relied upon fixed bases and not on mobility. They strove to move with caution and not with impetuousness, and they sought to rely upon fixed positions that used natural defensive features of the topography, most notably the steep gorges of the Yarmūk, the Wādī'l-Ḥarīr, and the Wādī'l Ruqqād, which also gave them access to ample supplies of water. The region was sufficiently valuable for both sides to risk battle for control of it.

The earlier analysis by Leone Caetani is the most plausible modern account of the battle. Not all of his detailed reconstructions are acceptable, but essential parts are, and in any case his are more persuasive than those of other scholars.[23] Many problems in modern interpretations of the battle

[23] Caetani, *AI* 3: 499–613; De Goeje, *Mémoire*² esp. 103–36. Glubb, *The Great Arab Conquests* 173–80. See Yūsuf Ghawanmā, *Ma'arakat al-Yarmūk* (Irbid: Dār Hishām l'il nashr w'al Tawzī', 1985) for a reconstruction of the battle. He has personal familiarity with much of the area, has read many of the relevant Arabic sources, but he ignores the researches of Leone Caetani, *Annali dell'Islam.* He uncritically accepts statements from Pseudo-Wāqidī, such as, p. 35, the presence of *Rūs* [sic] at the battle of the Yarmūk, which weakens his investigations. He provides a suggestive and ingenious reconstruction of five days of battle and a sixth of Muslim pursuit of the Byzantines. His reconstruction shows ignorance of Caetani's arguments for the decisive location of the principal Byzantine forces between the Wādī'l Ruqqād and the Wādī'l 'Allān; Ghawanmā's reconstruction has serious topographical flaws. Ghawanmā's reconstruction cannot be read alone. It requires critical

derive from the failure of modern historians to read the detailed analyses and conclusions of Leone Caetani;[24] invariably they must go back over material that Caetani worked out and proved early in the century. Whether or not one agrees with Caetani, it is essential to have read and analyzed his arguments about the topography of the battlefield.[25] He visited the scene of the military operations in a period of peace when it was possible to traverse the region without much difficulty.

THE RELEVANCE OF BYZANTINE MILITARY DOCTRINE

The overwhelming amount of evidence indicates that both sides waged war with cleverness at the Yarmūk, not merely with zeal due to religious devotion, or economic or tribal considerations. The location of the battle, too, was not accidental. Instead it was carefully chosen by both sides. The battle of the Yarmūk conforms to known Byzantine military doctrine, especially as revealed in the *Strategikon* of Maurice.

Byzantine military doctrines about the camp and its placement may have contributed to the lapse of the Byzantines (otherwise hard to explain) in allowing themselves to be lured into the impossible military situation in which they found themselves at the battle of the Yarmūk. Thus the Armenian historian Ghevond criticizes the Byzantines for leaving their camp separate from the main body of their troops.[26] Yet such a procedure conforms to the advice of the *Strategikon*, according to whose author it was dangerous to

comparison with other analyses of the topography and military operations. Poorly documented – with few references to sources and again none to the great work of Caetani – is the otherwise plausible schema of M. Ṭalās, *Sayf Allāh, Khālid ibn al-Walīd* (Damascus 1978) 387–431, whose maps at the end of his volume provide a more reasonable reconstruction of the battle. Yet he fails to give a critical assessment of the primary and secondary literature. Aḥmad ʿAdil Kamāl, *al-Ṭarīq ilā Dimashq* (Beirut 1982) 403–507 uses sources uncritically and again fails to consult Caetani. His maps, figures 29–33, which are located between pp. 476 and 492, are, however, not implausible reconstructions.

24 More bluntly put, many modern historians appear to have little or no knowledge of Italian and therefore have avoided using Caetani's weighty tomes.

25 John W. Jandora, "The Battle of the Yarmūk: A Reconstruction," *Journal of Asian History* 19 (1985) 8–21; this provocative recent interpretation does not employ all of the modern bibliography or all of the primary sources, esp. on Byzantine strategy and tactics. The term "cataphract," for example, on pp. 14–15, is not very relevant to this period of Byzantine military history; cf. Lawrence Conrad, "Seven and the Ṭasbīʿ," *JESHO* 31 (1988) 54–5.

26 Ghevond, *History of Lewond the Eminent Vardapet of the Armenians*, trans. by Rev. Zaven Arzoumanian (Wynnewood 1982) 48–9; *Histoire des guerres et des conquêtes des arabes en Arménie* trans. by Garabed Chahnazarian (Paris: Librarie de Ch. Meyrueis et Compagnie, Editeurs, 1856) 3–4. Sebēos, *Sebēos' History*, trans. by Robert Bedrosian (New York 1985) 125, and *Histoire d'Héraclius* c. 30 (97–8 Macler). Sebēos (131 Bedrosian, 102 Macler) claims that his information derives from prisoners; cf. Heinrich Hübschmann, *Zur Geschichte Armeniens und der ersten Kriege der Araber* (Leipzig 1875) 18, n. 3. Bedrosian does not show awareness of Hübschmann's remarks on the difficulties in interpreting this passage.

place the camp too near the place of battle because of the danger of its becoming prey to the enemy and not giving the cavalry adequate room for maneuver.[27] Maurikios implies that the Persian practice contrasts with that of the Romans or Byzantines. The decision of the Byzantine commanders at the Yarmūk to locate their camp some distance from the anticipated scene of battle may have been wrong, but in doing so they were following standard Byzantine military doctrine. The author of the *Strategikon* also advises placing the camp on the enemy's side of a bridge. Such was the location of the Byzantine camp in relation to the Wādī'l Ruqqād during the maneuvering of the battle of Jābiya-Yarmūk.[28] It appears that one motive for the location of the Byzantine camp near the river and ravine was to provide a secure area in which the soldiers might relax.[29] But the Muslim operations in 636, as did their others, eliminated distinctions between the front and rear. There was no longer any secure area, except by explicit verbal or written arrangement with the foe.[30]

The Christian Arab historian Eutychius reports that noise played a prominent role in the battle of the Yarmūk. He states that Manṣūr, who was in charge of fiscal affairs at Damascus, claimed that he could not raise an amount of money sufficient to feed so many Byzantine troops as Vahān brought. He had already incurred the anger of the Byzantine government for paying so much tax money to the Persians during their occupation of the region. They sought to recover it from him and were angry with him about that past action on his part. Local officials had long sought to divert Byzantine and late Roman armies from their localities because of the burden they would impose on the local populations. Manṣūr's action conforms perfectly with the problem mentioned in Novel 130 of Justinian I and with arguments that it was local officials, not the praetorian prefecture, who collected and distributed rations and maintenance for soldiers. He did try to find an excuse to divert the Byzantine army from Damascus. He had men raise noise with cymbals and drums that frightened Byzantines into thinking that Muslims were coming from that unexpected direction.[31]

27 *Strategikon* 11.1.

28 *Strategikon* 5.3, for keeping baggage some distance from battle; esp. 9. 1 (94 Dennis trans), 12.B22, on placing camp on enemy's side of river and the importance of securing bridges to permit unrestricted passing of Byzantine troops from battle areas where necessary. Yet Fredegarius, *Chron*. 4.66, ed. by Bruno Krusch (MGH Scriptores Rerum Merovingicarum, T. 2 [Hanover 1888; repr. 1984]) 153–4, states that both camps were located not far away from each other.

29 Roman manuals recommended placing the camp so that a river or stream bordered it on one side or the other: Pseudo-Hyginus, *Des fortifications du camp* c. 57, ed. and trans. by Maurice Lenoir (Paris: Les Belles Lettres, 1979) 22; cf. Carl von Clausewitz, *Vom Kriege*, ed. by W. Hahlweg (Bonn: Ferd. Dümmlers Verlag, 1973) 525.

30 'Abd al-Ḥamīd b. Yaḥyā, *Risāla* 4: 521–3 = Schönig, *Sendschreiben* 62–4.

31 Just. Nov. 130.1–3. Eutychius, *Ann*. 278–9 (135–7 Breydy edn., 114–15 Breydy trans.).

Sixth-century Byzantine military treatises advise using noise to mislead the enemy[32] and to cover the actions of spies,[33] in conformity with Eutychius' report that Manṣūr used noise to frighten the Byzantine troops away from Damascus. Manṣūr's actions can plausibly have had as much negative effect on the Byzantine armies as Eutychius claims. Noise was regarded as a kind of warning indicator that could cause men to abandon their positions. Decisive events in the battle took place at night, according to several accounts. Eutychius indicates that Manṣūr's noisy demonstration frightened the Byzantines into flight at night.

NARRATIVE SOURCES

The earliest extant recorded account of the battle appears to be the brief one of the Frankish historian Fredegarius, in the late seventh century (*c.* 658), who more vaguely speaks of a decisive divine blow against the Byzantines at night so that they were unwilling to fight the following day. Fredegarius correctly reports that the Muslims were led by two commanders, although he does not identify them by name:

> The latter, under two commanders, were approximately 200,000 strong. The two forces had camped quite near one another and were ready for an engagement on the following morning. But during that very night the army of Heraclius was smitten by the sword of the Lord: 52,000 of his men died where they slept. When, on the following day, at the moment of joining battle, his men saw that so large a part of their force had fallen to divine judgment, they no longer dared advance on the Saracens but all retired whence they came.[34]

The sources of Fredegarius for his short account of this battle are probably Byzantine or, more likely, Christian Oriental, but in any case, his is the earliest surviving account, one in which numbers of soldiers and casualties are already wildly exaggerated.[35]

[32] Anonymous Byzantine Treatise on Strategy, c. 29, ed. in: G. T. Dennis, *Three Byzantine Military Treatises* (Dumbarton Oaks Texts, 9 [Washington, DC: Dumbarton Oaks, 1985]) 90–1.

[33] *Strategikon* 7B.10 (71–2 Dennis trans.), 11.B22 (159 Dennis trans.); cf. Leo VI warned in his *Tactica* 18.112 = *PG* 107: 972, that the Arabs or "Saracens" use cymbals and make sounds that upset their enemies. He repeats this, *Tactica* 18. 141 (*PG* 107: 981), recommending that commanders accustom their horses to noises of drums and cymbals and to the sight of camels. *Strategikon* also advises that foragers are to flee in haste back to camp if certain signals are given. Byzantine troops indeed may have mistook the noise made by Manṣūr's men as an indication of the approach of the enemy, as the *Strategikon* says that it might be.

[34] Fredegarius, *Chron.* 4.66 (153–4 Krusch) = (55 Wallace-Hadrill); Kusternig, *Quellen* 232–4; cf. 9–13. The "sword" may mean Khālid.

[35] Ekkehart Rotter, *Abendland und Sarazenen* (Berlin: De Gruyter, 1986) 153–70. But Rotter makes no use of Caetani, *AI*, on the battle; he only uses Caetani's other volumes on *Chronographia islamica*. Rotter dates some material in the Fredegarius chronicle to c. 659:

Ibn 'Asākir's important account also stresses that the Muslims apparently seized the Byzantine camp at night, and by daybreak the Byzantines had broken and fled or been destroyed. This was unusual because later the Byzantines assume that Arabs do not like to fight at night. This is a rare but decisive occasion on which the Byzantines' enemy resorted to an unexpected practice for invaluable results.[36] In any case, events at night unsettled the Byzantines and contributed to their breakdown of morale and cohesion, including their will to fight.

Armenian and Arabic sources agree that the Byzantines used infantry at the battle of the Yarmūk. Sebēos emphasizes that the exhausted Byzantines attacked the Muslim camp on foot and were then forcefully and decisively counterattacked by Muslims who had been lying in hiding. The Byzantines probably did not use infantry exclusively, as the Armenian historians Sebēos and Ghevond (eighth-century writer who reused parts of Sebēos' materials) claimed. They probably also used cavalry, as several Arabic sources, including al-Ṭabarī and Ibn 'Asākir report.[37]

al-Ṭabarī's and Ibn 'Asākir's descriptions of some maneuvers of Khālid b. al-Walīd are reminiscent of actions reported in the Maurice *Strategikon*. In particular, the Byzantines may well have used the so-called mixed or convex formation when they left their safe areas beside the Wādī'l Ruqqād in order to pursue the apparently fleeing Muslims. The author of the *Strategikon* specifies a particular mixed formation when the troops are roused to action. The mixed formation required the infantry to maneuver in complex formation to allow the cavalry to pass through their lines, after which time the infantry were to close ranks again. The infantry were to create a temporary gap in their ranks once again when the cavalry retired. This appears to have been what happened.

Byzantine attacks against the Muslim right flank first, and then their left, failed successively but forced the Muslims to retreat to their camp. There a concerted defense by Muslim infantry, possibly cheered and aided by women in the camp, drew Byzantine cavalry away from supporting infantry and

p. 149. Rotter fails to appreciate that Fredegarius is the oldest extant source, however garbled, on the battle.

36 Fredegarius, *Chron.* 4.66(166 Krusch); Eutychius, *Ann.* 278–9 (136–7 Breydy); Ibn 'Asākir 1: 534, 544, 550. On night-fighting, see Leo VI, in his *Tactica*, 18. 117 (*PG* 107: 973), who claims that "Saracens" fear night-fighting and nighttime attacks on their camps. Late Umayyad fears about fighting at night: 'Abd al-Ḥamīd ibn Yaḥyā, *Risāla* 4: 523–4, 526 = Schönig, *Sendschreiben* 64–6. It is likely that Muslims also harbored such fears in the preceding (seventh) century.

37 Byzantine use of infantry at the battle: Sebēos, *Hist.* c. 30 (125 Bedrosian, 97 Macler); cf. the derivative tenth-century history of Thomas Artsruni, *History of the House of the Artsrunik'*, trans. by R. W. Thomson (Detroit: Wayne State, 1985) 167–8; al-Ṭabarī i 2089, 2099–100; Ibn 'Asākir 1: 538–9, 547. Recommendation for carefully drawn-up infantry formations against the Persians: *Strategikon* 11.1 (114 Dennis trans.).

allowed a Muslim cavalry counterattack, supplemented by those Muslim foot who had been hiding, causing the Byzantine cavalry to flee and scatter. al-Ṭabarī (following traditions of Sayf, from Abū 'Uthmān Yazīd b. Asīd al-Ghassānī) states that Khālid finally managed to maneuver his cavalry between the Byzantine cavalry, who then scattered in the plain, and the Byzantine infantry, whom he then attacked and overwhelmed; then he proceeded to storm the key Byzantine camp. His maneuvers appear to have exploited the potential danger of using the complicated Byzantine mixed or convex formation, which classical strategists warned could expose its practitioner to the separation of cavalry and infantry, with disastrous consequences. This appears to have been a critical element among many in the Muslim annihilation of the Byzantines. The mixed formation was always a difficult one, and the Byzantine armies of 636 were not the only ones in history to have difficulty with it.[38]

Arabic references to cases of Byzantine soldiers at Yarmūk being chained together to prevent flight have been misinterpreted. They may, of course, merely be a *topos*. But they may transmit some traces of historical reality. They probably refer to Byzantine soldiers locking shields tightly in order to form the tightest and most solid possible resistance to assault by infantry or cavalry. These maneuvers are mentioned in the *Strategikon*. Muslim sources concede that Byzantine troops fought bravely in the early part of the battle. Their morale only declined later in the course of the battle. In no sense were they cowardly at the beginning.[39]

The camps of both sides have a prominent place in narratives of the battle. Muslim women played an unusually important role in stiffening resistance against the Byzantines by shaming and even fighting against those Muslims who were fleeing. Descriptions of the Muslims' storming of the Byzantine camp at Yarmūk appear to be plausible.[40] The sources emphasize the role of

[38] Muslim historians report actions of Byzantine armies that appear to involve the so-called mixed formation of the *Strategikon* 12.1–7 (127–36 Dennis trans.): al-Ṭabarī i 2099; Ibn 'Asākir, *TMD* 1: 547. Difficulties with combining horse and foot: Arthur Ferrill, *The Fall of the Roman Empire: The Military Explanation* (New York: Thames and Hudson, 1986) 63, on the battle of Adrianople (378); Raimondo Montecuccoli, *Memoire del General prencipe di Montecucculi*... (Colonia 1704?) 37–8; cf. Monsieur le Comte Turpin de Crissé, *Commentaires sur les Mémoires de Montecucculi*... (Paris: Lamcobe, Lejay, 1759), 1: 42, 102–3, 111–12, 190–1, 204–9, 231–6; yet Marshall De Saxe, *Reveries*, in: T. N. Phillips, *The Roots of Strategy* (repr. Greenwood Press, 1985), 136–7.

[39] Balādhurī 135, references to Byzantine soldiers being chained together probably denote the locking of shields in the standard Byzantine so-called mixed formation: *Strategikon* 12.7 (134 Dennis trans.); cf. *Strategikon* 12A.16 (146 Dennis trans.).

[40] Bravery of Byzantine soldiers early in battle: Ibn 'Asākir 1: 537; al-Ṭabarī i 2097–9; Azdī 222–3, 225–7. Camps: Fredegarius, *Chron.* 4.66 (153–4 Krusch); Ghevond [Lewond], *Histoire des guerres et des conquêtes des arabes*, trans. by G. V. Chahnazarian (Paris 1856) 3–4. Muslims storm Byzantine camp: Ibn 'Asākir, *TMD* 1: 534, 540–3; al-Ṭabarī i 2088–100.

psychology and morale and fear and volatility in affecting the outcome of the battle, not merely sheer numbers of casualties inflicted. The real objective and achieved outcome was the destruction of the fighting effectiveness of the Byzantine army, irrespective of the actual numbers killed. The Muslims do not appear to have taken prisoners from the ranks of Greeks and Armenians, although they welcomed the desertion or side-switching of some Arabs. Some Byzantines who fled from the scene of the battle to other regions were captured rather soon, but the Muslims did not take prisoners on the actual battlefield itself, perhaps because of their fury at their own losses in the ferocity of the combat. Similar slaughter has frequently taken place in many contexts after hard-fought battles.[41]

MUSLIM STRATEGY

From the start of the Muslim invasions it was reportedly the strategy of Caliph Abū Bakr to engage in actions that would compel the Byzantines to send large numbers of troops to Syria so that the Muslims could defeat them decisively there.[42] In other words, the Muslims, in contrast to the Byzantines, sought decisive victory on the battlefield. They, not the Byzantines, wanted battle. This description of Muslim strategy appears to be accurate. It was not inevitable that the Byzantines suffer a defeat at Jābiya-Yarmūk. The Muslim leaders drew them into a situation that at some point made a Muslim victory overwhelmingly probable, but that outcome was not a certainty at the beginning of the campaigning and maneuvering.

Ibn 'Asākir also reports that the Muslims deliberately lured the Byzantines into attacking them by noisily breaking up camp and withdrawing.[43] In the meantime, groups of soldiers had been hidden to spring into action at the appropriate time. The Byzantines were lured into assaulting the Muslim camp but then were taken off balance by the Muslim counterattack, which came with sufficient force that it prevented them from effectively regrouping for a competent defense. The battle involved the Muslim use of much planning and craft, and excellent use of the topography, not mere hurling of masses of bodies against the Byzantines in order to overwhelm them.

The battle was not of the type in which two armies blunder into each other and accidentally come to a great clash. Here both armies had been maneuvering for considerable time before the battle, on topography of which the general contours were well known, or should have been well known, to both. In addition, the Byzantines dominated the highest ground and possessed areas that appeared to present good defensive features if there were a crisis.

[41] Richard Holmes, *Acts of War: The Behaviour of Men in Battle* (New York 1985) 381–92.
[42] Azdī 15.
[43] Ibn 'Asākir, *TMD* 1: 531–3.

Yet events demonstrated that possession of the high ground, including the Golan Heights, did not provide the Byzantines with certain victory. Possession of fixed positions with their deceptively attractive protected flanks did not determine the outcome of what was to be a classic battle of maneuver. If anything, the Byzantines did not act aggressively in the early stages of the battle. The Muslim commanders made most of the decisive moves to lure the Byzantines into the killing ground.

BYZANTINE COMMAND AND CONTROL

It is impossible to penetrate the mind of Heraclius himself, who was far away from the battle scene, presumably at Antioch, although some traditions place him at Ḥimṣ. No relevant military memoranda survive from his reign. No memoirs of Heraclius' advisers or other relevant archival material survive about the battle of Yarmūk. No Byzantine source provides the wealth of details that some Muslim sources, such as Ibn Aʿtham al-Kūfī, Ibn ʿAsākir, and Azdī provide in a somewhat conflicting fashion.

Sources do not explain how the Byzantines planned their order of battle at Yarmūk. Byzantium had no general staff or war college for the formulation of military strategy. In all likelihood, it was Heraclius and his most intimate advisers, especially his brother Theodore, and a small group of generals who included Niketas, the son of the Persian general and short-lived King Shahrbaraz, who decided some of the outlines of strategy and operations. Vahān, as general, was expected to act in accordance with this broader plan, but he did not have good relations with Trithurios and Niketas. It was, of course, impossible to plan the Byzantine counteroffensive in every detail from the far-away headquarters of Heraclius at Antioch. The irascible and strong-willed Heraclius may have tried to control operations too closely. Balādhurī, Nicephorus, and the continuator of Isidore of Seville may correctly assert that the Byzantines resolved to give battle at the Yarmūk. This was a rare reversal of their propensity to try to avoid it, at least since their defeats at Dāthin and Ajnādayn.[44] A Latin tradition plausibly asserts that Theodore, the brother of Heraclius, and his Byzantines ultimately attacked the Muslims because they could not wait longer while the Muslims continued to gain more reinforcements.[45]

The Muslims were probably aware of the Byzantine preference to avoid combat at the hottest time of day and therefore attacked at that time.[46] Such

[44] Balādhurī 135.

[45] *Cont. Byz. Arab.*, MGHAA 11: 337–8 = *Crónica mozárabe de* 754, ed. by Jose Eduardo López Pereira (Zaragoza 1980) 30–1.

[46] *Strategikon* 11.1 (113–14 Dennis trans.); 12B.23 (162 Dennis trans.); also 7.17 (78 Dennis trans.).

problems played into the hands of the Muslims. The heat of the day, as well as dust storms, are mentioned by Byzantine sources concerning Byzantine soldiers' problems at the battle of the Yarmūk.

The Byzantines tried to communicate with the Muslim commanders, probably in order to learn more about them, to devise more effective tactics and stratagems, and probably to corrupt and win them over.[47] Such precedents conceivably were familiar to Byzantine commanders in the seventh century. Their broader efforts failed, even though there were some significant desertions. In the end it was the Byzantines who suffered the greatest number of desertions and lack of coordination between military units. al-Ṭabarī (via Sayf, and Abū 'Uthmān Yazīd b. Asīd al-Ghassānī) plausibly reports that Vahān and his commanders encamped at Yāqūṣa and wanted their men to become acquainted with, or adjusted to, the look of the Arabs. This indicates, of course, that some of their troops, especially the Armenian and Greek contingents, were not familiar with fighting or even seeing Arabs.[48] Vahān not only sought to calm the fears of his troops about the appearance of Arabs by waiting before battle but also tried to learn more about the Muslims, their strength, and the capabilities and intentions of their commanders, and any weakness or possibility for corruption of them or their troops. Such was typical Byzantine practice in fighting barbarians.

The Muslims on the eve of the battle of the Yarmūk were on the alert against the Byzantines' possible machinations – that is, clever tricks and stratagems. They knew, then, that the Byzantines were prone to try clever means to defeat them. In fact, they devised their own cleverer and ultimately successful stratagems against the Byzantines.[49]

The battle of the Yarmūk took place approximately two days' or one and a half days' distance from Damascus.[50] Eutychius mentions the distance in terms of days' travel or march from Damascus. It was an area which had been familiar, with its criss-crossing roads, since the Biblical era. The ultimate

47 Byzantines probably tried to contact Muslim leaders to try to win at least some of them over to their side: Ibn 'Asākir, *TMD* 1: 533. The author of the *Strategikon* recommends that Byzantine commanders who must fight strange people give their men some time to accustom themselves to these new foes, so that they lose any fright about them: 7.11 (67–8 Dennis trans.). Thus the assertion of some Muslim sources that Vahān deliberately gave his men some time to gain familiarity with the Muslims is very plausible and consistent with the recommendations of the prevailing Byzantine military treatise. In about AD 900, Emperor Leo VI recommended that Byzantine commanders accustom their horses, and presumably their men, to the noise of drums and cymbals and the sight of camels, all of which the Arabs used in battle, he emphasized: *Tactica* 18.112 = *PG* 107: 972; 18. 141 = *PG* 107: 981. This may explain the actions of the Byzantine commanders before the battle of the Yarmūk, including why they camped relatively close to the Muslims; cf. Polyaenus, *Strat.* 7.6.6, ed. by R. Vari (repr. Stuttgart: Teubner, 1970) 317.

48 al-Ṭabarī i 2088. See F. Ṭuqān, "Al-Wāqūsah," 1985 *Bilād al-Shām Proceedings* 2: 323–31.

49 Ibn 'Asākir, *TMD* 1: 531–3.

50 Eutychius, *Ann.* (136 Breydy edn, 115 Breydy trans. = Cheikho 2: 14).

flight of the Byzantines who did escape from the battle of the Yarmūk was reportedly to Ḥimṣ, whether via the Biqāʿ valley or via Damascus. There is no report of the immediate effects in Palestine, especially Galilee, but there very probably were immediate reactions and consequences. The distances are close. Word of the outcome of the battle probably reached Galilee and the rest of Palestine very quickly.

The statistics of the battle are misleading and probably without any sound empirical basis. It is possible that, on this rare occasion, the Byzantines enjoyed numerical superiority. Estimates of the number of Byzantine troops vary wildly and are improbably high. Given the small size of Byzantine armies in the early Byzantine and middle Byzantine periods, it is exceedingly unlikely that the Byzantine numbers at the battle reached the 40,000 or 80,000 that are at the low end of Muslim statistics for the Byzantines. Although it is possible to concede Byzantine numerical superiority, it is very doubtful that Byzantine forces, including Armenian and allied Christian Arab troops, foot and horse, exceeded 15,000 or 20,000 soldiers.[51] It was natural for later Christian sources to depict the Muslim forces as huge and growing daily, to help explain away the Byzantine defeat. It is not worth even attempting to determine the respective probability of any veracity in the various Christian and Muslim traditions. Their numbers simply bear no relation to what military historians can accept as plausible for this period for Byzantine troops. Their troops included Christian Arabs, especially those under the command of the Ghassānid King Jabala b. al-Ayham, and Armenians, especially those under Jarajis (George) and Vahān, as well as Greeks. It is unclear how important it was for the Byzantines to have Trithurios and Vahān's troops united, or whether the battle began before they united. It is likewise unclear whether all Byzantine troops reached the place of battle via the Biqāʿ valley, or whether some in fact came via Damascus.

Parts of the Byzantine armies at the battle of the Yarmūk fought without good coordination with other sections of their forces. This contributed to the Muslim victory and to the heavy Byzantine casualties. The dangers that were inherent in forming an army of so many disparate elements became real during the course of the protracted battle. The sources do not give a clear and detailed description of the location of the Byzantine commanders during the various stages of the battle, or indeed during any stage of it. There is some description of commands of various wings of their army but not the precise location of any of the wings.

[51] Donner, *EIC* 221, estimates "perhaps 20,000 to 40,000," which is conceivable, but definitely on the high side of what is reasonable for Byzantine troops in that impoverished Heraclian era. Unrealistically high are the estimates of Jandora, "The Battle of the Yarmūk" 14; cf. Lawrence Conrad, "Seven and the Ṭasbīʿ," *JESHO* 31 (1988) 54–5.

FRICTIONS WITHIN THE BYZANTINE ARMIES

Friction at several levels within the Byzantine army at Jābiya-Yarmūk resulted from mistrust between the Greeks, Armenians, and Christian Arabs. Within the ranks of the highest command, there was distrust between Trithurios and Vahān. Within Armenian ranks, there was mistrust between Jarajis and Qanāṭir (*Buccinator*).[52] All of this was extremely harmful to the Byzantines' ultimate combat effectiveness, military cohesion, and swiftness and smoothness of command and planning. The defects within the Byzantine army, therefore, were multiple on the eve of that fateful battle. This was not the only occasion on which Byzantine armies suffered from strife between commanders and different units. Its existence at the time of the battle of Jābiya-Yarmūk, however, was especially fraught with dangers for the well-being of the empire.[53]

The Armenian troops do not appear to have been deeply divided by controversies about Monophysitism and Chalcedon, even though their clerics were. Yet the strife within the Armenian church over the issue of union and Heraclius' policies cannot have helped morale among the soldiers. There is likewise no evidence of the controversies' influence on Armenian commanders. At a minimum the ecclesiastical strife was a potentially complicating issue that cast a pall over the important Armenian contingents at the battle of the Yarmūk. There is no evidence whether it caused any problem in securing chaplains or other clerics to encourage Armenian soldiers and minister to them before, during, and after the battle. It probably was a troubling factor in the background, but nothing more can be stated with any degree of confidence. Ibn 'Asākir reports traditions about friction and a tendency toward disobedience within the ranks of Armenian troops, indicating that Qanāṭir (presumably, as De Goeje argued, *Buccinator*, who was Armenian) on the right wing disputed with his superior, Jarajis (George), and declined to respect his orders. In particular, the narrative of Sayf b. 'Umar claims that an Armenian commander named George converted to Islam just before the battle of the Yarmūk. This account should be regarded as very suspect but perhaps an echo of the unrest that resulted in the alleged rebellion of Vahān. Abū Ḥudhayfa claims that George quarreled with "Qanāṭir." These are perhaps confused reminiscences of trouble within the Armenian troops and their leadership at the battle.[54] These Arabic sources do

[52] Friction between various Byzantine commanders: Theoph., *Chron.*, AM 6126 (637–8 De Boor), including the alleged revolt of Armenian troops in support of Vahān. Ibn 'Asākir, *TMD* 1: 541.

[53] W. E. Kaegi, *BMU* 64–88, 293–325.

[54] Theoph., *Chron.*, AM 6126 (3378 De Boor). Armenian ecclesiastical strife: G. Garitte, *La narratio de rebus Armeniae, Diegesis* 121, CSCO, Subsidia, T. 4 (Louvain 1952) 43, 302–4. Ibn 'Asākir, *TMD* 1: 541, 547; al-Ṭabarī i 2097–9. There is no confirmation from Byzantine

not specifically report any Armenian rebellion and proclamation of Vahān as Byzantine emperor, but they do indicate the presence of various kinds of disorder, including this disobedience, and the Byzantine troops' disorderly conduct and abuse of civilians in Syria.

Theophanes' and Nicephorus' source sought to explain away the crushing Byzantine defeat and avoid casting blame on Heraclius by claiming that there had been treasonous disobedience to Heraclius' orders to avoid open combat with the Muslims. That earlier propaganda became distorted into a claim by Theophanes and his source that some Byzantine troops not only disobeyed Heraclius' instructions but openly rebelled against him and abortively proclaimed General Vahān emperor, thereby wrecking the Byzantine effort in the battle. The brief account of Fredegarius, in which he emphasizes the failure of the Byzantines to fight after the sudden and mysterious death of so many Byzantine soldiers in camp the previous night, may be a distorted or garbled reporting of internal strife within the Byzantine army and its harmful consequences for the fighting effectiveness of the Byzantines. Azdī especially gives space to such reports of disorderly conduct. The disorderliness mentioned by Azdī and Eutychius reinforces the impression that the Byzantine army was dissolving on the eve of and during the battle, but no one else claims that Vahān was proclaimed emperor in an abortive plot.[55]

Theodore, the brother of Heraclius, reportedly had avoided the battle scene, for Heraclius angrily ordered him taken to Constantinople from Syria. After humiliation at Constantinople, Theodore disappears.[56] His failure, arrest, and disgrace tainted the reputation of the dynasty, imperiled the defense of Syria, but also made it more difficult for Heraclius to find anyone to whom he could delegate military responsibility for the establishment of any new defenses against the Muslims.

The Byzantines did not use allied Arabs as shock troops in the battle of Jābiya-Yarmūk at decisive points. The key desertion of Arabs was by those who were stationed near the bridge over the Ruqqād and between it and the village of Yāqūṣa. The Greek and Armenian troops appear to have been the ones who engaged in the earlier bloody fighting on horse and on foot. The

texts, except by a most liberal reinterpretation of Theophanes' account of Vahān and ascribing it to "George.".

[55] Friction among Armenian troops: De Goeje, *Mémoire*² 114–22. Ibn 'Asākir, *TMD* 1: 541. Later reports of friction between Monophysites and the presumably Monothelite brother of Heraclius, Theodore: Michael the Syrian, *Chronique* 11.5 (2: 418). Fredegarius implies friction in his account of unwillingness of the Byzantine soldiers to engage the Muslims on the decisive morning of battle: *Chron.* 4.66 (153–4 Krusch); Azdī 176–7; Eutychius, *Ann.* (131 Breydy edn, 111 Breydy trans.) on strict discipline of Muslims, under orders from Abū Bakr.

[56] Theoph., *Chron.*, AM 6125 (De Boor 337); Nicephoros, *Hist.* 20 (68–71 Mango). These events may have followed the battle of Ajnādayn. The accounts are muddled. But it appears that Theodore lost favor.

Byzantines probably preferred to avoid the same ethnic group in critical combat situations against their own people (despite the conventional wisdom of using Arabs to fight Arabs).[57] Ibn 'Asākir reports that the Byzantines, on learning that their Christian Arab allies had been defeated, so shouted, and fled. This incident emphasizes the role of volatility and fluctuating loyalties in the battle. Yet there were desertions on the Muslim side as well, as lists of unfaithful tribes demonstrate.[58]

LOGISTICS

The battle of Jābiya-Yarmūk was a rare occasion on which the Byzantines engaged in decisive battle. They generally wished to avoid such engagements. They finally were drawn into a situation where they had to fight, on land that was not to their advantage. Shock was present in the battle, unlike many other ones in which Byzantines participated. This is the rare battle where it is possible to gain some idea – at least according to some Muslim sources – of actual troop movements. It was a battle that can be analyzed in military terms, although there are also unmistakable aspects of military psychology and logistics and military finances involved as well.

The problem of the ration allotments in kind has a possible relationship to the battle of Jābiya-Yarmūk. The Byzantine logistical and financial system required that the Byzantine army move in areas where grain and foodstuffs could be requisitioned by traditional procedures. This required the troops to pass through the Biqā' valley and to encamp on the lush pasturage near the springs of the Golan Heights.[59] The outcome was friction of the Byzantine army with the Syrian population and with Manṣūr at Damascus, and hence the army's own restiveness in the Muslim and Greek accounts.

The Byzantine praetorian prefecture, or whatever vestige had survived it into the 630s, and its deputies, the local officials, had experience with planning supplies for large numbers of Byzantine troops in that area only in 614, when there was a major battle between Adhri'āt and Bostra. The

57 Azdī 176–7. Ibn 'Asākir, *TMD* 1: 534; al-Ṭabarī i 2347, reports desertion of Arab allies of Byzantines. The author of the *Strategikon* advises "Long before battle, troops of the same race as the enemy should be separated from the army and sent elsewhere to avoid their going over to the enemy at a critical moment" 7.15 (69 Dennis trans.). But Lakhm and Judhām abandoned the Muslims: De Goeje, *Mémoire*[2] 114.

58 Ibn 'Asākir, *TMD* 1: 534. For stress on the encouragement of desertion of one's enemies: 'Abd al-Ḥamīd b. Yaḥyā, *Risāla* 4: 531 = Schönig, *Sendschreiben* 71. This passage emphasizes the desirability of encouraging dissension and desertions and switching sides in the warfare of the mid-eighth century, but its advice may have some validity for the conduct of Muslims in encouraging desertion and switching by Arabs who had been allied with the Byzantines.

59 W. E. Kaegi, "The Annona Militaris in the Early Seventh Century," *Byzantina* 13 (1985) 591–6.

numbers of troops who were involved is not known at all. They may have been relatively modest in 614, even though the memory of that battle impressed itself on Arabs in the Arabian peninsula and was recorded in one Muslim tradition. Moreover, that battle involved supplying Byzantine forces who were retreating from the north toward the south. In 636 the praetorian prefecture had to arrange for inexperienced local officials to supply unprecedented numbers of Byzantine forces and their Christian Arab allies who were arriving from the north and proceeding southwards.

The battle of Jābiya-Yarmūk was fought over ground that belonged to two different late Roman provinces, Arabia and Palaestina II. In addition, two other provinces, Phoenice [Paralia] and Phoenice Libanensis, extended very close to the site of fighting and were probably the localities through which some Byzantine armies passed and some supplies were supposed to pass to those armies (Maps 2, 4). This complex of civilian jurisdictions might well have been overridden by emergency military improvisations, but it may nevertheless have complicated the process of communicating with the local population, handling various disputes, and procuring money and supplies. It is impossible to know how well these bureaucracies coordinated their actions in support of the Byzantine armies, but such coordination would have been a considerable challenge.[60]

Most Muslim sources and later Islamic and even Byzantine historians are not aware of late Roman and early Byzantine provincial boundaries and therefore ignore the possible significance of this fact. Indeed, one wonders whether another reason for the site of the battle was the effort to decide the fate of the province. A battle at this site would have immediate consequences for much of the province, especially those areas of it north of the Wādī'l Mūjib. Because the battlefield was part of and adjacent to several provinces, there were complications to supplying the Byzantine troops. It appears that the number of different jurisdictions immensely complicated coordination of supplies and the handling of any disputes or complaints between civilians and troops.

THE TOTALITY OF DEFEAT

There is a strange but not impossible report in the history of al-Ṭabarī and in the *Ta'rīkh Madīnat Dimashq* of Ibn 'Asākir that some Byzantines, including officers, when they perceived that they were defeated, sat down and refused (or were unable) to flee and were slaughtered in place by the

[60] Provincial borders: George of Cyprus, in: *Le Synekdèmos d'Hieroklès et l'opuscule géographique de Georges de Chypre*, ed. and comment. by E. Honigmann (Corpus Bruxellense Historiae Byzantinae, Forma Imperii Byzantini, fasc. 1 [Brussels 1939] 41–5, 66–70 and background, 1–9, 49–50, map IV.

Muslims. It is, if true, indicative of the despair and moral breakdown of the Byzantine army, and consistent with the disintegration of the morale of many of those who managed to flee as far as Ḥimṣ and beyond.[61] Similar psychological phenomena have taken place at major battles elsewhere in other periods.[62] It is symbolic of the magnitude of the defeat. There was a very important psychological dimension to the Byzantine defeat. Such conduct is a true symptom of profound and total defeat and its recognition and acceptance. There is always the possibility, however, that those who sat down expected to be captured as prisoners and possibly later ransomed, a not uncommon practice. If so, they were bitterly and disastrously and fatally deceived. The Muslims took no prisoners at the battle, although they did capture some during the subsequent lengthy pursuit.

The local inhabitants who served in the Byzantine armies at Yarmūk appear to have been the Ghassānids and other Christian Arab tribesmen. Although Heraclius encouraged local inhabitants to try to defend themselves, his intent was probably centered on procuring sufficient manpower to defend walled towns. There is no evidence, for example, that villagers or farmers from the Golan or from the Nāqūra or Adhri'āt or Nawā or any other nearby towns, such as Damascus or Ḥimṣ or Bostra, served in the Byzantine armies that fought at Jābiya-Yarmūk. Nor is there any report of villagers or townspeople from Galilee or the Balqā' serving there as Byzantine soldiers. Vahān's armies probably did include, as some Muslim sources claimed, Armenian and Greek soldiers who were recruited from and who had served in areas that were far away from the eventual battle at Jābiya-Yarmūk.[63]

Heraclius probably received initial reports of the battle's outcome by rapid courier in several days.[64] There is no evidence about the role of any civilians, whether townspeople or farmers, in the vicinity of the battle of the Yarmūk during the course of the fighting. Perhaps the most affected civilians were Ghassānid tribesmen who normally pastured their flocks in the area.

The success of the Byzantine strategy of reliance on walled towns depended on these town garrisons and townspeople holding out long enough for relief armies of mobile troops to strike decisive blows against the

[61] al-Ṭabarī (via Sayf, Abū 'Uthmān Yazīd b. Asīd al-Ghassānī) i 2099–100: Byzantine officers sit down, are slain. Widespread and far flight after the battle: Balādhurī 135.

[62] Cf. the defeat of the Roman army of P. Quinctilius Varus at the battle of the Teutoberg Forest, in AD 9, Cassius Dio, *Historiarum romanarum quae supersunt* 56. 22. 1, ed. by Ph. Boissevain (Berlin: Weidmann, 1898) 2: 534. Broader reflections: Richard A. Holmes, *Acts of War* 213–29, 381–2.

[63] Composition of Byzantine armies at Yarmūk, disparate recruitment: al-Ṭabarī, *Ta'rīkh* i 2081, 2347, 2394; Balādhurī 135, 164, 181–3; Azdī 28, 111, 125, 152, 174–7; Ibn al-Athīr (2: 308, 381 Tornberg).

[64] Azdī 235–7; cf. L. I. Conrad, "al-Azdī's History of the Arab Conquests in Bilād al-Shām: Some Historiographical Observations," 1985 *Bilād al-Shām Proceedings* 1: 28–62.

beduin. That had been the practice in earlier perturbations of beduin in the region on a smaller scale. The failure of that mobile force at Jābiya-Yarmūk exposed the vulnerabilities of the reliance on walled towns, which now could be picked off one by one, given the absence of truly significant numbers of troops in individual towns, and given the difficulties of communications between them as the military situations worsened. The failure also exposed the Byzantines' fallacious assumption that they were dealing with mere beduin, rather than the coordinated army of a new state.[65] That is a reason for the subsequent rapid surrender of so many of the remaining towns of Syria to the Muslims.

The role of Niketas, son of Shahrbaraz the Persian general, at the battle of Jābiya-Yarmūk is uncertain. It does appear that he was a rival of Trithurios and Vahān. He attempted to join the Muslims after they overtook him and some other fleeing Byzantine commanders and troops in the vicinity of Emesa/Ḥimṣ. Niketas' fluctuating loyalties may indicate that he did not resolutely fight at the battle of Jābiya-Yarmūk, but it is dangerous to claim that he betrayed the Byzantines. The exact character of the soldiers whom he commanded is likewise unknown.[66]

Some Christian sources speak of sand or quicksand at the battle of the Yarmūk.[67] It is quite possible that there was a severe duststorm at the time of the battle. Dust devils are a common occurrence throughout modern Jordan and southern Syria.[68] But the putative area of the battle is not desert and it is not covered with deep sand. There is soil, and it can be very dry in the month of August. But one should be cautious about chroniclers' claims that the Byzantine forces were overcome by sand. The terrain is just not of that type. The chroniclers may simply be imagining what kind of territory Arabs might prefer for battle, or they may have heard stories from defeated Byzantines who were trying to explain away their defeat by blaming the nature of the terrain and local conditions.

The Pseudo-Methodius *Apocalypse*, which was very probably written in upper Mesopotamia, in the Syriac language, in any case sometime between 650 and 690, is one of the oldest texts that mention the battle of the Yarmūk, although it refers to Gabitha or Jābiya. Its Syriac author "predicts" of the

65 Donner, *EIC* 48–9.

66 Niketas fled to Ḥimṣ, is slain: Michael the Syrian, *Chronique* 11.6 (2: 421 Chabot); C. Mango, "Deux Etudes sur Byzance et la Perse Sassanide," *TM* 9 (1985) 105–18. But Speck, *Das geteilte Dossier* 317–50, for skepticism about Theophanes' account of Niketas and his father Shahrbaraz.

67 Sebēos, *Hist.* (125 Bedrosian) and c. 30 (97 Macler); Theoph., *Chron.*, AM 6126 (337–8 De Boor). This may also be a distorting of a lost "eastern source" for both Muslim and Christian extant historical accounts, which may have spoken of a foggy day.

68 I have myself seen swirls of dust in late August (in 1984) near Ramtha, which is not far from the place of the battle.

Byzantines "so they will be destroyed in Geb'ut by Ishmael, the wild ass of the desert, who will be sent with fierce anger against [the whole earth:] men, wild animals, domestic animals, and even trees and plants."[69] It corroborates the statement of Ibn 'Asākir that the Muslims first concentrated at Jābiya. This appears to be the reason why the battle is often called that of Gabitha or Jābiya by the Christian authors of Syrian origin, and those other historians, such as Theophanes, who drew on such traditions.

The Greek Pseudo-Methodius' statement that the Byzantine commanders will fall into the mouth of the sword of the Muslims at the battleground may be nothing more than a literary phrase, but "fall" here can imply that they were drawn into the trap that Ibn 'Asākir mentions in his *Ta'rīkh madīnat Dimashq*. Yet Pseudo-Methodius' reference to the battle is very brief so the modern researcher should use caution in using this admittedly early text.[70]

BYZANTINE FLIGHT

It is erroneous to assume that it was absolutely impossible for any of the defeated Byzantines to escape from the triangle of land between the Wādī'l Allān and Wādī'l Ruqqād, or for anyone near Yāqūṣa to escape from the Muslims who attacked it from the east. It is possible for individuals to climb up and down the heights on both sides.[71] Some Byzantine soldiers could have fled through the gorge after descending the heights. Yet they may have known that it was theoretically scalable from certain points and not realized how dangerous it was at other points or at night.

In all likelihood those taking flight in this way would have lost their mounts and the weapons, and armor, or anything else that was heavy. But if

[69] Francisco Javier Martinez, "Eastern Christian Apocalyptic Tradition in the Early Muslim Period" (unpub. Ph. D. diss., Catholic University, 1985) 140, and comment. on pp. 186–7, accepts Kmosko's identification of Geb'ut Ramta with Jābiya, but does not understand how the entire region between Jābiya and Ramtha was the scene of the battlefield of the Yarmūk battle. The Syriac text correlates with information that Ibn 'Asākir gives. Cf. Harald Suermann, *Die geschichtstheologische Reaktion auf die einfallenden Muslime in der edessenischen Apokalyptik des 7. Jahrhunderts* (Frankfurt, Bern, New York: Peter Lang, 1985) 60–3; on p. 60, n. 322, he accepts identification of Gabaoth with "Stadt Gabitha beim Fluss Yarmūk"; Suermann, 159–61, dates Pseudo-Methodius between 644 and 674.

[70] Pseudo-Methodius, *Die Apokalypse*, Lolos edn., implies that the Muslims drew the Byzantines into a trap: 11.3 (96–7 Lolos); also, A. Lolos, ed., *Die dritte und vierte Redaktion des Ps.-Methodios* 11.3, in: Beiträge zur klassischen Philologie, H. 94 (Meisenheim am Glan 1978) 40–2. Theoph., *Chron.*, AM 6126 (337–8 De Boor). On Pseudo-Methodius, Paul J. Alexander, *The Byzantine Apocalyptic Tradition* (Berkeley 1985) 13–60; F. J. Martinez, "Eastern Christian Apocalyptic Tradition." On trapping the Byzantines: Ibn 'Asākir, *TMD* 1: 532–4, 549. al-Ṭabarī i 2088. Michael the Syrian, *Chronique* 11.6 (2: 420–1 Chabot).

[71] Professor Yūsuf Ghawanmā, of Yarmūk University, who had done so as a child from the Jordanian village of Saḥam on the southern side of the Yarmūk gorge, so informed me.

the Muslims were then in firm control of Gadara, they could have made it very difficult for more than a few to escape following the Yarmūk gorge. It appears that many were not trapped in the triangle but somehow fled toward Ḥimṣ, in the hopes of security or at least finding a point from which they could make their way more securely to the more familiar north.[72]

The Byzantines indubitably suffered the heaviest casualties, probably in the thousands, but the list of Muslim dead is also long. The battle's bloody character left a long imprint in the memory of both Byzantine and Muslim. In order to appreciate the magnitude of Yarmūk, one must look at how many Byzantine commanders fell or disappeared and at estimates of their losses of men. Only then can one turn to look at the actual strategic situation and its transformation as a result of the battle.[73] There are conflicting reports about the ultimate fate of Vahān – whether he fell on the battlefield, or whether, out of humiliation and shame at defeat he became a monk on Mt. Sinai, or whether he was pursued as far as Ḥimṣ, where he was overtaken and slain. In any case, he ceased to command.[74]

Many of the substantial number of Byzantine casualties at the battle of Jābiya-Yarmūk were suffered when the Byzantines lost cohesion and those who could then fled in scattered directions, no longer maintaining any rational discipline and order. This was the moment of the greatest human losses. Such proportions of losses have not been uncommon in other battles – that is, the greatest portion of loss took place when the losing side broke ranks and fled pell-mell, thereby no longer putting up serious resistance, and thus exposing themselves to the assaults of their foes. Troops are most vulnerable when they flee in disorder without maintaining a firm resistance, for even when retreating they can best protect themselves and hold down losses by keeping order and resisting.

One reason for the decisiveness of Jābiya-Yarmūk was the rapidity, thoroughness, ruthlessness, relentlessness, and determination with which the Muslims exploited their victory.[75] The Byzantines, by Muslim accounts, had no time to recover immediately following the battle. The Muslims maintained their organization, followed closely, and hunted down those who fled in every locality until they pursued them to Damascus and beyond to

[72] I visited the Jordanian side of the gorge in October, 1983, with the generous assistance of Professor Ghawanmā and Yarmūk University. I again visited the southern heights overlooking the Yarmūk near the village of Hartha, which is slightly east of Saḥam, on 24 March 1985.

[73] Bloodiness of the battle: Ibn 'Asākir, *TMD* 1: 542, 544; Azdī 230–1; Theoph., *Chron.*, AM 6126 (337–8 De Boor); al-Ṭabarī i 2091, 2099, 2104; Balādhurī 135; Fredegarius, *Chron.* 4.66 (153–4 Krusch). Anas. Sinait. *Sermo Adversus Monotheletas* 3 (60 Uthemann).

[74] Ibn A'tham al-Kūfī 1; 269–70. Eutychius, *Ann.* 279 (136–7 Breydy edn, 116 Breydy trans.).

[75] Carl von Clausewitz, *On War*, book 4. ch. 12, P. Paret trans. (Princeton 1978) p. 267 = *Vom Kriege* 480–1 W. Hahlweg ed.; cf. Clausewitz, 265 Paret and 474 Hahlweg.

Ḥimṣ. They did not halt after the battle to relax or quarrel over the booty. They concentrated on sound military goals, the destruction of the remaining Byzantine forces as organized armies, and only then worried about conquering and organizing rich lands and towns. These actions transformed what was merely a great victory into a very decisive one, and one of the worst of all Byzantine military disasters.[76] Only north of Ḥimṣ, in northern Syria, did the Byzantines have a chance to begin to regroup what was left of their shattered forces.[77]

One column under 'Iyāḍ b. Ghanm pursued the Byzantines as far as Melitēnē, which he captured, some 800 kilometers north of the battleground: "And when the Byzantines were defeated, Abū 'Ubayda sent 'Iyāḍ b. Ghanm in pursuit of them. He followed them passing through al-A'māq [district near Dabiq, between Aleppo and Antioch in northern Syria] until he reached Malatya. He made a treaty with its inhabitants for the payment of the head-tax [*jizya*] and he returned. When Heraclius heard about this he sent to his military forces and their commander and ordered them to Malatya. On Heraclius' orders Malatya was burned." A pursuit this far indicates how totally broken the Byzantines' order was immediately following the battle of Jābiya-Yarmūk. Yet this advance column was not followed up, because 'Iyāḍ b. Ghanm evacuated Melitēnē after giving terms to it, and Heraclius, who was furious that it surrendered, had it destroyed in order to punish its inhabitants and to deny it to the Muslims. The pursuit made it very difficult to defend other towns in Syria and Palestine immediately after the battle of Jābiya-Yarmūk.[78]

The Muslim military leadership showed strategic and military sense; they adhered to military priorities. There is an underlying military logic to the Muslim operations that immediately followed or developed out of the battle of Jābiya-Yarmūk.

[76] Proper pursuit of a fleeing enemy: 'Abd al-Ḥamīd b. Yaḥyā, *Risāla* 4: 526 = Schönig, *Sendschreiben* 66.

[77] Kūfī 1: 270. al-Ṭabarī i 2104, i 2349. Michael the Syrian, *Chronique* (2: 42 1 Chabot). Balādhurī 135.

[78] al-Ṭabarī (Ibn Isḥāq) i 2349. C.-P. Haase, *Untersuchungen zur Landschaftsgeschichte Nordsyriens in der Umayyadenzeit* (diss., University of Hamburg, 1972, publ. Kiel 1975) 27, accepts the genuineness of this tradition of the pursuit to Melitēnē, as does Nadine F. Posner, "The Muslim Conquest of Northern Mesopotamia: An Introductory Essay into Its Historical Background and Historiography" (unpub. Ph.D. diss., Dept. Near Eastern Languages and Literatures, New York University, 1985) 249–51. Both Caetani, *AI*, and De Goeje thought that this tradition was plausible, although they did not discuss it in detail, or the implications of it for interpreting other aspects of the conquests.

THE MAGNITUDE OF THE MUSLIM VICTORY

A late seventh-century observer, St. Anastasius the Sinaite, testified to the importance of the battle of Jābiya-Yarmūk as "the first and fearful and incurable fall of the Roman [Byzantine] army, I mean the bloodshed at Gabitha [Jābiya] and Yarmūk."[79] A few decades after the battle Byzantines looked back to it as the turning point, after which full recovery was out of the question.

The Byzantine commanders had no good fall-back position at Jābiya-Yarmūk other than their camp, which was stormed at a decisive point in the battle. This is surprising because all agree that the armies of both sides were massed in the vicinity of the battle for some time before coming to combat. There was plenty of time to have thought out the alternatives, including means of escape. It appears that the Byzantine commanders had not anticipated a major defeat here, which is normal, for otherwise they would not have allowed their soldiers to risk battle here. The battle took on entirely unanticipated dimensions.

The Byzantine traditions of the battle of Jābiya-Yarmūk implicitly absolve Heraclius of any responsibility for the debacle. Instead, they lay responsibility at the feet of the weather or alien ethnics, namely, the Armenians, or the Byzantine commanders who failed to follow the wise advice of Heraclius. It was necessary to shift any blame away from the reigning emperor or his dynasty. That tendency has complicated understanding the actual battle. The conclusion that one gains from reading the Muslim sources is that responsibility lies with Byzantine military leadership. On the other hand, they impute many positive qualities to the Muslim leadership and to the zeal and steadfastness of their soldiers and accompanying civilians, especially courageous women.[80]

There is an asymmetry in the Christian and Muslim descriptions of the battle. Christians attempted to emphasize that it was not a glorious military victory for the Muslims but one that they obtained through stealth and deceit rather than through honest martial success. The Muslims stressed that it was a decisive battle, one in which intelligence was used but also one in which Muslim valor and moral force were decisive. Again, the brief Christian explanations appear to have been part of an effort to apologize for the disaster and to deflect criticism from the military performance of the Byzantines, especially away from any responsibility of the reigning Emperor

[79] Anastasius the Sinaite, *Sermo adversus Monotheletas* 3.1.86–8 (60 Uthemann); Theoph., *Chron.*, AM 6121 (332 De Boor).

[80] Ch. 1, above and *Cont. Byz. Arab.*, MGHAA 11: 336–7 = *Crónica mozárabe de* 754 (30–1 López Pereira); Theoph., *Chron.*, AM 6126 (337–8 De Boor). Divine wrath: Fredegarius, *Chron.* 4.66 (154 Krusch).

Heraclius himself. Yet there is an irony here, because the Byzantines, if anyone, were supposed to excel at the use of cleverness in warfare. If anything, the lesson drawn is that the Byzantines were not sufficiently clever and perceptive in contriving the ways in which they fought against the Muslims at the battle of Jābiya-Yarmūk.[81]

There is no evidence that the Byzantines tried to convert any Muslims or Muslim commanders at the battle, but there were communications with the probable intent to corrupt the Muslim leadership or to cause its tribal groups to disintegrate by encouraging rivalries and by taking advantage of fluctuating loyalties. Only the Muslim sources give evidence of any religious polemics that might be intended to convert anyone. References in the sources to the religious chants of the Muslims at the battle of the Yarmūk are a reminder that the religious emotions of the Muslims and their degree of religious commitment should not be underestimated. Many Muslims at that battle were religiously motivated. Christian monks and presumably other clergy reportedly accompanied the Byzantine armies and attempted to increase their morale.[82] Yet there is no evidence that Byzantine soldiers who were captured were required to convert.

During the protracted period before the battle the Byzantines appear to have tried to use more traditional means of corrupting threatening barbarian leaders and their armed followers. It is not clear how seriously the Byzantines took the religious impulse among the Muslims and the Muslim leadership at that relatively early date. They had reportedly already known enough about it at the battle of Mu'ta for one Byzantine commander to try to exploit it for timing an attack on the Muslims. But at Jābiya-Yarmūk the Byzantines did not find any way to exploit Muslim religious proclivities to their own advantage. For that matter, they did not find it elsewhere.

The transmission of local traditions about the battle of the Yarmūk in both Syria and Jordan is obscure. Have they appeared recently, as a local response or assimilation of what learned or unlearned visitors have told or asked people, or are they truly indigenous? Some Jordanian traditions from the village of Hartha include a belief that a certain hill in present-day Jordan was the site from which Khālid b. al-Walīd viewed the battle, as well as that another hill was the site for massing certain troops. In Syria, there is a tradition of a hill "Tall al-Jumū'a," the hill of the gathering, where the Muslims allegedly gathered for their battle against the Byzantines (it, at least, is near the Roman road that goes to the critical bridge over the Wādī'l

81 *Cont. Byz. Arab.* reports cautionary advice of Heraclius, apparently from some ultimate Byzantine or Syriac source: MGHAA 11: 336–7 = *Crónica mozárabe de* 754 c. 8 (stealth: 28–9, warning of Heraclius: c. 9, 30–1 López Pereira).

82 al-Ṭabarī i 2089; Irfan Shahid, "Asrār al-naṣr al-'arabī fī futūḥ al-Shām," 1985 *Bilād al-Shām Proceedings* : 137–47.

Ruqqād). These traditions deserve to be collected, recorded, and evaluated for any possible historical value, but a skeptical attitude is warranted unless they conform to topographic realities and to the facts as the literary histories report them.[83]

The battle of Jābiya-Yarmūk was a turning point in the history of Byzantine warfare. Yet Byzantine traditional tactics and techniques and procedures had failed in a battle that had a long period of advance preparation, in which supposedly many alternative courses of action and many potential courses of action by their opponent had been weighed. Other means of warfare had to be explored when these had so dismally and emphatically failed. The Byzantines needed to find ways to defeat the Muslims, yet they lacked the time to develop the means to fight the Muslims in open or rolling country of the kind where they had just lost the battle of the Yarmūk. Such terrain, although much of it was much more poorly watered, stretched far to the north in Syria. All of this was so exposed that it had to be evacuated. The Byzantines reinforced their propensity to want strong cover and fixed positions which had already emerged in their stress on the defense of walled towns.

What is striking is that, despite all of the warnings in the contemporary and preceding military literature about the danger of being lured into traps by the enemy's feigned flight, this happened again at the battle. Perhaps the relatively vast amount of space over which this battle was fought contributed to the success of the Muslims' trap. It marked the death-knell of Byzantine search-and-destroy operations, for a long time. Henceforth the Byzantines attempted to avoid more such decisive tests on the battlefield, both because they lacked the manpower and will for such combat, and because they generally preferred other means of struggle than direct combat. It marked a turning point, and was so recognized by both sides and later historians of both sides. Yet no new tactics or weapons or technology emerged there. While it did force the Byzantines to avoid fighting out in the open, whenever possible, for a long time, that decision essentially reinforced already existing proclivities among the Byzantines. No Muslim or Byzantine historian even wrote a detailed description of the battle and the respective maneuvers of the generals of each side as an example of what to do and what not to do for any future battles or campaigning.

The battle of Jābiya-Yarmūk was the climactic battle in a series of battles in the Muslim conquest. Muslim sources mark many aspects of the conquest

[83] I visited the village of Hartha in 1987. Caetani, *AI* 3: 512, mentions, without comment, the location of Tall al-Jumū'a; he does not place it on his maps with an identification, although he clearly shows it unidentified. "Tall al-Jumū'a" is marked as "Tell ej Jemûah" on Sheet 7, *PEF Palestine*. It is located about two and one-half miles southwest of Nawā. Thus it was known before Caetani visited the vicinity of the battlefield a few years later.

in terms of battles, *waqaʿāt*, thereby emphasizing the military dimension and indicating their assumption that battles were very important. Yet there has been a tendency in some modern discussion and historiography, some of this oral discussion rather than published histories, to assume that there "must be" some other more profound explanation than warfare for these events. There is, then, a refusal or disinclination to accept the possibility of the importance of military causation. This is part of broader historiographical trends outside of Byzantine and Islamic history. Yet at Jābiya-Yarmūk the fate of Byzantine rule in Syria and Palestine, and perhaps of Transjordania as well, was hanging in the balance. Historians both Byzantine and Islamic are correct to assign great importance to this battle, even though there were necessarily other factors that contributed to the lack of Byzantine military cohesion at the battle of Jābiya-Yarmūk, and that lack of cohesion, reinforced by tensions with the local population, rivalries of Byzantine commanders, and logistical problems, all contributed to the ultimate disastrous outcome of the battle. Yet it was the actual combat there that in the final analysis was decisive – not the other factors.

BREAKTHROUGH AND THE IMMINENCE OF COLLAPSE

The Byzantine debacle at the battle of the Jābiya-Yarmūk ripped apart Byzantine defenses. Yet at the end of the battle the richest cities of Syria still remained in Byzantine hands, along with the most agriculturally productive and therefore tax-revenue producing regions. Most of the population of Syria still lay outside of Muslim control. The most important cultural centers of Syria, such as Antioch and Edessa in the north, were far removed from the scene of that battle. The ports of Syria and Palestine still remained in Byzantine hands. The inhabitants of these urban and rural areas, however, had no real training in defending themselves. Material resources still abounded, but the Byzantines lacked the human resources or the will to reverse the military situation.

Those Byzantine soldiers and commanders who escaped destruction at the battle of Jābiya-Yarmūk followed one of several options: (1) some Christian Arab tribes negotiated with and joined the Muslim forces, although not necessarily converting to Islam; (2) many soldiers and commanders simply fled north as fast as they could, following the principal direct roads north in the direction of Antioch, Edessa, and even to Melitēnē (modern Turkish Malatya); (3) some disgraced commanders and possibly some soldiers as well sought refuge in monasteries; (4) some soldiers, although it is difficult to ascertain their units and provenance, remained or sought refuge as members of garrisons of Syrian towns who either offered temporary resistance or sought to negotiate the surrender of their walled towns.

The Byzantine defeat at Jābiya-Yarmūk resulted in a military rout and a situation that was extremely fluid. All reliable calculations were in suspense. No modern media were present to record and probe the dimensions of the military collapse. Although some of the Syrian population, especially the Melkites, departed, there is no evidence for mass flight of the indigenous Syrian population. They may have experienced panic, but to judge from the sources, the greatest levels of panic gripped the Byzantine military. The means do not exist to measure that in neat quantifiable proportions, but the obvious symptom of it was the disappearance of any coherent defense and defensive line after the battle of Jābiya-Yarmūk. It was probably a combination of panic and paralysis.

Byzantine soldiers with good reason did not wish to find themselves cut off from escape far from more familiar territory in northern Syria, and Asia Minor. Having lost the topographic advantages of the Yarmūk River and Golan Heights areas, and badly shaken by their losses at Jābiya-Yarmūk, they probably had little relish for trying to make another stand in southern Syria. Even more important, their commanders did not attempt to create another defensive line below or just north of Damascus. That would not have been easy in any case. The efforts of individual walled towns, such as Damascus and Baʿlabakk, to hold out while their surrounding countryside was overrun were fated to be shortlived.

When a military front collapses it is natural for the leadership of the collapsing front to follow several courses of action: (1) seek a cease-fire; (2) replace commanders with new and more competent ones, or who at least are believed to have credibility with the soldiers, civilians, and the government; (3) reshuffle political leadership; (4) issue calls for more troops and recruits; (5) perhaps make emergency decrees to cope with a crisis situation to try to stabilize it; and (6) raise more funds to meet the emergency in different ways.

Byzantium, however, in 636 and the following years never became completely numb or inert because of Jābiya-Yarmūk. It was a thorough and catastrophic defeat, but it did not result in total defeat and overthrow. Territorial depth helped the Byzantines to trade territory for time to regroup and stabilize, but it was not the full explanation.

Even the negotiations and scattered resistance by garrisons and inhabitants of a few walled towns, e.g., Caesarea Maritima, helped to tie down Muslim forces and prevent them from concentrating on following the Byzantine forces north. That was, certainly, a very expensive trade: rich ports, cities, and fields of Syria in return for more time for the Byzantines to regroup, muster, and establish a defensive line or even counterattack.

EPILOGUE

Byzantine towns, cities, and countryside in Syria and Palestine reached arrangements with the Muslims after the battle of Jābiya-Yarmūk. Some cities, such as Damascus, fell rapidly. Others, such as Ascalon, Gaza, and Caesarea Maritima, held out for a while. Inland cities fell first to the Muslims after the battle. No unusual strategic or tactical innovations are present. There was no coherent Byzantine defense of Syria or Palestine after Jābiya-Yarmūk.[84]

A tentative chronology of some aspects of the Muslim occupation of the remainder of Palestine and Syria includes the following landmarks: the surrender of Damascus, in late 636 or early 637, to the Muslims, followed by the Muslim occupation of Ba'labakk and the Biqā' valley, and the surrender of Ḥimṣ (Emesa) sometime in 637. Jerusalem yielded to the Muslims also sometime in 637, as did Gaza, at the end of June or in early July, 637. The first surrender of Ascalon may have taken place in the summer of 637. In late 637 the Byzantines and Muslims consented to a truce at Qinnasrīn (Chalkis), after the defeat and death of the Byzantine General Menas. At the end of that truce, in 638, the Muslims occupied the remaining parts of northern Syria, including Antioch, Cyrrhus, Manbij (Hierapolis), Aleppo (Berrhoia) without encountering further armed resistance. Sometime in 638 Caliph 'Umar visited Jābiya and disposed of conquered properties and reorganized Muslim administrative structures in Syria. The Byzantine–Muslim truce continued to hold for Mesopotamia during 638. The Byzantine evacuation of fortifications northwest of Antioch on orders of Heraclius constituted the beginning of the creation of an empty zone or no man's land in 638 and 639. Meanwhile the Byzantines were regrouping in Anatolia. The Muslim conquest of Byzantine Syria terminated with their conquest of coastal cities, including Caesarea (640), followed by Beirut, Gabala, and Laodicea (al-Lādhiqiyya).

The reduction of these areas presented no special problems. There was no coherent Byzantine defense strategy for these posts, except to try to hold on to whatever was possible. This was a reasonable strategy if military relief could have come, but in the absence of it, hopes faded away as well as the will to resist. No Byzantine primary sources provide any clear historical understanding of these final moments of the Byzantine presence in Syria. The catalogue of these events underscores the decisiveness of the battle of Jābiya-Yarmūk.

84 The exact chronology is admittedly controversial. I have synthesized Christian and Muslim sources in determining this sequence of dates. I have omitted detailed citation of primary sources here to save space.

Chapter 7

THE BRIEF STRUGGLE TO SAVE NORTHERN SYRIA AND BYZANTINE MESOPOTAMIA

THE BYZANTINE ROUT AND DILEMMAS OF DEFENSE IN NORTHERN SYRIA AND MESOPOTAMIA

Byzantine flight after Jābiya-Yarmūk was understandable. As Clausewitz observed:

> When a battle is lost, the strength of the army is broken – its moral even more than its physical strength. A second battle without the help of new and favorable factors would mean outright defeat, perhaps even absolute destruction. That is a military axiom. It is in the nature of things that a retreat should be continued until the balance of power is reestablished – whether by means of reinforcements or the cover of strong fortresses or major natural obstacles or the overextension of the enemy. The magnitude of the losses, the extent of the defeat, and, what is even more important, the nature of the enemy, will determine how soon the moment of equilibrium will return.[1]

Among the many problems of historical explanation of the Muslim conquest of Byzantine territories in the seventh century is one that has been neglected: that is the role of Byzantine forces in northern Syria and Byzantine Mesopotamia after the battle of Jābiya-Yarmūk.[2] Mesopotamia here refers to areas now in northern Syria east of the Euphrates or in Turkey east of the Euphrates and, of course, west of the Tigris, in Arabic the Jazīra. It comprised the provinces of Osrhoene and Mesopotamia in sixth- and seventh-century Byzantine nomenclature,[3] and such cities as Callinicum

[1] Clausewitz, *On War*, book 4, ch. 13 (271 Paret) = *Vom Kriege* (486 Hahlweg).

[2] On region in later era: Michael Bonner, "The Emergence of the Thughūr: The Arab–Byzantine Frontier in the Early 'Abbāsid Age" (Unpub. Ph.D. diss., Princeton University, 1987).

[3] L. Dillemann, *Haute Mésopotamie orientale et pays adjacents. Contribution à la géographie historique de la région, du Ve s. avant l'ère chrétienne au VIe de cette ère* (Institut français d'archéologie de Beyrouth, Bibliothèque archéologique et historique, T. 72 [Paris: Geuthner, 1962]) esp. pp. 129–94 on roads, and pp. 198–240; Isaac, *Limits of Empire* 249–68, on the history of frontiers during Roman rule.

(Raqqa), Edessa (Urfa, al-Ruhā'), Monokarton, Amida (Diyarbekir), Dara, and Mardes (Mardin), as well as the Ṭūr 'Abdīn region (Map 3).[4]

al-Ṭabarī, repeating the tradition of Sayf b. 'Umar, plausibly states that Heraclius departed from Syria by way of Edessa and then Samosata, before proceeding to Constantinople.[5] Heraclius did visit Osrhoene; Edessa was the city that Heraclius needed to hold for a while to permit his Armenian troops to withdraw properly from Syria.[6] al-Ṭabarī's statement concerning Heraclius' departure from Syria via Edessa and Samosata (and not directly through the Cilician Gates from Antioch) may well be authentic. Heraclius does appear to have been trying to stabilize the military situation southeast of the Taurus Mountains before proceeding onto the Anatolian plateau and on to the Asian shores of the Bosphorus; he was not fleeing pell-mell after the defeat of his armies at the Yarmūk. The precise chronology is unclear.[7]

Reports of Heraclius' order for the recovery and destruction of Melitēnē (Malatya) and for implementation of a scorched-earth policy near Antioch and Cilicia indicate that he continued to try to build up defenses at the outer edge of Asia Minor and that he was not medically or mentally incapacitated soon after the battle of Yarmūk. Heraclius' anger at the *curator* John of Kateas' willingness to arrange a truce with the Muslims and his deposition and replacement by a more forceful military commander are consistent with the vigorous efforts reportedly made by Heraclius elsewhere to try to harden resistance and even to launch counterattacks.[8]

Heraclius did not attempt to defend Antioch more vigorously against the Muslims, although some might argue that if his motive were to stall the Muslims, prolonged resistance at Antioch might have served his purposes better than trying to hold exposed Mesopotamia. Antioch's retention would not have helped to spare his Armenians and Armenia very much. Heraclius could not, moreover, afford to lose large numbers of able-bodied men after Yarmūk in bloody struggles to hold some cities. Such men would have risked being encircled and bypassed and unable to assist the defense of Anatolia.

[4] For the situation in the year 600, best is George of Cyprus, *Le Synekdèmos d'Hieroklès et l'opuscule géographique de George de Chypre*, ed., trans., and comment. by E. Honigmann, 63–4; for *Synekdèmos*, p. 40; E. Honigmann, *Die Ostgrenze des byzantinischen Reiches von 363 bis 1071* (Corpus Bruxellense Historiae Byzantinae, 3 [Brussels 1935, repr. 1961]) 22–37.

[5] al-Ṭabarī i 2390–1. Azdī 237. Ibn al-Athīr (2: 384 Tornberg).

[6] J. B. Segal, *Edessa, the Blessed City* (Oxford: Clarendon Press, 1970).

[7] Donner, *EIC* 150. Kaegi, "Heraklios and the Arabs," *Greek Orthodox Theological Review* 27 (1982) esp. 119–29.

[8] al-Ṭabarī i 2349. Balādhurī 164. Michael the Syrian, *Chron.* 11.7 (2: 424 Chabot). On the route from Egypt to Melitēnē, see the schematization by K. Miller, *Itineraria romana*, ser. 98, on pp. 680–4. Theoph., *Chron.*, A. M. 6128 (340 De Boor). On alleged illness of Heraclius, Nicephorus, *Hist.* 24–5. 27 (72, 77 Mango). Kaegi, "Heraklios and the Arabs" 119–21.

Previous Byzantine immobilization in lower Syrian cities may have convinced him and his advisers of the risks that were inherent in committing large numbers of his diminishing supply of good soldiers to the defense of such large towns in relatively exposed military situations. There was more to be lost than gained in defending Antioch to the last man. He did not wish to risk another bloody encounter south of the Taurus Mountains. He sought to trade space to cut the rate of attrition of his forces and permit their survival and recuperation.

After the rout of Byzantine armies at the battle of the Yarmūk in 636, and their evacuation of Syria, Mesopotamia remained for a short time under Byzantine control and protruded in an overextended fashion into areas already conquered by the Muslims in Syria and Iraq until the Muslims under ʻIyāḍ b. Ghanm al-Fihrī overran it, others having already seized Iraq.[9] With so many questions remaining concerning the details and chronology of the Byzantine loss of Palestine, Syria, and Egypt, one may ask, why concern oneself with the details of the defense and loss of that southeasternmost Byzantine territorial outpost of the late 630s? In fact, the question of the defense of Byzantine Mesopotamia helps to illuminate larger questions of Byzantine priorities in trying to save the empire and find a way to halt the Muslims, as well as give the reader an understanding of broader issues of the survival of Byzantine authority in Asia Minor and its dissolution elsewhere.[10]

Mesopotamia had been one of the most troublesome regions for military unrest in the sixth and seventh centuries. Because of its strategic importance for defense against attack from Persia, it had always been heavily garrisoned, and special efforts were made to assure stocks of essential military supplies there.[11] Having passed through it more than once during and at the conclusion of his campaign against the Persians, Heraclius had occasions to appreciate its strategic importance and any local problems.[12]

[9] Balādhurī 172–7; al-Tabarī i 2505–9. Caetani, *AI* 4: 36–48. M. Cheïra, *La Lutte entre arabes et byzantins. La Conquête et l'organisation des frontières aux VIIe et VIIIe siècles* (Alexandria 1947) 47–50, on the conquest of Mesopotamia.

[10] On ʻIyāḍ b. Ghanm's campaigns: Theoph., *Chron.*, A. M 6128 (340 De Boor).

[11] *Just. Nov.* 134.1. *ND* Or. 35 (75–6 Seeck) on *dux Osrhoenae*; Or. 36 for *dux Mesopotamiae* (77–9 Seeck). Military unrest: Kaegi, *BMU* 64–88.

[12] Sebēos, *Histoire* c. 29 (116–17 Bedrosian, 91 Macler). Michael the Syrian, *Chronique* 11.3 (2: 410–12 Chabot). Ibn Khaldūn, vol. 12: 461 (Beirut edn, 1956). Stratos, Βυζάντιον 2: 647–52, 749. Azdī 237; al-Ṭabarī i 2391. Background: H. Manandian, "Marshrut'i persidskich pochodov imperatora Irakliy," *VV* 3 (1950) 144–6. Heraclius leaves for synod at Theodosiopolis, *La narratio de rebus Armeniae* 121, ed. by Gérard Garitte (CSCO, Subsidia, T. 4 [Louvain 1952]) 43. Date 632 or 633: Garitte, pp. 302–4; Stratos, Βυζάντιον 2: 750. Stratos, Βυζάντιον 2: 685–7, for Heraclius' travels in Mesopotamia (Manbij, Aleppo, *èn route* to Theodosiopolis) after visiting Jerusalem early in 630. Also, *Acta M. Anastasii Persae* (12.21a–26b Usener). Heraclius passed through Amida (Diyarbekir) and probably via Samosata and the Taurus passes on returning from campaigning in 624: Stratos, Βυζάντιον 1: 436–49.

The River Khābūr marked part of Byzantium's frontier with Persia, yet it was no impenetrable barrier. There are no reports of any tight patrolling or garrisoning of it against Muslim invasion from Iraq, but that eventuality never took place. Circesium marked the southeastern limits of the empire along the Euphrates, at the point at which the Khābūr flowed into it. The Khābūr was a valuable source of water for those who crossed the Euphrates. They could follow it to its sources at Rās al-'Ayn (Theodosiopolis) and beyond. Even the Euphrates was more of a marker than a real barrier, for it has some fords that are passable by men and horses. However, it was possible to string out manpower along the whole exposed length of the Euphrates and the Khābūr: such a defense would have been vulnerable because of the difficulty of rushing a mobile reserve to any crossing point: the rivers could be a trap for the defender.[13]

It was natural for the Muslims, having conquered Syria and Iraq, to wish to eradicate that salient or bulge of Byzantine Mesopotamia, which, theoretically at least, threatened the easiest and most convenient communication between Syria and Iraq. Its conquest was a prudent step in the consolidation of an empire. For Byzantium it was an agriculturally fertile and a rich province worth retaining.

Some facts are simple to understand. Byzantine retention of Mesopotamia first compelled Muslims in Syria and Iraq to divert troops from some other potential target, in particular Anatolia. Secondly, it helped to retain a forward base that could serve as a springboard for any possible Byzantine counteroffensive to recover territory lost to the Muslims, or for any attempt to make a joint counteroffensive in coordination with remaining Sassanian Persians, given Heraclius' recent good relations with Persians after the end of the long Byzantino-Persian War. Thirdly, it partially protected the Byzantine Empire's Armenian territories, which were valuable recruiting grounds for Heraclius' soldiers and commanders, from Muslim invasion and occupation. It was not clear that the Muslims would be able to consolidate their hold on Syria, and retention of Mesopotamia provided a good Byzantine listening post and a place from which either an attack or dissension could be spread among the inhabitants of the newly occupied territories. Fourthly, that retention of Mesopotamia could affect recruitment among Arab tribesmen for Heraclius' armies; he had used them extensively in the 620s for his successful comeback against the Persians. In addition to eliminating the Byzantine bulge or threat to Muslim communications, the Muslim conquest of Mesopotamia contributed to the elimination of any remaining trouble-

[13] "Ein höchst gefährliches Unternehmen," Carl von Clausewitz, *Vom Kriege*, ed. by Werner Hahlweg, 18th edn (Bonn: F. Dümmlers Verlag, 1973) 735.

some Persian resistance, helped to consolidate control of Iraq, and finally was indeed the necessary prelude to any effort to overrun the four Byzantine provinces of Armenia and thereby deny Heraclius access to Armenian recruits.[14]

Additional considerations resulted from the complex situation east and west of the Khābūr after the Persians capitulated in 628. The Persians did not fight extensively against the Byzantines in Byzantine Mesopotamia, as far as extant sources indicate. The apparent absence of a decisive battle there may have contributed to Heraclius' relative neglect of its military significance after his reoccupation of the region following the withdrawal of the Persian armies from Byzantine Syria and Mesopotamia. The situation appears to have been confused, with local strong men possibly having been conceded some *de facto* authority. The sources are poor and untrustworthy on this.[15]

BYZANTINES IN PERSIA AND PERSIANS IN BYZANTIUM

Byzantine history of the seventh century contains many mysteries, and among the most deserving of investigation is what Byzantines were doing in Persia and what Persians were doing in the Byzantine Empire after 628. Some conclusions may not be entirely satisfying – that is, it may not be possible to offer definitive and exhaustively documented answers to some of these problems. But it is worth trying. Only the Arabic and other non-Greek sources provide even an inkling of the existence of any problem.

Byzantium's eastern frontier with the Persians had not been entirely clearly delimited after the end of Heraclius' war with the Persians. The problem was not so much disagreement on the frontier's location, but Byzantine concern for the internal strife within the Persian Empire. Some Byzantine military units probably remained stationed in western or especially northwestern areas of the Persian Empire even after Heraclius' return to Byzantine territory. According to some Arabic sources, Muslim invaders of Iraq

[14] Byzantine recruitment of Arabs from Mesopotamia, and its conquest: al-Ṭabarī i 2081, i 2347, i 2394; Balādhurī 135, 164, 181–3; Theoph., *Chron.*, A. M. 6125–6 (337–8 De Boor); Azdī 28, 111, 125, 174–7; Ibn al-Athīr (2: 308, 381–2 Tornberg).

[15] Several works of dubious quality attributed to al-Wāqidī narrate the Muslim conquest of Mesopotamia. In addition to the Pseudo-Wāqidī Beirut edn of the *Futūḥ al-Shām*, there is *Libri Wakedii De Mesopotamiae expugnatae historia*, ed. by G. H. A. Ewald (Göttingen: Dieterich, 1827), from a Göttingen manuscript, and Cod. Arab. CXXXVII from the Kongelige Bibliotheca of Copenhagen. The latter manuscript appears to contain fabulous material, and must be used only with the greatest caution and reserve. Both appear to be late in date, to judge from some terminology. The Copenhagen and Göttingen manuscripts contain similar material, but they do not appear to contain reliable information about the Byzantine authorities and commanders in Mesopotamia at that time.

encountered some Byzantine troops there during the invasions.[16] Thus there was a very confused territorial control at the time of Muslim conquests.

The Ba'labakk agreement of late 636 as well as a reference by al-Ṭabarī to *'ajam* (Persians) indicate that there were Persians who either were left behind there or fled from internal strife in Persia after the death of Chosroes (Khosro) II.[17] The explicit reference to Persians in al-Balādhurī's account of terms given by Abū 'Ubayda at Ba'labakk may indicate that these Persians in the mid 630s failed to join in the Persian withdrawal, or it may have been an anachronistic reference to other Persians later resettled in the Biqā' valley in the 'Umayyad or later period. Analysis of the Ba'labakk agreement adds credence to the possibility of a role played by Niketas, son of Shahrbaraz, and possibly another son, and adds more credibility to reports about the presence of Persians in Mesopotamia at that confused period. 'Iyāḍ b. Ghanm probably pursued the Byzantines as far as Melitēnē.[18] The scholarly logic in reaching these conclusions deserves review, but there is evidence in favor of the probability of 'Iyāḍ's having accomplished the conquest of Mesopotamia from Syria.

Some Muslim sources, notably Ibn al-Athīr and al-Ṭabarī, who use traditions that Sayf b. 'Umar transmitted, raise the problem of the population at Ḥimṣ rising against the Muslims in favor of Heraclius. Heraclius allegedly supported them by persuading troops from Byzantine Mesopotamia to come to their assistance.[19] This Byzantine relief effort for Ḥimṣ from Mesopotamia

[16] al-Ṭabarī i 2474–9; al-Ṭabarī, *Chronique*, trans. by H. Zotenberg (Paris 1871) 3: 420. Ibn al-Athīr 2: 407–10. Not analyzed much by Caetani, *AI* 3: 753–6; Nadine F. Posner, "The Muslim Conquest of Northern Mesopotamia" (unpub. Ph.D. diss., New York University, 1985), to whom I am very grateful for a copy of this important work; Posner, "Whence the Muslim Conquest of Northern Mesopotamia?," *A Way Prepared, Essays on Islamic Culture in Honor of Richard Bayly Winder*, ed. by Farhad Kazemi and R. D. McChesney (New York: New York University Press, 1988) 27–52. Cf. Michael the Syrian, *Chron.* 11.5, 13 (2: 416, 513 Chabot); and J. M. Fiey, "Tagrît: Esquisse d'une histoire chrétienne," *Communautés syriaques en Iran et Irak des origines à 1552* (London: Variorum, 1979) esp. 309–11; Fiey, "The Last Byzantine Campaign into Persia and Its Influence on the Attitude of the Local Populations towards the Muslim Conquerors," *1985 Bilād al-Shām Proceedings* 1: 96–103; Fiey, "Les Diocèses du 'maphrianat' syrien," *Parole de l'Orient* 5 (1974) esp. 138, 140–1.

[17] Balādhurī 130. Nadine F. Posner, "The Muslim Conquest of Northern Mesopotamia" 176–81, notes on 198–200, 316–17, 371, n. 24. Hill, *Termination* 84–99. On '*ajam*, al-Ṭabarī i 2508; Posner, "The Muslim Conquest of Northern Mesopotamia" 271; Posner, "Whence the Muslim Conquest of Northern Mesopotamia?" 32–48; A. I. Kolesnikov, *Zavoevaniye Irana arabami* (Moscow: Nauka, 1982).

[18] al-Ṭabarī i 2349; M. J. De Goeje, *Mémoire*[2] 134–5; Caetani, *AI* 3: 812, but 3: 788–9; 4: 45. Broad reconstruction: Posner, "The Muslim Conquest of Northern Mesopotamia" esp. 246–92. The situation was confused in Mesopotamia, because there apparently were some Byzantine troops in nominally Persian territory who resisted the Muslim invasion of Iraq: al-Ṭabarī i 2474–7; Agapius, *PO* 8: 453; Caetani, *AI* 3: 752–3.

[19] Yāqūt 2: 73; al-Tabarī i 2393–4, i 2498–503, 2594; al-Tabarī, *Chronique* (Zotenberg) 3: 425–30. Ibn al-'Adīm, *Zubdat al-Halab min Ta'rīkh Ḥalab* 1: 25–9; Balādhurī 149; Ibn al-Athīr (2: 413 Tornberg). Cf. L. I. Conrad, "The Conquest of Arwad," in: A. Cameron, L. I.

reportedly did not work because the Arab allies pulled back on news of a Muslim threat from Iraq to their own homelands in Mesopotamia. The confused situation in Mesopotamia and northern Syria complicates any effort to understand the genesis of a fixed and clear Byzantine–Muslim frontier. Yet there is inadequate information about the physical demarcation of the frontier. Some Muslim sources apparently assume that there could be some limited trade near or at the borders.

It is difficult to ascertain just how much Heraclius may have relied on Persians' experiences and policies and advice after persuading them to withdraw from the Levant. He may have taken notice of Persian views and experiences during their decade and a half of occupation even though he disliked them so much. Yet the overwhelming evidence is that Heraclius and the victorious Byzantines tried to restore the status quo ante in the Levant.[20]

Some Persian troops continued to remain in Byzantine Mesopotamia after Heraclius and Shahrbaraz arranged peace. The situation was complicated. Rās al-'Ayn (Theodosiopolis) may have been a point of control or base for one son of Shahrbaraz, Shahryāḍ.[21] Other Persian troops, who had no positive future in Persia because of their loyalty to the unsuccessful cause of a candidate, Shahrbaraz, for the Persian throne – that is, one who reigned only a very brief period before his assassination – were probably shifted south after his assassination, against the Muslim threat that was emerging in the 630s. They probably were a significant element in the bodyguard of Niketas, son of Shahrbaraz.[22] Thus some Persian troops on Byzantine territory were not resisting Byzantine authority or the plans for the demarcation of the Byzantine–Persian border after the settlement of 628. Some simply had lost out in Persian internal strife and had no secure place in Persia but were useful, so it appeared, to Heraclius. They were effectively armed exiles without a home. Their numbers and precise chain of command are unclear. It may have been dangerous to try to disarm them, and it was onerous to have to feed them, but they did supply additional manpower to Heraclius in a period when it was difficult and expensive to procure it by traditional means. Hostile memories of the Persian occupation in some areas of the Byzantine provinces of Syria and Mesopotamia may have detracted from these soldiers' value, but even then their experience may have been of some use to Heraclius. But they would not have come cost-free.

Conrad, *The Byzantine and Early Islamic Near East* (Princeton: Darwin, 1992) 382–3.

[20] W. E. Kaegi, "Notes on Hagiographic Sources for Some Institutional Changes in the Early Seventh Century," *Byzantina* 7 (1975) 61–70; reprinted in Kaegi, *ASRB*.

[21] Yet the principal authority for this control of Rās al-'Ayn by Shahryāḍ is the unreliable *Libri Wakedii De Mesopotamiae expugnatae historia*.

[22] Paul Speck, *Das geteilte Dossier* 317–41, 355–77, is too skeptical about Shahrbaraz, although I agree with his identification on p. 347–9 of Niketas as son of Shahrbaraz.

Any Byzantine attempt to create emergency defenses against the Arabs within the official borders of enfeebled Sassanian Persia along the lower middle Euphrates and the stretches of the Tigris at and above Takrīt required coping with the heat, the need for water and other provisions, and with rivers whose currents were too strong for boats to move upstream. It was possible to post modest numbers of Byzantine soldiers there, but they would have operated under very adverse conditions. Most of them were contingents from Byzantine-allied Arab tribes of Mesopotamia, plus a few Byzantine officers and soldiers. Any attempt to defend a line from the town of Hīt on the Euphrates to Takrīt on the Tigris was well intentioned, and would have sought to create an outer defensive line where a ridge of rising heights first permits good topographic defenses along both of those strategic river routes, and would have denied the Muslims access along those critical and indispensable invasion routes into Byzantine Mesopotamia. However, it was easier to conceive than to implement such a defensive line.[23]

The most logical explanation is that after conquering the Persians in 628, Heraclius left some kind of occupying force of Byzantine soldiers in northern Iraq, especially at Hīt, Takrīt, and Mosul, but their control probably did not extend much east of the Tigris.[24] The evidence, however, consists of a brief reference in the Persian abridgment of al-Ṭabarī that Zotenberg edited and translated, one tradition from Sayf b. 'Umar related by al-Ṭabarī, a reference in the *Nihaya* of al-Nuwayrī, and some inferences from later Christian Syriac and Arabic sources. There is no explicit early testimony in Arabic and none in Greek or Armenian. It is impossible to determine from known sources the numbers and nature of any continuing Byzantine military presence in Mesopotamia. The Byzantine commander at Takrīt was allegedly named "Anṭāq", very probably his original name was Antiochos. He had come with inhabitants of Mosul to Takrīt: "This commander had with him, apart from (his) Byzantine contingent, some tribesmen from the Iyād, Taghlib, and al-Namir tribes, as well as some local dignitaries." He has not been otherwise identified. Anṭāq and the rest of his Byzantine forces at Takrīt perished after a forty-day siege. Many of the above Arab tribesmen switched allegiances; some served as spies for the Muslims, who received additional help from Mārūtha, the Monophysite Metropolitan of Takrīt. Mār Emmeh, the Nestorian bishop, reportedly betrayed the city and citadel of Mosul to the

23 W. E. Kaegi, "Challenges to Late Roman and Byzantine Military Operations in Iraq (4th–9th Centuries)," *Klio* 73 (1991) 586–94.

24 J. M. Fiey, "Tagrît: Esquisse d'une histoire chrétienne," *Communautés syriaques en Iran et Irak des origines à 1552* (London: Variorum, 1979) esp. 309–11; Fiey, "The Last Byzantine Campaign into Persia and Its Influence on the Attitude of the Local Populations towards the Muslim Conquerors," *1985 Bilād al-Shām Proceedings* 1: 96–103; Fiey, "Les Diocèses du 'maphrianat' syrien," *Parole de l'Orient* 5 (1974) esp. 138, 140–1.

Muslims. Other Byzantine forces, again mostly Arabs from upper Mesopotamia whom Heraclius had dispatched, were defeated after they unsuccessfully defended Hīt. This poorly noted and anomalous material may have implications for understanding Byzantine policy with respect to Persia, Muslims, and the Arabs, and dissident Christians. Once again, the reliability of traditions transmitted by Sayf b. ʿUmar is at issue.[25]

Heraclius probably left some Byzantine troops in Persia, specifically in Iraq, in order to maintain Byzantine influence over the Persians, to try to provide a buffer on his own eastern frontier, and to stabilize the internal Persian situation in a manner favorable to Byzantine interests. It may have served as a necessary prop to a friendly but weak Sassanian government that he had installed in power and that was facing potential internal unrest and the risk of chaos.[26] Yet there were real limits to Heraclius' ability to control events and trends. The principal problem for the Byzantines was that such an extended Byzantine presence, however token, also potentially overstrained and overextended Byzantine communications, logistics, manpower, and finance. It could offer little real resistance to the Muslims.

Yet the Byzantine presence in northern Iraq made it even more desirable for Heraclius to try to hold on to upper Mesopotamia, to the provinces of Osrhoene and Mesopotamia, in order to preserve communications and the ability to reinforce Byzantine garrisons in Iraq. Because some Byzantine troops were stationed in Iraq, there was some temptation and hope, presumably, that perhaps some coordinated action against the Muslims could be arranged and successfully implemented. Of course, that never happened. The basic question is the trustworthiness of the accounts of

[25] Takrīt: al-Ṭabarī (Sayf) i 2475–7; al-Ṭabarī, *Chronique* (Zotenberg) 3: 420; al-Nuwayrī, *Nihāyat*, XIX, 236–8. Hīt: al-Ṭabarī i 2479. Mosul: Mārī b. Sulaymān, *Akhbār batarikat kursī al-Mashriq*, ed. by H. Gismondi (Rome 1899) 1: 62. Quotation: *The History of al-Ṭabarī*, 13: *The Conquest of Iraq, Southwestern Persia, and Egypt*, trans. by Gautier H. A. Juynboll (Albany: State University of New York Press, 1989) 54. Fiey was, however, primarily interested in the implications of this material for the understanding of the Nestorian and Monophysite churches, and did not pursue any investigation of the implications of these anomalies for the interpretation of the reign of Heraclius or other aspects of Byzantine history. George Rawlinson, *The Seventh Great Oriental Monarch* (New York: Dodd, Mead, n.d.) 2: 230, n. 5, noting that a Roman [Byzantine] general "Antiochus?" defended Takrīt, commented that "It is just possible that, on the collapse of the Persian power, Rome attempted to obtain a share of the spoil." Plausible, but Byzantine concern for defensive security probably also was a factor, and one that weighed even more heavily in Byzantine calculations.

[26] The clearest evidence for contemporary Byzantine anxiety about the Sassanian Empire, and the desirability of preserving it from falling into chaos, is Theophylact Simocatta's composition of a speech, written anytime between 628 and 640, which he attributed to ambassadors of Chosroes II to Maurice (in 590): Theophylact Simocatta, *Hist.* 4.13.9, 4.13.13. But it helps to illuminate the mood at Heraclius' court that could have stimulated the decision to keep some troops in Persia to try to hold some kind of friendly government together.

Byzantine presence in Persia and Persian presence in Byzantine territory. There are sufficient numbers of reported Byzantines to conclude that there probably was some overlapping presence. The losers in Persian civil strife probably found employment under the Byzantines. Heraclius probably did wish to draw on Persian advice about administering Syria and defending it from nomads. One would like to know more of the text of agreements between Shahrbaraz and Heraclius at Arabissos, in July 629, which is crucial for understanding the problems.[27] There probably were difficulties in ejecting all Persian troops from northern Mesopotamia. It was necessary for Theodore to besiege them at Edessa, it appears, in late 629 or 630. And it appears that some Persians remained in Syria, for example, in the Biqāʿ valley at Baʿlabakk, after the other Persians withdrew from areas they had previously occupied, in conformity with the agreement with Shahrbaraz at Arabissos in July, 629.

The numbers and quality of the Persian troops in Byzantine territory and of Byzantine troops in Persian territory cannot reliably be determined, but they were indisputably unable to develop successful resistance to the Muslim invaders. Yet they were not deemed to be so excellent that Heraclius withdrew them for redeployment elsewhere, when the pressures grew. There is no evidence of any flight of Persians to Byzantine territory after Muslim invasions or in the course of them, although a son of Shahrbaraz allegedly went over to the Muslims, or at least negotiated on the pretense of deserting, but was ultimately executed because he was suspect. Many problems await further scholarly investigation.[28]

In conclusion, the recent long war with the Persians had many legacies for the warfare between Byzantines and Muslims. This is especially true for Byzantine Mesopotamia. The existence of Byzantine officials in part of northern Iraq, as well as troops there, made it all the more desirable to try to hold on to Byzantine Mesopotamia in order to preserve communications and the ability to reinforce the others. Their presence made Mesopotamia and northern Syria and their roads and towns all the more vital. They also seriously complicated decision making on the defense of Byzantine Syria and Mesopotamia. It was much more difficult to decide to evacuate Mesopotamia when there was the recent experience of also occupying part of Iraq. The situation created a natural reluctance to give up all of this, even though that was the rational decision to make in those circumstances. Except for underscoring the provisional and volatile military and civilian and ecclesi-

[27] Ibn ʿAbd al-Ḥakam, *Futūḥ miṣr* (36–7 Torrey). On Arabissos: Friedrich Hild and Marcell Restle, *Kappadokien (Kappadokia, Charsianon, Sebasteia und Lykandos)*: *Tabula Imperii Byzantini* 2 (Vienna 1981) 144–5.

[28] Cyril Mango, "Deux études sur Byzance et la Perse Sassanide," *TM* 9 (1985) 105–18. I thank Cyril Mango for helpful advice.

astical situation in those areas, the identification of these Byzantine troops in Sassanian Persia and the presence of Persians in Byzantine territory does not, on balance, probably change very much of what we know. But it does provide a fuller and more nuanced historical understanding.

MESOPOTAMIA IN THE EYES OF HERACLIUS

To contemporaries, the recent victory of Heraclius over the Persians, despite the initially great negative odds, may well have strongly affected perceptions and calculations about strategy and military operations after the conquest of Syria. From the Muslims' perspective it was critical to prevent any repeat of successful Byzantine recruiting among Armenians and elsewhere in the Caucasus, which had proved so important to Heraclius in the 620s.[29] For Muslim military interests, in addition to eliminating the Byzantine bulge or threat to communications, the conquest of Mesopotamia was indeed the necessary prelude to any effort to overrun the four Byzantine provinces of Armenia and thereby deny Heraclius access to Armenian recruits. These motives are not mentioned in the sparse extant sources; they simply emerge from any reflection on the actual military situation in the 630s and the immediately preceding military historical events that would have formed the frame of reference for those making military decisions.[30]

The Byzantines, including Heraclius and his advisers, also may have been thinking, however vainly, of the possibility of some repetition of the dramatic recuperation and counteroffensives of the 620s. The result was to leave Byzantium, after evacuation of most of Syria, holding widely dispersed forces in Egypt and Mesopotamia, in addition to completely isolated garrisons in such Palestinian ports as Caesarea and Gaza. In short, the remaining Byzantine forces were scattered in extremely diverse directions, unable to concentrate.[31] The Muslims held a central position from which they could freely strike west, north, and northeast.

The continued Byzantine occupation of Mesopotamia in 637–8 and subsequent efforts to send more troops there under Generals Dawit' (David) Urṭaya and Titus, in 640, temporarily diverted the Muslims from more serious attacks into Anatolia or on Constantinople, and they may have helped to give important additional breathing space for the creation of

[29] Possible additional confirmation is the hypothesis that the famous Mardaites of the late seventh century may have been (1) stationed earlier in various parts of Armenia IV, including Mardes (Mardin) in upper Mesopotamia, and (2) originated near Theodosiopolis (Erzurum): Hratz Bartikian, "Ἡ λύση τοῦ αἰνίγματος τῶν Μαρδαϊτῶν," *ByzStratos* 1: 17–39. He makes a strong case.

[30] On the Muslim conquest of Armenia, see the following chapter.

[31] Wide dispersal of those who fled after the battle of the Yarmūk: Balādhurī 135.

scorched-earth policies in Cilicia as well as the more carefully thought-out fortification of key points in Asia Minor, including mountain passes and dispersal of troops to such critical defensive points. Nevertheless, Mesopotamia drew away important Byzantine forces and attention from the defense of Egypt, which was an even more tempting Muslim target of opportunity.[32] Mesopotamia was at the end of a complex line of communications through Armenia III and IV that was difficult to maintain after the loss of the rest of northern Syria (Euphratesia, Antioch).

The Byzantine decision to try to hold Mesopotamia was not part of any brilliant grand strategy. It was a vestige that temporarily was bypassed by the principal Muslim invasions. Under certain conditions that accidental survival of the salient could have been an embarrassment or grave threat to Muslim control of Syria and to the consolidation of control of it and even Iraq. It soon became apparent that the Byzantine Empire lacked the resources for a comeback comparable to that of the 620s against the Persians, but one could have been certain of that only in comfortable retrospect, not late in 636.

One should ask: Why did Heraclius try to hold on to Mesopotamia after the loss of Syria? Why not evacuate it at the same time as Syria – especially since he was overextended there? Arabs had served as major components of Heraclius' armies that fought to defend Byzantine Syria and Palestine. The struggle of Abū Bakr and 'Umar to gain control of all of the Arabs potentially deprived Byzantium of a major source of good military manpower that was an alternative to that of the Armenians.

Heraclius was the only reigning Byzantine emperor after Julian in the fourth century who actually visited both provinces of Osrhoene and Mesopotamia while they were still under Byzantine control (possible hasty military penetrations by emperors who were raiding in the eighth and tenth and eleventh centuries are not relevant here and do not invalidate this point). He had the opportunity to appreciate its strategic importance when he traversed it while campaigning in 624 and returning from Persia in 628/9 and while rebuilding the church of Amida *c.* 628–9, and again in 631 and 633 while determining the Byzantine–Persian frontier in Mesopotamia after the Persian evacuation and during his efforts to settle Christian religious disputes. His brother Theodore had also spent time besieging and recapturing Edessa from the Persians and from recalcitrant Jews. It was not easy to abandon the labor that he and his family had expended on Byzantine Mesopotamia.

One must give up a world perspective from Constantinople for the moment and think in terms of Heraclius' origins in Armenia, possibly even

[32] Michael the Syrian, *Chron.* 11.7, 10 (2: 424, 441–3 Chabot). Julius Wellhausen, "'Amr b. 'As in Ägypten,'" *Skizzen und Vorarbeiten* (Berlin 1899) 6: 93; C. H. Becker, *Cambridge Medieval History* 2: 349.

Armenian Theodosiopolis or modern Erzurum, Turkey; one must keep in mind as well Heraclius' father, Heraclius the Elder, who had spent an important part of his early military career in and around another Theodosiopolis, that of Byzantine Mesopotamia, where he gained considerable military prestige in 587. Heraclius the Elder very probably pointed out the strategic advantages and significance of Byzantine Mesopotamia to his son, the later Emperor Heraclius.[33]

THE TRUCE AT CHALKIS

The most important detail that has been neglected in the study of the Muslim mop-up in northern Syria is that everything did not succumb instantly to the Muslims in Syria immediately following the battle of the Yarmūk on 20 August 636. A flying column under the command of ʿIyāḍ b. Ghanm probably did reach as far as Melitēnē, but he could not hold it against strong Byzantine counterattacks. The critical north Syrian stronghold of Chalkis had been bypassed and remained in Byzantine hands until its *patricius* negotiated a one-year truce with Abū ʿUbayda that provided for its surrender to the Muslims at the expiration of that full year. The authority for this truce is Eutychius, who is a very credible source. Pseudo-Wāqidī, to be sure, a less credible source, and Agapius of Manbij also provide some details. The truce had implications for Mesopotamia.[34]

The Byzantine chronicler Theophanes as well as Michael the Syrian state that John Kateas, the Byzantine governor or ἐπίτροπος (*curator*) of the province of Osrhoene, who governed it from the city of Edessa, came to Qinnasrīn (ancient Chalkis, the modern village of Al-Is) in Syria, presumably in 637 (unless there is confusion with 638), and made a pact (ἐστοίχησε – "he arranged") with the Muslim general ʿIyāḍ b. Ghanm, agreeing to pay 100,000 gold *nomismata* (72 *nomismata* = 1 Roman pound) annually, and in return for this payment, as long as it was made, ʿIyāḍ and the Muslims agreed: "Not to cross the Euphrates, neither peacefully nor in a state of war, μήτε εἰρηνικῶς μήτε πολεμικῶς, as long as the Byzantines pay the amount of gold." The Greek text is probably an authentic reproduction of an original that included the Arabic prohibitions on crossing *ṣulḥan* or *ʿanwatan*, in peace or by force – that is, the Arabs agreed to peace for a truce arrangement.

33 Heraclius' Armenian consciousness: Henri Grégoire, "An Armenian Dynasty on the Byzantine Throne," *Armenian Quarterly* 1.1 (1946) esp. 6–17.

34 al-Ṭabarī i 2349. Eutychius, *Ann.* 282 (141–2 Breydy text, 120–1 Breydy trans.). Pseudo-Wāqidī, *Futūḥ al-Shām* (Beirut 1972) 1: 114–5; reference to *Malik al-Rūsiya* and to cavalry of the *Saqāliba* or Slavs, which is anachronistic, indeed chronologically impossible, thereby impugns the validity of all information in this printed text without rigorous verification from outside sources that are reliable: Pseudo-Wāqidī, *Futūḥ al-Shām* (Beirut 1972) 1: 162.

This agreement of the Muslims not to cross the Euphrates protected the Byzantine territories in Mesopotamia by guarding against any pretext of transhumant movement being used to introduce Arabs across the river.[35] Skeptically inclined Arabists may wonder whether the text, that is, the oriental source for Theophanes, is late, because of their assumption that the *ṣulḥan-ʿanwatan* tradition is a relatively late invention. When Heraclius learned of this agreement, he dismissed and exiled John Kateas and replaced him with Ptolemaios, τινα στρατηλάτην (a certain general), who refused at its expiration to renew the truce on the previous terms.

Ptolemaios' appointment and refusal to pay tribute immediately led to ʿIyāḍ b. Ghanm's invasion of the region: crossing the Euphrates, he seized Callinicum and Edessa, and then imposed similar capitulation terms on the rest of the towns of the area, all of which fell within a year.[36] Kūfī calls the patrician at Edessa "Mītūlus?," who is otherwise unknown.[37] Kūfī asserts that Heraclius had angrily placed "Copts" over Raqqa/Callinicum after recovering it from the Persians. That decision had angered the otherwise unknown patrician Bintus, who negotiated the terms with ʿIyāḍ, and some others of the local elite.[38] Antagonisms that dated to the harsh justice meted out at Edessa by Heraclius and his brother Theodore on recovering Edessa from the occupying Persians may have alienated portions of the local leadership and disposed them to consider making terms with the Muslims. Only a few towns required violent assault before the rest yielded to the Muslim invaders. This invasion took place in AH 17 or 18 or 19, that is, 638–40. ʿIyāḍ probably completed the conquest in 640. Tella, Dara, and Rās al-ʿAyn (Theodosiopolis) resisted violently; some of their inhabitants were slain, but they all fell.[39]

The Muslim conquest of Mesopotamia took very little time and, to judge from sources, involved no major battles or significant military innovation. The Byzantine forces were completely outnumbered, and their commander Ptolemaios surely did not wish to risk the annihilation of valuable remaining

[35] Theoph., *Chron*, AM 6128 (De Boor 340). Agapius, *PO* 8: 476–7. L. I. Conrad, "Theophanes and the Arabic Historical Tradition: Some Indications of Intercultural Transmission," *ByzF* 15 (1990) 1–45. D. Hill, *Termination* 84–99. Transhumant movement was common in the region. The concepts of *ṣulḥan* and ʿ*anwatan* may not be contemporary with the conquests: Albrecht Noth, "Some Remarks on the 'Nationalisation' of Conquered Lands at the Time of the Umayyads," *Land Tenure and Social Transformation in the Middle East*, ed. by Tarif Khalidi (Beirut: American University of Beirut, 1984) 223–8.

[36] Theoph., *Chron.*, AM 6128 (340 De Boor). Michael the Syrian, *Chron*: 11.7 (2: 426 Chabot). Agapius, *PO* 8: 476, wrongly calls him "Paul." Michel Kaplan, "Quelques aspects des maisons divines," 'Αφιέρωμα στὸν Νίκο Σβορῶνο esp. 79–96; occasionally, Kaplan, 89–90, this office of *curator* was combined with other offices including military responsibilities in Syria.

[37] Kūfī 1: 331.

[38] Kūfī 1: 326–9, esp. 328. Michael the Syrian, *Chron.* 11.7 (2: 426 Chabot). Posner, "Muslim Conquest" 336–8.

[39] Michael the Syrian, *Chron.* 11.7 (2: 426 Chabot).

manpower in a hopeless combat. Agapius reconfirms this information, although he identifies the governor as Paul, whom he asserts was punished for making peace by being exiled to Africa.[40] It is incorrect to assume that local kinglets or dynasts, who lack independent confirmation, ruled the various towns of Byzantine Mesopotamia on the eve of the Muslim conquests: such conditions are inconceivable there after the Byzantine reoccupation.[41]

Heraclius probably wanted John Kateas to hold on to Mesopotamia without fighting: "Let no one engage in any more fighting with the Taiyyayê [Arabs]; but let him who can hold his position remain in it."[42] This instruction is consistent with his earlier order to Theodore Trithurios to avoid open battle with the Muslims before the battle of the Yarmūk. Heraclius may simply have been angry at John for arranging a peace without authorization or he may have wished to maintain pressure everywhere and thus prevent Muslims from releasing troops from the Euphrates region to use against other exposed Byzantine positions.

The historical background has been distorted by a number of problems, including the lack of accurate understanding of late Roman and Byzantine place-names in Syria, in particular, that ancient Chalkis became medieval Qinnasrīn. Inconsistent and contradictory understanding of the identification impeded scholarly appreciation of the true significance of Chalkis in the sources' narratives of events.[43] John Kateas signed the truce that temporarily protected Mesopotamia at Chalkis. The Muslim signatory was Iyāḍ b. Ghanm, or, according to Eutychius, Abū 'Ubayda, who was 'Iyāḍ b. Ghanm's superior commander.[44] Its scope embraced not only Mesopotamia but apparently also some of northern Syria; in any case it included the strategic region around the nodal point of Chalkis/Qinnasrīn.

The conquest of Bālis and Qāṣirīn by Abū 'Ubayda, accompanied by the withdrawal of many of the Greeks there to the Byzantine Empire, Mesopotamia, and Jisr Manbij, is probably part of the same truce and withdrawal arrangement made at Qinnasrīn by Abū 'Ubayda. Abū 'Ubayda

[40] Agapius, *PO* 8: 476–7.

[41] Posner, "The Muslim Conquest of Northern Mesopotamia," wrongly asserted that such cities as Edessa, Harrān, Mardīn, and Circesium "were ruled by local dynasts and kinglets" (p. 179).

[42] Michael the Syrian, *Chron.* 11.7 (2: 424 Chabot); cf. Agapius, *PO* 8: 471–2.

[43] Caetani, *AI* 4: 46, where incorrectly identified. But see 4: 814, where correctly identified.

[44] Eutychius, *Ann.* 282 (141–2 Breydy text, 120–1 Breydy trans.). Pseudo-Wāqidī, *Futūḥ al-Shām* (Beirut 1972) 114–15. There is reference to another one-year truce proposal for Rās al-'Ayn in the history of another false Wāqidī, *Libri Wakedii De Mesopotamiae expugnatae historia*, ed. by G. H. A. Ewald (Göttingen: Dieterich, 1827) 20. Again, the terms mentioned in this last proposal included a one-year delay, after which the Byzantines would either convert to Islam or withdraw to "*bilād al-rūm*" – namely, to Byzantine Anatolia, an echo of the same treaty that Eutychius cites. But this is a late text of doubtful credibility.

probably advanced as far as the Euphrates in 637, where he halted. This preceded any Muslim crossing of the Euphrates as well as the peace that Theophanes states that the Byzantines made at Qinnasrīn for the protection of Byzantine Mesopotamia. The report by Balādhurī on Bālis and Qāṣirīn became separated in historical memory from the events at Qinnasrīn.[45] There were two truces made at Qinnasrīn. The one to which Eutychius refers preceded the one that Theophanes, Michael the Syrian, and Agapius mention.[46] Yet it is possible that there was only one truce and that chronological errors have created the dubious foundation for a supposition of two truces. The patrician who made the truce at Qinnasrīn in 637 originally may or may not have had Heraclius' permission to make such an agreement.

The Byzantines, at least nominally, still controlled Chalkis at the time of the signing of the peace. There was still an anonymous Byzantine *patricius* at Chalkis, and presumably he was different from John Kateas, who came there from Osrhoene to sign the truce agreement. It involved not only Mesopotamia but also part of Syria, as is clear from Eutychius, whose account tends to hide the truce's coverage of Mesopotamia, perhaps because Eutychius was primarily interested in events in Syria. In both cases these truces – or maybe they were specific components of one truce – temporarily stabilized a military situation that was dangerously in flux. They deterred the Muslims from exploiting the possibility of a deep penetration and breakthrough. The Muslims received money and the opportunity to consolidate their gains as well as to rid themselves of segments of the local populations who were potentially hostile to their new regime.[47]

The military significance of the region of Chalkis for early Byzantine defenses has long received recognition, even though investigators were unable to disentangle fortifications and structures of varying periods with absolute clarity.[48] The conclusions of Mouterde and Poidebard appeared too late for Caetani or other early Orientalists to consult when they were analyzing the Muslim conquests. Chalkis was a vital crossroads, which dominated the intersection of east–west communications between Antioch and the Euphrates, and north–south ones, between Ḥimṣ, Damascus and other inland Syrian cities, and Edessa and Melitēnē and other northern Syrian and other military strongholds and nodal points. It was a logical place

45 Balādhurī 150.

46 Theoph., *Chron.*, AM 6128 (340 De Boor); Michael the Syrian, *Chron.* (2: 426 Chabot); Eutychius, *Ann* 282 (141–2 Breydy Arabic text, 120–1 Breydy trans.); Agapius, *PO* 8: 476–7. Pseudo-Wāqidī, *Futūḥ al-Shām* I (Beirut, 1972) 114–16. Consistent with the chronology of D. Hill, *Termination of Hostilities* (London: Luzac, 1971) 67, 81, 92.

47 Caetani failed to discuss the relationship.

48 R. Mouterde and A. Poidebard, *Le Limes de Chalcis. Organisation de la steppe en Haute Syrie romaine* (Paris: Geuthner, 1945) 1: 21–3.

to attempt to stabilize a secondary Byzantine defense line that protected much of northern Syria after the debacle of the battle of the Yarmūk. Its control preserved for the Byzantines, however temporarily, the valuable agricultural and olive-producing areas of the "Massif Calcaire" of northern Syria and also helped to protect Byzantine Mesopotamia.[49] It was strategically sound to try to hold it by means of a truce.

The duration of the peace terms was extended in the trans-Euphrates Byzantine territories, that is, Mesopotamia and Osrhoene, until 639, when the Muslims invaded on the pretext of the Byzantine failure to pay the stipulated tribute. These improvisations had their political aspects. The Muslims probably knew that Byzantine requests for a truce could have had as an ulterior motive the desire to bring up more men for a Byzantine counterattack or counteroffensive. Yet the temporary truce lines traversed routes that transhumant Arabs often had used before the Muslim invasions. Thus the frontier agreed for in Mesopotamia was one that the Byzantine authorities accepted because they were afraid of Arabs peacefully crossing it and then inflicting harm on the Byzantine forces, the authorities, and the region.

Dissatisfaction with General Manuel in Egypt and with the governor of Osrhoene and Mesopotamia, John Kateas, reinforced Heraclius' resolve to maintain tight central imperial control over the empire's borders. He did not wish diplomatic relations to fall into the hands of the local authorities, especially if they failed to consult him about important matters.[50] He wanted to clear and approve them himself. In similar fashion, by issuing his order for local officials to hold out as long as possible against the Muslims, but not to attack them out on the open battlefield, Heraclius was attempting to establish a common policy and guideline for local administrators, to prevent harmful local *ad hoc* arrangements with the Muslims whenever possible.[51] That was also part of the process of creating a very clear imperial authority's reach directly to the limits of the frontier.

The Chalkis agreement also prevented trade and thus applied a certain economic, especially commercial pressure. This was consistent with the agreement at Ba'labakk mentioned by al-Balādhurī, in which Greeks cannot trade beyond regions that have made peace terms, *ṣulḥ*, with the Muslims. These subtle commercial, transportation, and economic pressures worked in

[49] G. Tchalenko, *Villages antiques de la Syrie du Nord*, 3 vols. (Paris 1953–8).

[50] Theoph., *Chron.*, AM 6128 (340 De Boor); Michael the Syrian, *Chron.* 11.7 (2: 425–6 Chabot); cf. Agapius, *PO* 8: 476–8; cf. 8: 471–2, Theoph., *Chron.*, AM 6126 (338–9 De Boor), on Egyptian peace, with 'Amr b. al-'Āṣ. But note the skepticism of P. Speck, *Das geteilte Dossier* 182–5, 190, 398–403, 410–12. D. R. Hill, *Termination of Hostilities in the Early Arab Conquests* (London: Luzac, 1971) 84–99.

[51] Michael the Syrian, *Chron.* 11. 7 (2: 424–5 Chabot).

favor of the Muslims, although they also suffered somewhat from such disruptions. Muslim leaders were probably aware of the important role of economics in the conquest. During their conquests of Palestine and Syria the Muslims cut off trade in order to pressure the Byzantine defenders.[52] Their actions contributed to the ultimate subjugation of localities.

The fifty-year treaty between the Persian Empire and Byzantium in 561 had required Saracens [Arabs] to abide by the other provisions: not to attack the Byzantines or Persians, and Saracen merchants were not to travel by strange roads or cross into foreign territory without official permission. The aim of these provisions was control of the movement of beduin in a manner similar to the provisions of the Chalkis treaty between the Muslims and Byzantines, which probably was effective in 638/9. Thus there was a longer heritage to these diplomatic negotiations and to efforts to develop comprehensive security and control of the beduin. The region in question in 638/9 overlapped, in fact, with that covered by the Byzantine–Persian treaty of 561.[53]

The agreement, *ṣulḥ*, made by commander Abū ʿUbayda at Baʿlabakk is an important parallel and possible confirmation of the agreements at Qinnasrīn or Chalkis. It does not specifically confirm the date, but it provides additional documentation for specific and relatively long periods during which Greeks [*Rūm*] might peacefully evacuate, which is a distinctive feature of the truce at Qinnasrīn, according to the above Christian authors. The agreement at Baʿlabakk probably was made in late 636, after the fall of Damascus in December 636, and provided for the Greeks to have the ability to winter in the Baʿlabakk region and only to move in May–June 637 = Rabīʿ II and Jumādā I. These dates are consistent with a date of 637 for an agreement, made by Abū ʿUbayda or ʿIyāḍ b. Ghanm with a Byzantine patrician at Qinnasrīn, for a year's truce at a defined line to enable Greeks to evacuate.[54]

The terms involve segregating the Greeks, *Rūm*, in the Baʿlabakk region from the rest of the local population. They are not to move near the city or leave until approximately May 637, or inhabit fortified or settled places, presumably because they might use these to entrench themselves. Of course,

[52] Azdī 165. Lawrence I. Conrad, "Al-Azdī's History of the Arab Conquests in Bilād al-Shām: Some Historiographical Observations," *1985 Bilād al-Shām Proceedings* 28–62.

[53] Menander, frg. 6.1 (Blockley 70–3). Irfan Shahid [Kawar], "The Arabs in the Peace Treaty of AD 561," *Arabica* 3 (1956) [repr. as VII, in Shahid, *BSOBRI*] esp. 192–200, explains why it was necessary to make explicit reference to Arabs in the treaty, to insure their uncontested and full compliance with its provisions in 561. The same concerns were valid in 639 along the Euphrates. There was no desire to find beduin claiming exemption from provisions of the treaty of 638/9, as had happened in 539 when there was a dispute concerning whether the treaty of 532 explicitly covered activities of Arabs: Procopius, *Hist.* 2.1.1–15.

[54] Balādhurī 130. Date: L. Caetani, *AI* 3: 435; N. A. Miednikov, *Palestina ot zavoevaniya eie arabaye* 1: 486–9.

if the northern border were closed to movement, that would have required making the Greeks stationary until it was time to open it. Allowing them to move, together with their animals, risked clashes with tribes, disputes over food supplies, and transient pasturing rights. The Ba'labakk agreement shows that the Muslims did permit Greeks, *Rūm*, to move in staged withdrawals with mutual concern for the welfare of those inhabitants who wished to leave.[55]

Muslim strategy allowed those non-Muslims who so wished to evacuate conquered regions, in some cases with movable property. They could depart where they wished, for example to Byzantine territory. Their departure of course allowed the Muslims to seize and redistribute, if they wished, their landholding in the countryside and in the towns. Such policies were not necessarily unique creations of Muslims, but elaborations of policies that late Romans, Byzantines, and Persians had followed even in the fourth century.[56] This was a good escape valve: it cleared regions of as many unfriendly people as possible and was a fitting background to later efforts to create a zone of devastation between the Byzantines and Muslims. It was better to allow hard-core non-Arab opponents of the regime to depart, and avoid becoming a disgruntled fifth column behind Muslim lines. The evacuation of Greeks from newly conquered areas appears to have been handled with great care by both sides at a number of locations.

The issue is not whether the Muslims wanted a permanent frontier with Byzantium. They unmistakably did not want such a permanent frontier. But references in a number of primary sources from several different ethnic traditions indicate that Muslims did agree to, for a number of reasons, or even desired some temporary frontier between the newly conquered Muslim-controlled areas and those that still belonged to Byzantine authority.

The truce line presumably started somewhere south of Qinnasrīn. A portrait of a seated Heraclius on a stela or shaft, or *'amūd*, marked the demarcation line, presumably – although the sources do not say so explicitly – along a road or some kind of well-traveled route where people would see it. It was apparently a representation drawn on the pillar, not a bust or statue, located somewhere in northern Syria and was not merely the course of the Euphrates River, otherwise the report of the location of the bust of the emperor would make no sense. Yet the erection of such a portrait on a shaft is a valuable detail that underscores the Byzantine zeal and sensitivity to protect the honor and prestige of the emperor, especially in the circumstances of an

[55] A. J. Butler, *The Arab Conquest of Egypt*, rev. by P. M. Fraser (Oxford: Oxford University Press, 1978) 207–9, 481–3. Theoph., *Chron.*, AM 6126 (338 De Boor). But al-Balādhurī and Byzantine sources failed to mention the Qinnasrīn arrangements that Eutychius, Agapius, and Pseudo-Wāqidī report.

[56] Ammianus Marcellinus, *Hist.* 25.7.9–13.

embarrassing, indeed humiliating, military withdrawal from valuable territory. Eutychius reports that a Muslim accidentally defaced the eye of Heraclius on that image while playing on horseback, causing Abū 'Ubayda to agree, in response to the Byzantine protest, to allow an image of himself to be created and its eye to be mutilated.[57]

The above story from Eutychius has some earlier historical parallels and should not be regarded as fanciful. First, the sixth-century Syrian chronicler John Malalas states that in the reign of Diocletian "They raised stelae to the emperor and the Caesar on the *limes* of Syria."[58] Another source reports that the destruction of statues and busts of Constantine I in the frontier zone at Emona (modern Ljubljana, Yugoslavia) in 324 had been a pretext for Constantine's declaration of war against Licinius.[59] The sixth-century Monophysite ecclesiastical historian John of Ephesus reported that in contemporary Persia there was such veneration and fear of a statue of Emperor Trajan in Sassanian Persia that no one dared to pass in front of it on horseback. Indeed, the statue had provoked such Byzantine–Persian controversy about the alleged implicit Persian recognition of Roman authority that Chosroes I ordered the statue to be demolished.[60] More important, the author of the seventh-century *Doctrina Iacobi nuper baptizati* speaks of pillars or boundary stones of brass and marble to mark the far-flung borders of the empire.[61] There were precedents for marking imperial boundaries and for foreign horsemen respecting imperial Byzantine statues a few decades before the alleged incident at Chalkis.

Finally there is a report of the flaying alive of two officials and the massacre of the population of Tiflis in reprisal for the malicious caricature and deforming of an image of Heraclius' ally, the Khazar Khan,[62] which is somewhat similar to Eutychius' narrative of the truce at Chalkis. Both emphasize the sensitivity of seventh-century sovereigns to insults to their respective images. The stories are sufficiently different, however, to rule out any mere copying. In the account of Tiflis, the image is made as a deliberate caricature and elicits a very harsh reprisal because of the willful, not

[57] Eutychius, *Ann.* 282 (141–2 Breydy text, 120–1 Breydy trans.). Pseudo-Wāqidī (Beirut 1972) 114–15.

[58] Malalas, *Chron.* (Dindorf 308); cf. trans. of Elizabeth Jeffreys, Michael Jeffreys, Roger Scott *et al.*, *The Chronicle of John Malalas* (Byzantina Australiensia, 4 [Melbourne: Australian Association for Byzantine Studies, 1986]) 168.

[59] *Origo Constantini Imperatoris* [*Excerpta Valensiana*] 15.

[60] Joh. Ephes., *Hist.* II 3. 6. 23 (245–6 Brooks).

[61] στῆλαι: *Doctrina Iacobi nuper baptizati* (62 Bonwetsch). No such markers have been found, I believe. The reference to brass and marble ones may be a *topos*.

[62] Movses Dasxuranci, *History of the Caucasian Albanians* 2.11–12, 14, trans. by Charles J. F. Dowsett (London: Oxford University Press, 1961) 86, 94–5; Eutychius, *Ann.* 282 (141–2 Breydy text, 120–1 Breydy trans.); C. Toumanoff, *Studies in Christian Caucasian History* (Washington: Georgetown University Press, 1963) 391, n. 7.

accidental, insult to the prestige of the Khazar Khan in 627. The ultimate fate of the inhabitants of Tiflis was a terrible one and strikingly different from the positive and pacific outcome of the truce at Chalkis that was preserved despite the accidental mutilation of the portrait of Heraclius. It is possible that the reports of the horrible consequences of the recent caricaturing of the khan sensitized the Muslims to avoid angering Heraclius.[63] If anything, the incident that Eutychius reports is evidence of a less strident tone in the Byzantine war against the Muslims than in the earlier war against the Persians and their King Chosroes II and his allies, one that may have reduced the willingness to resist to the end. The striking difference in the two campaigns is characteristic of the differing Byzantine attitudes to the two respective opponents, Persian and Muslim, although, to be sure, the ridiculers of the Khan were inhabitants of Tiflis, in Georgia.

The truces at Chalkis were somewhat comparable to the one that the Byzantine governor of Egypt, Cyrus, purchased for the protection of Egypt, according to Theophanes and Agapius. Skeptics of the historicity of that truce have failed to note the existence of these other truces in other areas in the path of the Muslim advance. Although it may be hard to believe that the Muslims rationally would have accepted such truces, there may well have been a desire on their part to consolidate as well as the monetary temptation of the actual tribute that persuaded them to do so. The description of these truces by Agapius, Theophanes, Michael the Syrian, and Eutychius – all of whom may derive their information from a single source of probable Syrian Christian origin – seriously undermines the arguments of skeptics against any truce agreement between the Byzantines and the Muslims with respect to the security of Egypt. It is foolish to dismiss all of these. Some details of the truce for northern Syria and Mesopotamia are credible, even though many questions remain unclear. There was a truce, indeed a series of truces, on various fronts.[64]

MILITARY COMMANDERS REPLACE CIVILIAN GOVERNORS

Theophanes and Agapius – or more properly, their source – state that Heraclius became angry with both Byzantine governors, with John Kateas in Osrhoene and with Cyrus in Egypt. His anger arose from several causes, perhaps first of all the expense and concomitant loss of tax revenue for the

[63] Siege at Tiflis: Baynes, "Military Operations," *United Service Magazine* n.s. 47 (1913) 668. The story of Movses Dasxuranci contrasts very sharply with the efforts of the Muslim leadership to avoid any offense whatsoever to the prestige of Heraclius.

[64] Major critic of the truce: A. J. Butler, *The Arab Conquest of Egypt*, rev. by P. M. Fraser (Oxford 1978) 202–3, 480–2. Note the *urkūn* or ἄρχων of Cyprus who negotiated a separate peace with Mu'āwiya in 648/9: Balādhurī 153.

Byzantine Empire at a time of great fiscal exigency because both officials had purchased expensive truces with the Muslims. He also removed these officials because they had made these arrangements without his permission. He replaced John Kateas with the military commander Ptolemaios, who was an unspecified στρατηλάτης (*magister militum* is the normal rendering, although at this late date it could be a more generic term for a military commander). He likewise replaced Cyrus with Manuel, who boasted that he was not ἄοπλος, "unarmed," but ἔνοπλος, "armed."[65] These are both cases of replacement of civilian with military commanders and add credibility to the statements of Kūfī and Azdī about Heraclius' appointment of military commanders over cities at an earlier stage in the Byzantine effort to resist the Muslims. It was ostensible imperial displeasure with unauthorized contacts by civilian officials with the Muslims that caused Heraclius to make these two particular appointments, and he apparently made another one of Menas to rule over Chalkis/Qinnasrīn.[66]

Military commanders were not likely to attempt independent deals with the Muslims that might run counter to the wishes or interests of Heraclius. Their appointments helped to secure absolute coordination of local town authority with the supreme military and imperial authority. Independent civilian officials might not be as readily subject to military command and to military interests. There had been a long history in Syria, as the history of patronage in the vicinity of Antioch, for example, shows, of conflict between military and local officials and elites.[67] Its continuation at the time of the Muslim invasions of the 630s was understandable but very harmful to the creation of any viable resistance. Heraclius may well have decided that payment of tribute to the Muslims simply increased their ability to raise more soldiers who would make it even more difficult for the Byzantines to resist, at the same time that the money created more visible momentum and prestige for the Muslims. It turned out to be a bad agreement.

The identity of the *patricius* Menas, who once commanded Chalkis/ Qinnasrīn and perished in combat against the Muslims near it, is important yet uncertain.[68] He may be identical with the στρατηλάτης Menas

[65] Theoph., *Chron.*, AM 6126, 6128 (338, 340 De Boor), first reference for Manuel's statements about now being armed. Cf. Agapius, *PO* 8: 471–2; Speck, *Das geteilte Dossier* 182–5, 190. Theophanes' information about the appointment of an armed commander gains credibility when compared with traditions reported by Azdī 28–9; al-Ṭabarī i 2104; Kūfī 1: 100–1.

[66] Menas: Ibn al-'Adīm, *Zubdat al-Ḥalab min Tarīkh Ḥalab* (Damascus 1951) 1: 25–6. al-Ṭabarī i 2393–4. Balādhurī 130, 144–5. Caetani, *AI* 3: 791–3.

[67] Liebeschuetz, *Antioch* (Oxford 1972). R. M. Price, "Military Men" (unpub. diss., Oxford, 1974); G. Downey, *History of Antioch* (Princeton 1961) 422–3; L. Harmand, ed. and trans., *Libanius, Discours sur les patronages* (Paris 1955).

[68] Ibn al-'Adīm, *Zubdat al-Ḥalab min Ta'rīkh Ḥalab* (Damascus 1951) 1: 25–6; al-Ṭabarī i 2393.

whose lead seal reads, Θεότοκε Νουμερικ[ῶ]ν βοήθ[ει] Μη[ν]ᾶ στρατηλάτου (Virgin of Noumerika, Help Menas the Magister Militum).[69] It probably came from Noumerika, a town with probable military associations, and probably dates from the seventh century.[70]

SIGNIFICANCE OF THE TRUCE OF 637

The provinces of Osrhoene and Mesopotamia may have been administratively dependent at that time on Chalkis/Qinnasrīn, as the Muslim jurist al-Ya'qūbī claims. That may be why John Kateas of Osrhoene went to Qinnasrīn to sign the articles of the truce agreement. The sources do not say explicitly, but the truce probably had at least two parts, one for Chalkis and vicinity, perhaps extending to the northernmost limits of Syria, and one for the provisions that applied to Osrhoene and Mesopotamia, for which John Kateas signed. There is no report that Heraclius disapproved of any provisions for Syria itself, even though he objected to the participation of John Kateas for Osrhoene and Mesopotamia. The precise reasons are uncertain, although extant sources may simply provide an inadequate understanding of the entire truth. The truce probably took effect for both areas simultaneously. Theophanes indicates that the truce for Mesopotamia was renewable on full payment of the stipulated tribute, while Eutychius describes the provisions for the vicinity of Chalkis as having a very finite and terminal period of one year, without any presumption of the possibility of renewal. It is uncertain whether there were two distinct truce agreements, or one agreement with different provisions, and it is difficult to determine which alternative is the more probable.[71]

Nothing is known of the soldiers and officers who were under the command of Ptolemaios. The character, number, and quality of the existing Byzantine troops in upper Mesopotamia is likewise unknown. The area had long supported substantial Byzantine garrisons for protection against the Persians. It had been heavily fortified and presumably had good warehouses

[69] Zacos and A. Veglery, *BLS*, no. 934C (Basel 1972) 1: 637.

[70] It was within Bithynia, but perhaps near its border with Galatia, at the beginning of the seventh century: *Vie de Théodore Saint de Sykéôn* c. 152, ed. and trans. by A. J. Festugière (Subsidia Hagiographica, 48 [Brussels 1970] 1: 122). Noumerika may refer to the *numeri* or military units (often 300–500 men), possibly even ones of the imperial guard, who may have been stationed in part in the outlying districts away from but not too far from Constantinople; became bishopric in the ninth century: Mansi, *Sacrorum Conciliorum Nova et Amplissima Collectio* (Venice 1771) 16: 193; M. Le Quien, *Oriens Christianus* (Paris 1740) 1: 661–2.

[71] al-Ya'qūbī, *Ta'rīkh* 1: 177; Theoph., *Chron.*, AM 6126, 6128. Disjointed is Caetani, *AI* 3: 789–92, 799–800, 814–15; 4: 32–48.

and logistical backup, given the lengthy local tradition of major Byzantine armies being stationed there. Muslim sources state that a substantial number of troops who fought against them came from the Christian Arab tribes of the area.[72] It is unclear how many non-Arab Byzantine soldiers were there. It was located very close to Armenia, so that it was easy to recruit hardy Armenians to serve there.

It is conceivable that Heraclius merely used the lack of previous consultation by governors as a pretext to cancel agreements that he had passively accepted at an earlier critical moment. He may have simply repudiated these agreements when he believed that it was expedient to do so. It is even possible that he planned to do this before his officials were permitted to sign the agreements. There is some Byzantine precedent for such practices. He may have allowed his subordinates to make such agreements: he and his empire enjoyed the respite that such agreements provided, and then he repudiated the agreements and sent military governors to replace the civilians who had accepted such terms. It is not impossible, but such an explanation is a little too ingenious and convoluted. The greatest problem with such an explanation or policy, if it really was his plan, was its quick and unambiguous failure to protect the provinces that the agreements originally covered. It did give Heraclius and his subordinates time to regroup and create secondary defense lines for the better protection of the Byzantine hinterland. Only in those terms could such a cynical use of agreements make sense.

The truce suited the Byzantines for many reasons. Chalkis was, foremost, a strategically intelligent place for the Byzantines to try to make or persuade the Muslims to halt their advance, at least temporarily, at a very vulnerable moment for the Byzantines. It temporarily removed the chance for a Muslim breakthrough. It gave the Muslims a chance to receive much financial gain as well as to consolidate their very considerable territorial gains thus far, so it was not a stupid decision on their part to accept it. It was somewhat risky although tempting for them to continue their full and relentless pursuit of the Byzantines at that time. The unreliable *Futūḥ al-Shām* of Pseudo-Wāqidī (but not that of Azdī) gives one version of this truce in detail but dates it earlier in the history of the conquests, namely, before the battle of the Yarmūk. In this source Abū 'Ubayda and his advisers understand that the Byzantines are seeking a lengthy truce in order to gain time for more Byzantine reinforcements to arrive. Therefore they place restrictive conditions, according to this account, on the lucrative truce that they ultimately concede to the Byzantines. Yet Pseudo-Wāqidī confirms the plausibility of a

[72] Muslim sources on Byzantine recruitment from Mesopotamia, presumably from the region's Christian Arab tribes: al-Ṭabarī i 2393–4, 2498–504, 2594; Balādhurī 149; Azdī 152: Ibn 'Asākir 1: 531–2.

potential Byzantine desire to gain time for another possible offensive, not merely to alleviate the suffering and inconvenience of civilians who were caught in the middle of the fighting.

THE FLIGHT OF JABALA

Raqqa or Callinicum was the first of the cities of Byzantine Mesopotamia to fall. In addition to the previously mentioned broad strategic reasons making it desirable or obvious for the Muslims to capture Mesopotamia, as well as the lure of money, tribute, booty, and possibly military glory, there was another neglected reason: one Muslim tradition mentions that the last Ghassānid king, Jabala b. al-Ayham, fled from the Caliph ʿUmar to Heraclius via Raqqa: "He [Jabala b. al-Ayham] proceeded until he entered the land of Raqqa and reached Heraclius."[73] Other sources report that up to 30,000 Arabs (! – from his tribe of Ghassānids) accompanied Jabala and ultimately settled near Kharšana or Charsianon Castron, in Cappadocia, where the geographer al-Iṣṭakhrī mentions them in the tenth century.[74] One of the motives of those directing early Islamic conquests was the consolidation of control over Arab tribes not yet Islamicized.[75] The hitherto neglected case of the escape route of the last Ghassānid monarch graphically underlines how intolerable and dangerous the continuation of Byzantine control of Mesopotamia was for consolidation of caliphal control over Arab tribes.

The specific escape route of the Ghassānid king apparently lay through the region of Raqqa or Callinicum to Heraclius. Whether Jabala b. al-Ayham was accompanied at that time by large numbers of Arabs fleeing from Muslim authority, or whether these fleeing Arabs joined him somewhere else within Byzantine territory – and the sources al-Balādhurī and al-Yaʿqūbī indicate that they fled together with him from caliphal territory – his escape route in AH 17 could tempt other recently conquered Arabs to use it either as an escape route for themselves or as a conduit for maintaining communications outside of caliphal control, or possibly as a center for subversion of those Christian Arabs who stayed within caliphal territories.

[73] Bilād Raqqa: al-Aṣmaʿī [attribution], *Taʾrīkh al-ʿArab qablʾal-Islam*, ed. by Muḥammad Ḥasan al-Yāsīn (Baghdad 1959) 111–12. Yet the source in its present form may not date to the early Arab lexicographer Āl-Aṣmaʿī, who died in AD 828 or 831, but to the tenth century, according to Jaroslav Stetkevych. Other references to Jabala's flight, without these details: al-Yaʿqūbī, *Taʾrīkh* (2: 168 Houtsma).

[74] al-Iṣṭakhrī, *Viae regnorum*, *Bibliotheca Geographorum Arabicorum*, ed. by M. J. De Goeje (repr. Leiden: Brill, 1961) 1: 45. Charsianon Castron: Dejanira Potache, "Le Thème et le fortresse de Charsianon: recherches dans la région d'Akdagmadeni," *Geographica Byzantina*, ed. by H. Ahrweiler et Collaborateurs (Paris 1981) 107–17; I. Beldiceanu-Steinherr, "Charsianon Kastron/Qalʿe-i Harsanōs," *Byzantion* 51 (1981) 410–29; and esp. F. Hild, *Kappadokien* (Vienna: Akademie der Wissenschaften, 1981), 163–5.

[75] Donner, *EIC* 116–19, 251–71.

Raqqa and Mesopotamia were conquered in that (638) or the following year, AH 18 (639–40), or possibly AH 19 – because until Raqqa and Mesopotamia were conquered, one could not prevent Arabs inside the caliphal realm from making easy contact with the still feared Byzantine authorities, with whom such tribesmen had often arranged relationships in the past. For this reason Raqqa could not be permitted to remain in Byzantine hands. Reports of the concern of early Muslim conquerors that inhabitants of northern Syria give information about Byzantine troop movements and other useful intelligence to the new Muslim conquerors, who definitely still feared the Byzantines, reinforce this reasoning. Secondly, there are explicit references in al-Ṭabarī that 'Umar and other Muslims demanded the return of those Arabs who had fled to Heraclius' control. Arabs joining the Byzantines even after the loss of Syria was still a serious problem for 'Umar.[76] The escape of the principal Byzantine Arab ally by way of Callinicum/Raqqa, let alone with up to 30,000 Arabs, underlined the danger of leaving that city and Osrhoene and Mesopotamia in Byzantine hands. It was a cause and catalyst for 'Iyāḍ b. Ghanm's invasion. Raqqa and Nisibis probably fell first to 'Iyāḍ b. Ghanm, who afterwards took Ḥarrān, Rās al-'Ayn, and Dara in AH 19. Edessa fell in AH 18 or 19. Circesium may have fallen as late as AH 22, after the Khābūr was overrun by the Muslims. Takrīt, Hīt, and Mosul may well have fallen to Muslims coming from Ctesiphon (al-Madā'in) under 'Abdullāh b. al-Mu'tamm.

The question of whether Mesopotamia was conquered from Iraq or Syria is not altogether simple to answer. It appears, however, that 'Iyāḍ b. Ghanm came from Syria for the principal thrust, even though there are three other versions of his alleged approach from Iraq. The intense heat of Iraqi summers and problems of the flooding of the Euphrates often twice a year would have complicated efforts to conquer upper Mesopotamia from Iraq, although it was theoretically feasible. It is possible, as stated above, that small contingents of Byzantine troops were at Hīt and Circesium (Qarqisiya), but it is exceedingly improbable that after the battle of the Yarmūk Heraclius could have spared many troops for those vulnerable towns, let alone any for Mosul.

Pseudo-Wāqidī provides a very questionable account of various complex negotiations and treachery leading to the fall of various Byzantine cities to the Muslims,[77] especially the alleged role of Yūqnā.[78] He describes a vigorous Byzantine defense led by Shahryāḍ b. Farūn, the master of Rās al-'Ayn, and

[76] al-Ṭabarī on 'Umar's demands for return of Arabs from Byzantium: i 2508–9.

[77] Pseudo-Wāqidī, *Futūḥ al-Shām* (Beirut 1972) 2: 104–64.

[78] Another anachronism in Pseudo-Wāqidī, *Futūḥ al-Shām*, is the reference to the name "Istanbul" as well as Constantinople: Pseudo-Wāqidī, *Futūḥ al-Shām* (Beirut 1972) 2: 155.

other local leaders. There is no independent confirmation of any of his account, in particular, that Heraclius permitted such local rulers to spring up in Mesopotamia, or that they ever existed. Thus the accounts of Theophanes Confessor and Agapius of Manbij are fundamental for understanding the essential sequence of events in the fall of Byzantine Mesopotamia, when used together with information from Eutychius, al-Ṭabarī, and Balādhurī. The narrative of Pseudo-Wāqidī is fanciful and bears no reasonable relation to historical realities of the middle of the seventh century. Some of the inhabitants and authorities in Mesopotamia may have supported some Byzantine effort to recover Emesa (Ḥimṣ) from the Muslims, aided perhaps by restive Christian Arab tribesmen within Emesa (Ḥimṣ) and its region.

THE CHALLENGE OF TRIBAL MIGRATION

Heraclius appears to have enjoyed prestige among Christian Arab tribesmen. Later Arabic sources speak of Christian Arab tribesmen seeking to flee to join "Heraclius." The sources may be exaggerating the personal role of Heraclius in attracting these tribesmen as Byzantine authority collapsed in Syria, but that is the way in which they describe matters. There were other cases of migration of Christian tribesmen than that of those who accompanied Jabala in AH 18 or 19. The Iyād b. Nazīr tribe departed "with bag and baggage" and entered Byzantine territory after the Muslims conquered Mesopotamia.[79] Again in AH 20, the Christian Arab tribe of Banū Taghlib threatened to leave the adjacent Syrian banks of the Euphrates for asylum in Byzantine territory. They were reportedly angered by Muslim efforts to tax them and the pejorative character of the tax. They had allegedly crossed the river, presumably the Euphrates, on their way to Byzantine territory when Caliph 'Umar forestalled the move by adjusting their tax obligations. Islamic historians of this incident have normally concentrated their attention on its information about early Muslim taxation of non-Muslims, but for the Byzantinist the incident underlines the volatility of tribal allegiances, the attraction or at least reasonable alternative of a move to Byzantine territory, and the desire of a caliph to prevent any such move.[80]

Some Monophysite Christians did acquiesce in the Muslim conquest of Byzantine Osrhoene and Mesopotamia but there was no widespread disloyalty to the Byzantine Empire. Only a few towns put up much violent resistance, and that was crushed. But the Christian Arab tribes who fled or unsuccessfully strove to flee to Heraclius were Monophysite Christians, and yet they did not wish to be subjects of the new masters of Syria. Christian

[79] al-Ṭabarī i 2507 (Juynboll trans. *History* 88).
[80] Banū Taghlib threaten to leave caliphal territory in AH 20: Balādhurī 181–3.

sectarian differences did not cause the failure of Byzantine resistance, or in any case they surely were not the primary cause.[81]

The problem of tribal migration is a fundamental dimension of the truce agreement for Mesopotamia. The phrase in Theophanes' chronicle about crossing the Euphrates peacefully should be understood in terms of the practice of migration of Arab tribal groupings in that region. The chronicler does not preserve the full text of the agreement, but it is very possible that to prevent 'Iyāḍ b. Ghanm's Arabs from crossing into Byzantine Osrhoene and Mesopotamia, all Arabs, including ones traditionally friendly to Byzantium, may have been forbidden to cross the river. We do not know, because the complete text is not given. That would help explain Heraclius' anger against John Kateas for signing such an agreement, in addition to John's paying the not inconsiderable sum of 100,000 gold *nomismata* annually to prevent invasion.

'Iyāḍ's Arabs in any case were not to cross peacefully as Arabs had customarily done in earlier years. If Arabs had not been accustomed to cross the Euphrates into Osrhoene and Mesopotamia it would have been unnecessary to stress that they could cross neither in a hostile nor in a peaceful fashion or manner. The agreement was untenable in the long run. Either tribal jealousies would have been exacerbated by permitting some tribes to cross the Euphrates and not others, or if the agreement was understood to forbid all Arabs from crossing it would have unwittingly undermined long-term Byzantine friendships and ties with specific tribes and would have embarrassed Heraclius and created a bad precedent for future Byzantine relations with whatever remaining friends they had among Arab tribes. It likewise created an expensive and humiliating precedent for relations with tribes under the control of Muslims. Theophanes' text is credible.

The struggle for Mesopotamia not only involved that lush pasturage and the important trade routes but also affected whether, in effect, Byzantium could retain a significant hold on and access to traditionally or potentially friendly and useful Arab tribes, as she had generally managed to do since, indeed before, the fourth century. In retrospect, that short struggle may have seemed stupid and impractical for Heraclius to attempt. Yet even the maintenance of Byzantine control for the year or two longer after the evacuation of Syria did permit a significant contingent of Arabs under the last

[81] J. Moorhead, "The Monophysite Response to the Arab Invasions," *Byzantion* 51 (1981) 579–91; Stephan Gerö, "Only a Change of Masters? The Christians of Iran and the Muslim Conquest," *Transition Periods in Iranian History. Actes du Symposium de Fribourg-en-Breisgau (22–24 mai 1985)* [*Studia Iranica*, book 5, 1987] 43–8; Friedhelm Winkelmann, "Die Quellen zur Erforschung des monoenergetisch-monotheletischen Streites," *Klio* 69 (1987) 515–59.

Ghassānid king, Jabala b. al-Ayham, to escape successfully into Byzantine territory, and it is unclear whether they would have been able to escape otherwise, for they might have been cut off and destroyed, as were some other Arab tribesmen who attempted to flee to Heraclius by way of the mountain passes to the northwest of Antioch.

IMPLICATIONS OF THE LOSS OF MESOPOTAMIA

The loss of Mesopotamia cut off Byzantium from friendly Arab tribes and their manpower and contributed significantly to the need to develop new sources of military manpower and more effective strategies and tactics for fighting Arabs; it was clear by now, in contrast to a century earlier, that the empire could no longer fight Arabs by merely hiring other Arabs. The empire had to change its ways of waging war against the Arabs. The picture that one gains from the sources is of a rapidly changing situation that was still in flux but forming a drastically different relationship between Byzantium and the Arabs. Byzantium and some of Byzantium's long-time Arab allies were desperately striving to maintain or restore old ties, while the new masters of the lands south and west of the Euphrates were at least equally determined to sever irrevocably those old ties between Byzantium and some Arabs. Finally, the loss of Mesopotamia prevented Byzantium from taking any possible action with the Persians against the Muslims, and it prevented Byzantium from helping to save the collapsing Persian Empire. (Byzantine aid to friendly Persian rulers was not out of the question, as events had proved in 590–1, and 628–30.)

One may legitimately ask whether in the long run it really mattered whether the Byzantine commanders secured truces from the Muslims in 637 or thereafter, for the Byzantines soon lost these territories irretrievably (except for a partial reconquest of some parts in the late tenth and early eleventh centuries in a very different situation). The truces did not save Syria, Mesopotamia, or Egypt, but they did give Heraclius and his officials and commanders a respite in which to recover their balance, at a very precarious and dangerous moment, in order to prepare the ultimately successful defense of what was to become the empire's Anatolian heartland.

Those who departed with the Byzantine armies from those provinces – and little is known about the social and economic composition of the non-Arabs – have plausibly been assumed to include primarily individuals whose careers and prospects were closely connected with the Orthodox (Melkite) church and the Byzantine government, and possibly a few other ethnic Greeks and wealthy merchants and craftsmen. Although some individuals who departed may have possessed valuable skills, their departures do not appear to have disrupted the society and economy of their former towns and regions of residence. Greek sources say little of them, except for a few monastic and other ecclesiastical refugees. Muslim sources do make particular mention of Christian Arab refugees, both individuals and tribes or parts of tribes, who sought asylum in Byzantine territory. There are, of course, no reliable statistics, though as we have seen the number of Christian Arabs in the tribe of Ghassān who fled with Jabala is said to have totaled 30,000. The timing of the truces was therefore quite important for the survival of the Byzantine Empire, although not for the survival of Byzantine authority in Syria, Mesopotamia, and Egypt.[82]

IMPLICATIONS FOR INSTITUTIONAL DEVELOPMENTS

The case of Mesopotamia has relevance for the development of Byzantine institutions of the middle Byzantine period. Heraclius was implementing some kind of militarization of governmental authority. Azdī reported that Heraclius "appointed as his deputies over the cities of Syria commanders from his army" (*khallafa umarā' min jundihi 'alā madā'in al-Shām*). This is a reference to the sudden creation of certain emergency military authorities over specific cities in Syria and Palestine.[83] He was doing this in response to the growing Muslim threat. The description of his actions in Mesopotamia conforms to the ones that Azdī, Kūfī, and Ibn 'Asākir (or, more correctly, their sources) state that he had attempted in Syria. Fragments of this process can be followed in the Arabic and Greek and Syriac sources. The scraps of information from reports about these twilight moments of Byzantine Mesopotamia are extremely valuable. They help to elucidate part of the historically contingent *ad hoc* process by which special emergency improvisations in the appointment of military commanders replaced unsatisfactory traditional late Roman civilian officials and thereby intensified and accelerated the transformation of late Roman institutions into middle Byzantine ones. It is impossible to understand this process without considering the evidence from Byzantine Mesopotamia, fragmentary though it is. These commanders may have been *vicarii*.

[82] On the problem of the flight of refugees from Syria and elsewhere into Byzantine territory there is, surprisingly, no general study of satisfactory quality. Scattered references in the primary sources make research difficult although far from impossible: Balādhurī, 163–8 De Goeje; Ibn al-Athīr (2: 386 Tornberg). Melkite church: Hugh Kennedy, "The Melkite Church from the Islamic Conquest to the Crusades: Continuity and Adaptation in the Byzantine Legacy," *Major Papers, The 17th International Byzantine Congress* (New Rochelle, NY: Caratzas, 1986) 325–43; Sidney Griffith, "Stephan of Ramlah and the Christian Kerygma in Arabic in Ninth-Century Palestine," *Journal of Ecclesiastical History* 36 (1985) 23–45; Griffith, "Theodore Abu Qurrah's Arabic Tract on the Christian Practice of Venerating Images," *JAOS* 105 (1985) 53–73; Robert Schick, *Christian Communities of Palestine.*

[83] Azdī 31; Ibn al-Athīr 2: 311, 317–18; al-Ṭabarī i 2104.

From another historical perspective, Heraclius' creation of these special military commanders is just another example of *ad hoc* experimentation with the unification of civilian and military powers in the hands of one official. This had already been happening in the era of Justinian.[84] These references in Azdī and other sources are rare examples of militarization that can be traced in at least fragmentary fashion, just as they were being created. There were explicit reasons for needing emergency unified authority to act unhesitatingly as Heraclius desired to assure coordination of local and imperial strategy and operations. The creation of these special military authorities at this time in Mesopotamia is especially significant. Mesopotamia was always one of the most vital areas for the Byzantines to defend against the Persians.

The fact that Heraclius had not already created such a military district or special commander for that area during or immediately following his wars against the Persians is extremely important because this is the area where one would have done it first of all, given its critical importance for defense against Persia. It was the most threatened region, it was rich, and it was located on the usual invasion route. If the motive for the creation of special military commanders had been protection against the Persians, a certain candidate for inclusion at the start would have been Mesopotamia. Yet it was later, at the time of the imminent withdrawal from Syria, that Heraclius replaced the governor there with a military commander, Ptolemaios.

Byzantine rule probably left some institutional traces in Mesopotamia, however. The Muslim imposition of a tax in Mesopotamia for support of an army on inhabitants of the countryside and not on the townspeople of Mesopotamia, which Abū Yūsuf reports, may well be a continuation of the late Roman and Byzantine tax procedures. At a minimum, it is a striking parallel in that same area to what is specifically mentioned in the legislation of Justinian I,[85] who explicitly made inhabitants of that region responsible for supplying the army. Later Muslim commentators did not understand the origin of this tax custom in the persistence of some institutional practices of the sixth century up to the end of Byzantine authority.

CONTINUING MILITARY OPERATIONS

The details on the capture or the reduction of the remaining towns and localities of Byzantine Mesopotamia are the subject of a number of Muslim traditions that present no special difficulties of interpretation. But an

[84] Ralph-Johannes Lilie, "Die zweihundertjährige Reform. Zu den Anfängen der Themenorganisation im 7. und 8. Jahrhundert," *Byzsl* 45 (1984) 27–39; Haldon, *Byzantium* 209–10.

[85] Abū Yūsuf Ya'qūb, *Kitāb al-Kharāj*, ed. by Iḥsān 'Abbās (Beirut: Dār al-Shirūk, 1985) 136–8, allusion to taxes in kind which are reminiscent of the *annona*, Just. *Nov.* 134.1.

exception is the dubious reports that Muslims from Iraq played a decisive role in the conquest of Byzantine Mesopotamia. There have been recent attempts to argue for the plausibility of these Iraqi traditions. It will probably take some time to reevaluate this whole problem. There may have been some raids into Byzantine Mesopotamia from Iraq, but the principal starting point for the conquest of that area was probably Syria. Perplexing and even more difficult to refute are the reports of Byzantine counterattacks into Mesopotamia and northern Syria.[86] These require serious investigation, but it must be a separate and thorough one on another occasion. What is clear is that there was no extensive fighting away from walled towns in Mesopotamia. Although Byzantine commanders obeyed Heraclius' orders that they should not attempt to fight the Muslims in the open country there but should try to hold on to existing positions wherever possible, such a strategy did not save Byzantine Mesopotamia. Efforts to pursue a strategy of defensive positional warfare were to prove no more successful in holding Mesopotamia than they had been in Syria.

A controversial historical problem is whether there ever was a Byzantine effort to recover Ḥimṣ from Mesopotamia after the Byzantines lost it to the Muslims a second time, after the battle of the Yarmūk. Some Iraqi traditions claim that the Byzantines thrust at Ḥimṣ from Mesopotamia – that is, from the trans-Euphrates area – and even that Heraclius participated in such a land campaign. Yet no Byzantine source corroborates this tradition. Wellhausen had rejected its authenticity because of his theories about the self-serving motives of some historians of what he hypothesized was an Iraqi school. This tradition assumes an uprising of a *ḥāḍir* or camp of Arabs of the tribe of Tanūkh at Qinnasrīn, in support of a Byzantine effort to retake Ḥimṣ with the aid of expeditionary forces from Mesopotamia. It is plausible that there was a *ḥāḍir* at Qinnasrīn, but it is uncertain whether the Byzantines remained sufficiently strong and energetic after their debacle at Yarmūk to be able to contemplate and to attempt a major reconquest of such a vital nodal point of communications as Ḥimṣ was.[87] Other Muslim sources explicitly claim that there were no battles in Syria after that of the Yarmūk, an assertion that calls into question the authenticity of traditions about an unsuccessful Byzantine thrust to recover Ḥimṣ. In any case, such traditions cannot be accepted at face value without critical scrutiny. The most that can

[86] al-Ṭabarī i 2501–2. J. Wellhausen, *Skizzen und Vorarbeiten* (Berlin 1899) 6: 81–8; cf. Nadine Posner, "The Muslim Conquest of Mesopotamia," *passim*.

[87] Balādhurī 144–5. Wellhausen, *Skizzen und Vorarbeiten* 6: 81–8. N. Posner assumes the authenticity of this tradition: "Muslim Conquest" 258–82; I. Shahid, *BAFOC* 402–7, 481–5. Byzantinists have generally ignored these Muslim reports, although A. Stratos, Βυζάντιον 3: 84–6, is rightfully skeptical about these reports of a Byzantine recapture of Antioch, Aleppo, Qinnasrīn, and other cities by Constantine, son of Heraclius.

be said is that many inhabitants of northern Syria, including Arabs, did not welcome the Muslims. The truce at Chalkis encouraged their restiveness and unrealistic hopes, perhaps abetted by a few Byzantine intrigues and military repositionings and limited movements in contested border areas. In later traditions those circumstances became distorted into wholly unhistorical major Byzantine expeditions to recover Ḥimṣ and Syria by land or sea.

The inability of Byzantine forces from Egypt to coordinate their military actions with other Byzantine forces in Mesopotamia and Syria had already been demonstrated in 613 when Niketas, cousin of Heraclius, had been unable to aid Heraclius in fighting the Persians near Antioch, Syria.[88] The brief Byzantine effort to hold Mesopotamia may have diverted some attention and some human and material resources away from the critically exposed and soon to be lost Byzantine Egypt, but it was not the cause of the Byzantine loss of Egypt. If anything, the holding of Mesopotamia helped to divert Muslim attention away from Byzantine Asia Minor. The outcome was a short but probably vital breathing spell that permitted Heraclius and Byzantine commanders to regroup soldiers, scatter garrisons, and think about strategy and tactics and problems of holding the Taurus mountain passes against the Muslims.

In other words, the attention of the new Muslim rulers of Syria was diverted briefly to consolidating communications with Iraq and eliminating any possibility of a Byzantine or Byzantine and Christian Arab thrust to recover Syria, and thus it delayed a Muslim assault on Asia Minor and, ultimately, Constantinople. Those years are so obscure that it is difficult to make a confident judgment, but the jockeying and maneuvering in Byzantine Mesopotamia, and around Samosata and Melitēnē, should not be overlooked in trying to understand how certain historical contingencies contributed to the survival of Byzantine Asia Minor despite Byzantine military catastrophes in Palestine and Syria. What Heraclius and his advisers and generals needed most after the debacle in Syria was time. Their insistence on trying to resist and retain – even for a fleeting time – Chalkis/Qinnasrīn, Osrhoene, Mesopotamia, and such cities along the Euphrates as Melitēnē contributed, whether intentionally or not, to providing some of that valuable time.

Although both Byzantine and Muslim antagonists had good reason for still believing in the importance of Osrhoene and Mesopotamia in the late 630s, still bearing in mind the role of those regions in the border warfare of the fourth, fifth, and sixth centuries, the conditions that had produced that strategic frame of mind were to disappear permanently. Although the

[88] *Vie de Théodore Saint de Sykéôn* c. 166, lines 22–4 (1: 154 Festugière); Sebēos, *Histoire* c. 24 (95 Bedrosian, 67–8 Macler). N. H. Baynes, "The Military Operations of the Emperor Heraclius," *United Services Magazine* 47 (1913) 196.

Byzantines temporarily regained Edessa and what had once been known as Osrhoene, they never recovered the province of Mesopotamia after losing it in AH 17/18. With that irrevocable loss disappeared any conception of the area as the essential pivot for warfare such as it had had in the long Byzantine–Persian (and Roman–Parthian) wars. It was replaced by the tedious and very difficult struggle for the Taurus mountain passes and the access points to the Anatolian plateau, a new eastern frontier.[89]

[89] John Haldon and Hugh Kennedy, "The Arab–Byzantine Frontier in the Eighth and Ninth Centuries: Military Organisation and Society in the Borderlands," *ZRVI* 19 (1980) 79–116. For one hostile Christian perspective from north Mesopotamia on the Byzantines: S. P. Brock, "North Mesopotamia in the Late Seventh Century. Book XV of John Bar Penkaye's *Rīš Mellē*," *JSAI* 9 (1987) 51–75.

Chapter 8

BYZANTIUM, ARMENIA, ARMENIANS, AND EARLY ISLAMIC CONQUESTS

THE CONTEXT

The Muslim invasions and conquest of Byzantine Armenia in the seventh century become intelligible only in light of the Muslim conquest of Byzantine Mesopotamia and, to a lesser extent, of northern Syria. Byzantine Armenia was not initially an object in and of itself, even though it possessed some valuable assets. Armenia did contain rich pasturelands, despite its formidable winters. It possessed livestock, minerals, timber, and manpower, which was even more valuable because of the loss of Mesopotamia with its recruiting ground for friendly Arabs, and it dominated some key trade routes as well as strategic mountains. Booty in Armenia was probably not the main Muslim objective, at least at the strategic level. Its timber may have been too difficult to transport out of Armenia on a cost-effective basis. The Muslim invasion and conquest of Armenia was a consequence of and inextricably connected with the consolidation of power in Mesopotamia and made strategic sense. The Muslim invasion and conquest of Georgia derived from opportunities discovered in the wake of the conquest of Armenia.

The evidence for Heraclius' interest in Armenia and his fellow Armenians is overwhelming. Although his birthplace and his exact date of birth (*c.* 575) are uncertain, his father, also named Heraclius, may have come from Theodosiopolis (Erzurum).[1] Heraclius summoned and personally attended a synod at Theodosiopolis in 633 to unify the Armenian church with his Monothelite one.[2] He extensively recruited Armenians for his campaigns against the Persians in the 620s,[3] and gave them a major role in his campaigns

[1] Theophylact Simocatta, *Hist.* 1.1.1. I thank R. W. Thomson, R. Hewsen and R. W. Edwards for help. C. Mango, "Deux études sur Byzance et la Perse Sassanide," *TM* 9 (1985) 114, remains unconvinced about the identification of the birthplace of Heraclius.

[2] *Narratio de rebus Armeniae* 121–2, ed. by Gérard Garitte (CSCO, vol. 132, Subsidia, T. 4 [Louvain 1952]) 43, 302–11.

[3] Baynes, "Military Operations"; Kaegi, "Two Studies in the Continuity of Byzantine and Late Roman Military Institutions," *ByzF* 8 (1982) 87–113.

against the Muslims. However, Heraclius was not more of an Armenian than a Byzantine. He unquestionably placed the empire's interests high, as he understood them. Armenian generals and troops remained prominent in the succession crisis that followed the death of Heraclius.[4] They were an important but not, however, the exclusive bloc of support, especially military support, for the Heraclian dynasty and for efforts to defend Armenia against the Muslims.

Heraclius did not receive unanimous support from Armenians. His ecclesiastical policies aroused considerable opposition from many Armenian clerics and monks.[5] Armenians may have influenced some of his policies, such as the desire to defend Mesopotamia and certain military strong points on the edge of northern Syria, but their influence was certainly not unlimited. He did not decide questions of policy exclusively in terms of their repercussions or acceptability among Armenians inside or outside of Armenia.

Armenians had spread out in areas adjacent to but beyond the limits of historical Armenia in the early seventh century. The lack of population statistics makes it impossible to determine the relative percentage of the population who were Armenian in any province or town. Although there were able-bodied Armenians, it is impossible to know how many of them were potentially available for service in Heraclius' armies, or indeed how many were serving at any time in his armies, or what percentage of total military personnel in the Byzantine armies, infantry and/or cavalry, at that time or later, was Armenian.[6] The Byzantine forces were unable to retain control of the eastern regions of Armenia that Heraclius had briefly brought within the potential reach of some kind of Byzantine authority. They did succeed, however, in retaining some areas inhabited by Armenians that ultimately became known as the Armeniak Theme. Geography hindered the delivery of Byzantine assistance (or the imposition of Byzantine authority) and, if anything, favored the Muslims in Mesopotamia, who probably had slightly better access to Armenia than did the Byzantines.

The contentiousness of Armenians made it impossible to organize an effective defense against the Muslims. Some Armenians, such as Theodore Reshtuni, found it in their interest to switch to the Muslim side, or even to

[4] Peter Charanis, "The Armenians in the Byzantine Empire," *Byzsl* 22 (1961) 196–240; repr. Calouste Gulbenkian Foundation, Lisbon.

[5] Sebēos, *Hist.* c. 29–38 (115–78 Bedrosian, 90–149 Macler); *Narratio de rebus Armeniae* 121–50 (43–7, 258–350 Garitte).

[6] Cf. A. P. Kazhdan, *Armiane v sostov gospodstvuiuschchego klassa Vizantiiskoi imperii v 11–12 vv* (Yerevan: Akademii Nauk Armen. SSR, 1975); P. Charanis, "The Armenians in the Byzantine Empire," and "How Greek was the Byzantine Empire?," both reprinted (V: 196–240; XXII: 101–16, esp. 113–15) in his collected essays: *Studies on the Demography of the Byzantine Empire* (London: Variorum, 1972).

help Muslim forces defeat Armenian resisters. Although ecclesiastical disagreements concerning Chalcedon and Monotheletism had some real effect, and their ecclesiastical leaders, the Catholicos Ezr and then Nersēs, definitely influenced events, the fundamental local impetus favoring the Muslims was internal division and strife between Armenians, making it impossible for them to present a unified resistance, with or without Byzantine assistance, against the Muslims.[7]

Heraclius passed much of his life in greater proximity to Armenia and Armenians than would any other emperor until the tenth century. Not only did he spend his youth there, campaign there against Persians, recruit there, and summon a synod there, but his lengthy stay in Syria and even his flight via Edessa and Samosata kept him closer to Armenians and Armenian problems than he would have been if he had stayed, as his predecessors had for two centuries, at Constantinople. He did not, of course, possess total knowledge of affairs in Armenia, although for many years in the 620s and 630s he was located in or close to areas of Armenia and to Armenians coming to and from their homeland.

An appreciation of the role of Armenia and solicitude for Armenians is essential to understanding the waning years of Heraclius, whose reign was one in which some Armenians were intellectually prominent, e.g., Ananias of Shirak.[8] Armenians served as cavalry for the Byzantines, but presumably not exclusively as cavalry. They were capable of using a wide variety of weapons. Although militarily important, they possessed no inherent advantage in fighting the Muslims in open country. If anything the Muslim conquests made Armenians even more strategically important than before for the Byzantines.[9]

Armenia differed from Syria and Palestine in that many of its inhabitants were armed, and much, but not all, of its terrain favored defense against invaders. The Byzantine government probably never successfully enforced its

[7] It is inappropriate to review Byzantine–Armenian ecclesiastical history during the reign of Heraclius here. Old is L. Bréhier, in: *Histoire de l'église depuis les origines jusqu'à nos jours* (Paris: Bloud and Gay, 1938) 103–24, 131–43, 155–60; L. Duchesne, *Eglise au VIe siècle* (Paris 1925) 385–97; Jan Louis Van Dieten, *Geschichte der Patriarchen von Sergios I. bis Johannes VI. (610–715)* (Amsterdam: Hakkert, 1972) 28, 35, 70. V. Grumel, "Recherches sur l'histoire du monothélisme," *EO* 27 (1928) 15–16, 277; C. Toumanoff, *Studies in Christian Caucasian History* (Washington: Georgetown University Press, 1963) 476–7, n. 171. Karekin Sarkissian, *The Council of Chalcedon and the Armenian Church* (London: SPCK, 1965), and N. Garsoïan, "Some Preliminary Precisions on the Separation of the Armenian and Imperial Churches," Καθηγητρία 249–85, for surveys of earlier background.

[8] H. Berbérian, "Autobiographie d'Anania Sirakc'i," *REArm* n.s. 1 (1964) 189–94; Paul Lemerle, "Note sur les données historiques de l'autobiographie d'Anania de Shirak," *REArm* n.s. 1 (1964) 195–202.

[9] W. E. Kaegi, "al-Balâdhurî and the Armeniak Theme," *ASRB*, which is a revised version of article publ. in *Byzantion* 38 (1969) 273–7. On this, see Laurent, *L'Arménie* 566 n. 3.

prohibition against the possession or purchase or sale of weapons by private individuals in its Armenian territories. The terrain and remoteness of the area, together with local traditions, probably hindered any such enforcement. In theory, Armenians were therefore better able than any other Byzantine provincials to develop local armed resistance against the Muslims and to resist religious conversion.

CHRONOLOGICAL ASSUMPTIONS

This is an outline of the Byzantine attempts to defend and the ultimately successful Muslim efforts to conquer Armenia, not a detailed narrative and evaluation of the history of Armenia. Here Armenia designates both the regions that traditionally lay within the Roman/Byzantine borders, for the most part west of the upper Euphrates, and those that lay to the east, in former Sassanian spheres of influence.[10] We must first review what is proposed to be the chronological framework, although some parts of it remain controversial.

The alert and aggressive Muslim commander ʿIyāḍ b. Ghanm overran Byzantine Mesopotamia in 639/40 while other Muslims under ʿAmr b. al-ʿĀṣ began their invasion of Egypt in December 639. In the following year, in 640, Muslims invaded Byzantine Armenia from Mesopotamia under the command of ʿIyāḍ b. Ghanm. In the same year, 640, Byzantine Generals Dawitʿ (David) Urṭaya and Titus made an abortive campaign in Mesopotamia and there may have been, although the report is probably false, some kind of Byzantine raid toward Ḥimṣ. The year 640 also experienced the fall of Caesarea in Palestine. On 11 February 641 Heraclius died, followed on 20 April or 20–24 May 641 by the death of Heraclius Constantine or Constantine III, and the intensification of the Byzantine succession quarrel. In late (probably November) 641 Martina and her son Heraclonas were overthrown, which left Constans II as sole Byzantine emperor. In early 642 the Byzantine Empire suffered from the abortive revolt of General Valentinus, and the loss of Egypt, and the beginning of the Muslim invasion of Cyrenaica. In 642–3 the second Muslim invasion of Armenia took place. The Byzantine government's attention was diverted from Armenia in 644 by the first Muslim expedition to Amorion, in 647 by the unsuccessful revolt of

[10] The chronology is the composite of my own reflections on the sources and modern scholarship. I do follow some of the basic conclusions of H. Manandian about the dating of Muslim invasions: see below for details; cf. P. Speck, *Das geteilte Dossier* 44–50. On the borders, see Honigmann, *Ostgrenze* 16–37; *Le Synekdèmos d'Hieroklès et l'opuscule géographique de Georges de Chypre*, ed. trans. and comment. by Ernst Honigmann (CBHB, Forma Imperii Byzantini, fasc. 1 [Brussels: Editions de l'Institut de Philologie et d'Histoire Orientales et Slaves, 1939]) p. 37 (nos. 702.9, 703.6), pp. 64–6.

Gregory the Exarch in Africa, and in 649 by the Muslim raid and invasion of Cyprus. The year 650 marked the third Muslim invasion of Armenia, which concluded with a three-year truce negotiated by the Byzantine envoy Procopios with Muʿāwiya, governor of Syria. In 652 there was a conspiracy of some Armenian commanders and troops in the Byzantine army. Developments reached their culmination in 653 when Theodore Reshtuni pledged the subjugation of Armenia to Muʿāwiya, governor of Syria. In 653 Emperor Constans II left Armenia after campaigning there indecisively, effectively conceding that the Muslim conquest of Armenia would be accomplished by Ḥabīb b. Maslama. The Byzantine authorities' attention was diverted in 655 by the naval battle of Phoenix ("Battle of the Masts"). That year the Muslims consolidated their control of Armenia by capturing Theodosiopolis and deporting Theodore Reshtuni, who died in Syria in 656. Between 654 and 661 Hamazasp Mamikonian was supreme commander of the Armenians, and in 656, during the outbreak of Muslim civil war, he attempted rebellion. In 659 Caliph Muʿāwiya negotiated an expensive truce with Byzantium. In 661 Ḥabīb b. Maslama invaded Armenia. Finally, in 662, Muʿāwiya recognized Grigor Mamikonian as commander of Armenians and Armenia paid tribute to Muʿāwiya. The first stage in the Byzantine–Muslim struggle for control of Armenia had resulted in a Muslim triumph.

THE PROMINENCE OF ARMENIANS IN SYRIA AND MESOPOTAMIA

Armenians were prominent passive and active contemporaries of events in the 630s and 640s. While this is not the proper occasion for a total reexamination of Byzantine–Armenian questions in the seventh century, extant sources permit some reconsiderations and new conclusions.[11] Of particular importance is Heraclius' concern for Armenians and Armenia immediately after the debacle of his armies at the Yarmūk.[12]

Armenians were prominent in Syria, Palestine, and Egypt after Heraclius' recovery of those provinces from the Persians. Unsettled conditions prevailed

[11] Chr. [Hratz] M. Bartikian, Βυζάντιον εἰς τὰς Ἀρμενικὰς Πηγάς. Byzantina Keimena kai Meletai, 18 (Thessaloniki: Center for Byzantine Studies, 1981). There is, unfortunately, no study of Byzantine images of the Armenians in the sixth and seventh centuries, except: S. Vryonis, "Byzantine Images of the Armenians," in: *The Armenian Image in History and Literature*, ed. by Richard G. Hovannisian (Studies in Near Eastern Culture and Society, 3 [Malibu: Undena, 1981]) 65–81.

[12] Despite the title, there is very little on the initial Muslim conquests of Armenia in Aram Ter-Ghewondyan [Ghévondian], "L'Arménie et la conquête arabe," *Armenian Studies/Etudes Arméniennes in Memoriam Haïg Berbérian*, ed. by Dickran Kouymjian (Lisbon: Calouste Gulbenkian Foundation, 1986) 773–92. He accepts Manandian's chronology of Muslim invasions in the summer of 640, again in 642–3, and in 650 via Atropatenē, p. 773. Broad survey: Gérard Dédéyan, *Histoire des Arméniens* (Toulouse: Privat, 1982) esp. 177–214.

in parts of Armenia in the early 630s. The civil strife in Persia after the assassination of Chosroes II, and the troubles connected with the Persian slowness to evacuate the Byzantine territory they had occupied, probably were contributing causes. Many Armenians visited holy places in those regions as religious pilgrims. St. Anastasius the Sinaite states that Armenians were particularly numerous in the Sinai just before the Muslim conquest. Some of those pilgrims probably came not directly from Armenia proper but from posts, whether military or civilian, in Syria, Palestine, and Egypt.[13] Heraclius appears to have relied heavily on his fellow Armenians in the selection of appointees, especially major officials and military commanders.[14] However, a list of seventh-century Armenian monasteries in Jerusalem may be inauthentic.[15]

ARMENIAN TROOPS DURING THE MUSLIM CONQUEST OF SYRIA

Allegations that a revolt of Armenians in support of General Vahān's candidacy to be emperor and a supporting revolt by his Armenian troops caused the disaster of Yarmūk are probably false attempts to find scapegoats and deflect blame from the Heraclian dynasty. Arabic traditions do mention disorderly conduct among Vahān's troops, but no rebellion. It is quite possible that some of these Armenians did manage to escape from the battle and make their way north toward their Armenian homelands. The Armenian

13 Michael E. Stone, "Holy Land Pilgrimage of Armenians Before the Arab Conquest," *Revue Biblique* 93 (1986) 93–110; E. W. Brooks, "An Armenian Visitor to Jerusalem in the Seventh Century," *EHR* 11 (1896) 93–7. Stone convincingly redates the travels of Yovsep' and Mxit'ar from Armenia to Jerusalem and back via the Byzantine-controlled Taurus to the late or possibly the early 630s, not the 660s, as Brooks had done. There is no direct evidence that the troubles for travelers derived from Arabs, whether Muslim or otherwise. They could merely reflect chaos in Persia because of the internal strife about the royal succession after the death of Chosroes II: *The History of the Caucasian Albanians by Movses Dasxuranci*, trans. by Charles Dowsett, c. 50, London Oriental Series, vol. 8 (London: Oxford University Press, 1961) 181–3. Also, Robert W. Thomson, "A Seventh-Century Armenian Pilgrim on Mount Tabor," *JTS* 18 (1967) 27–33.

14 F. Nau, "Le Texte grec des récits du moine Anastase," *Oriens Christianus* 2 (1902) 81–2, 78. Musele: "Passio LX martyrum," *AB* 23 (1904) 303; Henri Grégoire, "An Armenian Dynasty on the Byzantine Throne," *Armenian Quarterly* 1.1 (1946) 4–21; Cyril Toumanoff, "Caucasia and Byzantium," *Traditio* 27 (1971) 149, for a partial list of prominent Armenians in the imperial service in the reign of Heraclius.

15 On Armenian monasteries in Jerusalem, see *The History of the Caucasian Albanians, by Movses Dasxuranci*, book II, c. 52, trans. by C. J. F. Dowsett (London: Oxford University Press, 1961) 184–5. List of seventh-century Armenian monasteries in Jerusalem: R. Nisbet Bain, "Armenian Description of the Holy Places in the Seventh Century," *Palestine Exploration Fund Quarterly Statement* (1896) 346–9, which is a very questionable, indeed very legendary source: Avedis Sanjian, "Anastas Vardapet's List of Armenian Monasteries in Seventh-Century Jerusalem: A Critical Examination," *Le Muséon* 82 (1969) 265–92.

historian Sebēos claims to have gained his information about Byzantine–Muslim clashes in Syria and Armenia through conversations with former prisoners.[16]

Much of Heraclius' effort after the Byzantine defeat at the battle of the Yarmūk was intended to stabilize the military front, regroup, and play for time in order to establish a new defensive line somewhere in the north but also to permit the largest possible number of Armenians, both soldiers and civilians together with clergy and monks, to flee to safety. Ibn Isḥāq claimed that 12,000 Armenians fought in the Byzantine armies at the battle of the Yarmūk. This was part of the reason why Heraclius ordered his troops to cut the roads and fight hard to recover and then destroy Melitēnē. In addition to Byzantine territory, he wished to protect his homeland of Armenia and its valuable manpower from the ravages and horrors of invasion.[17]

A substantial number of the Byzantine troops who attempted to defend Byzantine Mesopotamia against the Muslims probably were of Armenian origin.[18] A prominent Armenian commander of the defense of Mesopotamia was allegedly "Rūbīl al-Armanī," although the source, a false Wāqidī, is suspicious.[19] Another commander, reportedly of 4,000 Byzantine soldiers, was Yūryak the Armenian ("Yūryak al-Armanī"), who is otherwise unknown.[20] He supposedly assisted the unsuccessful defense of Circesium against the Muslims. Pseudo-Wāqidī also claims that "Kīlūk" the Armenian was ruler ("*ṣāḥib*") of Edessa, but there is no other source for this doubtful information.[21] Another supposedly famous unsuccessful combatant against the Muslims, this time in the defense of Ḥarrān, was "Arjūk" the Armenian.[22] The lord of Akhlāṭ reportedly sent 4,000 cavalry under his daughter Ṭāryūn to Shahryāḍ b. Farūn for the defense of Rās al-'Ayn against the Muslims.[23] This relief force passed through Bitlis and Ḥiṣn Kayf and thereby underscored their military importance for the campaigning in Mesopotamia. Armenia could not, if these reported actions have any historical reality, be ignored by the Muslims.

If the above reports were true, it would be easier to comprehend how the Muslims' campaign to overrun Mesopotamia necessarily involved their military commanders in the conquest or neutralization of strategically

16 Sebēos, *Hist.* c. 30 (131 Bedrosian, 102 Macler). The prisoners probably were Armenian, not Greeks or Arabs or Persians, because that is the language that Sebēos could have most easily used to converse with them. Yet his phrasing is vague.

17 12,000 Armenians at the battle of the Yarmūk: al-Ṭabarī (Ibn Isḥāq) i 2347.

18 *Libri Wakedii De Mesopotamiae expugnatae historia*, ed. by G. H. A. Ewald (Göttingen: Dieterich, 1827) 18. See also Pseudo-Wāqidī, *Futūḥ al-Shām* (Beirut 1972) 111.

19 *Libri Wakedii De Mesopotamiae expugnatae historia*, ed. by G. H. A. Ewald (Göttingen: Dieterich, 1827) 19.

20 Pseudo-Wāqidī, *Futūḥ al-Shām* 106.

21 Pseudo-Wāqidī, *Futūḥ al-Shām* 129.

22 Pseudo-Wāqidī, *Futūḥ al-Shām* 128.

23 Pseudo-Wāqidī, *Futūḥ al-Shām* 131.

relevant areas of neighboring Armenia. It is impossible at this time to find independent confirmation of the historical reality of these personages, but later Muslim traditions attributed a major role to Armenians in the final moments of the Byzantine defense of Mesopotamia. Although the actual names and particulars may be confused, and it is impossible to ascertain their numbers or proportions in the Byzantine army, it is plausible to assume that Armenians were prominent in political and military roles in the waning period of Byzantine rule in Mesopotamia. Armenians probably fought in its defense as soldiers, and other Armenians probably exercised prominent political and military authority.

Armenia and Armenians had provided the springboard for Heraclius' successful efforts to create a Byzantine military recovery against the Persians in the 620s. A reasonable observer in the late 630s might have anticipated that Heraclius and Byzantium might be capable of repeating such a recovery against the Muslims, at least as long as the Byzantines retained control of Mesopotamia and Byzantine Armenia. Yet this was another question of historical repetition that did not fulfil itself in such a simplistic pattern.

ARMENIA ON THE EVE OF THE MUSLIM CONQUESTS

Unlike Palestine, Syria, Egypt, and Mesopotamia, Byzantine authority prior to the Muslim conquests had been very limited at the local level in many parts of Armenia. Heraclius had campaigned there extensively in the 620s and had devoted much effort to drawing all of it, not merely those areas that were formerly late Roman provinces, into dependency on him and identification with his church and empire. He enjoyed personal familiarity with much of Armenia. The initial Muslim invasions of Palestine and Syria arrested that process of Byzantinization and centralization of power by diverting Heraclius' attention away from tightening his control over Armenians, in particular those who were formerly in areas dependent on the Sassanians. In fact, the Muslim invasions probably contributed, paradoxically, to the preservation of Armenian distinctiveness, and in any case they slowed down and then reversed the incipient process of Byzantinization.[24] Yet the Muslim invasions made the Armenians and Armenia even more important to Heraclius and his immediate successors for manpower and for the strategic value of its topography. Those in power at Constantinople in the middle of the seventh century could not afford to lose their power base among Armenians, however tenuous it was and however many problems Armenians created for them. There are historical parallels between the agreement made

[24] A conclusion made by N. Garsoïan and others.

by Theodore Reshtuni and the Muslims and the long-standing duties of the Armenians toward their Sassanian rulers; the earlier military obligations come out clearly in the *History* of Elishē. It was this continuation of customary obligations that made it easier for Armenians to acknowledge Muslim control, especially since the latter did not impose any religious tests – unlike the imposition of Chalcedonian orthodoxy by Byzantines or attempts at imposing Zoroastrianism by Sassanians. Estimates of the number of Armenian troops in Byzantine Armenia in the decades before the Muslim invasions range from 15,000 to 30,000.[25] Their commander was probably the *magister militum per Armeniam*. The Muslims imposed a levy of 15,000 Armenian soldiers in their negotiations with Theodore Reshtuni in 653.

In no other region of the Byzantine Empire, and certainly no other one then exposed to the threat of Muslim invasion, did the local inhabitants have a tradition of being so well armed and prone to rely on themselves and their own family groupings and notables. The situation was exceptional and created a different situation for Muslim invaders and those Byzantines who tried to devise some viable military defenses.

The Muslim conquest of Mesopotamia in 639/40 immediately compelled the Muslim leader of that conquest, ʿIyāḍ b. Ghanm, to take measures to secure his newly won territory from attack from Armenia. Furthermore, Armenia itself had suffered much recent turbulence and was a tempting target for conquest itself. Its *naχarars*, or local lords, were engaging in destructive strife among themselves. There was dissent because of Heraclius' efforts to compel unification of the Armenians to his Monothelite church, a rash of court conspiracies late in the reign of Heraclius, the succession crisis, the drain of Byzantine attention and giving priority to the defense of Syria, and of course, the weakness and vacuum within the Sassanian Empire, all of which encouraged independence on the part of Armenian *naχarars* and their powerful and proud families.

All these conditions encouraged a surge of Armenian internal strife and striving for independence on the eve of the Muslim invasions. They contributed to Armenia's vulnerability and to the relative ineffectiveness of the Byzantine military effort against the Muslims there.[26] So many Byzantine troops had perished in Syria, and so many were tied up defending or holding what remained of the empire that no single-minded Byzantine defense of Armenia was possible at the beginning of the 640s. The ruinous succession dispute and the minority of Constans II (aged twelve at his accession in 641)

[25] Marius Canard, revision of Joseph Laurent, *L'Arménie entre Byzance et l'Islam depuis la conquête arabe jusqu'en 886* [henceforth cited as *Arménie*²]. New revised and enlarged edn. Armenian Library of the Calouste Gulbenkian Foundation (Lisbon: Bertrand, 1980) 93, 110 n. 23.

[26] René Grousset, *Histoire de l'Arménie des origines à 1071* (Paris: Payot, 1973) 256–95.

exacerbated the situation. As had been the case in Mesopotamia, the Byzantine army was in no shape to offer major resistance to the Muslims at the beginning of their invasion of Armenia in 640.

The Byzantine government at Constantinople did not enjoy absolute control of all of Armenia even late in the reign of Heraclius, although at that time it was probably more able to dominate local events than at any previous point in time. The succession crisis and the youth of Constans II, as well as the strife concerning the ambitions of General Valentinus, weakened Byzantine authority there at the time of the initial Muslim penetrations. A glance at the empire's internal situation in 640 and 642–3 underscores the limited ability of Constans II and his entourage to determine the course of events. Yet he perceived the importance of Armenia to his power, and that is why he campaigned there in person in 652–3.

A quick review of some of the personalities will suffice. Heraclius had given support to the general of the Greek region (whom he had raised in 629 to the rank of *išχan* or prince), Mžêž Gnuni, who met death at the hands of Davith Saharuni in 635, who then replaced him as *curopalates* from 635 to 638, when other Armenian *naχarars* forced him to flee.[27] Heraclius also supported Varaztirots' Bagratuni, *marzpān* (viceroy) of Armenia, and rival of Theodore Reshtuni. He honored Varaztirots' with a palace and supreme honors.[28] But Varaztirots' became implicated in a plot of Heraclius' bastard Athalaric and was exiled with his wife and sons to an island. At that time there was no general around whom Armenians were willing to rally.

Heraclius was attempting to rule Armenia in part by encouraging each of the prominent *naχarars* to seek favors, honors, and protection from him personally, thereby exploiting the competition of these rival family leaders for the benefit of his own imperial power. Such a game was possible as long as a powerful emperor who understood Armenia and Armenians was on the throne, but it always depended on his own political strength and the empire's external military situation, which began to deteriorate rapidly under the weight of the Muslim invasions of Syria.[29]

Theodore Reshtuni emerged as the *išχan* or prince and *sparapet* or commander-in-chief of Armenian forces, who united eastern and western

[27] Sebēos, *Hist.* c. 29 (118–20 Bedrosian, 93–4 Macler). A. Ter-Ghewondyan, "L'Arménie et la conquête arabe" 773. On the *išχan* of Armenia, trans. by Cyril Toumanoff as "Presiding Prince," see Toumanoff, "Caucasia and Byzantium," *Traditio* 27 (1971) 118–21, 139–40. See Laurent, *Arménie*[2] 116–17.

[28] Sebēos, *Hist.* c. 29 (118–19 Bedrosian, 92–3 Macler). Laurent, *Arménie*[2] 401.

[29] C. Toumanoff, "The Heraclids and the Arsacids," *REArm* 19 (1985) 431–4, repudiates his earlier attribution of the Heraclids to the Armenian Mamikonian family, "Caucasia and Byzantium," *Traditio* 27 (1971) 157–8; cf. D. Kouymjian, "Ethnic Origins and the 'Armenian' Policy of Heraclius," *REArm* n.s. 17 (1983) 635–42; I. Shahid, "The Iranian Factor in Byzantium During the Reign of Heraclius," *DOP* 26 (1972) 293–321, esp. 308–11.

parts of Armenia in 639, using the island of Aght'amar as his center of authority, just as the Muslims were conquering nearby Mesopotamia. Aght'amar is in the territory of the Reshtuni family, so Theodore was operating from his home base. All of this internal strife facilitated the Muslims' ability to find information and support, and profit from their opponents' divisions.[30] It was a disunited Armenia in which Byzantine influence fluctuated wildly and was at that moment at a low ebb.

Armenia possessed certain choke points which could serve to check an invader from the south, but there was no recent experience with conducting a defense against such an invasion. Critical were the passes, which required garrisons to block them. It was essential to maintain observation posts to perceive the route and intentions of any potential raiding party. The Bitlis Pass, Balouos Kastron, Xarperd (Kharpert, Harput), and Kamachon (Arabic, Kamkh, modern Kemah) are some of the important check points against invaders from the south, assuming the loss of upper Mesopotamia, including Martyropolis, Samosata, and Arsamosata. The Byzantine–Persian borders *c.* 600 have been ascertained to have run just east of Theodosiopolis (Erzurum), then south along the Göniksuyu, then south along the Nymphios (Batmansuyu today), then east along the Tigris to just beyond Kephe or Ḥiṣn Kayf, and then south in Mesopotamia along the Khābūr to the Euphrates at Circesium.[31] Yet there was no obvious defensible southern line. The difficult task of defense required organization, cooperation, vigilance, and readiness to act swiftly.

THE PROBLEM OF THE MUSLIM INVASIONS OF ARMENIA

There have been serious scholarly disputes about the correct chronology, direction, nature, and causes of the earliest Muslim invasions and conquest of Byzantine Armenian areas. The actual late Roman provincial divisions recognized Armenia I, II, III, and IV; however, Armenians populated other provinces in considerable numbers too.[32]

30 On the *sparapet*, Laurent, *Arménie*[2] 118 n. 138. On Thedore Reshtuni: Laurent, *L'Arménie* 401–2.

31 See Armenian maps prepared by Robert Hewsen for *Tübinger Atlas des Vorderen Orients*; map I, "Mesopotamia et Armenia Quarta," in: Honigmann, *Ostgrenze*. See Sebēos, *Hist.* c. 3 (27 Macler), for a description of the territorial cessions by Chosroes II. Place-names, H. Hübschmann, "Die altarmenischen Ortsnamen," *Indogermanische Forschungen* 16 (1904) 197–490.

32 Nina Garsoïan, s.v., "Armenia, Geography," *DMA* 1 (1982) 470–4. Out of date is H. Hübschmann, *Zur Geschichte Armeniens und der ersten Kriege der Araber* (Leipzig 1875). H. Thopdschian, "Armenien vor und während der Araberzeit," *Zeitschrift für Armenische Philologie* 2 (1904) 50–71. Caetani, *AI* 7: 67–85. Useful material in the text ascribed to Moses of Chorene: *Géographie de Moïse de Corène d'après Ptolemée*, ed. and trans. by P. Arsène Soukry (Venice: Imprimerie Arménienne, 1881) 36–46, for Armenia.

The basic chronology of the Muslim invasions and conquest was first established by Ghazarian,[33] and was reconfirmed by Manandian,[34] Der Nersessian,[35] Ter Ghewondyan,[36] Canard,[37] and Garsoïan.[38] This chronological structure is essentially satisfactory. Stratos' chronological revisions of Manandian are excessively ingenious and not entirely persuasive. Yet Stratos rightly emphasizes the importance of Mesopotamia as the starting point for Muslim invasions of Armenia. Stratos concludes that there were two separate Muslim invasions in 641 and 642, and he rejects Manandian's argument for dating the first invasion to late 640. Yet Manandian's chronology is reasonable for this date of 'Iyāḍ's first expedition, not necessarily, as Manandian thought, to Dvin but at least to Bitlis and Akhlāṭ, which accepted 'Iyāḍ's terms.[39]

'Iyāḍ probably penetrated no further than Bitlis and Akhlāṭ on the first Muslim expedition into Armenia. It is uncertain but possible that the first expedition, which probably started as a pursuit of retreating Byzantine troops of Armenian origin, extended as far as Dvin. Yet the Muslims faced difficult terrain and probably had a limited initial goal of consolidating control over Mesopotamia and preventing raids against it. Of course, 'Iyāḍ b. Ghanm was sufficiently opportunistic to take advantage of opportunities for enriching himself and his men by plundering Armenian towns and countryside.

The first and most serious Muslim invasions came not from the direction of Persia and Azerbaijan, or even from Iraq, but from Syria and Mesopotamia.[40] Yet some Armenian troops had fought in support of the Persians

[33] M. Ghazarian, *Armenien unter der arabischen Herrschaft* (Marburg 1903); E. Filler, "Quaestiones de Leontii Armenii Historia," *Commentationes Philologicae Ienenses*, vol. 7, fasc. 1 (Leipzig: Teubner, 1903) 9–11.

[34] Hacob A. Manandian, "Les Invasions arabes en Arménie," *Byzantion* 18 (1948) 163–92.

[35] Accepted (without citation) by Sirarpie Der Nersessian, "Between East and West: Armenia and Its Divided History," in: *The Dark Ages*, ed. by David Talbot Rice (London: Thames and Hudson, 1965) 76, who dates Arab invasions to 640, 642/3, and 650.

[36] Aram N. Ter-Ghewondyan, "L'Arménie et la conquête arabe," *Armenian Studies/Etudes Arméniennes in Memoriam Haïg Berbérian* 773–92. See also, Aram Ter-Ghewondyan, *The Arab Emirates in Bagratid Armenia*, trans. by Nina Garsoïan (Lisbon: Bertrand, 1976) 1–31, 46–7.

[37] Laurent, *Arménie*^{2} esp. 44, 55–6, 125, 236, 401–2. Also, Canard, "Arminiya," *EI*^{2} 1 (1960) 634–6. Grousset, *Histoire de l'Arménie* 296–8.

[38] Nina Garsoïan, s.v., "Armenia, History of," *DMA* 1 (1982) 478.

[39] A. Stratos, Βυζάντιον 4: 24–37, esp. 30–1, also his appendix IV, 276–8, used no untranslated Arabic sources. Gérard Dédéyan, *Histoire des Arméniens*, accepts, on p. 187, the date of 6 October 640 for the Muslim capture and pillage of Dvin.

[40] No new information on Armenia in R.-J. Lilie, *Die byzantinische Reaktion auf die Ausbreitung der Araber* (Munich 1976) 23–6, or elsewhere in his book, which has as its focus areas to the west. The text of Vardan published and studied by Joseph Muyldermans, *La Domination arabe en Arménie* (Louvain, Paris: J.-B. Istas, P. Geuthner, 1927), esp. 82–8, is a derivative chronicle.

against the Muslims at Qādisiyya, where the Muslims won a decisive victory in 637. Armenian troops who had served in both Byzantine and Persian armies had fled from engagements against the Muslims and were fearful of them. Among their concerns was awareness that Muslims remembered their recent military service against them.[41]

The first well-attested Muslim invasion of Armenia took place in 640 under the leadership of the formidable Muslim commander, 'Iyāḍ b. Ghanm, who had just completed the conquest of Mesopotamia. He probably began the expedition in the late summer of 640 as an extension, indeed part of the consolidation, of the Muslim seizure of Mesopotamia, especially of Byzantine Mesopotamia. Departing from his base in former Byzantine Mesopotamia, 'Iyāḍ b. Ghanm struck against the only forces – Armenians – who could threaten what had been Byzantine Mesopotamia. He penetrated as far as the cities of Bitlis and Akhlāṭ, which he compelled to accept his terms. He apparently also penetrated the region of Taron, Bznunik', Aliovit, the valley of Berkri, and the region of Ararat. At a minimum one can accept Balādhurī's account of 'Iyāḍ b. Ghanm's penetration as far as Akhlāṭ. He may have pushed further to the Ararat region and even to Dvin.[42]

An Armenian renegade, Vardik, prince of Mokk', allegedly helped the invading Muslims to cross the Mecamor River to Dvin, which they may have temporarily captured on 6 October 640, taking many captives. The tradition is suspicious. The Muslims successfully fought off Armenian ambushes on the way back to Mesopotamia. Theodore Reshtuni was unable to organize effective resistance. There is no evidence that Byzantine troops offered serious resistance to that raid. Any active resistance came from local Armenians. This invasion resulted in no immediate territorial occupation or conquest by the Muslims, although it revealed Armenian vulnerability.[43]

'Iyāḍ b. Ghanm then departed for Mesopotamia, where he passed through Raqqa and then went on to Ḥimṣ in Syria, where 'Umar appointed him governor. His expedition terminated at Ḥimṣ, where later 'Abd al-Raḥman b. Khālid b. al-Walīd would return after an expedition to Anatolia. This emphasizes the desire of central authorities to maintain control over such expeditionary forces.[44] 'Iyāḍ b. Ghanm died almost immediately, in 641, after the conclusion of this campaign. Theodore Reshtuni was then appointed commander-in-chief of Armenian forces by Constans II and was given the

[41] Note Sebēos, *Hist.* c. 30 (126–7 Bedrosian, 98–9 Macler).

[42] Sebēos, *Hist.* c. 30 (128–9 Bedrosian, 100 Macler). Manandian believes that this raid penetrated as far as Dvin, which he asserts that the Muslims captured: Manandian, "Les Invasions arabes" 176. 'Iyāḍ may have led more than 5,000 troops.

[43] Hacob Manandian, "Les Invasions arabes en Arménie" 168–9, 176–7.

[44] Balādhurī 176. Sebēos, *Hist.* c. 30 (128–30 Bedrosian, 100–1 Macler).

title of *patrikios*. The chronology is controversial.[45] The confused report in the *Chronicle* of Michael the Syrian about an abortive Byzantine military thrust into Mesopotamia by General Dawit' (David) Urṭaya, who was probably Armenian, and General Titus, indicates that Muslim fears of a Byzantine return in force were not entirely groundless.[46] Muslim traditions of unsuccessful Byzantine efforts to retain Ḥimṣ probably derive from that abortive campaign, which has received exaggerated fame in Muslim historiography.

Power shifted away from Mediterranean coastal cities to cities of the interior of Syria after the Muslim capture of the Levant.[47] Any potential threat from Armenia was all the more dangerous to a Muslim state whose center was now located in the interior. It was essential to protect that northern border. Whether or not Armenia was conquered, it was essential to weaken or neutralize or coopt the potential military strengths of Armenians.[48]

Constans II appointed another Armenian, Theodore, to command his military forces. Theodore in turn successfully appealed for Constans II to release and return Armenians who had been exiled to Africa. Theodore also sent Thuma to Armenia, where he illegally seized Theodore Reshtuni and brought him to Constans II, who, however, had him released.[49] Also released from Africa was the *aspet* Smbat, who refused to take allegiance to Byzantine control. After difficult negotiations he agreed to take an oath, but he died. Constans II promoted Smbat's son Smbat Bagratuni to be *aspet* and *drungarios*, and, probably in 649, he made Theodore Reshtuni general-in-chief.[50] Constans II sent Procopios to negotiate peace with Mu'āwiya at Damascus in 650. Mu'āwiya insisted on receiving Gregory, son of Theodore, brother of Heraclius, as hostage.[51] Gregory died a hostage in 652 at Hierapolis/Manbij, and his remains were returned to Constantinople for proper burial rites.

45 Sebēos, *Hist.* c. 30 (101 Macler). Marius Canard, "Arminiya," *EI*² 1: 634–6; Caetani, *AI* 4: 49–53, 165, 510–14; 5: 34; E. Dulaurier, *Chronol. Arm.* 357, 231. Asolik says 18 June 646/17 June 647: Dulaurier, *Chron. Arm.* 229. Dated to 642 by Thopdschian, "Armenien vor und während der Araberzeit" 64–71.

46 Michael the Syrian, *Chron.* 11.10 (2: 443–4 Chabot).

47 Hugh Kennedy, "The Last Century of Byzantine Syria: A Reinterpretation," *ByzF* 10 (1985) 141–85, and his "From Polis to Madina: Urban Change in Late Antique and Early Islamic Syria," *Past and Present* 106 (1985) 3–27.

48 Arab occupation, see Kh. 'Athamina, "Arab Settlement during the Umayyad Caliphate," *JSAI* 8 (1986) 194–5.

49 Sebēos, *Hist.* c. 32 (137–9 Bedrosian, 106–7 Macler). See Manandian, "Les Invasions arabes" 190–2.

50 Sebēos, *Hist.* c. 32 (138–41 Bedrosian, 108 Macler). Date: Manandian, "Les Invasions arabes" 191, 194.

51 Theoph., *Chron.*, AM 6143 (344 De Boor). P. Peeters, "Πασαγνάθης-Περσογενής," *Byzantion* 8 (1933) 418–19.

Constans II removed Theodore Reshtuni from his duties but still sought his aid against the Muslims. A confused account by Theophanes has led to an incorrect belief that Theodore Reshtuni's son Vardik – in prearranged concert with his father Theodore – betrayed a bridge that he was supposed to guard,[52] and even that this defection caused the panic and destruction of the Byzantine forces at the hands of the Muslim invaders.[53]

The exact borders between Byzantine and Muslim authority in Armenia are obscure, but the town of Derzene (Δερζηνή, Deižan, Wiǧan, Bizan, which is modern Turkish Tercan, Τερτζάν, Derǧan or Deičan, southwest of Theodosiopolis or Erzurum), probably was located at the limits of what the Muslims regarded as appropriate Byzantine authority in Armenia, for it is there that they sent envoys in 652 to warn Emperor Constans II to go no further.[54] In effect, this unsuccessful Muslim diplomatic mission sought to restrict Byzantine control to those areas of Armenia Minor under Roman control before 387, even though the envoys were probably not aware of the historical precedents. The Muslims apparently wished to keep the Euphrates as an approximate eastern limit for Byzantine authority – in that region, more than 50 kilometers west of the former Byzantine–Persian border *c.* 600.[55]

The Muslims may not have sought to garrison their portion of Armenia in the vicinity of Derzene, but, as in case of northern Syria, strove to create some empty no man's land, however temporary, between the two powers. The Muslims were claiming authority over virtually all of what had been the Byzantine province of Armenia I. The incident indicates that Constans II had temporarily lost control of it and was explicitly trying to reassert his control there. But there is no explicit text other than the brief testimony of Sebēos concerning the delineation of any frontier between Muslim and Byzantine zones of authority in the middle of the seventh century. At that time Theodosiopolis lay outside of the zone of Byzantine occupation – until Constans II reoccupied it. But the precise list of towns and precise limits of

[52] Hacob Manandian, "Les Invasions arabes en Arménie" 168–9, 176–7. On the identification: Paul Peeters, "Πασαγνάθης-Περσογένης," in: *Byzantion* 8 (1933) 416–17, who did not know the conclusions of Manandian.

[53] Sebēos, *Hist.* c. 30, 35 (128–30, 158–9 Bedrosian, 100–1, 132–3 Macler). See also, Pseudo-Shahpuh, *Istorija Anonymnogo Povestvovatelya*, ed. and trans. by M. H. Darbinyan-Melik'yan (Yerevan 1971) 96–100.

[54] Sebēos, *History* c. 35 (160 Bedrosian, 134 Macler, 31 n. 5 Hübschmann); on the location, Nicholas Oikonomides, *Listes de préséance byzantines* 267, but esp. 358; cf. Oikonomides, "Organisation des frontières" 75; Constantine VII Porphyrogenitus, *DAI* 53.507, ed. by G. Moravcsik and trans. by R. Jenkins (Washington: Dumbarton Oaks, 1967) 1: 284; Honigmann, *Ostgrenze* 19, 53 n. 6, 54 n. 8, 64, 156, 181, and his maps. Joseph Laurent, *L'Arménie* 41. Derzene was in upper Armenia.

[55] See map I, "Mesopotamia et Armenia Quarta," in: Honigmann, *Ostgrenze*.

the zone of control remain vague. The Byzantines did not accede to the Muslim wishes.

It is reasonable to accept the dating of the second and third invasions of Armenia respectively to 642–3 and 650.[56] Both of these originated from the region of Atropatenē. The definitive Muslim conquest of Armenia took place only after the breakdown of the peace of 650–3. That final conquest occurred in 654.[57] It was accomplished by Ḥabīb b. Maslama al-Fihrī[58] whom Mu'āwiya sent to Armenia in response to reports of Byzantine troop concentrations. He and Syrian troops were initially reinforced by 8,000 Kūfan soldiers, followed by 6,000 under Salmān b. Rabī'a b. Yazīd b. 'Umar, who was killed at Balanjar in Armenia in AH 29, 30 or 31.[59] These traditions suspiciously accentuate the role of Iraqi soldiers. With the assistance of Salmān, Ḥabīb was able to defeat and kill the Byzantine commander Maurianos with his 8,000 (allegedly 80,000 Byzantines and Turks/Khazars) troops who initially had endangered Ḥabīb's Muslim troops. Maurianos apparently had sought out and found Ḥabīb and his troops, who then successfully attacked him at night, probably near Dvin.[60]

The Byzantines, despite the critical situation of the empire on other borders, such as to the north in the Balkans, did not write off Armenia. It was too important. The young Constans II returned with a large army in 652, wintered at Dvin in 652–3, and temporarily restored Byzantine authority. His unsuccessful efforts to impose Monotheletic or Chalcedonian doctrines offended local clergy and *naχarars*. But in 653 Theodore Reshtuni and the Muslims drove out the Byzantine troops whom Constans II left in Armenia, which now once more recognized Muslim overlordship.[61]

The terms of Theodore Reshtuni's agreement with Mu'āwiya, governor of Syria, in 653 are significant. The Muslims agreed not to station troops or any

[56] Marius Canard, "Arminiya," *EI*² 1: 636.

[57] Caetani, *AI* 7: 379–87, 453–4, 515; Johannes Kaestner, *De imperio Constantini III (641–668)* (diss., Jena, publ. at Leipzig: Teubner, 1907).

[58] al-Ṭabarī (Abū Mikhnāf) i 2806–7 misdates the invasion to 644/5; *History* 15: 8–11. Caetani, *AI* 7: 86–101, did not use Kūfī 2: 108–16, whose own sources appear to try to emphasize the Iraqi role, in contrast to that of the Syrians, in the Muslim conquest of Armenia. For that reason, Kūfī's account requires careful critical and skeptical scrutiny. Although Khalīfa b. Khayyāṭ al-'Uṣfurī, *Ta'rīkh* (Baghdad 1967) 1: 130, mentions Ḥabīb b. Maslama al-Fihrī, who replaced 'Iyāḍ b. Ghanm as governor of Mesopotamia, and was given control of Mesopotamia together with Armenia and Azerbaijan, under the year AH 33, he does not narrate in detail the conquest of Armenia.

[59] Ibn 'Asākir, *TMD Mukhtasar*, ed. by Riyāḍ Abd al-Ḥamīd Murād (Damascus 1984) 10: 56–8; Ibn Sa'd, *Ṭabaqāt* 6: 90. Ibn 'Asākir, *TMD Mukhtasar* 6: 189–92, on Ḥabīb b. Maslama b. Mālik al-Akbar.

[60] al-Ṭabarī (Abū Mikhnāf) i 2808; Theoph. *Chron.*, AM (345 De Boor); Balādhurī 199. Sebēos, *Hist.* c. 36, 38 (138, 145–6 Macler). Ibn Sa'd, *Ṭabaqāt* VII/2: 130, says that Ḥabīb died in Armenia in AH 42.

[61] Sebēos, *Hist.* c. 35 (158–9 Bedrosian, 132–3 Macler). A. Ter-Ghewondyan, "L'Arménie et la conquête arabe" 774–5.

officers in Armenia. The Armenians agreed to make available 15,000 horsemen in Armenia, but they were not to be required to serve in Syria. The Armenians were responsible for provisioning them with food. The Muslims promised to avoid levying tribute for seven years in return for this agreement. They also agreed to support the Armenians against the Byzantine emperor by sending troops wherever the Armenians requested.[62] These terms theoretically gave the Armenians freedom from direct Muslim or Byzantine control, in return for limited military service for and alliance with the Muslims, and of course these terms denied Armenia, including its manpower and strategic location, to the Byzantines.

Yet the Muslims won only limited control of Armenia at that time, and only gained control of the high plateau late in the seventh century. Maurianos, the commander of the Byzantine Armeniak forces, had unsuccessfully sought to reconquer Armenia for Byzantium.[63] In 655 the Muslims took Theodosiopolis (modern Erzurum, Arabic Qālīqalā, Armenian Karin) but also took Theodore Reshtuni with them to Syria in 655, where he died in 656.[64] They replaced him with Hamazasp Mamikonian, who, to their surprise, favored Byzantium.[65] He became *išχan* of Armenia in 654 and was recognized by Byzantium as governor of Armenia and *curopalates*. He remained prince from 654 to 661, when his brother Grigor Mamikonian succeeded him and ruled as prince, recognizing the suzerainty of Muslims and, in particular, of Mu'āwiya, from 662 to 681.[66] That act was a watershed in Armenian relations with Byzantium and the Umayyads.[67]

OBSERVATIONS ON THE STRUGGLE FOR ARMENIA

Muslim invasions of Armenia were an integral part of the Muslim pursuit of fleeing hostile troops. This was true when Muslims pursued Byzantine troops who were probably Armenian as far as Melitēnē immediately following the battle of the Yarmūk.[68] Other Muslim troops had pursued Armenians who had fought in the losing armies of the Sassanians. The same pattern was repeated by 'Iyāḍ b. Ghanm in 640 when he invaded Armenia, probably in support of his efforts to consolidate control over Byzantine Mesopotamia.[69]

The initial Muslim invasions from Atropatenē occurred in the hot pursuit

[62] Sebēos, *Hist.* c. 35 (133 Macler); Ghazarian, "Armenien unter der arabischen Herrschaft" 30–1.

[63] Sebēos, *Hist.* c. 35 (166–7 Bedrosian, 138 Macler), c. 38 (177 Bedrosian, 145–6 Macler).

[64] Sebēos, *Hist.* c. 38 (176–7 Bedrosian, 145–6 Macler).

[65] Sebēos, *Hist.* c. 38 (180–1 Bedrosian, 146 Macler). J. Laurent, *L'Arménie* 402.

[66] Laurent, *Arménie*² 402.

[67] W. E. Kaegi, "Observations on Warfare Between Byzantium and Umayyad Syria," *1987 Bilād al-Shām Proceedings* 2: 49–70.

[68] al-Ṭabarī i 2349.

[69] Balādhurī 176, 197–8; Yāqūt 1: 206.

of the last remnants of the Sassanian forces, whose ranks included Armenians.[70] It was understandable that Armenian soldiers in both Byzantine and Sassanian armies would flee in search of safety to their mountainous homelands and their fellow Armenians. It is equally understandable that Muslim commanders were concerned that such fleeing forces should not be able to reconstitute themselves and form new threats to the new regime.

The Muslim invasions of Armenia deserve some comparative historical remarks. Balādhurī reports that Muslim conquerors in northern Syria imposed an obligation on some villagers to report on Byzantine activities, presumably military ones.[71] Sassanian military authorities had previously profited from similar reports about Byzantine troop movements that Nestorian clergymen in border territory made for them.[72] The pursuits revealed the area's vulnerability and attractiveness for conquest. Initially, the Muslims of the early 640s were pursuing remnants of Byzantine and Armenian soldiery, when they suddenly realized the opportunities and the strategic significance of Byzantine Armenia, which they could not ignore or allow to remain in strong hostile hands.

The fall of Armenia to the Muslims resulted more from political and ethnic than military causes. The problem of civilian populations' passivity toward Muslim invaders had typified reactions in Syria, Palestine, and Mesopotamia. Presumably the previous military experiences of Muslim victories and Byzantine defeats in Syria, Palestine, Egypt, and Mesopotamia had created a momentum in favor of the Muslims in Armenia which discouraged local resistance, since it had not proved to be effective in those regions; Armenia was in fact a better example of local ethnic antagonisms and religious differences with Byzantium and local ambitions discouraging resistance to the Muslims than the more often cited cases of Syria and Egypt. Yet Armenia's population generally did not convert to Islam or become assimilated to Islamic and Arabic civilization.[73] Its peripheral location and impulse to local autonomy contributed to that lack of assimilation. Yet the church and the will to remain distinctively Armenian were the most important reasons for non-assimilation. When the Muslims later pressured

[70] Nadine Posner, "The Muslim Conquest of Northern Mesopotamia" 261–92, esp. 346–8, 359–62.

[71] Balādhurī 150, 159. N. Posner, "Muslim Conquest of Mesopotamia" 364. This will also be a later obligation of the inhabitants of Tiflis, and the region of the "Bāb" [Bāb al-Abwāb, Darband], according to al-Ṭabarī i 2665–6. See Laurent, *L'Arménie* 582–3, 647–8.

[72] *Histoire Nestorienne = Chronique de Séert PO* 13: 438. See Nina Garsoïan, "Le Rôle de l'hiérarchie chrétienne dans les relations diplomatiques entre Byzance et les Sassanides," *REArm* 10 (1973) 119–38.

[73] Armenian understanding of Islam: R. W. Thomson, "Muhammad and the Origin of Islam in Armenian Literary Tradition," *Armenian Studies/Etudes Arméniennes in Memoriam Haïg Berbérian* 829–58.

for conversion and for the imposition of higher taxes, the Armenians united in revolt. And one may doubt that Muslims initially placed any high priority on converting Armenians, who were able to continue to play their long-lived role of exploiting their situation on the edges of two larger empires to benefit themselves.

Armenia's winter climate was not hospitable to the Muslims, who also were probably less familiar with its topography and other useful local details. The Armenians did not welcome the Muslims with open arms. The Muslim conquest was violent and destructive. A few Armenians did collaborate with Muslims from the beginning, for various motives. But chroniclers such as Sebēos describe the conquest as a calamity, not a liberation.[74] What is important is that, despite these apparently prevailing negative perceptions and fears about the Muslims, Armenian military resistance was essentially ineffective. Armenian and non-Armenian sources, however, do not attribute any superior military technology or tactics to the Muslims in their campaigning in Armenia. Extant primary sources do not provide detailed descriptions of the number and character of the Muslim expeditionary forces in Armenia.[75] The number of Muslim invaders was probably significant, but not unlimited – in the thousands, perhaps, but not in the tens of thousands.

Armenians cannot have been encouraged to resist violently by the precedents of the swift subjugation of Palestine, Syria, and Mesopotamia to the Muslims. Those conquests had created their own momentum and impression of irrepressible victory. It is unclear whether any coherent plans for the defense of Armenia had been made by Armenians themselves, or just how thoroughly Byzantine commanders, after the death of Heraclius, had thought out the defense plans for Armenia. Although Armenia had experienced many invasions in its history, its recent history provided few examples of military invasions from Mesopotamia. The absence of such precedents cannot have helped anyone who attempted to plan a defense against any possible Muslim attack from Mesopotamia. There is no record of any serious effort to coordinate and implement such a plan.

Ethnic antagonisms between Armenians and Greeks and ecclesiastical differences over the Heraclian dynasty's Monothelite policy inhibited the dynasty's efforts to mobilize full Armenian support against the Muslims. There was no strong Byzantine army there attempting to direct its defense against the Muslims, after the fall of Mesopotamia and the death of Heraclius. Only Heraclius' grandson Constans II attempted to make a major effort to assert Byzantine control, but he encountered Armenians who

[74] Sebēos, *Hist.* c. 32 (134–6 Bedrosian, 104–5 Macler).

[75] It is risky to project back from a description of an Arab camp organization in Armenia at the beginning of the ninth century to the situation in the seventh: Ibn ʻAsākir, *TMD* 1: 261.

preferred Muslim rule. Here surely the older Armenian tradition of shifting allegiances between Rome/Byzantium and Parthia/Sassanian Empire created proclivities on the part of some to prefer a power other than Byzantium as nominal supreme authority. The earlier history of the region differed so much from that of Syria, Palestine, and Egypt that it was not surprising that its fortunes in the course of the Islamic conquests differed from those of those regions, which were nearer to centers of Arab population and power. Logistical challenges were always present of course, for Byzantine armies operating in Armenia, at the tenuous end of a long line of communications.

Armenia possessed sufficient human and material resources to attempt to defend itself against the Muslims, but erroneous Byzantine policy measures and the strife of its prominent families and their leaders made it impossible to develop a coherent resistance. Yet there was more local violent resistance in Armenia than there had been in Syria and Palestine and Egypt, but no imperial army was in shape or in a position to come to its assistance in the critical early 640s. By the early 650s, when Constans II had secured tighter control of the governmental and military apparatus, it was too late for Byzantium to do much. The Muslims had developed enough local ties and familiarity with the local situation that – together with the rising number of Muslim troops available for combat and conquest in Armenia – the odds had risen against the prospects for imposition of solid Byzantine authority. Yet the switching of sides by some Armenians, even the collaboration, did not lead Armenians to convert to Islam. Here again, their experiences differed from many of the Christian inhabitants of Syria, Mesopotamia, and Egypt.

IMPLICATIONS FOR BYZANTIUM

No great battles that involved large masses of troops determined the fate of Byzantine authority in Armenia. Portions of former areas of control remained Byzantine and came, in a still controversial process, to constitute first the Armeniak Theme.[76] But the areas that the Byzantines lost fell by lack of appropriate local resistance and insufficient aid from Byzantine mobile expeditionary forces. There were efforts to hold out in strong points, such as forts and walled towns, as well as attempts at improvisations of ambushes against the Muslims. But there do not appear to have been any new inventions of tactics or techniques to fight the Muslims, at least none that won any success. It is difficult to assess just how Heraclian emperors and their commanders and advisors drew any conclusions or lessons from their

[76] Lilie, Ralph-Johannes. "Die zweihundertjährige Reform. Zu den Anfängen der Themenorganisation im 7. und 8. Jahrhundert," *Byzsl* 45 (1984) 27–39; W. E. Kaegi, "Al-Balâdhurî and the Armeniak Theme," *ASRB*, 273–7.

military and political experiences in Armenia, or even how they received information on military action there.

In those early years of Byzantine–Muslim strife in Armenia the Byzantines had not won decisive tests against the Muslims. They may have gained valuable experience and insights about fighting the Muslims, but any such results were not yet evident in the military and political struggles there of the 640s and 650s. The situation was volatile, and it was unclear whether the Byzantines would succeed in developing effective tactics against the Muslims and in winning the commitment of the population to resist the Muslims. The fall of most of Armenia to the Muslims demonstrated the continuing failure and vulnerability of Byzantine military and political leadership and the continuation of old grievances and fissures among Armenians.

There is much controversy about the origins of the Armeniak Theme. It appears that Maurianos commanded the embryonic Armeniak unit in the middle of the 650s. The unit surely evolved from the army of the Byzantine *magister militum per Armeniam*. Its numbers are uncertain, but immediately following the restoration of Byzantine authority and the determination of the borders between Byzantium and Sassanian Persia after the conclusion of hostilities, Mžêž Gnuni commanded Armenians. Extensive warehouses existed for their support, which were an awkward burden on the local population. It appears that at least parts of the old system of payments in kind were continuing in Byzantine-controlled Armenia after the restoration, that is, immediately before the Muslim conquest.[77] There was no social and economic transformation that accompanied the restoration of Byzantine authority in the final decade and a half of Heraclius' reign. What is clear in Byzantine Armenia is that however much of an embryonic theme the Armeniak corps was constituting at the end of the 630s and at the beginning of the 640s, its institutional structure provided no magical answer to the challenge of the Muslim invasions. No effective Byzantine military institutional answer had been found at the moment of the early Muslim invasions.

Yet the Byzantine problem in Armenia was not simply tactical and strategic. It was political, ethnic, religious, and logistical as well. Whatever successes Armenians won against the Muslims did not depend upon Byzantine military structures. It is conceivable, however, that previous Roman and Byzantine experiences in developing the defense of passes against the Persians may have inspired local defenses in Armenia against both Byzantines and Muslims.

It is uncertain how Heraclius' initial experiments with the appointment of

[77] Sebēos, *Hist.* c. 29 (117 Bedrosian, 92 Macler); W. E. Kaegi, "Variable Rates of Change in the Seventh Century" 191–208.

emergency military commanders in Syria and Egypt affected his policies for organizing the military strength of Armenians and in Armenia in the final years of his reign. In fact, the ultimate willingness of Theodore Reshtuni to negotiate with the Muslims and accept the subjugation of his land and people to them was an additional confirmation of Heraclius' fears about local officials arranging their own terms with the Muslims. Theodore Reshtuni was able to do what John Kateas and Cyrus, patriarch and Augustalis of Egypt, were unable to do in Mesopotamia and Egypt. Heraclius was able to dismiss them, but neither he nor his successors could dismiss Theodore Reshtuni and make that dismissal effective. Theodore Reshtuni was following the ancient Armenian tradition of accepting the inevitable in order to gain some degree of local political and religious autonomy.

The Muslim policy toward Armenia in the Caliphate of 'Uthmān should be regarded as similar to that for northern Syria. The Muslims wished to create some very temporary no man's land or buffer, although a friendly and not a neutral one, between their area of control and that of the Byzantines. That is another reason, in addition to the difficulty of the terrain and the intractability and formidable character of the Armenians, for their pledge to Theodore Reshtuni not to send any Muslim ("Arab") soldiers or officers to Armenia. As in the case of Arabissos (and probably Melitēnē), they wished to make arrangements with the local people to gain reports about Byzantine troop movements and cooperation against the Byzantines. Muslim policy in Armenia, like that in Cyprus, should not be regarded in isolation. There were special features to the Armenian situation but there were also common features with trying to establish Muslim policy in other frontier zones against the Byzantines. They wanted a demilitarized zone, but only in the first phase of the conquests. It was only after the expiration of the three years' truce in 653 that Ḥabīb b. Maslama, under the instructions of Caliph 'Uthmān and Mu'āwiya, who was then governor of Syria, raided and directly subjugated Armenia and Georgia. Ḥabīb's successes created a new situation and new opportunities, which led to a modification of the initially more cautious Muslim military probes and accompanying diplomacy and financial arrangements.

On the other hand, the Byzantines under Constans II did not want the emergence of a buffer state on their borders, especially one created out of former Byzantine territory. Constans II and Heraclius did not favor the emergence of local centrifugal authorities, whether Armenian or not. That was the greatest danger for Byzantium, because such a process could accelerate. Constans II vainly attempted to prevent this movement in the case of Armenia. But terrain, ethnic and religious hostilities, and miscalculations about policy all contributed to his failure.

The Muslim experience in Armenia encouraged hope for more breakaway dissident movements that could assist Muslim expansion and the weakening of the Byzantine Empire. It probably encouraged Muslim hopes for persuading other Byzantine military units to switch allegiance to the Muslims. In particular, it probably encouraged them to seek to persuade the commanders and soldiers of the embryonic Armeniak corps to defect and offer submission of themselves and their region to the Muslims.[78] The kinds of subversion that ʿAbd al-Ḥamīd b. Yaḥyā advocated using against the Kharijites in the eighth century appear to have been similar to the kinds of offers of governorships, preservation of property, gifts, and encouragement that Muslims, and Muʿāwiya in particular, offered to Armenians for splitting away from the Byzantines in the middle and late seventh century. This type of action was a model of the kinds of cunning that Muslims hoped, usually unsuccessfully, to employ elsewhere to woo desertions of prominent leaders and groups within the Byzantine Empire.

Experiences with such events as the defection by Theodore Reshtuni and other Armenians to Muʿāwiya probably increased apprehensions within Constantinople and within the Byzantine military leadership about the vulnerability of troops on the Armenian frontier to possibly more defections. In fact, Theodore Reshtuni's delivery of the allegiance of Armenia to Muʿāwiya probably did increase tensions within the Byzantine Armeniak forces and tempted some to reconsider allegiances, which actually temporarily happened in the subsequent abortive rebellion of the commander Saborios in 667.[79]

Armenia represented the first instance of the defection of the armed leadership of some Christians, and the soldiers and civilians under their authority, to Muslim authority, without any immediate expectation of their conversion to Islam. The question, however, remained open whether other elites within the Byzantine Empire would follow the examples of these *naχarars* and embark on serious negotiations with the Muslim authorities in Damascus in contemplation of withdrawing their allegiance from Byzantium and bringing their forces and territory under Muslim authority. Such drastic realignments would realistically result only if the interests of those elites, and specific military commanders, were direly threatened in some fashion by central authority in Constantinople.

Muslims probably gained intelligence about the Byzantines from Armenians. Armenia was an important sounding post for information about

[78] Encouragement of desertion of one's enemies: ʿAbd al-Ḥamīd b. Yaḥyā, *Risāla* 4: 531 = Schönig. *Sendschreiben* 71.

[79] P. Peeters, "Πασαγνάθης-Περσογενής," in: *Byzantion* 8 (1933) 404–23; Kaegi, *BMU* 166–7, 182, 201, 234, 302, 320.

Byzantine intentions, troop movements, strengths and weaknesses, and capabilities. Muslim occupation of Armenia and negotiations with Armenians probably greatly improved Muslim understanding of Byzantine ways of waging war.

Armenia is an exceptional case in which centrifugal local forces did successfully, if briefly, emerge to make separate arrangements with the Muslims. But here it was armed military officers, not traditional civilian officials (indeed there were no traditional civilian officials in the Armenian society of the time), who accomplished this independent negotiation. Historically, this was always the case in Armenia. Of course, historians of Armenia will evaluate these events exclusively from the perspective of Armenian history and its precedents. But it is possible to evaluate them from the reaction of eastern provincial Byzantine officials to the Muslim invaders. In this light, Theodore Reshtuni succeeded where others failed – and provided the government at Constantinople with yet another reason to fear local autonomy.

Chapter 9

CONTROVERSY AND CONFIDENCE IN THE SEVENTH-CENTURY CRISIS

THE CHALLENGE OF FLUCTUATING MOODS

Seventh-century Byzantine perceptions of the critical sequence of genuine military and political disasters in Asia and Europe took shape in an empire already convulsed with religious controversies. Texts that were contemporary or almost contemporary with the Islamic conquests provide clues to contemporary moods, attitudes, and responses. Seventh-century sources of any kind are rare, and among the rarest are those that attempt any explanation or rationalization.

Soon after the loss of Palestine, Syria, and Egypt seventh-century Byzantines recorded some of their impressions about these disasters. Their brief mentions of events contributed to the creation of the later historiography of what had happened. They believed that decisive battles had marked the key stages of their losses and eventual ruin at the hands of the Muslims. Thus St. Anastasius the Sinaite (d. *c.* 700 or shortly after) expressed it: "the first and fearful and incurable fall of the Roman [Byzantine] army, I mean the bloodshed at Gabitha [Jābiya] and Yarmūk and Dathesmon [Dāthin], after which there were the captures and burning of [provinces of] Palestine and Caesarea and Jerusalem, then the Egyptian destruction, and in order the imprisonments and incurable devastations of the peninsulae and islands of all Romania."[1] It was disastrous battles that stood out in the memory of contemporaries as the initial part of the Byzantine catastrophe. They did admit that other disastrous conditions followed in the wake of these battle defeats, and they attributed all of these military defeats, as well as other lost battles, such as the naval defeat at Phoenix, to erroneous religious policy.[2] Those, of course, were not merely perceptions. Battles had

1 Anast. Sinait., *Sermo adversus Monotheletas* 3.1. 86–92 (60 Uthemann). St. Anastasius the Sinaite probably wrote these words in the late seventh century, well before 700, to judge from other evidence about contemporary events in this sermon. Influence on later historiography: Theoph., *Chron.*, AM 6121 (332 De Boor).

2 Anast. Sinait., *Sermo adversus Monotheletas* 3. 1.93–101 (60–1 Uthemann).

been important in ejecting the Byzantines from Palestine, Syria, and Egypt. It is impossible to ascertain how much specific information about those battles was in the possession of later seventh-century contemporaries other than the remaining survivors themselves.

There were efforts, which remain very difficult to trace, to divert responsibility for the military debacle away from the Emperor Heraclius or from the ordinary Byzantine soldiers. Instead, responsibility is laid at the hands of other Byzantine commanders who failed to heed the wise warnings of Heraclius, or responsibility is laid on Muslim tricks rather than virtue on the battlefield. There was an implicit unreadiness and refusal to concede that the Muslims had conquered by superior military generalship, tactics, morale, and strategy. Yet the allegation that the Muslims had conquered by the use of stealth may have blinded Byzantine observers to any lessons that might have been learned from those disasters, and moreover, they ironically appear to concede superiority to the Muslims in the sphere of the use of brainpower in warfare, something that they normally reserved to themselves. An eighth-century Latin chronicle from Spain, which has some oriental or Byzantine source, claims that "Saracens, influenced by their leader Muḥammad, conquered and devastated Syria, Arabia, and Mesopotamia more by stealth than by manliness and not so much by open invasions as by persisting in stealthy raids. Thus with cleverness and deceit and not by manliness they attacked all of the adjacent cities of the empire and later they shook off the yoke on their neck and openly rebelled."[3] This source deflects any criticism from Heraclius, and then minimizes the Muslim achievements by ascribing their victories to military trickery rather than to honest and manly military merit, even though the Byzantine military manuals had often advised commanders to resort to military trickery. Its author rationalizes Byzantine defeat and Muslim success by claiming the Muslims had not fought fairly.

Seventh-century Greek patristic literature contains some scattered allusions to political and military affairs, but the investigator must then decide whether these glimpses into the seventh century form any configuration or common trend. There is little evidence that in the seventh century there was any assimilation into Byzantine military literature of the lessons or results of reflecting on the Byzantine Empire's military defeats at the hands of the Muslims. At least nothing has survived in extant books of military tactics and strategy. The extant historical writings of the conquests have not been written with a military didactic purpose in mind. None of this means that the

[3] *Crónica mozárabe de* 754 c. 8 (28–9 López Pereira) = *Cont. Byz. Arab.*, MGHAA 11: 336–7. See c.. 9 (30–1 López Pereira) for Heraclius' warning to Theodore to avoid battle with the Muslims.

Muslim victories had no permanent effects on Byzantine warfare, but they left no noticeable traces in Byzantine military literature.

ANXIETIES

Anxiety over the condition of the Byzantine Empire emerged at the beginning of the seventh century and intensified during its course. An anonymous Life of the late Emperor Maurice includes a report that his murderer and successor, the Emperor Phocas, had exploited resentment against him by charging that Byzantium's enemies "took a great part of our provinces because of his negligence and weakness," that unless Maurice were overthrown, the Byzantine Empire would entirely perish because it would lack strength and its enemies would not be reduced.[4] This was, in fact, a description of much that did take place. The *Vita* of St. John the Almsgiver reports that Niketas, the cousin of Heraclius, had remarked: "The empire is hard pressed and needs money" ['Η βασιλεία στενοῦται καὶ χρημάτων ἐπιδέεται].[5] Sophronius of Jerusalem wrote a lament on the destruction of Jerusalem and hoped for divine vengeance on the Persians in the form of the destruction of their empire.[6] The author of the Jewish Apocalypse "Prophecy and Dream of Zerubbabel" appears to anticipate the destruction of Heraclius' empire. Later writers retrospectively pointed to astral portents of the impending disaster.[7]

Anxiety about the future existence of the empire had plagued Byzantium during the Sassanian Persian invasions, as the inscription *Deus adiuta Romanis* ("God help the Romans") on the silver hexagram (Plate I, nos. 1–2),[8] a prophecy ("The Byzantines have been defeated in the neighboring part of their land, and a few years after their defeat they will be victorious")

[4] F. Nau, "Histoire de Saint Maurice, Empereur des Romains," *PO* 5: 776

[5] *Vie de Syméon le Fou et Vie de Jean de Chypre* c. 10, line 5, ed. and trans. by A.-J. Festugière, L. Rudén (Bibliothèque Archéologique et Historique, Insitut français d'Archéologie de Beyrouth, T. 95 [Paris 1974]) 356.

[6] Greek text and translation: A. Couret, "La Prise de Jérusalem par les Perses, en 614," *ROC*, ser. 1, vol. 2 (1897) 140–3.

[7] Brannon Wheeler, "Imagining the Sassanian Capture of Jerusalem: 'The Prophecy and Dream of Zerubbabel' and Antiochus Strategos' 'Capture of Jerusalem'," *Orientalia Christiana Periodica*, 57 (1991); cf. Israel Lévi, "L'Apocalypse de Zorobabel et le roi de Perse Siroès," *Revue des Etudes Juives* 68 (1914) 129–60; 71 (1920) 57–65. Muslim apocalyptic texts about Byzantium: Wilfred Madelung, "Apocalyptic Prophecies in Ḥimṣ in the Umayyad Age," *Journal of Semitic Studies* 31 (1986) 146, 155, 156 n. 64, 158–74, 180–1, 183–4; Lawrence I. Conrad, "Portents of the Hour," *Der Islam*, forthcoming; Jewish apocalyptic literature: Benjamin Z. Kedar, "The Arab Conquests and Agriculture: A Seventh-Century Apocalypse, Satellite Imagery, and Palynology," *Asian and African Studies. Journal of the Israel Oriental Society* 19 (1985) 3–5. Stars: Theoph., *Chron.*, AM 6124 (336 De Boor); Extract from the Chronicle of Zuqnīn, in: A. Palmer, *Chronicles*, part 1, no. 10: AG 937.

[8] Ph. Grierson, *DOCat* (Washington 1968) II, part 1: 270–4, nos. 61.1–68.

1 Heraclius, Hexagram. AR. *DOCat* 61.2 Constantinople. Obverse: seated Heraclius and Heraclius Constantine. Reverse: DEUSADIUTAROMANIS. Whittemore Collection. Date: 615–38. (Photograph courtesy of Dumbarton Oaks)

2 Constans II and Constantine IV. Hexagram. Constantinople AR. *DOCat* 55.3. Reverse: DEUSADIUTAROMANIS. Date: 654–9. (Photograph courtesy of Dumbarton Oaks)

3 Heraclonas. Follis. AE. *DOCat* 5a. Constantinople. Obverse: Heraclonas overstrike on bust of Constans II. Reverse: M [40], ΑΝΑΝΕΟΣ. Date: 641. Dumbarton Oaks. (Photograph courtesy of Dumbarton Oaks)

4 Heraclonas. Follis. AE. *DOCat* 5b. Constantinople. Obverse: Facing bust. Heraclonas Overstrike]ONIKA (from ENTOYTONIKA). Reverse: M [40], ΑΝΑΝΕΟΣ. Date: 641. Dumbarton Oaks. (Photograph courtesy of Dumbarton Oaks)

5 Example of genuine Byzantine solidus (*AV*) with cross potent on base and four steps on reverse before Muslim transformation; Heraclius and Heraclius Constantine on obverse. *DOCat* 271a. Ravenna mint. Date: 613–29. Whittemore Collection. (Photograph courtesy of Dumbarton Oaks)

Plate I
Contemporary allusions on Byzantine coins

6 Three standing figures. Solidus/dinar. AV no mint mark. Latin inscription. Transformed cross. Walker, *British Museum Catalogue Arab-Byzantine Coinage* Plate V, no. 54. (Courtesy of Trustees, British Museum)

7 Two figures. Solidus. AV no mint mark, Damascus? Transformed cross. (Photograph courtesy of American Numismatic Society, no. 1983. 122.1)

8 Three figures. Solidus. AV no mint mark. Damascus. Transformed cross. (Photograph courtesy of American Numismatic Society, no. 1002.1.107, on permanent loan from University Museum, Philadelphia)

9 'Abd al-Malik. AV Standing Caliph. Dinar. No mint mark. Damascus. Transformed cross. (Photograph courtesy of American Numismatic Society, no. 1970.63.1)

10 Dinar. AV no mint mark. Damascus. Post-Reform. (Photograph courtesy of American Numismatic Society, no. 1002.1.406, on permanent loan from University Museum, Philadelphia)

Plate II

Muslim imitations of Byzantine coins and reformed coinage

in a famous Sūra of the *Qur'ān*,[9] and a contemporary description of the Avaro-Persian siege of Constantinople in 626 all eloquently attest.[10] Uncertainties changed to euphoria when Heraclius decisively crushed the Persians. In an official victory bulletin from the field he claimed that his victory was a certain proof of the truths of Christianity.[11] George of Pisidia reaffirmed a connection between the empire's military successes and divine aid.[12] The author of the description of the transfer of the corpse of St. Anastasius the Persian from Persia to Constantinople, who was writing in the 630s, testified to that "greatest joy and indescribable happiness" (μεγίστη χάρα καὶ ἀδιήγητος εὐφροσύνη), concerning the restoration of the relics of the cross to Jerusalem and the first visit of a reigning Christian emperor to Jerusalem.[13]

INITIAL REACTIONS

The unanticipated Arab Muslim victories of the last decade of Heraclius' life not only involved the conquest of Byzantium's provinces and the shattering of her armies but, in the minds of some men, called into question any assumptions about the eternity of the empire, its divine support, and the very soundness of the Christian faith. The few texts from the third decade of the seventh century which refer to the Arab victories interpret Byzantine reversals as the result of the removal of divine protection of Byzantine Christians, or more simply, divine wrath, due to the sins and negligence of Christians. These are reminiscent of earlier Christian opinions. Such is, in 637, the view of Patriarch Sophronius of Jerusalem:

> Whence occur wars against us? Whence multiply barbarian invasions? Whence rise up the ranks of Saracens against us? Whence increases so much destruction and plundering? Whence comes the unceasing shedding of human blood? Whence birds of the heavens devour human bodies? Whence is the cross mocked? Whence is Christ Himself, the giver of all good things and our provider of light, blasphemed by barbarian mouths...?

9 *Qur'ān*, Sūra 30: 2–3.

10 L. Sternbach, "Analecta Avarica," *Rozprawy, Polska Akademii Umiejetnosci, Wydzial Filologiczny*, ser. 2, vol. 15 (Cracow 1900) 298–9, 308, 312, 317, 320.

11 *Chronicon Paschale*, ed. by L. Dindorf (Bonn 1832) 1: 729, lines 6–8.

12 George of Pisidia, *Exp. Pers.* 1. 13–16, 3. 385–461 and *Heraclias* 1. 1–79 (*Poemi*, I: *Panegirici epici*, ed. by A. Pertusi [Ettal 1960] 84–5, 133–6, 240–3); D. F. Frendo, "Classical and Christian Influences in the *Heracliad* of George of Pisidia," *Classical Bulletin* 62.4 (1986) 53–62.

13 'Επάνοδος τοῦ λειψάνου τοῦ ἁγίου μάρτυρος 'Αναστασίου ἐκ Περσίδος εἰς τὸ μοναστέριον αὐτοῦ, *Acta M. Anastasii Persae* (12.28a Usener); cf. F. Halkin, "Un discours inédit du moine Pantaléon sur l'élévation de la Croix, *BHG* 427 p.," *OCP* 52 (1986) 257–70; E. Honigmann, "La Date de l'homélie du prêtre Pantoléon sur la fête l'Exaltation de la Croix (VIIe siècle) et l'origine des collections homiliaires," *Bulletin de la Classe des Lettres et des Sciences Morales et Politiques* (Académie royale de Belgique, 5 sér, T. 36 [1950] 547–59, esp. 556–7).

Sophronius concludes, "The defiled would not have achieved or gained such strength to be able to do and to utter such things, if we had not first insulted the gift and if we had not first defiled the purification, and by this we injured the gift-giving Christ and impelled this wrath against us."[14] For Sophronius, the Arabs or "Saracens," as he called them, had "risen up unexpectedly against us because of our sins and ravaged everything with violent and beastly impulse and with impious and ungodly boldness."[15] Maximus the Confessor, the foremost apologist for Orthodox Christology, similarly condemned Arab success in overrunning Byzantine territory as "serious," "terrible," "piteous," and "fearful."[16]

The terminology of the anti-Jewish apologetical treatise known as *Doctrina Iacobi nuper baptizati*, written *c.* 634, is nervous and severe in its judgment on the condition of the empire: "humiliated" (ταπεινωθεῖσαν), "diminished and torn asunder and shivered" (μειωθῇ καὶ διαιρεθῇ καὶ συντριβῇ), "fallen down and plundered" (καταπεσοῦσαν καὶ ἁρπαζομένην), "Romania is shivered and divided"[17] (συντριβομένης τῆς Ῥωμανίας καὶ διαιρουμένης). Yet its author had not written off the empire, for in one section of the dialogue, Jacob the newly baptized asks, "'How does Romania [i.e., the Byzantine Empire] appear to you? Does it stand as from the beginning or is it diminished?' Justus [his unbaptized Jewish interlocutor] answers, 'Even if it is diminished a little, we hope that it will rise again.'"[18] The author employs very forceful verbs – συντρίβω, ταπεινόω, διαιρέω, καταπίπτω, ἐλαττόω, μειόω – to describe the empire. The same author spoke with shock of news of the death of Sergios at Dāthin in 634: "They said 'The candidatus is slain!' And we Jews rejoiced very much. They said that the prophet appeared coming with the Saracens and proclaimed the arrival of one to come, the expected one, the anointed [the Christ]." The author claimed that the convert Justus continued, "'And what do you tell me concerning the prophet who appeared among the Saracens?' And he groaned a lot and said 'That he is false. For do prophets come with sword and chariot? These are the works of confusion today... And inquiring Abraham heard from those who had met the prophet that you will find no truth in the said prophet, except for the bloodshed of men. For he says that he possesses the keys of paradise, which is false.'" These remarks, however distorted, give some

[14] Sophronius, Λόγος εἰς τὸ ἅγιον βάπτισμα, Ἀνάλεκτα Ἱεροσολυμιτικῆς Σταχυολογίας, ed. by A. Papadopoulos-Kerameus (St. Petersburg 1898) 5: 166–7.

[15] Sophronius, *PG* 87: 3197D.

[16] Maximus the Confessor, *epist. 14, ad Petrum illustrem*, *PG* 91: 540.

[17] *Doctrina Iacobi nuper baptizati* (62, 63, 70 Bonwetsch). The Ethiopic text of Sergius of Abarga in *PO* 13 is derivative and not the best medium for understanding the original.

[18] *Doctrina Iacobi* (60 Bonwetsch). V. Déroche edn. in *TM* 11 (1991) appeared too late to use.

feeling for the strong impressions that those events made on some Jewish contemporaries in northern Palestine in 634, shortly after the battle of Dāthin,[19] – the oldest Byzantine reference to Muḥammad.

It is possible that Theophylact Simocatta, the historian of the court of Heraclius, may be referring to the collapsing Sassanian Empire's defeat at the hands of the Muslim Arabs in inserting in a speech attributed to the ambassadors of Chosroes II to Emperor Maurice in spring or summer of 590: "Thus what good fortune would befall the Roman [Byzantine] Empire if the Persians were stripped of their power and domination were transferred to another race."[20] It is possible that Theophylact is merely referring to the desirability of preserving Persia when defeated by Heraclius in 628. It is a significant text, which can help to explain Byzantine solicitude for the preservation of a Persian Empire after the long wars from 603 to 628, but is not explicitly a reference to the Muslim Arabs. Nevertheless, the prophecy that "Thus, even if the Persians were to be stripped of their power, it would immediately shift to other men," is indicative of contemporary (*c.* 630–40) Byzantine anxiety.[21] Theophylact demonstrates consciousness and worry about the fortunes of Persia, and concern if it should disappear as an empire.

Nervous and fearful uncertainty is the mood that these writings of the 630s convey. None of these authors pretended to know just what was happening or what would be the ultimate outcome of the swift sequence of military events taking place.

Primary sources are even scarcer from the decades that immediately followed the death of Heraclius in 641. Not long after 641, the monk George included in his biography of St. Theodore of Sykeon (d. 613) a harsh description of the empire's fortunes in the form of a prophecy of St. Theodore:

> ... many hard and perilous things for us. For it signifies the fluctuation of our faith and apostasy, the invasion of many barbarian peoples, the shedding of much blood, universal destruction, captivity and desolation of the holy churches, the halt of divine praise, and the fall [πτῶσις], and overthrow of the empire and much uncertainty and the crisis of the state. It predicts, then, that the coming of the Enemy is near.[22]

19 *Doctrina Iacobi* (86–7 Bonwetsch).

20 Theophylact Simocatta, *Hist.* 4. 13. 13, ἑτέρῳ δὲ παραπεμπόντων φύλῳ τὸ τύραννον. Peter Schreiner's assertion that the text alludes to the Persian defeat by the Muslims at the battle of Qādisiyya, Theophylaktos Simokates, *Geschichte*, trans. and comment. by Peter Schreiner (Bibliothek der griechischen Literatur, 20 [Stuttgart: Anton Hiersemann, 1985] 303 n. 591), is possible but not certain.

21 Theophylact Simocatta, *Hist.* 4. 13. 9.

22 *Vie de Théodore de Sykéôn* c. 134, ed. by A.-J. Festugière (Subsidia Hagiographica, n. 48. [Brussels 1970] 1:106). George the monk began to compile the biography while St. Theodore of Sykeon still lived: *Vie* c. 165, 170. George was born in the last decade of the sixth century. He wrote the final version of the biography after Emperor Heraclius died, because he knows the length of Heraclius' reign: *Vie* c. 166, lines 32–4 (1: 154 Festugière). Cf. W. E. Kaegi, "New Evidence on the Early Reign of Heraclius," *BZ* 66 (1973) 308–30.

The stark use of πτῶσις is the earliest use of the verbal noun "fall" in Greek to describe the situation of the empire, although there are earlier instances of the verb πίπτω, or "fall," itself in descriptions of the empire.[23] A few decades later, Antonios, a seventh-century biographer of St. George of Choziba, the ascetic who lived in the Judaean wilderness and who died around 625, describes St. George's fears and anxiety about the Byzantine Empire and its present and future condition: "I, my sons, am afraid and tremble because of the evils that are coming to the world."[24]

SEVENTH-CENTURY SEARCHES FOR SCAPEGOATS

Various persons and groups, in the critical decades after the loss of Syria, Palestine, and Egypt (decisively lost by 642), disputed the responsibility for the military debacle. Not surprisingly, efforts to ascribe culpability became intertwined with the contemporary religious disagreements concerning Christology, that is, among proponents of Monothelitic, Monophysitic, or Chalcedonian (i.e., Orthodox or Catholic) doctrines. Contemporary Monophysite judgments are found in the *Chronicle* of the late seventh-century Coptic historian John, Bishop of Nikiu (Egypt), who interprets Arab victories as evidence of divine wrath for the sins of Byzantine Christians and their rulers.[25]

Far away in Gaul at the end of the 650s Fredegarius likewise attributed the destruction of the Byzantine army at Yarmūk to "the sword of God," while claiming that Heraclius' adherence to Eutychianism, that is, to Monophysitism, and his improper marriage to his niece Martina, harmed Heraclius' situation and prospects.[26]

The late seventh-century Armenian historian Sebēos related the appearance of the Arabs to the prophecies of Daniel:

> But who would be able to tell of the horror of the invasion of the Ishmaelites [= the Arabs], which embraced land and sea? The fortunate Daniel foresaw and prophesied

[23] W. E. Kaegi, Jr., "Gli storici proto-bizantini e la Roma del tardo quinto secolo," *Rivista Storica Italiana* 88 (1976) 5–9; repr. in *ASRB* 6: 5–9.

[24] "Sancti Georgii Chozebitae Confessoris et Monachi Vita Auctore Antonio eius discipulo," *AB* 7 (1888) 117. This text may date approximately to 638, according to its editor, p. 95.

[25] John, Bishop of Nikiu, *Chronicle* 120.33, 121.2, 121.11, 123.5, trans. by R. H. Charles (London, Oxford 1916) 195, 200, 201, 202. See also the attribution to divine wrath of the Christian sufferings in the tract of Pseudo-Athanasius (*c.* 691–750), which Francisco Javier Martinez has edited and translated, "Eastern Christian Apologetic in the Early Muslim Period" (Ann Arbor, MI: University Microfilms, 1985) 510–31. On Pseudo-Methodius: P. J. Alexander, "Psevdo-Mefodii i Efiopii," and "Medieval Apocalypses as Historical Sources," repr., with additions, in his *Religious and Political Thought in Byzantium* (London: Variorum, 1978), respectively, XI: 21–7a; XII: 53–7; and XIII: 1003, 1006–8.

[26] Fredegarius, *Chron.* 4. 66 (154 Krusch). Perhaps sword of God is a *double entendre* for Khālid b. al-Walīd and may be an indication of the eastern provenance of the source for this section of the chronicle.

evils similar to those which were to take place on earth. By four beasts he symbolized the four kingdoms which must arise on earth. First, the beast with a human form, the kingdom of the west, which is that of the Greeks [the Byzantine Empire]. That is clear by his saying "Its wings fell and it was effaced from the earth." He is referring to the destruction of diabolic idolatry. "And it made to stand as on human feet, and a man's heart was given to it." And here is the second beast, similar to a bear. It was raised up on one side, the eastern side. It signifies the kingdom of the Sassanids. "And having three sides to its mouth" – he means the kingdom of the Persians, Medes, and the Parthians. This is evident by the fact that one says to him: "Arise, devour several bodies." As, moreover, the world knows he devoured them so thoroughly. "And the third beast, like a leopard, with wings of a bird on him and four heads of a beast." He means the kingdom of the North, Gog and Magog, and their two companions, to whom was given the power to fly with force in their time from the northern direction. "And the fourth beast, terrible, dreadful, his teeth of iron, his claws of bronze; he ate and crunched and trampled the rest underfoot." He is saying that this fourth kingdom, which rises from the south [east], is the kingdom of Ishmael. As the archangel explained it, "The beast of the fourth kingdom will arise, will be more powerful than all of the kingdoms and will eat the whole world. His ten horns are the ten kings who will arise, and after them will arise another who will surpass in evil all of the preceding ones."[27]

Sebēos also reports an account of the alleged original Muslim demands on the Byzantines before their conquests of Byzantine Palestine and adjacent territory commenced: "God gave this land [the land of Israel] to our father Abraham and to his posterity after him. We are the children of Abraham. You have possessed our land long enough. Cede it to us peacefully, and we shall not invade your territory. If not, we shall take back from you with usurious interest what you have seized."[28]

Sebēos provides in these passages some insight into the mood of some late seventh-century Christians concerning Muslim military victories. He blames Heraclius for rejecting this initial Muslim appeal to evacuate peacefully. He claims that Heraclius had arrogantly replied to the Muslim demand by saying, "This land is mine, your inheritance is the desert. Go in peace to your country."[29]

The *Chronicle* of the twelfth-century Syrian Jacobite bishop Michael the Syrian also included some incidents that appear to provide authentic reports

[27] Sebēos, *Hist.* c. 32 (104–5 Macler, see also trans. by Bedrosian, p. 135).

[28] Sebēos, *Hist.* c. 30 (96 Macler, see trans. of Bedrosian, p. 124). This passage is reminiscent of Muslim arguments. It is possible that Sebēos reproduces contemporary Muslim apologetical arguments that justified their conquests. Although a Monophysite, this argument contains no special Monophysite pleading or point of view. For later Armenian views on Muhammad: R. W. Thomson, "Muhammad and the Origin of Islam in Armenian Literary Tradition," *Armenian Studies/Etudes Arméniennes in memoriam Haïg Berbérian*, ed. by Dickran Kouymjian (Lisbon: Calouste Gulbenkian Foundation, 1986) 829–58.

[29] Sebēos, *Hist.* c. 30 (124 Bedrosian, 96–7 Macler).

about seventh-century Monophysite reactions. His reports may derive from rumors that circulated soon after the Arab conquest of Syria. He asserts, for example, that Heraclius' brother Theodore had vainly promised a Chalcedonian stylite ascetic that he would persecute the Jacobites (Monophysites) after returning from a campaign to vanquish the invading Arabs *c.* 636. After his humiliating defeat at the hands of the Arabs, according to Michael, a Monophysite Byzantine soldier mocked him and asked "What then, Theodore, where are the promises of the stylite that you would return with a great name?" Theodore allegedly became ashamed and fled into hiding.[30] Michael also claimed that after Heraclius evacuated Antioch, one of his Chalcedonian commanders named Gregory executed Epiphanius, a Monophysite bishop, for refusing to accept the official Monothelite creed in Cilicia (which still remained under Byzantine control), and the outcome was the death of Gregory in battle against the Arabs on the following day.

Michael's passages, therefore, emphasize Chalcedonian–Monophysite tension in the midst of Byzantine efforts to develop defenses against the Arabs. His judgment on events may be his own or it may reflect seventh-century Monophysite opinions: "For he who is intelligent, justice permitted what happened, because in place of fasting, of the vigil, of psalmsinging, Christians delivered themselves to intemperance, drunkenness, dancing, and other forms of debauchery and luxury during the feasts of the martyrs, and irritated God. And for that He has justly struck and chastised us in order that we correct ourselves."[31]

The seventh-century Syriac treatise called *The Gospel of the Twelve Apostles* speaks of, indeed ostensibly predicts, the difficulties that resulted from the Muslim invasions:

> He [Ishmael] shall lead captive a great captivity amongst all the peoples of the earth and they shall spoil a great spoil, and all the ends of the earth shall do service and there shall be made subject to him many lordships; and his hand shall be over all, and also those that are under his hand he shall oppress with much tribute: And he shall oppress and destroy the [rulers of the] ends [of the earth]. And he shall impose a tribute on [the earth], such as was never heard of... he that has shall be reckoned in their days as though he had not, and he that builds and he that sells as one that gets no gain.[32]

For the late seventh-century Pseudo-Methodius, it was a very pessimistic vision:

[30] Michael the Syrian, *Chron.* 11.5 (2: 418 Chabot); Friedhelm Winkelmann, "Die Quellen zur Erforschung des monoenergetisch-monotheletischen Streites," *Klio* 69 (1987) 515–59.

[31] Michael the Syrian, *Chron.* 11.6 (2: 422–3 Chabot).

[32] *The Gospel of the Twelve Apostles Together with the Apocalypses of Each One of Them*, ed. and trans. by James Rendall Harris (Cambridge: Cambridge University Press, 1900) 36–7.

The path of their advance will be from sea to sea, [and from the East to the West] and from the North to the desert of Yathrib. It will be a path to calamities; old men and women, rich and poor, will travel on it, while they hunger and thirst, and suffer with heavy chains to the point that they will bless the dead. For this is the chastisement of which the Apostle spoke... Men will be persecuted; wild animals and cattle will die; the trees of the forest will be cut; the most beautiful plants of the mountains will be destroyed; opulent cities will be laid waste, and they will capture places because there is no one passing through them. The land will be defiled with blood, and its produce will be taken away from it.[33]

In similar fashion, John Bar Penkāyē in the late seventh century interpreted the Muslim military achievements as reflections of divine wrath:

We should not think of the advent (of the children of Hagar) as something ordinary, but as due to divine working. Before calling them, (God) had prepared them beforehand to hold Christians in honour; thus they also had a special commandment from God concerning our monastic station, that they should hold it in honour. Now when these people came, at God's command, and took over as it were both kingdoms, not with any war or battle, but in a menial fashion, such as when a brand is rescued out of the fire, not using weapons of war or human means, God put victory into their hands in such a way that the words written them might be fulfilled, namely, "One man chased a thousand and two routed ten thousand." How otherwise, could naked men, riding without armor or shield, have been able to win, apart from divine aid, God having called them from the ends of the earth so as to destroy, by them "a sinful kingdom" and to bring low, through them, the proud spirit of the Persians.[34]

Again: "Their robber bands went annually to distant parts and to the islands, bringing back captives from all the peoples under the heavens."[35]

Who can relate the carnage they effected in Greek territory, in Kush, in Spain and other distant regions, taking captive their sons and daughters and reducing them to slavery and servitude. Against those who had not ceased in times of peace and prosperity from fighting against their Creator, there was sent a barbarian people who had no pity on them.

Again:

And so, when God saw that no amendment took place, He summoned against us the Barbarian kingdom – a people that is not open to persuasion, which acknowledges no

[33] Pseudo-Methodius, in Martinez, "Eastern Christian Apocalyptic" 143–4; cf. Harald Suermann, *Die geschichtstheologische Reaktion auf die einfallenden Muslime in der edessenischen Apokalyptik des 7. Jahrhunderts* 174, 190–2. G. J. Reinink, "Ismael, der Wildesel in der Wüste. Zur Typologie der Apokalypse des Pseudo-Methodios," *BZ* 75 (1982) 336–44; date: 338.

[34] John Bar Penkāyē, in: S. P. Brock, "North Mesopotamia in the Late Seventh Century. Book XV of John Bar Penkāyē's *Rīš Mellē*," *JSAI* 9 (1987) 57–8.

[35] John Bar Penkāyē, in: S. P. Brock, "North Mesopotamia in the Late Seventh Century. Book XV of John Bar Penkāyē's *Rīš Mellē*," *JSAI* 9 (1987) 61.

treaty or agreement, which accepts no flattery or blandishment, whose comfort lies in blood that is shed without reason, whose pleasure is to dominate everyone, whose wish it is to take captives and to deport. Hatred and wrath is their food; they take no comfort in what they are offered.[36]

There was at least one Monothelite attempt to shift the blame for the empire's recent territorial losses away from Emperor Heraclius and his dynasty and from Monothelitism. A *sakellarios* of Heraclius' grandson, Constans II, charged Maximus the Confessor, the resolute apologist for Chalcedonianism, in a legal proceeding of 653, with responsibility for the loss of several provinces: "For you alone betrayed Egypt and Alexandria and Pentapolis and Tripoli and Africa to the Saracens." He explained that when Peter, commander of the Byzantine army in Numidia, received an order from Heraclius to assist the defense of Egypt against the invading Arabs, he asked the advice of Maximus, "And you wrote a reply to him, saying, 'Do not do this, since God does not favor assisting the Roman state during the reign of Heraclius and his family.'"[37]

Maximus' denials of this charge evoked another charge, namely that he revealed a subversive dream in which he heard angels shouting in the east and west respectively, "*Constantine Auguste, tu vincas*" [Constantine Augustus, may you conquer] and "*Gregori Auguste, tu vincas*" [Gregory Augustus, may you conquer] and that ultimately those acclaiming Gregory overcame those of Constantine (signifying that the usurper Gregory in Africa would overcome Emperor Constans II).[38] Gregory was a Chalcedonian but fell in battle against the invading Muslims in Africa during 647.

Whatever one believes of the charges and Maximus' rebuttals, it is evident that in the early 650s the recent territorial losses remained sore issues in Constantinople. Scapegoats were sought, and it was all the more convenient if they were already opponents of the government's religious policies. The charges against Maximus raise the question, although lack of other sources forbids any answer, just how much advantage Chalcedonians may have

36 John Bar Penkāyē, in: S. P. Brock, "North Mesopotamia in the Late Seventh Century. Book XV of John Bar Penkāyē's *Rīš Mēllē*," *JSAI* 9 (1987) 58, 60.

37 *Relatio motionis factae inter domnum abbatem Maximum et socium ejus atque principes in secretario*, *PG* 90: 112.

38 *Relatio*, *PG* 90: 112–13. This accusation has some plausibility. The contemporary Egyptian historian John of Nikiu reports that another general, John of Barca, was ordered to move and did move, unsuccessfully, to resist the Muslims in Egypt; he fell in combat. If Byzantine troops from Barca were sent against the Muslims, it is probable that there was an attempt to commit those from Numidia as well: John of Nikiu, c. 111.1–3 (178–9 Charles); Nicephorus, *Hist.* 23 (70–1 Mango). Also: John Haldon, "Ideology and the Byzantine State in the Seventh Century: The 'Trial' of Maximus the Confessor," in: *From Late Antiquity to Early Byzantium*, ed. by V. Vavrinek (Prague: Academia, 1985) 87–91; John Haldon, "Ideology and Social Change in the Seventh Century: Military Discontent as a Social Barometer," *Klio* 68 (1986) 139–90.

taken from the military reversals of the Monothelite-dominated government at Constantinople. Sources do not permit us to know whether Chalcedonian lack of enthusiasm or outright disloyalty may have damaged Byzantine defense efforts in those crucial years, yet it is interesting to note that officials made such accusations against a Chalcedonian leader, Maximus.

Coins reflect the crisis and the need for divine aid. Constans II also issued bronze folles with the Constantinian inscription Ἐν τούτῳ νίκα ("By this conquer" (Plate I, no. 4). A puzzling question concerning intellectual moods of the middle of the seventh century involves another numismatic problem. A rare inscription ANANEOSIS [ΑΝΑΝΕΩΣΙΣ], that is, renewal, exists on some of the bronze coins of Constantine III, or according to some scholars, Constans II, or Heraclonas[39] (Plate I, nos. 3–4). ΑΝΑΝΕΩΣΙΣ can mean "revival" or "renewal," yet it is uncertain how this is to be understood in the middle of the seventh century. It is not a normal term for Byzantine coins of the immediately preceding reigns. It may well be a reminiscence of the wish for a golden age of restoration, such as Constantine I's fourth-century coinage inscription *Fel(ix) temp(orum) reparatio*. It may or may not have an ideological message for seventh-century contemporaries.

THE WORLDVIEW OF THE SIXTH ECUMENICAL COUNCIL

Another group of religious references to the condition of the empire is clustered around the year 680, which is when the Sixth Ecumenical Council began its sessions. Several letters preserved in its acts stress the continuing expectation and necessity of divine protection for the empire's military well-being. Thus Emperor Constantine IV in 680 began his letter to George, Patriarch of Constantinople, which authorized the summoning of the council at Constantinople:

[39] *DOCat* 2, part 1: 101, 106; DOCat 2, part 2: 391–4, 396–8 (Heraclonas, no. 5a, 5b, 5c, 5d.1–2, 5e.1–4), p. 399, no. 9a; *DOCat* 2, part 2: 406, 443–62, nos. 59a–93b.3. Léon Matagne, "La Succession d'Héraclius," *Revue Belge de Numismatique et de Sigillographie* 122 (1976) 87–96, esp. 95–6. Bates' dating is the most convincing. George F. Bates, "Constans II or Heraclonas? An Analysis of the Constantinopolitan Folles of Constans II," *ANSMN* 17 (1971) 141–61. P. Grierson, in J. Yvon and H. M. Brown, eds., *A Survey of Numismatic Research 1966–1971* II (Medieval and Oriental Numismatics [New York 1973]) 8. Alois Wenninger, "I*n*PER CO*n*ST – Ein Beitrag zur Follisprägung des Konstans II.," *Jahrbuch für Numismatik und Geldesgeschichte* 27 (1977) 75–8. Wolfgang Hahn, *Moneta Imperii Byzantini*, 3: *Von Heraklius bis Leon I.* (Österreichische Akademie der Wissenschaften, Philosophisch-Historische Klasse [Vienna 1981]) 3: 136–40, accepts the attribution to Constans II and believes on p. 136 that the issue does reflect a new ideology. Unnoticed but interesting and relevant is a quotation from Eusebius, *Demonstratio evangelica* 1.9.4.7: ἀνανεώσεως τε καὶ παλιγγενεσίας αἰῶνος ἑτέρου. This is the only instance in Eusebius' work of the Greek usage of ἀνανέωσις in any sense as renewal (other than architectural renewal or renovation). I thank P. Grierson for the opportunity to discuss these issues with him in 1974, 1979, and 1980.

Although Our Serenity is unyieldingly occupied with military and political concerns, since all affairs of our Christ-loving state are placed second to our most Christian faith, which is our champion in wars and which we have possessed for our Christ-loving armies, we have judged it to be necessary in our pious presence to make use of our letter to your paternal beatitude, [and] through the act of urging it forward, we authorize your paternal beatitude to gather all of the holy metropolitans and bishops under its most holy throne in this God-guarded and imperial city of ours.[40]

Some of the delegates' acclamations of the emperor at the council identified the welfare of the faith and the sovereign, but more emphatic than any Greek document was the affirmation of Pope Agatho in his letter to Constantine IV:

the living tradition of Christ's Apostles ... which preserves the Christian Empire of Your Clemency, which brings great victories from the Lord of Heaven to Your most pious Fortitude, which accompanied you in battles and defeats enemies, which protects on every side as an invincible wall your Empire, which God has preserved, which smites enemy nations with terror and casts them down by divine wrath, which, in wars, grants the palms of triumph from Heaven through the dejection and conquest of enemies, and, in peace, always guards secure and joyful your most faithful principate.[41]

In a second letter to Constantine and his two brothers Heraclius and Tiberius (who shared the throne with him at that time), he stressed the ability of divine power to subjugate barbarian nations to the empire and to the faith.[42] If anything, Agatho's correspondence encouraged Constantine IV and ecclesiastics to expect, despite the military defeats of the past decades, divine assistance for the state if it adhered to appropriate doctrine and conduct. In no sense had Persian, Avar, Slavic, or Arab victories silenced all hope for divine assistance to right-thinking and right-acting Christian sovereigns.

The overwhelming bulk of the proceedings of the Sixth Ecumenical Council is not concerned with the military and political situation of the Byzantine Empire. There is, however, a short reference to a military reversal that occurred not on the empire's southern or eastern frontier with the Arabs but instead on its northern, or Danubian, frontier. Early in the sessions of the council a Syriac-speaking priest by the name of Constantine from Apamaea, Syria, insisted on being heard: "I came to your sacred synod to instruct you, since if I had been listened to, we would not have this year suffered what we did suffer in the war of Bulgaria." After briefly examining him the council shouted him down and anathematized and expelled him for his vain attempt

40 J. D. Mansi, *Sacrorum Conciliorum nova, et amplissima collectio* 11: 201.

41 Acclamation of Constantine IV: Mansi 11: 656. Letter of Pope Agatho: Mansi 11: 239E–242A, trans. from K. F. Morrison, *Tradition and Authority in the Western Church* (Princeton 1969) 148; cf. Mansi 11: 238B, 239B–C.

42 Mansi 11: 286C–D.

to halt the impending restoration of a Chalcedonian Christology.[43] The priest Constantine had sought to exploit the Bulgarian defeat of the Byzantines earlier in 680 to demonstrate that it expressed divine wrath against a restoration of Chalcedonianism. It is a fleeting reference in the acts, and the argument obviously was unpersuasive to the assembled clergy and officials. Yet a priest who did not come from the Balkans attempted to make a religious issue out of a major Byzantine defeat at the hands of the Bulgars, which opened the way for the Bulgars to settle south of the Danube.

THE PROBLEM OF ANTI-JEWISH POLEMICS

Seventh-century anti-Jewish tracts provide some of the most explicit discussions of the religious implications of Byzantine military defeats. The *Doctrina Iacobi nuper baptizati* is only one of several such apologetical works written in the seventh century. A tract entitled *The Trophies of the Divine Church and the Truth of the Invincible God Accomplished Against the Jews in Damascus*... describes a debate between Christians and Jews which allegedly occurred in the same year in which the Sixth Ecumenical Council began, that is, AD 680. It probably was written in that year or soon thereafter.[44] Although most of the arguments involve theological and biblical questions, one section indicates that someone – Jewish, Muslim, Monophysite, or otherwise (one need not assume that any genuine debate occurred with Jews) – had been asking troubling questions about the relationship of recent military defeats and wars to the truth of the Christian gospel.[45]

In the late seventh century, Orthodox Christians who remained within the caliphate probably had much need of an apologetical treatise that could rebut Muslim, or possibly Jewish or Monophysite accusations. The Jewish debaters allegedly ask:

[43] Proceedings: Mansi 11: 617–20; quotation: Mansi 11: 617. For the significance of the incident for Bulgarian history: G. Cankova-Petkova, "Über die Bildung des bulgarischen Staates," *Beiträge zur byzantinischen Geschichte im 9.–11. Jahrhundert*, ed. by V. Vavrinek (Prague 1978) 473.

[44] G. Bardy, "Les Trophées de Damas. Controverse judéo-chrétienne du VIIe siècle" *PO* 15 (1927) 175–8. A. Scharf, "Byzantine Jewry in the Seventh Century," *BZ* 48 (1955) 103–15; A. Sharf, *Byzantine Jewry: From Justinian to the Fourth Crusade* (London 1971); A. L. Williams, *Adversus Judaeos* (Cambridge 1935); Maryse Waegeman, "Les Traités *Adversus Judaeos*. Aspects des relations judéo-chrétiennes dans le monde grec," *Byzantion* 56 (1986) 295–313. See also, Anonymi Auctoris *Theognosiae (saec. IX/X). Dissertatio contra Iudaeos*, ed. by Michiel Hostens (CC, Series Graeca, 14 [Brepols-Turnhout: Leuven University Press, 1986]).

[45] David Olster, *Roman Defeat, Christian Response, and the Literary Construction of the Jew* (Philadelphia: University of Pennsylvania Press, 1993). Also, Vincent Déroche, "L'Autenticité de l''Apologie contre les Juifs' de Léontios de Néapolis," *BCH* 110 (1986) 655–69.

If things are as you say, why have captivities befallen you? Whose lands are devastated? Against whom have so many wars been raised? What other race has been at war as much as the Christian? Therefore it is difficult for us to believe that Christ has come. For when He has come, the prophets Isaiah and Micah say that the earth will be at peace...[46]

The Christian replies:

The question is two-fold and the rebuttal must be two-fold. As for the prophets' saying that the coming of Christ would pacify the earth, [it is] not peace as you understand it, but it means that most men would take rest from idolatry and would know the Lord. That is one solution; however, the church was at peace for many years and our empire possessed profound peace, because it has not been fifty years yet that the present wars have risen.[47]

The Christian concludes this section by arguing:

This is the most incredible thing, that the church after having fought, remained invincible and indestructible, and while all struck it, the foundation remained unmoved. While the head and the empire stood firm, the whole body could be renewed, but a people without a head would completely die.[48]

The *Trophies of Damascus* demonstrates that, although Christians might have been shaken by the empire's military defeats in the seventh century, there still remained a confidence in the correctness of their faith, and some still retained the ability to place a positive interpretation upon their contemporary circumstances.

THE AUTHENTICITY AND PURPOSE OF AN ANTI-JEWISH TREATISE

An even fuller exposition of the rationalization that Orthodox Christians developed to explain the misfortunes of the Byzantine Empire and Christian communities is found in another Greek treatise against the Jews which, like the *Trophies of Damascus*, was written in the late seventh century by a Christian who lived within the territories of the caliphate. Its Greek title is Διάλεξις Κατὰ 'Ιουδαίων ["Argument," "Discourse," "Conversation," or "Dialogue" "Against the Jews"], although it is often cited by its Latin one, *Adversus Iudaeos Disputatio*. The manuscripts identify its author as "Anastasius the Abbot" or "Anastasius," and scholars initially ascribed it to St. Anastasius the Sinaite, who lived in the second half of the seventh century and who died *c.* AD 700.[49] Like other Byzantine anti-Jewish treatises, the tract has received little scholarly investigation, and for more than two

[46] *Trophées* 3.1 (220 Bardy).
[47] *Trophées* 3.2 (221 Bardy).
[48] *Trophées* 3.4 (222 Bardy).
[49] *Adversus Iudaeos Disputatio*, *PG* 89: 1203–72.

centuries scholars have doubted that it could have been written by the enigmatic Anastasius the Sinaite, whose authorship of many treatises has been contested, because it was noticed that twice in the treatise there are statements that 800 or more years have now passed since the lifetime of Christ and since the destruction of Jews by Titus and Vespasian. For this reason, most of the relatively few scholars who have examined the treatise have dated it to the late ninth century.[50] Another reference to "the empire of the Persians having been swallowed up by these barbarian Turks" has led two other scholars to misdate the work to the eleventh century.[51]

Despite these seemingly formidable arguments, at least one section of the *Adversus Iudaeos Disputatio* derives from and describes conditions in the late seventh century. St. Anastasius the Sinaite definitely did write a treatise against the Jews, for he refers to it in another tract, the *Hexaëmeron*, which virtually all scholars concede to be genuine.[52] It is unnecessary here to determine irrevocably the date and authorship of the entire treatise *Adversus Iudaeos Disputatio*, but it is worth showing why certain sections, despite possible later interpolations or corruptions, date from the late seventh century or, at the latest, from the initial years of the eighth, and what these sections reveal about one Christian's views on the condition of the Byzantine Empire and church.

The author of the *Disputatio* argues from historical facts after having made some theological points: "let us present this to you not only in words, but from the facts, that which has been cried out and witnessed in the entire inhabited world."[53] He then makes several historical arguments against the Jews, including one that no barbarian people has prevailed against the empire.[54] He rebuts criticism of the contemporary condition of Christians who had fallen under alien domination:

> Do not say that We Christians are afflicted and taken prisoner. What is significant is that while persecuted by and fought by so many, our faith stands and will not cease nor is our empire rendered impotent [or overcome] nor are our churches closed. But in the middle of the peoples who dominate and persecute us, we have churches and we erect crosses and found churches.[55]

[50] 800 years since Christ: *PG* 89: 1225D; since Vespasian and Titus: *PG* 89: 1237B. Scholarship in favor of a ninth-century date summarized by J. Kumpfmüller, *De Anastasio Sinaita* (diss., Würzburg, 1865) 147–8; K. Krumbacher, *Geschichte der Byzantinischen Litteratur* (2nd edn Munich 1897) 66; H.-G. Beck, *Kirche und Theologische Literatur im Byzantinischen Reich* (Munich 1959) 443; esp. S. Sakkos, Περὶ 'Αναστασίων Σιναϊτῶν (Thessalonica 1964) 194–9, 188–9.

[51] *PG* 89: 1212B–C; cf. A. L. Williams, *Adversus Judaeos* (Cambridge 1935) 175, accepted by G. Podskalsky, *Byzantinische Reichseschatologie* (Munich 1972) 44, n. 272.

[52] *PG* 89: 933; Sakkos, Περὶ 'Αναστασίων Σιναϊτῶν, 196–8; J. B. Pitra, "Anastasiana," *Juris eccles. Graecorum hist. et monum* (Rome 1868) 2: 244, n. 2.

[53] *PG* 89: 1220D.

[54] *PG* 89: 1223D.

[55] *PG* 89: 1221C–D.

Archaeological investigations confirm Christian construction within caliphal territory in the late seventh and early eighth centuries.[56]

The author of the *Disputatio* lays out another point:

> And we see that there will not be found from the beginning of time a people fought by all for so many years that was not annihilated, except for the nation of the Christians alone, who, however, would not have remained intact while fought by so many nations if the hand of the Lord did not protect it and does not still protect it intact.[57]

The next argument refers to a historical context that, as far as is known, no Byzantine historian, in contrast to textual and theological scholars, has ever studied. The following statement, unless garbled in transmission (and this would not make sense in the context), cannot have been uttered by anyone for the first time in the late ninth century:

> And another point, no Christian emperor has ever suffered death at the hands of barbarians, even though so many barbarian nations fought the empire. They not only failed to eliminate the emperor, but failed to eliminate his picture with the cross from the *nomisma*, even though some tyrants attempted to do so. Do not consider this a simple and mean thing, that the embattled faith is standing and not fading. For unless God had chosen and loved our nation, He would not have protected it from the wolf-like nations.[58]

NUMISMATIC EVIDENCE IN THE ANTI-JEWISH TREATISE

Neither McGiffert's *Dialogue of Papiscus and Philo* nor the *Quaestiones ad Antiochum Ducem* of Pseudo-Athanasius (date not determined), which both repeat some of the historical arguments of the *Adversus Iudaeos Disputatio* attributed to Anastasius the Sinaite, is as complete as the *Disputatio*; they probably depend on it.[59] Above all, the numismatic evidence is cited in much

[56] Fr S. J. Saller, "An Eighth-Century Christian Inscription at el-Quweisme, near Amman, Transjordan," *Journal of the Palestine Oriental Society* 21 (1948) 138–47; A. Grabar, *L'Iconoclasme byzantin. Dossier archéologique* (Paris 1957) 53–7; Michele Piccirillo, "The Umayyad Churches of Jordan," *ADAJ* 28 (1984) 333–41; Piccirillo, *Chiese e mosaici della Giordania Settentrionale, Studium Biblicum Franciscanum*, 30 (Jerusalem: Franciscan Printing House, 1981), and especially the early eighth-century dated mosaic from Umm al-Raṣāṣ: Piccirillo, "Le iscrizioni di Um er-Rasas-Kastron Mefaa in Giordania I (1986–1987)," *Liber Annuus Studium Biblicum Franciscanum* 37 (1987) 177–239; Robert Schick, *Christian Communities of Palestine*.

[57] *PG* 89: 1224A; cf. *Trophées de Damas*, *PO* 15: 222; Ps.-Athanasius, *Quaestiones ad Antiochum Ducem*, *PG* 28: 624.

[58] *PG* 89: 1224A–B.

[59] McGiffert, *Dialogue* c. 10, pp. 61–2; Pseudo-Athanasius, *Quaestiones ad Antiochum Ducem*, *PG* 28: 624. A. L. Williams unpersuasively ascribes the *Quaestiones* to the sixth century, but he fails to note the poor quality and unintelligible character of the numismatic reference, in contrast to that of the "Anastasius" *Disputatio: Adversus Judaeos* 160. The tract has received virtually no study since Casimir Oudin argued that it was not a genuine work of St. Athanasius: *Trias dissertationum criticarum... Secunda, De Quaestionibus ad Antiochum Principem...* (Leiden 1717) 73–135. McGiffert could not understand his text's

more detail by the author of the *Disputatio*. Up to this point, for example, the numismatic argument of the *Disputatio* appears in Pseudo-Athanasius, *Quaestiones ad Antiochum Ducem*. The author of the *Disputatio* then cites material which no other Greek anti-Jewish tract contains:

How is it that no one was strong enough to deny or to remove the seal of gold [τὴν τοῦ χρυσίου σφραγίδα] from us? How many kings of the Gentiles, Persians, Arabs, tried this and did not prevail at all? So that God could show that, even if we Christians are persecuted, we reign over all. For the gold sign of our empire [σημεῖον τοῦ χρυσίου τῆς βασιλείας] is a sign of Christ Himself [σημεῖον τοῦ χριστοῦ αὐτοῦ]. Tell me then, if it is not a sign that the faith and the empire of the Christians is eternal, invincible, and indelible, why have you lapsed from it – you who all hate and blaspheme the cross of Christ?

Why are you not able to abandon the cross of gold, but eagerly receive it, and yet if you see gold without the cross, you curse it and turn away?... Why do you desire what you make war against, and [why do you] eagerly receive, being [thereby] unexpectedly conquered, what you curse? And if you have sense and understanding, this sign would suffice for all of you, to show and to persuade you that the faith and the cross of Christ will reign forever through the ages.[60]

The above passage, neglected by numismatists, celebrates the prestige of the Byzantine *nomisma* coin, and is reminiscent of another famous passage on the prestige of the *nomisma*, that of Cosmas Indicopleustes in his *Christian Topography*, who speaks of the *nomisma* as a "sign of the empire of the Romans."[61] The medieval Latin translation of the *Disputatio* emphasizes the numismatic character of the gold *signum numismatis imperii nostri*, and *crucem in numismate* and *si quem nummum cruce carentem*.

Another late seventh-century literary text contributes to the dating of the numismatic references in the *Disputatio*. A Maronite chronicle that terminates in 664 referred to the Umayyad Caliph Mu'āwiya's unsuccessful attempt to issue gold and silver coinage without the traditional features of Byzantine coinage in AD 661: "He also minted gold and silver, but the populace did not accept it because there was no cross on it."[62] The Maronite

reference to a "sign of Christ" and a "gold cross": "Whether these words refer to a specific golden cross, or whether... I do not know" (*Dialogue*, p. 89).

60 *PG* 89: 1224C–1225A.

61 Cosmas Indicopleustes, *Topographie chrétienne* 2.77, ed. and trans. by W. Wolska-Conus (Sources Chrétiennes, 141 [Paris 1968]) 1: 393–5. Also note, from a century earlier, Quodvultdeus, "auream monetam cum eodem signo crucis fieri praecipit," *Livre des promesses et des prédictions de Dieu* III.xxxiv (36), ed. and trans. by René Braun (Paris: Editions du Cerf, 1964) 2: 558–60. But cf. Introduction, n. 1, 1: 70. This is an indication of how old is the apologetic effort to argue proofs from alleged coins with the cross. The *nomisma* or solidus is the standard gold coin of the empire, weighing 1/72 of a Roman pound, approximately 4·5 grams, and usually having a purity of about 22·5 carats. For more background, see Ph. Grierson, *DOCat* 1, part 1: 8–11.

62 Th. Nöldeke, "Zur Geschichte der Araber im 1. Jh. d.H. aus syr. Quellen," *ZDMG* 29 (1875) 96. "Extract from the Maronite Chronicle," in Palmer, *Shadow*, part 1: text 4, AG 971.

chronicle may not be referring to the same coin issue, but it is referring to the same reluctance of inhabitants of the Caliphate to accept imitations of Byzantine coins as is indicated in the above passage from the *Adversus Iudaeos Disputatio*. The two sources complement and corroborate each other. They confirm the existence of popular resistance to Islamic imitations of Byzantine gold coins which lacked a familiar symbol, the cross, and, according to the *Disputatio*, sometimes lacked the portrait of the emperor as well. Kmosko surprisingly made no use of the Maronite chronicle in his discussion of the numismatic passage in the *Disputatio*, but it helps to confirm his argument that this section of the *Disputatio* dates from the seventh century.

Pseudo-Athanasius, a Christian Egyptian text dated to *c.* AD 700, also takes note of the Muslim destruction of the cross on gold coinage, but without any aim to exalt Christian endurance: "that nation will destroy the gold on which there is the image of the cross of Our Lord, Our God, in order to make all the countries under its rule mint their own gold with the name of a beast written on it, the number of whose name is six hundred and sixty-six."[63] This text is additional evidence for the strong effect of numismatic changes on at least some of the Christian public, even though it appears to refer to a different numismatic alteration than that to which the *Disputatio* refers.

The progress of numismatic studies, as well as of Byzantine and Umayyad historical studies, enables the contemporary scholar to understand much more fully the historical context of the *Disputatio*'s numismatic passage than could the scholars of the nineteenth and earlier centuries or even scholars of the early decades of the twentieth century. Numismatists have succeeded in identifying a variety of Arab imitations of Byzantine gold coinage, all of which date from the late seventh century, although there is no scholarly consensus on the chronological limits of their minting.[64] Some of these issues do omit the standard Byzantine cross on the reverse and the cross on the globus cruciger in the hands of the emperor on the obverse, by removing the

[63] Pseudo-Athanasius, in edition and translation by Francisco Javier Martinez, "Eastern Christian Apologetic in the Early Muslim Period" 529–30.

[64] Basic: J. Walker, *Catalogue of the Arab-Byzantine and Post-Reform Umaiyad Coins* (London 1956) p. xxv, and in general, pp. xxii–xxvi. Also: P. Grierson, *DO Cat* 2, part 1: 60–2; Grierson, "Monetary Reforms of 'Abd al-Malik," *JESHO* 3 (1960) 242–4. The most convenient review of the scholarly literature together with new arguments: G. C. Miles, "The Earliest Arab Gold Coinage," *ANSMN* 13 (1967) 205–29. Important also is Cécile Morrisson, "Le Trésor byzantin de Nikertai," *Revue belge de Numismatique et de Sigillographie* 118 (1972) 29–91, esp. 58–64, concerning circulation of Byzantine gold in Muslim Syria; cf. William E. Metcalf, "Three Seventh-Century Byzantine Gold Hoards," *ANSMN* 25 (1980) 96–101, who modifies the conclusions in the publications of C. Morrisson and G. Miles.

bar of the cross. Numismatists have described these issues as "transformed cross" types (Plate I, no. 5, Plate II, nos. 6–9).

The author of the numismatic passage in the *Disputatio* is referring to some recent unsuccessful attempt to issue coinage that removed the emperor as well as the cross. The vague phraseology does not permit the identification of any known issue of Islamic imitations that scholars term "Arab-Byzantine" coinage. The numismatic references would not have made sense in the late eighth, ninth, or subsequent centuries, because the cross appeared on the reverse of the *nomisma* only between the reign of Tiberius II and 720. Such coins would not have continued circulating at a much later date. The *Disputatio*'s author is aware that there had been earlier Sassanian gold issues (which he, probably incorrectly, interpreted as imitations of Byzantine types) as well as Arab ones. It is unclear whether he is referring to any specific known type of "Arab-Byzantine" issues.

Specialists on Byzantine and Umayyad coinage believe that the numismatic passage must date from the late seventh century or the beginning of the eighth century at the latest.[65] The author of the *Disputatio* does not specifically refer to the imperial or standing caliph issues of Damascus in the 690s (Plate I, no. 9). Because he speaks of past failures, it would be possible to assume that he wrote at a time when no attempt was under way to issue standing caliph coins. It would be premature to state that no tyrant had succeeded so long as the standing caliph coins were being issued. Moreover, one could not make such an argument in the time of the issue of imperial coins with Greek or Arabic inscriptions, because one could not know whether the coins would succeed until they were terminated. These would be numismatic arguments for a possible date of the text before 692.

It is not clear whether the reference to popular resistance to the imitations in the *Disputatio* confirms the early date of 661 that is given in Nöldeke's chronicle. The passage in the *Disputatio* was written after 661 but possibly around 690 (the date most Islamicists believe was the approximate time of the minting of the "Arab-Byzantine" issues), or very soon after 'Abd al-Malik issued his (696/7) reformed coinage (Plate II, no. 10) – at a time, that

[65] Professor Philip Grierson and Dr. Michael Bates both answered my descriptions and inquiries. Letter of Ph. Grierson to me, dated 14 August 1974, and letters of Dr. Michael Bates, Curator of Islamic Coins, American Numismatic Society, dated 10 October 1975 and 29 September 1987. Correspondence with Dr. Bates in late 1978 and discussions in Paris with Dr. Cécile Morrison during 1978–9 have helped to clarify problems. See unpub. paper by Dr. Michael Bates, "The Umayyad Coinage of Damascus, 692–750," lent to me by kindness of author, dated 5 December 1986. See also Michael L. Bates, "History, Geography and Numismatics in the First Century of Islamic Coinage," *Revue Suisse de Numismatique* 65 (1986) 239–42, 250–3; Bates, "Coinage of Syria under the Umayyads, 692–750" *1987 Bilād al-Shām Proceedings* 2 (Eng. sect.) 195–228. For additional observations on this text and evidence for its late seventh-century date, see appendix I of this chapter.

is, when older Arab imitations of Byzantine issues were still somewhat familiar to the public. The attribution of the section of contemporary historical arguments in the *Disputatio* to the late seventh century does not necessarily solve the larger problems of the date and authorship of its entire five books. It may be a work, with the exception of a few interpolations and corruptions, which dates from the seventh century, and one may recall that is the period in which St. Anastasius the Sinaite flourished. It is possible – but far from certain – that the author was, after all, St. Anastasius the Sinaite himself. Such a conclusion would simplify many other problems concerning the corpus of writings ascribed to St. Anastasius the Sinaite, but a number of textual problems require further investigation.

The *Adversus Iudaeos Disputatio*, to return to the main subject, does provide at least a glimpse into the mood of the late seventh century. It reveals the need for Christians to explain away the century's Arab victories and Byzantine reverses. It shows that at least one Orthodox Christian was still able to take comfort from recent historical experiences and to find cause for confidence in the eternity of the Byzantine Empire and the survival of Christian communities under Muslim domination. It testifies to the continuing prestige of the Byzantine *nomisma* within Muslim-controlled territories and to the problems the early Muslim authorities faced in trying to remove familiar Christian symbols from their coinage, and thus it provides additional background for the conflict of coinages between Emperor Justinian II and Caliph 'Abd al-Malik. It shows that Arab military successes might potentially embarrass Christians, yet Christians were sufficiently resourceful to develop rationalizations, however unsophisticated or unpersuasive, to maintain their belief in the rectitude of their faith and in the eternity of the Byzantine Empire.[66]

IMPERIAL CONFIDENCE AND THE FAILED REBELLION OF SABORIOS

The *Chronographia* of Theophanes includes a story from the late seventh century that served to magnify the prestige of the Byzantine Empire and the majesty of its emperors in the face of internal strife and external threats from caliphs at the Umayyad capital of Damascus. The abortive rebellion of Saborios, the *strategos* [commander, general with civil and military authority within the military district] of the Armeniaks [this Byzantine Armenian region's capital as theme at one time was Coloneia; it included Theodosiopolis or modern Erzurum], failed in 667/8, despite negotiations with

[66] Michael McCormick, *Eternal Victory. Triumphal Rulership in Late Antiquity, Byzantium, and the Early Medieval West* 36–252.

Caliph Mu'āwiya at Damascus.[67] True, a fall from horseback accidentally killed Saborios, and quelled his rebellion, but his was a rare phenomenon.[68] This story was repeated in Byzantine and Syriac chronicles, which underscored the terrible fate that could await those who attempted private or personal diplomacy with Mu'āwiya, or other successor caliphs at Damascus, while emphasizing the advantages to all, including the Muslim leadership in Damascus, from direct diplomacy between Byzantine imperial and caliphal authorities.[69] According to Theophanes,

> the general of the Armeniaks Saborios (who was of the Persian race) rebelled against the Emperor Constans. He sent his general Sergios to Mu'āwiya, promising to subject Romania [= Byzantine Empire] to him if he would ally with Saborios against the Emperor. When the Emperor's son Constantine IV learned of this, he sent Andrew the *cubicularius* to Mu'āwiya with gifts so that he would not cooperate with the rebel.

Theophanes reports that Mu'āwiya declared "'You are both enemies, I will help him who gives the most.' Andrew told him 'You should not doubt, Caliph, that it is better for you to get a little from the Emperor than a greater deal from a rebel. Do this after all, as you are friendly.'" Mu'āwiya allegedly advised Saborios' envoy Sergios not to bow to Andrew. In the next audience, Sergios insulted Andrew as a eunuch. Andrew refused to match Sergios' promise to Mu'āwiya that his master, the rebel Saborios, offered to hand over the entire public revenues of the Byzantine Empire to Mu'āwiya. So Andrew left Damascus without having persuaded Mu'āwiya. But he successfully ordered the capture of Sergios at a mountain pass near Arabissos, and then had Sergios castrated and hanged. Saborios died in a subsequent accident. Thanks to the revolt of Saborios, the Muslims succeeded in temporarily capturing Amorion and raiding to the Bosphorus, but during the following winter the Byzantines annihilated the Muslim garrison at Amorion.[70]

The story of Saborios also emphasized the many techniques that the imperial government employed, including use of skillful and ruthless eunuchs, to enforce the authority of the emperor on the frontier, and to punish and liquidate those who attempted to become separatists. Arabic sources appear to neglect or ignore the revolt of Saborios, but it appears from the chronicles of Theophanes and Michael the Syrian that the revolt of

[67] Stratos, Βυζάντιον 4: 246–57; P. Peeters, "Pasagnathes-Persogenes," *Byzantion* 8 (1933) 405–23.

[68] Kaegi, *BMU*, esp. on Saborios: 166–7, 182, 201, 234; cf. John Haldon, "Ideology and Social Change in the Seventh Century: Military Discontent as a Barometer," *Klio* 68 (1986) 139–90.

[69] Michael the Syrian, *Chron.* 11.12 (2: 451–3 Chabot); Theophanes, *Chron.*, AM 6159 (348–51 De Boor).

[70] Theoph., *Chron.*, AM 6159 (350–1 De Boor); but cf. al-Ṭabarī ii 84–6 (AH 47–9).

Saborios marked the culminating point of Umayyad Syrian diplomacy in trying to win control of the Byzantine Empire through negotiations with local Byzantine commanders. Saborios, however, was not a civilian governor, he was one of the relatively new thematic *strategoi* [commanders]. For the Byzantines, the story of Saborios provided lessons and a warning against attempting separate deals with Damascus. The fate of Saborios and his supporters encouraged the belief that death and destruction was the consequence of revolt against Constantinople or direct negotiations with the Muslims.[71]

CONFIDENT SEVENTH-CENTURY ATTITUDES: AN OVERVIEW

Some larger outlines of seventh-century Byzantine political and religious attitudes are at least dimly perceptible. Although the last two decades of the first half of the seventh century may have been permeated by nervous doubt and recriminations, a small group of texts contemporary with or immediately subsequent to the period of the Sixth Ecumenical Council shows the existence of a confidence in the empire and of a faith despite adversities. The decisions of that council, as well as the empire's successful weathering of the first Arab siege of Constantinople, may have contributed to that mood, although it was natural for contemporaries to seek out positive interpretations of their experiences and circumstances. It is uncertain whether the mood of Christians inside and outside the empire differed in the reign of Constantine IV from that of his father, Constans II, although in a sermon St. Anastasius the Sinaite did perceive an improvement in the fortunes of the empire due to its shift to a correct Christological (Chalcedonian) position.[72]

The extant sources, not surprisingly, fail to reveal any sophisticated attempt to understand, explain, and cope with recent political and military developments. The overwhelmingly religious character of the surviving sources may explain the attempts of their authors to interpret events almost exclusively within a religious frame of reference, whether Orthodox, Monothelite, Monophysite, or Jewish. Yet in the total volume of their writings, references to historical events and conditions occupy a very minor position. These arguments display little originality; they resemble in part religious explanations of the empire's condition which had already become prevalent in an earlier imperial crisis, that of the fifth century.[73]

[71] Yet military revolts continued: W. E. Kaegi, *BMU* 186–208.

[72] Anastasius Sinaita, *Sermo adversus Monotheletas* 3. 1. 67–112 (59–61 Uthemann). First Arab siege of Constantinople: M. Canard, "Les Expéditions des Arabes contre Constantinople dans l'histoire et dans la légende," *Journal Asiatique* 208 (1926) 67–80.

[73] W. E. Kaegi, *Byzantium and the Decline of Rome* (Princeton 1968), and L. C. Ruggini, "Pubblicisticà e storiografia bizantine di fronte alla crisi dell'Impero romano," *Athenaeum* n.s. 51 (1973) 147–83. John Haldon, *Byzantium* 281–443.

The implications of these controversies for the broader rural and urban population of the empire, let alone for the Christian populations outside of the empire and under caliphal authority, are difficult to fathom. One can only speculate, because there are no proper sources to determine whether or how these elite reactions circulated among the broader population, and if so, in what form and with what consequences. It is also uncertain whether there was any uniformity to the spread of such reactions among broader sections of the population. Rural and even mountainous villages cannot have remained completely unaware of Muslim victories and the deterioration of security, even their local security. But sources do not indicate explicitly whether villages debated and commented on these events in a fashion similar to the better educated and often better traveled theologians. It is likewise difficult to know what broader segments of the lay population of Constantinople or Thessalonica thought about these events, or how they affected daily Christian beliefs and practices. One cannot run market surveys or polls of a twentieth-century type to determine popular responses or trends in the rate of change of popular responses: the sources do not exist. Even saints' lives, local histories, and correspondence are scarce. The gaps make it difficult to measure popular spirituality and its responses to the Muslim conquests. Some late seventh-century eschatological arguments continued to receive further elaboration in the early eighth century.[74]

[74] Klaus Berger, *Die griechische Daniel-Diegese* 1–9 (Studia Post-Biblica, 27 [Leiden: Brill, 1976] 12–14). H. Schmoldt, *Die Schrift 'Vom jungen Daniel' und 'Daniels letzte Vision'* (Theol. diss., Hamburg, 1972); Wolfram Brandes, "Apokalyptisches in Pergamon," *Byzsl* 48 (1987) 1 n. 2.

AUTHOR AND DATE OF THE ANTI-JEWISH TREATISE

More than two centuries ago the ecclesiastical historian Jacob Basnage commented in his essay *De Anastasio Observatio* that some of the *Disputatio's* arguments would appear unconvincing to contemporary Jews:[75]

He uses various arguments to silence the Jews which are sufficiently solid. However some arguments occur to which a Christian will not easily give assent. For who will conclude that the Christian religion was established by divine providence by the proof that no Christian emperor was delivered into the hands of the barbarians and was slain? Does the author not remember either Valens or Nicephorus who was slain by the Bulgars? Even if it were true, would it effect the consequences against the Jews that he infers from it? It is astonishing that he adds indeed frequently emphasizes that the Gentiles were unable to abolish the image or sign of the cross from the coinage of the Christians *although not a few tyrants have tried to do it, however this is the greatest argument for the truth that we hold.*

Basnage did not realize that the precise arguments that appeared so strange to him in the eighteenth century were those that provide evidence for the historical context of the treatise, or at least of this section. It seems inconceivable that the author of the *Disputatio* would have composed the above arguments late in the ninth century without qualifying his remarks to take note of and to explain away the slaying of Emperor Nicephorus I at the hands of the non-Christian Bulgarians, an event of shocking impact to the contemporary Byzantines.[76] One might recopy such an argument in the ninth century from an earlier text, but one would not create such a thesis at that time.

The author of the passage in the *Disputatio* very probably lived within the territory of the caliphate.[77] It is unclear whether he was seeking to counter

[75] Jacobus Basnage, *De Anastasio Observatio*, in his *Thesaurus Monumentorum Ecclesiasticorum et Historicorum sive Henrici Canisii Lectiones Antiquae* (Antwerp 1725) II, part 3: 10–11. The translation is my own. The italics appear in the original Latin.

[76] Dujčev, "La Chronique byzantine de l'an 811," *TM* 1 (1965) 205–54, collects the data.

[77] J. Kumpfmüller, *De Anastasio Sinaita* 147–8; cf. *Disputatio*, *PG* 89: 1221B–C, 1221D, 1236A.

actual contemporary arguments of Jews against Christians, but such debate would have been inconceivable inside the borders of the Byzantine Empire. The author of the *Disputatio* developed arguments about the condition of the empire and the survival of the faith which would have been potentially useful to buttress the confidence of Christians against Muslims as well as Jews.[78] The events that he had in mind (if indeed he had anything in mind besides a general impression that someone had tried to issue gold coins and failed) may have been the Sassanian gold or unofficial issues by local Muslim governors. His arguments appear to refer to timeless and general wisdom. It is therefore difficult to make a specific attribution to historical events.

The eminent western medievalist Charles Homer Haskins questioned, in an article in *Byzantion* whose title did not mention Anastasius the Sinaite, whether scholars should rely so much on the reference to 800 years since Christ as the *terminus post quem* for the *Disputatio*. He observed: "On this point we need further manuscript evidence, because the copyists of the Latin translations seem to have sought to bring this statement down to date, and the Greek scribe may have made a similar emendation." Haskins' skepticism about the ninth-century date received little attention.[79]

The Orientalist M. Kmosko also briefly mentioned the *Disputatio* in a subsequent volume of *Byzantion* and, for different reasons, also questioned its attribution to the ninth century. He took no account of Haskins' argument but perceived a numismatic reference in the *Disputatio* which dated before the Caliph 'Abd al-Malik reformed Islamic gold coinage (*c.* 694). Kmosko rebutted another argument against the value of the *Disputatio*. Late in the nineteenth century, A. C. McGiffert, an American scholar, had edited another Greek anti-Jewish tract, the *Dialogue of Papiscus and Philo*. He noted that there were some similarities between his text and that of the *Disputatio*, but he concluded from the ninth-century attribution of the *Disputatio* that the *Dialogue* was the source for much of the *Disputatio*, although he conceded that some might draw contrary conclusions. Kmosko perceived that the references to gold coinage in McGiffert's *Dialogue* were so abbreviated and confused as to be unintelligible, while those of the *Disputatio* were comprehensible and fit an historical context of which McGiffert, who

[78] B. Blumenkranz, *Juifs et chrétiens dans le monde occidental, 430–1096* (Paris, The Hague: Mouton, 1960) 68–84, argues for the actual use of polemical literature in debates and discussions in the west; cf. also, B. Blumenkranz, *Les Auteurs Chrétiens latins du moyen âge sur les juifs et le judaïsme* (Paris, The Hague 1963).

[79] C. H. Haskins, "Pascalis Romanus, Petrus Chrysolanus," *Byzantion* 2 (1925) 232. Dr. Otto Kresten has also suggested this explanation (in a letter to me) for the date in the extant manuscript. Professor Peter Herde, in some discussions with me at the Institute for Advanced Study in the Autumn Term, 1984, observed that the scribe could simply have made a mistake.

was not an historian, had no awareness. Kmosko concluded that the *Disputatio* really dated from the seventh century.[80] He buried his arguments, as had Haskins, in an article in *Byzantion* whose title did not even mention Anastasius the Sinaite. In fact, he briefly stated his conclusions only in connection with his exploration of the complicated textual history and historical background of the Pseudo-Methodius apocalypse, which dates from the seventh century and which contains one passage that also appears in the *Adversus Iudaeos Disputatio* but is little known.[81]

Other scholars of St. Anastasius the Sinaite were apparently unaware of Kmosko's observations; they did not comment on them. It will require considerable labor, and there may be no definitive results. One manuscript of the *Adversus Iudaeos Disputatio*, a complete one which has been tentatively dated to the fourteenth century, still remains unedited at the Karakallou monastery on Mt. Athos.[82]

The language and style of the *Disputatio* appears to resemble that of the unedited Greek text of St. Anastasius' *Hexaëmeron*, according to Sergios Sakkos, who has studied the manuscript. In the *Hexaëmeron*, St. Anastasius refers to a point he had elaborated in his treatise against the Jews concerning the creation of man, but in the extant text of the *Disputatio* the exact passage appears in the first book, not the second book as he had claimed. Sakkos, who assumed that both treatises belonged to the ninth century because of the date in the treatise against the Jews, believed that both were written by the same author and that the first section of the original treatise had been lost, resulting in the relevant passage, which supposedly was in the second book, appearing in book one of the present text. This observation needs more research.[83]

The relationship of the *Disputatio* to the *Dialogue of Papiscus and Philo*

[80] M. Kmosko, "Das Rätsel des Pseudomethodius," *Byzantion* 6 (1931) 293–5; *Dialogue between a Christian and a Jew*, ed. by A. C. McGiffert (diss., Marburg, publ. at New York 1889) 17, 35–7. For garbled numismatic passage, *Dialogue* c. 10, p. 61.

[81] I did not discover his remarks until I had independently reached the same conclusions.

[82] One fourteenth-century manuscript of the Κατὰ Ἰουδαίων has received little attention for establishing the text: Lampros no. 1573 = Karakallou no. 60, subs. 3, Lampros, *Cat. Greek Mss. Mt. Athos* 1: 134. Examination of a microfilm copy revealed no new evidence about the author or his date.

[83] Sakkos, Περὶ Ἀναστασίων Σιναϊτῶν, theorized that the writings that manuscripts ascribe to St. Anastasius the Sinaite really belong to seven different authors, pp. 38–43 and *passim*. G. Weiss negatively reviewed the analysis of Sakkos, but did not discuss the *Adversus Iudaeos Disputatio*, *BZ* 60 (1967) 342–6. Sakkos did examine the still unpublished Greek text of the *Hexaëmeron* and concluded that its vocabulary and style are identical to the *Adversus Iudaeos Disputatio*, 196–8. He concluded that the *Disputatio* must be the anti-Jewish tract mentioned by the author of the *Hexaëmeron* even though the subject which the *Hexaëmeron* states will be treated in the second book of the *Treatise Against the Jews* appears in the present first book; Sakkos hypothesizes that part of the original text may have been lost; cf. E. Chrysos, "Νεώτεραι Ἀπόψεις Περὶ Ἀναστασίων Σιναϊτῶν," Κληρονομία 1 (1969) 121–44.

and to the *Quaestiones ad Antiochum Ducem* also requires a thorough reexamination. Indeed, Byzantine anti-Jewish works have suffered general neglect.[84] The reference to the Turks is not a late interpolation or corruption, but part of a late seventh-century reference to Turks (proto-Bulgars?) and Avars. However, it raises the problem of the interrelationship of the *Disputatio* with another Greek religious tract, the Pseudo-Methodius apocalypse, which was first written sometime in the middle or late seventh century in Syriac and then translated into Greek and Latin with additions. The reference to "Turks" and Avars is found in the Syriac, Greek, and Latin copies of the Pseudo-Methodius apocalypse. Pseudo-Methodius provides a lengthier text of this passage, but it refers to Τοῦρκοι as synonymous with Avars and kindred tribes. This is the normal seventh-century usage of the term for that people. This section appears in a much abbreviated form in the "Anastasian" *Disputatio*, whose author may well have borrowed it from Pseudo-Methodius, and it is possible that a later Greek copyist no longer understood the seventh-century usage of the word "Turk" to describe the Avars, who no longer existed, and therefore shortened and altered the text to fit later circumstances. This is only a conjecture that does not warrant pressing. Although Pseudo-Methodius dates from the seventh century, it is unclear whether his apocalypse antedates the *Adversus Iudaeos Disputatio*.[85]

Finally, there is the problem of the year 670, which appears in one but not the other of A. C. McGiffert's manuscripts of the *Dialogue of Papiscus and Philo*: do this and the other dates in the manuscripts (670, 800, 1070) depend on some other text from which the author of the *Dialogue* borrowed material, or did he supply the initial date? Subsequent scholars have recognized the unconvincing and inadequate character of McGiffert's analysis of the *Dialogue*'s manuscript history, but they have not considered whether there may be implications for the study of the "Anastasian" *Disputatio*. It is sufficient for the purposes of this inquiry to have established the overwhelming probability of a late seventh-century date for the section of

[84] Except for A. L. Williams, *Adversus Judaeos*, which is inadequate. Robert Wilken, *John Chrysostom and the Jews: Rhetoric and Reality in the Fourth Century* (Berkeley: University of California Press, 1983); David Olster, "Roman Defeat, Christian Response, and the Literary Construction of the Jew."

[85] In the *Disputatio*, reference to Turks appears at *PG* 89: 1212, which corresponds for unknown reasons to a passage concerning Turks and Avars which is found in the Syriac Pseudo-Methodius apocalypse: Martinez, "Eastern Christian Apocalyptic" 76, 139; Latin: E. Sackur, *Sibyllinische Texte und Forschungen* (Halle 1898) 79 n. 4 and 5, and in the actual text, lines 2–4 on p. 80; Greek text, Antonios Lolos, *Die Apokalypse des Pseudo-Methodios*, 1. Red. X, 5, p. 94. Date: 20–2. It is an old apologetical reference to Khazars and Avars in the sense of Altaic European steppe nomads, not to eleventh-century Seljuk Turks. It does not relegate the *Disputatio* or Pseudo-Methodius to the eleventh century.

the *Disputatio* that refers to recent events, thereby justifying the earlier skepticism of C. H. Haskins and M. Kmosko.[86]

[86] A. C. McGiffert, *Dialogue* 41–4. G. Bardy, in his thorough introduction to his edition of the *Trophées de Damas, PO* 15: 185–8, notes the deficiencies and incompleteness of McGiffert's researches. Cf. John Haldon, "The Works of Anastasius of Sinai," in: A. Cameron, L. I. Conrad, *The Byzantine and Early Islamic Near East* (Princeton: Darwin, 1992) 107–47. Also: G. Dahan, "Paschalis Romanus. Disputatio contra Judaeos," *Recherches Augustiniennes* 11 (1976) 161–213.

Chapter 10

ELEMENTS OF FAILURE AND ENDURANCE

STRATEGIC FAILURE

The sixth-century Byzantine diplomat Peter the Patrician prophetically anticipated seventh-century events when, in 562, he warned another eastern power who threatened the Byzantine Empire, namely, the Persian Empire: "We have our fill of war before war has its fill of us... As long as men are evidently winning over their adversary, their courage is cultivated. But when it is obviously failing to destroy their enemies, they waste their own strength and as a result they lose to those who should not conquer them."[1]

Heraclius had eighteen years in which to find the proper strategy and tactics for crushing the Persians. But he did not have the leisure of eighteen more years to devise or improvise the proper tactics and defenses and counterstrategy against the Muslims. The initial Muslim invasions surprised the military defenders and civilian inhabitants of Syria and Palestine, who were not anticipating any major military activity from the direction of the Arabian peninsula, even though in retrospect modern observers may find warning signs.[2] It is impossible to prove whether Heraclius could have devised an effective strategy against the Muslims if he had possessed more time. He unsuccessfully tried to develop what one may term one variant of a strategy of positional warfare, that of a defense in depth. Such a strategy depends on the control of fixed fortified points and sieges, and a principal object is the control of territory and population in that territory. That strategy did not succeed. The problem did not lie in the fixed positions but in the lack of available adequate mobile forces together with an appropriate plan of operations and training for their coordination with those forces in the fixed positions or strongholds.[3] As it was, Heraclius died in early 641, some

[1] Peter the Patrician, frg. 6.1, in: *The History of Menander the Guardsman*, ed. and trans. by R. C. Blockley (ARCA, 17 [Liverpool: Francis Cairns, 1985]) 59. My own translation.

[2] Sophronius, *PG* 87: 3197D.

[3] For an evaluation of alternative strategies: Archer Jones, *The Art of Warfare in the Western World* (Urbana: University of Illinois Press, 1987) 662–716.

seven years after the serious emergence of the Muslim menace, or less than twelve years after the first serious clash at Mu'ta. His failure in the 630s in no way negates his great achievements in warfare against the Persians between 610 and 628. But in the 630s his was a strategic failure.

Heraclius consciously devastated the border areas along the southern approaches to the Taurus Mountains in 637–41, for he strove to create a free-fire no man's land of destruction and emptiness as part of his defense-in-depth against the Arabs. No individual local Byzantine heroes or families emerge from the earliest formative period of the frontier. No sources evoke the spirit of the culture of that emerging frontier, which became so prominent in subsequent centuries.[4]

The early conquests were not merely a sequence of battles and lesser clashes but included various diplomatic contacts and truces. Negotiations interrupted battle, whether or not under the impulse of sincere motivations or guile and intent to exploit for other purposes, such as creation of opportunities for ruses and gathering intelligence, or to capture or eliminate the opponents' leadership. There was a sequence of truces of unequal scope with respect to time and geographic extension. Byzantines and Muslims agreed to such truces for the purpose of demarcation, stalling for time, and alleged (and, at least occasionally, genuine) concern for relief of civilian hardships. There was a calculating quality to these truces, which were themselves a part of the larger struggle for the territories in question. Fighting and talking tended to alternate in part with the hope that delays might allow some new, perhaps unanticipated development – without the expenditure of many lives and much money – to accomplish the major aims of the war. These suspensions of hostilities and pursuit of formal or informal contacts created another chance for continuing war by means other than heavy bloodshed. Warfare had already assumed an uneven tempo in the sixth century on the eastern frontier, and that unevenness persisted even during the Byzantine wars with the Muslims in the 630s and 640s. War was seldom waged at its maximal intensity of fury; at times it became slow-motion warfare with deliberate delays, sluggish tempo, and a conscious unwillingness to risk pressing for a decisive test in battle.[5]

There had been various earlier potential defensive lines that had fallen but

[4] H. Ahrweiler, A. Kazhdan, N. Oikonomides, and A. Pertusi, and others, *Frontières et régions frontières du VIIe au XIIe siècle*, *Rapports*, *XIVe Congrès International des Etudes Byzantines* (Bucharest 1971), II.

[5] 'Abd al-Ḥamīd b. Yaḥyā, *Risāla* 4: 473–533, esp. 495–533 = Schönig, *Sendschreiben* 38–73; and on his knowledge of Greek, p. 106. He emphasizes craft and winning over key elements within the opposing army (instead of resort to open combat) a little more than a century after the conquest; the methods described were probably also prevalent among Muslims at the time of the conquests.

which could have served as frontiers: the Wādī'l Ḥasā, the Wādī'l Mūjib or Arnon River, the Wādī'l Zarqā', and, of course, the River Yarmūk. But the Muslims had crossed each one of them, which had successively failed to serve as a barrier beyond which they were not to pass. There was a desire to create a point beyond which the partisans of one side or the other were not to pass that was at the core of these early truce arrangements (in addition to monetary payments, fear, and potential exercise of military power). In principle, other potential fall-back positions existed for the creation of secondary defense lines than the ones that the Byzantines actually created. Yet the Byzantines had never given their frontiers with the Arabs the attention and thought that they had given to those with the Sassanians. It was only when the Muslims reached the northern part of Syria that a struggle developed concerning a secondary defense line, and the need to find a demarcation line of some kind, whether a line or a zone in depth. These fall-back lines could have been along the Lebanon mountains, anticipating those of the Crusades, or they could have retained more of northern Syria, including Antioch and its vicinity, as the Byzantines did in the late tenth and early eleventh centuries, and as the Crusaders subsequently managed to do. The reasons for withdrawing as far as the Taurus involved available Byzantine manpower and the desire to avoid as much bloody fighting as possible with the Muslims, even though such withdrawals only briefly postponed bloodshed and, moreover, increased the resources of the Muslims.[6]

Heraclius' efforts to recover Melitēnē [Malatya] from the Muslims, his anger at the inhabitants' negotiations with the Muslims, and his order for the destruction of the town were not exceptional actions but conformed to his larger policy of prohibiting inhabitants and leaders of various localities from making their own unauthorized settlements or terms with the Muslims. His destruction of Melitēnē helped to make an example out of it and also helped to create a zone of destruction and demarcation between Byzantines and Muslims.[7]

The Byzantine–Muslim frontier emerged in part out of the conditions of the conquest and truce arrangements made in Syria as well as those of Mesopotamia.[8] The relevant chronological limits are those of the conquest of

[6] C.-P. Haase, *Untersuchungen zur Landschaftsgeschichte Nordsyriens in der Umayyadenzeit* (diss., University of Hamburg, 1972, publ. at Kiel 1975) 1–32.

[7] al-Ṭabarī i 2349. Destruction, evacuation: Michael the Syrian, *Chron.* 11.7 (2: 424 Chabot).

[8] Michael Bonner, "The Emergence of the Thughūr: the Arab–Byzantine Frontier in the Early 'Abbāsid Age" (unpub. Ph.D. diss., Princeton University, 1987) 4–12; E. Honigmann, *Die Ostgrenze des oströmischen Reiches von 363 bis 1071* (Brussels 1935); Haldon, *Byzantium* 215–51; R.-J. Lilie, *Die byzantinische Reaktion auf die Ausbreitung der Araber* (Munich 1976) 40–96, 287–360; R.-J. Lilie, "Die zweihundertjährige Reform. Zu den Anfängen der

Syria and its immediate aftermath, that is, primarily the 630s and 640s, in particular the caliphate of ʻUmar I, or ʻUmar bin al-Khaṭṭāb (634–44), and the succeeding several decades. The Muslims did not allow their foes to have truces except on terms that were extremely advantageous to Muslims. Their practices involved a complex combination of diplomatic and military initiatives and threats that were coordinated and tended to reinforce each other. In negotiating terms, the Muslims often tried to by-pass the enemy military commanders. Instead they tried to make contact with local civilian officials and leaders. They wanted to negotiate terms with those who were willing to avoid waiting for official approval of their negotiations. They wanted to encourage breakaway local officials and populations, who were willing to sever ties with the former imperial authority and now switch over to recognize the authority of the Muslims, although not necessarily convert to Islam. One might characterize this strategy as "salami slicing" with the ultimate objective of the total reduction or disappearance of their opponents.

There is no reason to engage in semantic quibbles about the definition of "frontier," which can be a line or a zone, even a devastated zone. A frontier can serve to check not only external enemy movements but also the threat of unauthorized movement from within one's own borders to the territory of one's foe. Byzantine conceptions of the frontier antedated the rise of an Islamic threat and in fact were already in existence in late Antiquity. The Byzantine concept τὰ ἄκρα, or extremities for frontier regions, implies lands at the extremity, outer edge, or limits of Byzantine control. Procopius used the more traditional term ἐσχατιαί to refer to the extremities of the empire. The comparable Muslim concept of *ḍawāhi al-Rūm*, means "the exterior districts of the Greeks,"[9] or, as did the Byzantine τὰ ἄκρα, the extremities.[10]

The Muslims on their part sought to deter Byzantine incursions, raids, and espionage.[11] They wished to prevent their own fellow Arabs, whom they valued very highly and who might be non-Muslims, such as (but not necessarily) Christians, from fleeing to the Byzantine Empire. Neither side ever succeeded in making that frontier completely impervious to penetration. ʻUmar and Heraclius both wished, at least temporarily, to create a frontier along the passes of the Taurus and Antitaurus. Subsequently most willful

Themenorganisation im 7. und 8. Jahrhundert," *Byzsl* 45 (1984) 27–39. Cf. W. E. Kaegi, "The Frontier: Barrier or Bridge?," *Major Papers, The 17th International Byzantine Congress* (New Rochelle, NY: Caratzas, 1986) 279–303.

[9] Edward William Lane, *An Arabic–English Lexicon* (repr. Beirut 1968), part 5, book I, p. 1774. Procopius, *De aed.* 2.1. 2, *Anecd.* 24.12. Benjamin Isaac, "The Meaning of the Terms *Limes* and *Limitanei*," *JRS* 78 (1988) 135–6; cf. Suda, *Lexicon* 2: 432 Adler; Malalas, *Hist.* (308 Dindorf = 168 Jeffreys-Scott).

[10] J. Wellhausen, "Die Kämpfe der Araber mit den Romäern in der Zeit der Umaijiden," *Göttinger Nachrichten*, Philol.-Hist. Klasse (1901) 415.

[11] Duties imposed on Dulūk, Raʻbān inhabitants by their Muslim conquerors: Balādhurī 150.

contact of a nonmilitary kind between Islam and Byzantium passed by sea, not through the land frontiers, despite occasional famous embassies to Damascus.

THE PASSES

The geographical limits of the Byzantine Empire shrank to the Taurus mountain zone on the southeastern edge of Cappadocia and areas just above and below it, including parts of what is traditionally called northern Syria, as well as to Cyprus. In addition to Cyprus, in western Asia the frontier area includes territory that lies south of Iconium (Konya) and Caesarea (Kayseri), north of Aleppo (Ḥalab) and Antioch (Antakya), respectively in northern Syria and southeastern Turkey, and north or west of Melitēnē (Turkish Malatya) as well as lands to the east that were inhabited by Armenians. These regions belonged to the late Roman (Justinianic) provinces of Armenia I, II, III, and IV, Cilicia I and II, Isauria, Euphratensis, Osrhoene, and Mesopotamia. They comprised all or parts of the modern Turkish vilayets of Adıyaman, Adana, Antakya, Elâziğ, Erzincan, Gaziantep, Kayseri, Konya, Malatya, Maraş (Ar., Mar'ash), Mersin, Niğde, Sivas, and Urfa, and the modern Syrian *muḥāfizāt* (provinces) of Ḥalab, Raqqa, Ḥasaka, Idlib, and Ḥamā. All of these regions experienced direct and repeated Muslim raids and invasions and those that remained Byzantine faced threats of still more raids and invasions and insecurity. In those regions it was very hard for the inhabitants to cope with survival and maintenance of continuity. The price of survival for some communities was endurance of tenuous and virtually intolerable conditions, especially from the 630s to the middle of the ninth century (Map 5).

Important passes across the Taurus and Antitaurus Mountains include the Cilician Gates between Cilicia and Cappadocia; the Adata (al-Ḥadath) Pass through the Antitaurus between Germanikeia (Mar'ash) and Elbistan and the Arabissos region, which permitted travel into Armenia, northern Syria, Commagene, and northern Mesopotamia; two routes, the Pyramos (modern Ceyhan) River gorge as well as the Eyerbel Pass, between Kukusos in the Elbistan plateau to Germanikeia; the Mazgaçbel Pass from Kukusos to Phlabias (Kadirli). Another route ran from Kukusos to the Meryemçilbel Pass and via Andırın to Kastabala (Bodrum). Very difficult was the road from Caesarea of Cappadocia to Melitēnē through the passes of the Antitaurus Mountains, especially the route Caesarea to Arassaxa to Komana to Arabissos to Lykandos to Arka. Formidable on this route was the Karahan Geçidi Pass between Lykandos, Plasta and the route to Arka, Keramision, Sama, and Melitēnē (Malatya). Finally, another significant route ran from Develi to Bakırdaği then via Gezbel to Saimbeyli, Feke and thence to Sision

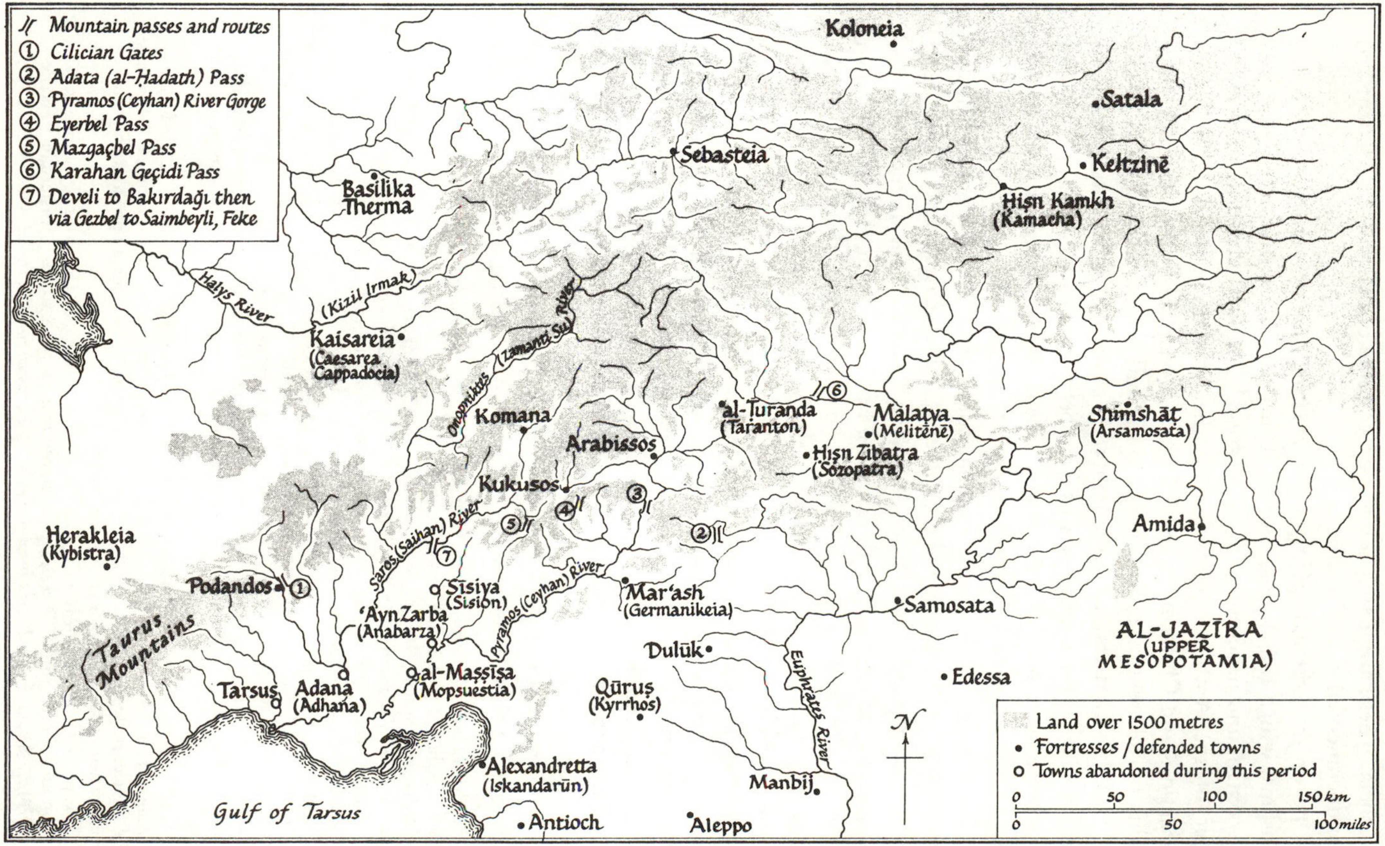

Map 5. Frontier zone between Byzantium and Islam in the Taurus Mountains (adapted from John Haldon, *Byzantium in the Seventh Century*, map V)

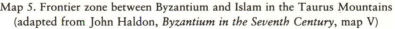

in Cilicia. These are merely a selection of some of the most prominent and best documented routes and passes.[12]

One of the essential elements in creating the new frontier with the Muslims, which ran through former Roman and Byzantine territories, was the control and penetration of the passes.[13] That act terminated the initial stage of the Arab conquests and of the Muslim pursuit of the fleeing Byzantines and Christian Arabs. The passes were seized as a symbol and a reality of the creation of new limits to the authority and freedom of people to travel, as barriers for both military and civilian elements, similar to Heraclius' decision to create a wasteland between the two regimes.[14] Muslim spearheads were naturally the first to engage in the struggle for the passes, which was not, at first, part of any formal agreement.

The struggle for the passes became both barrier and a means of hostile penetration, both obstacle and objective.[15] For this struggle long traditions of Roman and Byzantine border wars with the Persians on the upper Euphrates, ways of cutting off roads and defending heights, as well as Heraclius' own labors in 613 and in the 620s, were more relevant than much of the earlier Roman experience with the Arabs, which did not involve mountain warfare.[16] Although the κλεισοῦραι (mountain passes or the small Byzantine border military districts that contained prominent passes, from which the districts obtained their respective names) are critical elements for the understanding of this problem, it is tempting to assume but unclear whether the Muslim *thughūr* were the consciously created counterparts of the Byzantine στόμια (mouths, openings) or of the κλεισοῦραι, or how much of the frontier was firmly set before the Caliphate of Hārūn al-Rashīd. By the late seventh century a κλεισουροφύλαξ or "guardian of the pass" had appeared.[17] Yet little information exists about the actual conditions of routes

[12] Friedrich Hild, *Das byzantinische Strassensystem in Kappadokien* (Vienna 1977) 84–103.

[13] al-Ya'qūbī, *Ta'rīkh* 2: 161 Houtsma; Azdī 237.

[14] Michael the Syrian, *Chronique* 11. 6–7 (2: 422, 424 Chabot); Balādhurī 163–4. al-Ṭabarī i 2396. Yāqūt/Wüstenfeld 1: 928. Ibn al-Athīr (2: 384, 386 Tornberg). Pseudo-Methodius, who apparently wrote in the late seventh century, emphasizes the significance of the Muslim seizure, "he will seize the entrances of the North," i.e., the passes: in Francisco Javier Martinez, "Eastern Christian Apocalyptic" 142, cf. 58–205. For the Greek: Anastasios Lolos, *Die Apokalypse des Ps.-Methodios*, 1. Red. XI, 13, *Beiträge zur Klassischen Philologie* 83 (Meisenheim am Glan: Verlag Anton Hain, 1976) 104–5.

[15] For broader perspectives on some problems of military fortification and use of passes in this region: Robert W. Edwards, *The Fortifications of Armenian Cilicia* (Washington: Dumbarton Oaks, 1987) esp. 3–50.

[16] N. H. Baynes, "The Military Operations of the Emperor Heraclius," *United Service Magazine* n.s. 47 (1913) 36–8, 195–201. A. Stratos, "La Première Campagne de l'Héraclius contre les Perses," *JÖB* 28 (1979) 63–74; H. Manandian, "Marshrut'i persidskich pochodov imperatora Irakliy," *VV* 3 (1950) esp. 144–6.

[17] Theophanes, *Chron.*, AM., 6159 (350 De Boor). J. Ferluga, "Le Clisure bizantine in Asia Minore," *ZRVI* 16 (1975) 9–23, repr. *Byzantium on the Balkans* (Amsterdam: Hakkert, 1976) 71–85; cf. F. Hild, *Das byzantinische Strassensystem in Kappadokien* (Vienna 1977).

or passes through the frontier regions for the few who wanted to or had to travel. Heraclius wanted some kind of frontier that did not involve massive battle engagements in the open country. Once the fortified towns of Syria had been lost, what remained of defensible posts were located along the mountain ranges and their passes.

Seizure of the passes involved geographic realities as well as the will, sense of timing, and readiness to resist. Geography alone does not explain the Muslim halt at the end of the 640s. The Muslims were able to resist the vague threats of Byzantine counterattacks on their own heartland, i.e., Damascus, while it was always beyond Byzantine ability to mount any offensive into the Arabian peninsula. They were not successful in devising effective answers to Byzantine creation of a defense in depth of mountain passes in the Taurus and Antitaurus mountain range at the southeastern edge of Anatolia. They failed to develop an effective strategy for operating on the Anatolian plateau. They fell victim to their hope of a strategy to draw away major Byzantine leaders whom they expected to switch to political loyalty to themselves. That process never achieved the degree of success and acceptance that they originally anticipated. The result was that they became much more totally dependent on military solutions. They also penetrated areas where there was no longer any Arab population with whom they might hope to make special arrangements and from whom they might receive special cooperation and guidance against the Byzantines. Geography and logistics contributed to making their task progressively more difficult.

The Muslims came closest to achieving their goals in the first two to three decades of the eighth century, after which their expansion slowed. They did completely overrun the Persian Empire. The first three Arab civil wars, 656–61, 680–92, 747–51, drastically hampered the Muslims' offensive ability and their ability to pursue their strategic program. Their failure resulted more from their own internal dissensions than from the recuperative powers and military adaptations of their opponents in the seventh and early eighth centuries. The high-water mark of military expansion against Byzantium was probably the first or second siege of Constantinople (674–8, or 717–18), although others might argue for their zenith at the time of their operations north of the Pyrenees in the early eighth century. In any case, the first Muslim civil war seriously arrested the growing military momentum of the Muslims.

PRECEDENTS FOR CONTACTS

The negotiated surrender of various Syrian and Mesopotamian towns to the Muslims in the 630s and 640s contributed to the creation of a more homogeneous population within Byzantine and Muslim borders. Yet these populations in fact were not homogeneous at all; they were simply more homogeneous than they had previously been in Syria. The Muslim and Byzantine campaigning probably made Anatolia less homogeneous, because of the resettlement of certain refugees.

The last expedition of ʿUmar's caliphate took place in AH 20 under Maysara b. Masrūq and was the first against Byzantine territory, *arḍ al-Rūm*, that penetrated Asia Minor. al-Yaʿqūbī adds that Ḥabīb b. Maslama al-Fihrī hesitated because of fever, and so explained his conduct to ʿUmar when he inquired about the reason for the delay. This enraged the caliph: "ʿUmar said, whenever he spoke of the Byzantines, 'I would like God to make the passes burning coals [or embers], *jamra*, between us and them, this side [of the passes] for us and what is behind [the passes] for them.'"[18] Attribution to ʿUmar gave this statement special significance because of his great reputation.[19] At the least, this is a revealing characterization of the frontier that was circulating in the late ninth century.

Relations with Byzantium in ʿUmar's caliphate, after the great initial victories, have received little attention.[20] ʿUmar's remark indicates support for the creation of a frontier as a barrier at the passes. It is consistent with Balādhurī's report of ʿUmar's command to destroy the city of Arabissos because of its inhabitants' refusal to give information on the Byzantines to the Muslims.[21] ʿUmar wished to create a zone of destruction. The case of Arabissos may in fact be one of the instances that caused him to reach that determination.

According to al-Yaʿqūbī, serious Muslim expeditions into Asia Minor resumed after the death of ʿUmar. Yet there were expeditions across the passes into Asia Minor in 643, so this tradition is erroneous. ʿUmar's alleged statement is also a justification for the creation of a no man's land of destruction between the two empires, which met the needs for consolidation. Both Byzantines and Muslims probably feared the possibility of further incursions from the other side. Both sides may have wished to draw a clear line to prevent the enemy from nibbling away at their own territory. Presumably any transgression of the border zone, however minor or even accidental, would stand out and thereby permit the defender to strike back

[18] al-Yaʿqūbī (2: 178–9 Houtsma). An alternative interpretation of the text might render *jamra* as "white-hot coals" and lead one to believe that he means that the passes will be "hotly" contested, not that a zone of destruction is to be created. This report only exists in the history of al-Yaʿqūbī, who does not give his source.

[19] Yet it is possible that ʿUmar was simply a favored peg upon which all sorts of anachronisms are hung. Such stories may simply involve projecting back from late ʿUmayyad or early ʿAbbāsid times, when much of this material was formulated.

[20] E. W. Brooks omitted the passage from al-Yaʿqūbī in "The Arabs in Asia Minor (641–750), from Arabic Sources," *JHS* 18 (1898) 182–208, esp. 182–3; Brooks, "Additions and Corrections," *JHS* 19 (1899) 31–3.

[21] Balādhurī 156–7.

with full force.[22] It reflects a profound and apparently unbridgeable enmity in each side's conception of the other, with important implications for understanding the ideological aspects of relations between Byzantium and early Islam.[23]

al-Ya'qūbī claimed that there were no more expeditions during the caliphate of 'Umar by land against Byzantium after the first one across the passes in AH 20. Yet this first one really aimed at cutting off fleeing Arabs at the passes, which was accomplished.[24] It was not a raid deep into Anatolia. al-Ya'qūbī may be reflecting views of his own time instead of that of the caliphate of 'Umar (634–44).[25] There was also a potential conflict in reports about the caliphate of 'Umar because there are a number of well-attested reports that there was an expedition in 644 across the passes, indeed to Amorion, perhaps led by Mu'āwiya.[26]

Early Muslim expeditions across the passes into Byzantine Anatolia are obscure. No geographer or historian has conveniently recorded a detailed description of their formation, seasonality, constituents, and routinization of procedures, if any. It does appear that some early expeditions included troops from as far away as Egypt. The *jund* (military district and its army) of Ḥimṣ became an important concentration point for some early expeditions, at least until the death of 'Abd al Rahmān b. Khālid b. al-Walīd in 666. Ḥimṣ had already begun to be a critical nodal point under Heraclius. Its substantial Christian population probably created conditions for religious tensions at the time of massing of Muslim expeditionary forces, and increased the likelihood of intelligence about impending Muslim expeditions reaching the Byzantines, by one means or another.[27]

22 For some late Umayyad military advice – but ostensibly for fighting against the Kharijites: 'Abd al-Ḥamīd bin Yaḥyā, *Risāla* 4: 473–533, esp. 495–533. The author emphasizes the need for strong security measures, watchfulness, protection against night attacks, the dangers of enemy espionage, and the need for the use of tricks rather than battle. For him the choice and securing of encampments is important, as is strict discipline, creation of a strong rearguard, avoidance of risky combat, use of cleverness, and selection of trustworthy officers.

23 Balādhurī 165, 167.

24 Balādhurī 164.

25 al-Ya'qūbī, *Ta'rīkh* 2: 178–9. Moreover, it may not have been 'Umar I but 'Umar II (ibn 'Abd al-Azīz) who said something like that.

26 Ibn 'Abd al-Ḥakam, *History of the Conquest of Egypt*..., ed. by C. Torrey (New Haven 1922) 108; al-Ṭabarī, i 2594, 2798; Ibn al-Athīr (2: 444; 3: 60 Tornberg); Balādhurī 136–7; Michael the Syrian 11.8 (2: 431 Chabot). For analysis: W. E. Kaegi, Jr., "The First Arab Expedition to Amorium," *BMGS* 3 (1977) 19–22 = *ASRB* 14. For other references to this tradition, also from the traditionist Layth b. Sa'd (713–91): al-Fasawī (wrongly entitled al-Basawī, d. 277/890), *Kitāb al-ma'rifa wa'l ta'rīkh*, ed. by A. D. al-'Umarī (Baghdad 1976) 3: 307; Ibn Ḥajar al-'Asqalānī, *Al-Iṣāba fī tamyīz al-ṣahāba* (Cairo 1939) 2: 533. On Layth b. Sa'd: A. Mérad, "Layth b. Sa'd," *Encyclopedia of Islam* (2nd edn [1986]) 5: 711–12; R. G. Khoury, "al-Layth b. Sa'd," *Journal of Near Eastern Studies* 40 (1981): 189–202.

27 al-Ṭabarī ii 82–3 [AH 46 = AD 666/667] = *The History of al-Ṭabarī Between Civil Wars: The Caliphate of Mu'āwiya*, trans. by M. G. Morony (Albany: State University of New York Press, 1987) 88–9. Theoph. *Chron.*, AM 6157 (348 De Boor). H. Lammens, "Etudes

The Caliph ʿUmar bin al-Khaṭṭāb (634–44) probably was correct that the Muslims needed to consolidate before any resumption of conquests, despite reports that "In one of the villages of Ḥimṣ the inhabitants hear the barking of [the Byzantines'] dogs and the squawking of their chickens." Because he apparently wished to have a pause after the great Muslim territorial expansion of the initial years of his caliphate, and because of exaggerated reports about the dangers of the sea, he allegedly declined to authorize naval expeditions: "How can I bring the troops to this troublesome and infidel being [the Mediterranean]? By God, one Muslim is dearer to me than all the Byzantines possess." Reports[28] that ʿUmar restrained Muʿāwiya from earlier invasions of the island of Cyprus are consistent with the well known tradition that ʿUmar also tried to restrain the very able military commander ʿAmr b. al-ʿĀṣ from invading Egypt.[29]

Caliph Muʿāwiya favored and implemented a much more aggressive policy against the Byzantines because of his calculation of his own interests as well as those that he believed would accrue to Islam, by land and sea, after the death of ʿUmar. By that time the Muslims had consolidated their authority in Syria, but the Byzantines had also gained even more valuable time to pull themselves together and develop new ways to resist the Muslims. Muʿāwiya, governor of Syria, and later caliph, gained experience in fighting the Byzantines and familiarity with their territory. In 640/1 he led Muslim troops on a raid with the initial objective of Byzantine Cilicia, which ultimately extended as far as Euchaita.[30] He referred to Anatolia in a speech to his troops "We are ascending into a country which is full of gold and riches of every kind; the Lord will deliver it into your hands because of the sins of its inhabitants."[31] Responsibility for major expeditions had not yet fallen exclusively into the hands of commanders on or very close to the border.[32]

Most significant is the early raid by the Muslim commanders Abū'l-Aʿwar al-Sulamī and Wahb b. ʿUmayr in AH 23, or AD 644, against the important Byzantine Phrygian city of Amorion. It heralded the beginning of major Muslim expeditionary campaigns onto the Anatolian plateau with strategic as well as predatory aims. Whether or not he joined this expedition,

sur le règne du Caliphe Omaiyade Moʿawia Ier," *Mélanges de la Faculté Orientale, Université de Saint-Joseph* 1 (1906) 3, 14.

28 al-Ṭabarī (Sayf) i 2820-1; trans. from *History* (R. S. Humphreys) 15: 26, 27; Balādhurī 152.

29 Balādhurī 212.

30 Michael the Syrian, *Chron.* 11.8 (2: 431 Chabot); Frank R. Trombley, "The Decline of the Seventh-Century Town: The Exception of Euchaita," *Byzantine Studies in Honor of Milton V. Anastos*, ed. by Speros Vryonis, Jr. (Malibu 1985) 65–90.

31 Michael the Syrian, *Chron.* 11.8 (2: 431 Chabot).

32 On Muslim raids into Anatolia, see Wolfram Brandes, *Die Städte Kleinasiens im* 7. *und* 8. *Jahrhundert* (Berlin: Akademie-Verlag, 1989) 44–80.

Mu'āwiya personally participated in other expeditions into Byzantine Anatolia. From those experiences in Anatolia, at the very moment in which Byzantine resistance was beginning to harden, contemporary with the obscure yet important efforts of the Byzantine Emperor Constans II to fortify cities and strongholds and develop a coherent resistance, Mu'āwiya probably gained valuable experience in how to fight and negotiate with the Byzantines. He probably also gained an appreciation of the terrain and logistical problems of Anatolia. No other caliph had so much personal military experience against the Byzantines. Affairs were in flux when Mu'āwiya was governor of Syria and caliph. It is conceivable that the Byzantines could have collapsed, but they did not.

Mu'āwiya's offensive campaigns against the Byzantines resulted in no permanent Muslim conquests in Anatolia (Asia Minor) between 643 and his death in 680. There were almost annual Muslim raids, sometimes in the winter, sometimes in the summer, in fact sometimes raids during both seasons in the same year – even penetrations up to a thousand kilometers deep into Anatolia. Many of these raids started from the Syrian base of Ḥimṣ (the ancient town of Emesa), while others jumped off from Antioch still further north. These raids at a minimum contributed to the prestige of Mu'āwiya, but they also enriched Muslims, attracted more tribesmen to participate, and seriously harmed their Byzantine opponents, who suffered devastation of territory, loss of property and human lives and captives, and diminution of commerce and agriculture. The total Muslim casualties probably remained relatively modest. These operations also kept the Byzantines off balance by diverting their attention to defense and removing any hope of embarking on major offensive strategic policies against Muslim Syria.

Although they accomplished no permanent strategic goals the Muslim raids into Anatolia compelled their opponents to devote much time and effort to developing countermeasures. Mu'āwiya's governorship of Syria and his caliphate did extend Muslim territorial controls: Cyprus and most of Armenia fell under Muslim influence. In addition, they had another conscious or unconscious strategic effect: paralysis of the Byzantine government's ability to do much in defense of extremely exposed positions in North Africa, especially the coastal areas near Carthage and the coastal strip from Carthage to the Straits of Gibraltar. In other words, Muslim pressure on Anatolia, Cyprus, and other eastern Mediterranean and Aegean islands smoothed the way for the Muslim attainment of another strategic goal, the eventual conquest of the extensive and rich North African littoral.

Mu'āwiya's aggressive strategy attempted to exploit a number of Byzantine vulnerabilities. He exploited the unexpected by exposing dangerously false and smug Byzantine assumptions about Arabs. In the years between 661 and 680, Muslim raiders frequently embarked on winter expeditions into Byzantine Anatolia and sometimes they actually passed the entire winter in Anatolia. In addition to the obvious goal of bringing the reality of war into the Byzantine heartland that strategy almost certainly counted on taking advantage of the normal arrogant Byzantine assumption that Arabs, like the earlier Byzantine stereotypes of the Persians, could not fight in cold weather and instead became phlegmatic. These winter expeditions brought home to the Byzantines just how erroneous their stereotypes were about Muslim capabilities to make war. Their expectations had proven to be false in Syria, near Ḥimṣ, not to mention Armenia and Iran.[33]

The winter campaigns were costly to both sides, but they unquestionably deeply disturbed the Byzantines and compelled them to stay on the defensive. It was, however, a risky strategy to gamble the lives of Muslim soldiers in a totally hostile environment for a prolonged period. Moreover, the Muslims probably also profited from doing the unexpected in other ways. There was no tradition of Arab or Muslim seafaring. Yet there were major Muslim naval expeditions in 649 (naval expedition against Cyprus), 655 (naval victory of Phoenix or "The Battle of the Masts"), 673 (conquest of Rhodes), and a lengthy unsuccessful assault and naval blockade on Constantinople from 674 to 678. The Byzantines received some warning about some Muslim preparations for these expeditions, but the Muslim decision to embark on combined naval and land strategies, especially under the sponsorship of Muʿāwiya, underscored the readiness of Muslims to adapt to new strategies and techniques of war. At this date, the Muslims were still innovating and surprising their opponents.

THE STRUGGLE FOR THE CONTROL OF POPULATION

The population transfer arrangements that the Byzantines and Muslims made at the time of the conquests were a prelude to and a part of the larger problem of creating or developing a frontier. Creating a frontier required defining subjects, and, for the Muslims, that involved attempting to gain control of all Arabs, as one sees in ʿUmar's efforts to demand the return of Arabs, probably nomads, who had fled to Byzantine control, or even to the

[33] al-Tabarī i 2390–1 refers to Heraclius' attempt to take advantage earlier at Hims of the Arabs' dislike of cold. Leo VI, *Tactica* 18.124 = *PG* 107: 976, advises that the cold bothers Arabs and therefore one should attack them in cold weather. Sebēos, *Hist.* c. 38 (176 Bedrosian, 145 Macler), mentions the cold in Armenia because of which "the Arabs were unable to engage them [the Byzantines] in war" (176 Bedrosian). This passage from Sebēos' *History* helps to confirm that in the seventh century there were instances when the Byzantines did benefit from the Arab dislike of cold weather.

Byzantine court, such as, in one spectacular case, Jabala b. al-Ayham, the last king of the Ghassānids, the former Byzantine federates.[34] The cases of individuals who crossed the frontiers appear to be relatively few.

'Umar wrote to Heraclius for the return of Arabs, possibly of the tribe of Iyād, who had fled to Byzantine territory. Heraclius apparently returned these, but not other Arabs, such as the Ghassānid remnants, who had fled to Byzantine territory. This correspondence took place in AH 20, that is, 640/1. al-Ṭabarī reported that 'Umar demanded that they return those Arabs from the tribe of Iyād who had fled to Byzantine territory, or he threatened to harm – or eliminate – Christians within his territory: "It has come to my notice that a certain group of Arab tribesmen has left our territory and has sought residence in your territory; by God, if you do not drive them back, we will surely dissolve our covenants with the Christians living under Arab sovereignty, and expel them." Pseudo-Wāqidī claimed 'Umar further warned the tribe of Taghlib "If you seek refuge with the Byzantines, I shall certainly write to them about you and I shall come and lead you away in captivity." This is a much harsher description of the demand for return of Arabs than Ibn Sa'd or al-Ṭabarī mention. Ibn Sa'd also states that the Caliph 'Umar wrote to Emperor Constantine (perhaps Constans II, not Constantine III) in support of the release of the captured eminent Muslim 'Abd Allāh bin Ḥudhāfa, who was in fact released in response to this caliphal request. Ibn al-Athīr also recounts the flight of part of the tribe of Iyād to Heraclius, but he states that 'Umar requested the return of Arabs in exchange for the return of Byzantines to the emperor.[35] Yet the flight of Arabs into Byzantine territory continued.[36] There were explicit as well as tacit agreements.

[34] Balādhurī 136–7, 163–4; al-Ya'qūbī, *Ta'rīkh* (2: 168 Houtsma). al-Aṣma'ī [attribution], *Ta'rīkh al 'arab qabl'al-Islam*, ed. by Muḥammad Ḥasan Āl-Yāsīn (Baghdad 1959) 111–12. al-Aṣma'ī's detailed knowledge of Islamic traditions: N. Abbott, *Studies in Arabic Literary Papyri*, III: *Language and Literature* (Chicago: University of Chicago Oriental Institute Publications [Chicago 1972]) 99–107. al-Ṭabarī i 2508–9. Ps.-Wāqidī, (Beirut 1972) 2: 112. al-Iṣṭakhrī, ed. by De Goeje, *Bibliotheca Geographorum Arabicorum* 1: 45. Ibn al-Athīr (2: 386, 414–15 Tornberg). Abū'l Fidā, *Annales*, ed. by Jo. Ja. Reiske (Copenhagen 1789) I: 234–6. Excellent background: Irfan Shahid, *BAFOC* 2–4, 13–16, 18–24, 117, 382–3, 474–6, 499–500.

[35] al-Ṭabarī, i 2508, trans. from al-Ṭabarī, *The History of al-Ṭabarī*, 13: *The Conquest of Iraq, Southwestern Persia, and Egypt*, trans. by Gautier H. A. Juynboll (Albany: State University of New York Press, 1989) 89, 91. Pseudo-Wāqidī 2: 111–12 on flight of the Iyād. There is also, 2: 155, anachronistic reference to Istanbul. Cf. Bakrī, *Mu'jam mā ista'jam* (Cairo 1945), p. 75 on 'Umar writing to Heraclius: al-Ṭabarī i 2508–9. Ibn Sa'd, *Ṭabaqāt* IV/1: 139–40, for reference to 'Umar's successful effort to regain a captured Muslim commander 'Abd Allāh b. Ḥudhāfa in his correspondence with Emperor Constantine, son of Heraclius. 'Umar's efforts to try to halt the migration of the Banū Taghlib to Byzantine territory, Balādhurī 181–3; al-Ṭabarī i 2509–11; Caetani, *AI* 4: 226–31.

[36] In Egypt in 661, reportedly 15,000 caliphal soldiers negotiated with Constans II, converted to Christianity, and allied themselves with Byzantium: Sebēos, *Hist.* c. 38 (182 Bedrosian, 149 Macler); "Now the army which was in Egypt united with the Byzantine emperor, made

TENTATIVE DIPLOMATIC CONTACTS AND EXCHANGES

al-Ṭabarī, probably via the traditionist Sayf b. 'Umar, reports a charming exchange of gifts between Caliph 'Umar's wife, Umm Kulthūm, and the Byzantine empress, who presumably was Martina, wife of Heraclius. It cannot have taken place before 638, when 'Umar married Umm Kulthūm, or later than the death of Heraclius in 641. It occurred during a respite in hostilities, after the Byzantine emperor "abandoned raiding." According to the story, Umm Kulthūm sent perfume by way of an ambassador to the Byzantine empress, who reciprocated by sending her a necklace. The incident triggered a controversy about whether this was her personal property or that of the government. It ultimately was given to the caliphal treasury, and Umm Kulthūm received monetary compensation by 'Umar from his personal account.[37] The incident, as well as several other anecdotes about witty and relaxed correspondence between 'Umar and Heraclius, which al-Ṭabarī appears to have taken from some collection of traditions about Byzantine–Muslim relations, reveals the existence of embassies at an early date between the two empires.[38] This is true only if the collection of traditions used by al-Ṭabarī was a corpus of accurate accounts. There are very many false reports of communications between the two sides over minor matters. The frontier was not unbreachable, but the cases also illustrate the need to keep exchanges under the strictest controls, irrespective of the importance of the persons involved.

The Byzantines and Muslims had arranged agreements from the period of their earliest contacts, which became precedents for diplomatic relations in subsequent centuries, even though the existence of diplomacy did not signify the permanent disappearance of a state of warfare between the two parties.

Restricting commercial entry reduced the possibility of espionage by those posing as merchants and, somewhat less important, could have restricted movements of weapons or other items that the other side may have needed. Accordingly, Byzantine law attempted to restrict contacts across the frontiers. The military codes listed a number of essentially older Roman

peace and was incorporated. The multitude of the troops, some 15,000 people, believed in Christ and were baptized."

37 al-Ṭabarī i 2822–3. This undated incident may involve the aftermath of an alleged and improbable Byzantine effort to attack Ḥimṣ by sea, or by a raid from Byzantine Mesopotamia, or perhaps diplomatic negotiations to smooth events after the failure of the expedition, in order to prevent a major outbreak of new warfare.

38 al-Ṭabarī i 2820–30. Yet here again the caliphate of 'Umar may merely have served as a convenient place on which to project later stories. Caution is essential in reading or interpreting any such anecdotal material, which reads very much like a later attempt to establish the distinction between a public and a private treasury. It could derive from the eighth or ninth century.

prohibitions concerning sale or delivery of weapons and iron to the empire's enemies as well as problems of the flight and possible return of soldiers and civilians across the frontier under various circumstances.[39]

The frontier later became a place for the exchange of prisoners and hostages and therefore was a place where outside influences, and spies in the guise of merchants, could sometimes, somehow pass the frontier to learn about imminent raiding plans and routes of Muslims.[40] But there is no evidence about this in the middle of the seventh century. Presumably some merchants at least occasionally engaged in trade, and commercial exchanges may have been accompanied by other less willful exchanges, for example, of culture and information about events, conditions, practices, and innovations in the other society and its neighboring governmental entities.

CREATION OF THE FRONTIER

Resort to diplomacy did not end with the caliphate of ʻUmar. There is a tradition that when Caliph Muʻāwiya was told that the Byzantines had raised an army, a governor had run off, and prisoners had escaped, the commander ʻAmr b. al-ʻĀṣ advised him not to worry: "This is not much [trouble] for you. As for the Byzantines, satisfy them with a few concessions with which you can restrain [dissuade] them ... And Muʻāwiya followed his advice."[41] This may be a hostile tradition that wishes to malign the alleged easy-going nature of the Umayyads; it may reflect the fact that Byzantine threats did not need to be taken too seriously, that it was possible to reach negotiated settlements with them, without having to recourse to battle. It was not only the Byzantines who always wished to avoid battle.

Both the Byzantine and the Muslim leadership wished to establish tight control over communications and the passage of persons or groups between the two governments' territories. To the extent that the frontier could serve to connect both polities in that early period, it was as an instrument for the strict control of communications and passage, under the supervision and

[39] Νόμοι Στρατιωτικοί, 19, 46, ed. by I. and J. Zepos, *Jus Graeco-Romanum* (repr. Aalen 1962) 2: 83.123–6, esp. 87.242–7, on weapons, but concerning desertion and return: c. 9 (2: 82 Zepos), and c. 24 (2: 84–5 Zepos); Leo III, *Ecloga* 8.2, 8.4.2, ed. by Ludwig Burgmann (Forschungen zur byzantischen Rechtsgeschichte, 10 [Frankfurt: Löwenklau, 1983]) 202.

[40] "Skirmishing" 7, in *Three Byzantine Military Treatises*, ed. and trans. by G. T. Dennis (Washington: Dumbarton Oaks, 1985) 162–3; = *Le Traité sur la guérilla de l'empereur Nicéphore Phocas* 7.2, ed., trans., and comment. by Gilbert Dagron, Haralambie Mihaescu (Paris: Editions du C.N.R.S., 1986) 51, 180, 249. Gilbert Dagron, "Byzance et le modèle islamique au Xe siècle. A propos des *Constitutions tactiques* de l'empereur Léon VI," *Comptes rendus, Académie des inscriptions et belles-lettres* (1983) 219–43.

[41] Balādhurī, *Ansāb al-Ashrāf*, ed. by Iḥsān ʻAbbās (Wiesbaden; F. Steiner, 1979) IV.1: 47; edn by Max Schloessinger and M. J. Kister (Jerusalem: Magnes, 1971) IVA: 36.

with the consent of central authorities, not locally made *ad hoc* arrangements on the part of local authorities. Caliph and emperor wished to control their enemies and their own subjects. A frontier emerged at that time at the Taurus Mountains because both leaderships consciously wanted, at least temporarily, to create a frontier.

Extant sources do not provide a clear and unambiguous picture of the process of the emergence of the frontier. The investigator must rely on scraps and traces. Ambiguities and many questions remain. The process did not involve any normally peaceful diplomatic and economic relations but limited arrangements on mutually advantageous terms. For both parties, these arrangements assisted the consolidation of power and authority and the ending of a state of extreme flux and rapid military change, with all of the attendant social, economic, and human consequences and distress. The process helped to define the subjects of both governments and accelerated an imperfect homogenization of the populations of both governments. In the longer term, the external frontier may have become less important than internal divisions within Byzantine society. The Byzantine frontier with Islam may have resulted in the development of a certain amount of imitation by both parties and a relative devaluation of the frontier's own importance, but that process had only begun by the late seventh century.[42]

The formation of a Byzantine–Muslim frontier was not due exclusively to any imperial or caliphal decision: at least in the early stages, there also were local initiatives, however tentative. If anything, the Byzantine imperial authorities became convinced that too much local initiative was taking place on the Byzantine side, that there were too many attempts to make contact or local *ad hoc* arrangements with the Muslims to avoid serious hostilities. Many of those local initiatives probably were consistent with the creation of earlier Byzantine commanders and local leaders, who had arranged various settlements with Persian invaders in preceding crises, indeed back into the first half of the sixth century. It was Heraclius who did not like those initiatives and successfully intervened to maintain centralized control of regions that still remained at least nominally under Byzantine authority.

Although a number of local governors attempted to make their own arrangements with the Muslims, no buffer states or independent or semi-independent states emerged between the two powers for a long time. To some extent, the Muslims sought in the early 650s to make Armenia into a buffer zone, although a friendly and not a neutral one, between themselves and Byzantium. That effort faced strong Byzantine opposition and required the Muslims to seek some alternative arrangement for that difficult region.

[42] G. Dagron "'Ceux d'en face' les peuples étrangers dans les traités militaires byzantins," *TM* 10 (1986) 211, 222–7.

The closest other example of a breakaway or buffer state was Cyprus, but even Cyprus was not really a breakaway state. According to Balādhurī, in AH 28 [AD 648/9] (or AH 29) the Byzantine governor or *urkūn*, or ἄρχων, purchased peace from the invading Muslims for an annual payment of 7,200 (Ibn Sallām says 7,000) dinars, reminiscent of the arrangements that John Kateas and Manuel had made with the Muslims in Mesopotamia and Egypt a little earlier.

The Cyprus agreement of 648/9 is genuine and shows that (1) Heraclius did not succeed beyond his lifetime in imposing his policies of no unauthorized local negotiations, but it also again shows (2) the perils of allowing local officials to make local special arrangements with the Muslims.[43] The source for Balādhurī probably was the earlier traditionist Abū ʿUbayd al-Qāsim b. Sallām (770–838), who was reportedly of Byzantine descent and who lived near the frontier, at Tarsus, from 807 to 825. He cites al-Awzāʿī (d. 774), who also reports that there was a treaty that imposed tribute on Cypriots in the time of Muʿāwiya and specifically before the caliphate of ʿAbd al-Malik.[44] He states that the island paid tribute both to Byzantium and to the Muslims. Moreover, the inhabitants of Cyprus were not to conceal from the Muslims any activities of their enemies, the Byzantines, nor conceal from the Byzantines any activities of the Muslims. This is somewhat reminiscent of the obligation of the inhabitants of Dulūk and Raʿbān in northern Syria and of the inhabitants of Arabissos to inform on the Byzantines.[45] This is an earlier source than Balādhurī, who died in 892.[46] Despite some modern critics' reservations,[47] the Muslim accounts of a

[43] Balādhurī 153.

[44] Abū ʿUbayd al-Qāsim b. Sallām, *Kitāb al-amwāl*, ed. by Muḥammad Khalīl Harās (Cairo 1968) 248, 253; Marius Canard, "Deux épisodes des relations diplomatiques arabo-byzantines au Xe siécle," *Bulletin d'Etudes Orientales de l'Institut français de Damas* 13 (1949–1950) 62–3; repr. in his *Byzance et les musulmanes du Proche Orient* (London: Variorum, 1973). Canard accepts the credibility of the account; W. Barthold, "al-Awzāʿī," *Der Islam* 18 (1929) 244.

[45] Balādhurī 150, 156–7. The Muslim tradition specifically compares the case of Cyprus to that of Arabissos, a point which some modern historians of Cyprus have ignored. Yet the similarity in obligations increases the credibility of the terms that allegedly were imposed on the Cypriots by the Muslims.

[46] H. Gottschalk, "Abū ʿUbayd al-Qāsim b. Sallām," EI^2 1 (1960) 157.

[47] See A. Stratos, Βυζάντιον (Athens 1972) 4: 46–8, who argues that Cyprus had no "ruler" at that time, that therefore Balādhurī must be incorrect. Stratos is wrong, because the *Taktikon Uspensky* in the middle of the ninth century does list an ἄρχων for Cyprus: N. Oikonomides, *Listes* 57, cf. 353–4; on a possible explanation of the post of ἄρχων as one involving naval responsibilities: H. Ahrweiler, *Byzance et la mer* (Paris: Presses Universitaires de France, 1966) 54–61; cf. Judith Herrin, "Crete in the Conflicts of the Eighth Century," Ἀφιέρωμα στὸν Νίκο Σβορῶνο, ed. by Vasiles Kremmydas, Chrysa Maltezou, Nikolaos Panayiotakis (Rethymnon: University of Crete, 1986) 1: 113–26. A. I. Dikigoropoulos, "The Political Status of Cyprus AD 648–695," *Report of the Department of Antiquities* (1940–8; publ. Lefkosia 1958) 94–114, also questions the veracity of the tradition. But Costas P. Kyrres,

Cypriot governor's treaty with Mu'āwiya in 648/9 are plausible when reviewed against the larger background of what had happened in Egypt and Mesopotamia: local efforts to reach settlements with the Muslims. Heraclius had not succeeded in preventing such future local negotiations. Whether the Cypriot settlement of 648/9 received approval from Constantinople is an important yet moot issue. The governor may well have made an unauthorized local arrangement.

Neither Byzantium nor the Muslim leadership wanted much local autonomy on the borders, and Heraclius' strong leadership, even late in his life, helped to assure that the central government maintained some reasonable degree of control over its borders. At a later date in Byzantine–Muslim relations, some buffer states emerged, but none emerged in the middle of the seventh century. Muslim policy in Armenia in the 650s allowed for non-occupation of Armenia by Muslim troops, but it required the recognition of the subjugation of Armenia to Damascus, and certainly did not countenance the creation of any neutral and independent state. Indeed, the devastation of the new border areas helped to discourage such an outcome. The fact is that 'Umar, Heraclius, and his immediate successors managed to assert central control over the newly developing frontier between Byzantium and Islam. They established precedents even though the tight controls that they envisaged remained imperfect and eventually loosened under the influence of subsequent pressures, opportunities, and changes.

Some temporary concession of limited and uneasy coexistence within a framework of extremely limited and strictly controlled exceptional official contacts and communications existed in the late 630s and 640s. But both Muslim and Byzantine leaderships made every reasonable effort to prevent private individuals or groups, such as tribes, from engaging in any form of local or private contact, or travel, whether personal, commercial, military, or otherwise. It was a grudging temporary coexistence of a sort. Neither government ruled out from the beginning occasional useful or necessary diplomatic contacts to settle or neutralize specific problems. This limited coexistence and occasional reciprocity or symmetry of policies – and it would be wrong to assume much symmetry – in no sense involved any concession by either leadership of ultimate principles and claims, which

"The Nature of the Arab–Byzantine Relations in Cyrpus from the Middle of the 7th to the Middle of the 10th Century AD," *Graeco-Arabica* 3 (1984) 149–76, repr. in abridged form in his *History of Cyprus* (Nicosia 1985) 176–85, agrees that a 648/9 date for such peace terms is conceivable. Excessively skeptical is A. Papageorgiou, "Les Premières Incursions arabes à Chypre et leurs conséquences," 'Αφιέρωμα εἰς τὸν Κωνσταντῖνον Σπυριδάκιν (Lefkosia 1964) 152–8. Nikolas Oikonomakis, "'Η ἐν Κύπρῳ κατὰ τὰς 'Αραβικὰς Πηγὰς...," Πρακτικὰ τοῦ Πρώτου Διεθνοῦς Κυπρολογικοῦ Συνεδρίου (Lefkosia 1972) 2: 193–4, apparently accepts the 648/9 date.

prevented or at least restricted any easy positive evolution toward genuine coexistence.[48]

FEATURES OF THE FRONTIER

Despite reports of Byzantine mobilizations, it is unlikely that the Byzantines could have sponsored major military expeditions back into Syria. The Byzantines could and did threaten Mar'ash and Melitēnē/Malatya, and they could use the Jarājima or Mardaites as valuable allies or surrogates. But they lacked the resources and willingness at that time to take sufficient risks to attempt the recovery of Antioch or other major northern strongholds such as Qinnasrīn, let alone points south of those towns. They could and did organize raids and descents at almost any point along the Mediterranean coast, but they could not hold such positions. Some Muslim sources claim that the population at Ḥimṣ rose against the Muslims in favor of Heraclius, who allegedly supported them by persuading troops from Byzantine Mesopotamia to come to their assistance.[49] This Byzantine relief effort for Ḥimṣ from Mesopotamia reportedly did not work because the Byzantines pulled back on news of a Muslim threat from Iraq to their own homelands in Mesopotamia. The confused situation in Mesopotamia and northern Syria complicates any effort to understand the genesis of a fixed and clear Byzantine–Muslim frontier.

It is unclear how quickly Byzantine familiarity with Syria faded in the seventh century after the evacuation. Older maps and records gradually became obsolescent, but there is no way to determine how coherent a picture of seventh-century events and conditions in Syria was ever held by the Byzantines. One reason for Byzantine caution with respect to offensive actions against Muslim Syria may have been the poor quality of their information about it.

The problem of the Mardaites in the late seventh century is not inconsistent with broader patterns; they did not form a breakaway Byzantine state. They created, with Byzantine governmental encouragement, a sufficiently troublesome threat to the caliphal government in northern and coastal Syria that it found it preferable to devise a diplomatic solution with the Byzantine

[48] Ahmad Shboul, "Arab Attitudes Towards Byzantium: Official, Learned, Popular," Καθηγητρία: *Essays Presented to Joan Hussey for Her 80th Birthday* (Camberley, Surrey: Porphyrogenitus, 1988) 111–28.

[49] Notably Ibn al-Athīr and al-Ṭabarī, who use traditions that Sayf b. 'Umar transmitted: Ibn al-Athīr (2: 413 Tornberg); Yāqūt 2: 73; al-Ṭabarī i 3393–4, i 2498–503, 2549; al-Ṭabarī (Zotenberg, 3: 425–30); also, al-Ṭabarī, *The History of al-Ṭabarī*, 13: *The Conquest of Iraq, Southwestern Persia, and Egypt*, trans. by Gautier H. A. Juynboll (Albany: State University of New York Press, 1989) 79–91; Ibn al-'Adīm, *Zubdat al-Ḥalab min Ta'rīkh Ḥalab* 1: 25–9; Balādhurī (149 De Goeje). See N. Posner, "The Muslim Conquest of Northern Mesopotamia" esp. 246–92.

government to eliminate the Mardaite problem. In fact, their removal in the reign of Justinian II further illustrates the unwillingness and unreadiness of both Byzantium and the Umayyad Caliphate to allow buffer states to appear and survive. Both states were able to reach diplomatic agreements to suppress the Mardaites.[50]

The frontier between Byzantium and the caliphate remained unstable, suspicious, and hostile. One tradition attributed to the Prophet Muḥammad claimed that "arrogance is divided into ten parts, nine of which are found in the Byzantines and one in all the other people."[51] The frontier that traversed Armenian areas was lengthy and experienced conditions that differed from those further southwest. It was an important exception. Its history in subsequent centuries sometimes involved circumstances of much looser control, weaker central governments, and more local initiatives and arrangements of precisely the kind that Heraclius abhorred. And ultimately it would be the one where buffer arrangements emerged in the wake of the deterioration of a strong Muslim authority.[52]

A GENERAL REASSESSMENT OF BYZANTINE LAND

The expenses for the unsuccessful Byzantine defense of the Levant are unknown, but they were very substantial, in terms of salaries, stipends, provisions, arms, logistics, and shipping. Of course the permanent loss of Byzantine tax revenues as a result of the Muslim conquests was enormous. It necessarily resulted in many changes in Byzantine fiscal and administrative structure.[53] The reconstitution of Byzantine defenses required adequate financing. Yet procuring the necessary finances for defense against the Muslims required ascertaining just what remained of Byzantine resources after territorial losses in Europe and Asia. The late thirteenth-century historical compendium or Σύνοψις Χρονική of Theodore Skutariotes reports that Heraclius "ordered that there be a tax assessment [ἀπογραφὴν] and all of the land of the Roman [Byzantine] Empire was to be surveyed [κηνσευθῆναι], by Philagrios, who was Koubikoularios (*cubicularius*) and Sakellarios."[54] It is probable that this new census of land took place in the

50 Hratz Bartikian, "Ἡ λύση τοῦ αἰνίγματος τῶν Μαρδαϊτῶν," *ByzStratos* 1: 17–39.

51 al-Ṭabarī i 2516; trans. from *The History of al Ṭabarī*, 13: *The Conquest of Iraq, Southwestern Persia, and Egypt*, trans. by Gautier H. A. Juynboll (Albany: State University of New York Press, 1989) 96.

52 Walter E. Kaegi, "Observations on Warfare Between Byzantium and Umayyad Syria," 1987 *Bilād al-Shām Proceedings* 2: 49–70.

53 Michael Hendy, *Studies in the Byzantine Monetary Economy* (Cambridge: Cambridge University Press, 1985).

54 Σύνοψις Χρονική [*Synopsis Sathas*], ed. by Constantine Sathas, in; Μεσαιωνική Βιβλιοθήκη (Vienna, Paris 1894) 7: 110. On this thirteenth-century source, Karayannopulos-Weiss, *Quellenkunde* 2: 462–3, no. 443. It contains occasionally valuable unique references to the

wake of the Byzantine defeat in Syria. It was necessary to ascertain what were the empire's surviving fiscal resources after those major military reverses and Muslim seizure and raiding of much Byzantine territory.

This hitherto unnoticed act probably was a census taken after the loss of much territory to the Muslims. Heraclius probably needed to ascertain what remaining financial resources existed for the support of his government after losses to the Muslims and Slavs and Avars. It is impossible to say whether this survey resulted in any controversial broader institutional changes. The date of the commencement of this census probably fell sometime between late 636 and January 641. The exact chronological limits of Philagrios as *sakellarios* (Treasurer) are unknown, but he held that office after Theodore Trithurios, who was *sakellarios* at the time of the battle of the Yarmūk in August, 636. Philagrios continued to be *sakellarios* after the death of Heraclius in February 641. He remained *sakellarios* until early in the reign of Constans II, when he was exiled to North Africa, in 642 or 643.[55]

Many mysteries would find solution, of course, if the notarial records of that census were extant. Theodore Skutariotes offers no other details. All that one can do is to hypothesize that this census was one governmental response to the still expanding military crisis in western Asia and Egypt and in the Balkans. How successful it was is unclear. It is uncertain how long it required to complete this census, or what were its results.

Theodore Skutariotes does not connect this reassessment to any military reforms although its implementation under the *sakellarios* underscores the consolidation of the power of that office and the weakening of the praetorian prefecture. The making of such a census could have facilitated the allocation of lands to soldiers, but Theodore Skutariotes does not state that such a measure accompanied or immediately followed the reassessment. The existence of such a census after the massive territorial losses in the east and in the Balkans could have provided valuable information for all sorts of decisions concerning military and other aspects of public finance in the first years after the death of Heraclius. It was a sensible measure to take under the circumstances. Its conception and implementation are indications that the government did not remain paralyzed, even though paralysis may well have been the situation of the troops and military command in Syria. It is another indication that Heraclius remained active late in his reign and that he was still

seventh century: Walter E. Kaegi, "New Evidence on the Early Reign of Heraclius," *BZ* 66 (1973) 311, esp. n. 9.

55 Lead seals – Zakos-Veglery, *BLS* no. 1365, I, part 2: 831; V. Laurent, *Le Corpus des sceaux de l'Empire byzantin*, T. 2: *L'Administration centrale* (Paris: Editions du C.N.R.S., 1981) 385–6, no. 740 – of Philagrios are known, as well as his activities on behalf of Constantine III as successor of Heraclius, Nicephorus, *Hist.* 29 (78 Mango), and his exile at the instigation of General Valentinus, Nicephorus, *Hist.* 30 (80 Mango), and John of Nikiu 120. 2–3 (191 Charles). This is the only reference to this act.

taking active responsibility or at least being credited with taking responsibility for major administrative initiatives. It is perfectly consistent with Muslim sources' claims that Heraclius remained very energetic until the end of his reign. The census of land, which was presumably the last in the reign of Heraclius, probably contributed to the marshaling of available resources for the defense of what remained of the Byzantine Empire. It is unique because there is no record of a general census of the entire empire, in contrast to local ones, since Diocletian had made one. It is uncertain whether Mesopotamia or northern Syria was included in this survey, because of the lack of other information, including a precise date for the survey. This act may have stimulated analogous registration across the border. Theophanes reports that Caliph 'Umar in 640 ordered a general assessment of "the entire world subject to him": "people, livestock, and plants." It is inconceivable that 'Umar and his advisers were unaware of the Byzantine census, which they probably imitated.[56] This is the establishment of a Muslim tax register, just as Philagrios had already begun to create a new Byzantine one.

BYZANTINE MISTAKES

Relations between Heraclius and the Sassanians during the Muslim conquests are important, yet obscure and entirely neglected by historians. It is impossible to state whether there was any effort to coordinate the resistance of the two empires against the Muslims. Distance, differing languages, separate bureaucracies, outlooks, and interests all combined to make such coordinated strategy and operations very difficult to accomplish. It is easy to ruminate on how effective such joint policies might have been, but the effort results in wholly speculative scenarios.[57] Crucial to any reasonable conclusion is the evaluation of the nature and scope of any Byzantine military and administrative presence within the former boundaries of the Sassanian

[56] Theoph. *Chron.*, AM 6131 (341 De Boor). AH 20 = AD 640: al-Ya'qūbī (2: Houtsma); Ibn Sa'd, *Ṭabaqāt* III/1: 213 (Muḥarram AH 20 or December 640/January 641). There may be Byzantine influence on the establishment of a general tax register, but the issue of the creation of a register or muster list of those soldiers entitled to stipends is a separate matter, for which see Gerd-Rüdiger Puin, *Der Dīwān von 'Umar* (Bonn 1970) 18, 27, 94. The word *dīwān*, or treasury, had original associations with creating a register: Lane, *Arabic–English Lexicon*, 1: 939, and that is precisely what Theodore Skutariotes and Theophanes are mentioning for both states in the final years of the reign of Heraclius. Last general census: Jean Durliat, *Les Finances publiques* 16.

[57] Contemporary sentiments in favor of preservation of the Persian Empire and warnings about the potential danger of its replacement by some other race if it disappeared: Theophylact Simocatta, *Hist.* 4. 13. 9, 4. 13. 13. Theophylact is insufficiently explicit about the identity of the race that might replace the Persians. Perhaps he means *any* other race, a grudging admission that only the Persians could be considered civilized and on a par with the Byzantines.

Empire, most notably in northern Iraq, after Heraclius returned to Byzantine territory from his victorious defeat of the Persians.

If, as it appears likely, the Byzantines were occupying part of northern Iraq, and if they had appointed friendly governors of some northern Iraqi districts, they would have necessarily been kept closely informed on the progress of the Muslim conquest of Iraq and would have possessed units who could assist or coordinate their actions with the Persians. They would have necessarily been directly involved, whether they wanted to be or not, in the events of the Muslim conquests of Iraq. At least some Byzantine officers and troops would have gained some understanding of the possibilities, opportunities, difficulties, and scope of the effort to help the Sassanian regime survive.[58] All of this raises the question of the attitude of the Byzantine government toward the kaleidoscopic changes of leadership and factions within the Sassanian Empire, whether the Byzantine government favored Siroes but was not enamored of other Persian rulers.

Muslim victories over the Sassanian Persians in Iraq probably had no great effect on the outcome of warfare between the Byzantines and Muslims in Syria. The battle of Qādisiyya in Iraq in 637, one of the greatest Muslim victories, took place after the decisive battle of the Yarmūk. The Byzantines cannot have remained oblivious to Muslim successes in Persia, which augmented the victorious Muslim momentum, and probably discouraged Byzantine resistance in Egypt, northern Syria, and in upper Mesopotamia. Armenians serving in the Persian army probably passed word about Muslim victories in Iraq to their Armenian confrères in the Byzantine armies in Syria and Mesopotamia and Asia Minor.

The Byzantines failed to develop an effective strategy to cope quickly and decisively with the Muslim propensity to concentrate their attacks from the poorly guarded periphery against nodal points, choke points or pressure points, rather than the centers of population where most Byzantine troops and their leadership were based. The Byzantines retained control of centers of population until the outcome of battle elsewhere made their control of population centers no longer tenable. They were unable to exploit their control of the mass of the population to defeat the Muslims. Responsibility for large numbers of civilians may actually have reduced their freedom to conduct military operations. The civilian population was psychologically unprepared and untrained to cope with the invasions. There was no coherent Byzantine strategy and whatever passed for strategy did not incorporate Byzantine civilians into its larger perspectives.

The Byzantines tried to maintain control of commanders, to avoid the

[58] On the Muslim defeat of the Sassanians, A. I. Kolesnikov, *Zavoevanie Irana Arabami* (Moscow: Nauka, 1982).

risks and danger of military operations forever. Likewise Muslim conquests in Syria and Mesopotamia avoided the danger of operations forever, because of reasonably close communication with higher Muslim leaders. The principal limitation on Muslim operations forever was the Muslim motivation in much of the conquests; that was a religious impulse, not just the egos and ambitions of various adventuresome military leaders.

THE LIMITS OF BYZANTINE POWER: THE ABSENCE OF MILITARY EXPERIENCE AND WEAPONS AMONG THE CIVILIAN POPULATION

The more one reflects on the historical situation after 628, the more obvious it is that Byzantium simply lacked the human and material resources to hold the entire *oikoumene* of Byzantines and Persians together. Any effort to try to do this required calling – ironically – on the assistance of various friendly Arab tribes and groupings to make it possible. The Greek and Armenian and Latin sections of the population could not easily provide sufficient manpower and leadership, given the empire's other widespread needs. Heraclius' strategy had more relevance for Byzantine towns and cities than it did for the large numbers of people who lived in villages in the countryside outside the towns. There are no reports of Byzantine efforts to train the hitherto inexperienced civilian population in the use of weapons. Although Heraclius allegedly had encouraged civilians to resist, there is no report of precisely what he expected them to do in combat against the Muslims.

The imperial government had striven in fact to prevent private individuals from possessing arms, for the sake of public order and the avoidance of the creation of virtual private armies by large landowners. To the extent that this policy was successful, it prevented individuals from possessing the weapons and the experience with weapons that might have encouraged them to try violent resistance of their own against the Muslims.[59] The government had probably been unable to prohibit individuals from possessing arms in its border Arab and Armenian territories, but the policy on balance probably contributed to the disinclination or inability of the local populace to organize local self-resistance. It may have also resulted in a shortage of weapons, because the government had sought to restrict their manufacture to government-approved weapons factories. Although there is no specific mention of any weapons shortage affecting the outcome of the fighting, the policy probably resulted in fewer civilians possessing weapons or familiarity in their use. It is unrealistic to have expected, in these circumstances, that the

[59] Just. Nov. 85; Priscus, *Hist.*, ed. by L. Dindorf, Historici Graeci Minores (Leipzig: Teubner, 1870) 306; Denis Feissel, Ismail Kaygusuz, "Un mandement impérial du VIe siècle dans une inscription d'Hadrianoupolis d'Honoriade," *TM* 9 (1985) 397–419, esp. 410–15; Stein, *HBE* 2: 245, 465.

civilian population would have been likely to offer enthusiastic and effective mass armed resistance to the Muslims.[60]

Although Byzantine economic resources, however weakened by the recent and protracted wars with the Persians, and however exacerbated by Avaric and Slavic raids, were still far greater that those of the Muslims at the start of the Muslim conquests, the Byzantines were unable to convert them into a decisive military advantage. Heraclius was trying to juggle too many commitments on the periphery of his empire at the moment of the Muslim penetrations. He was unable to handle the challenge. Yet one could not have predicted the Byzantine military failure from examining the commercial, industrial, and financial balance sheets of the empire.[61] Sheer quantitative superiority in economic resources did not insure ultimate military victory. Fortunately for the Byzantines, one material resource – territorial depth – did allow for the possibility of survival and partial recovery.

Technological disparities do not explain the Byzantine defeat. The Byzantines possessed superior skills in siege warfare and benefited from their heritage of Graeco-Roman military experience and literature. One eighth-century Muslim military manual implicitly concedes the superiority of Byzantine weapons.[62] The camel was important to the Muslims, but no Byzantine source attributes Muslim victories to their mastery of the camel.

THE ROLE OF HISTORICAL CONTINGENCY

Decisive in confirming the loss of Byzantine territories in the Levant was the succession crisis at the end of the reign of Heraclius, from 4 July 638 (date of coronation of Heraclonas as Augustus) to November 641 (the date of the fall of Martina and her son, the Emperor Heraclonas, in favor of Constans II, the son of Heraclius Constantine). It climaxed with the death of Heraclius on 11 February 641. The revolt of General Valentinus against Martina and Heraclonas and in favor of Constans II further exacerbated internal strife at a delicate moment. Heraclius' controversial second marriage, with his niece Martina, the rivalry for the succession by his children from his first marriage, most notably the sickly Heraclius Constantine, who briefly succeeded Heraclius on 11 Februrary to 24 May 641, and his own son Constans II, and Martina's ambitions for her sons Heraclonas and David, the unsuccessful plot of Heraclius' bastard son Athalaric – all combined to make rational and

[60] For sensible emphasis on the ultimately important role of military force, not internal strife, in determining the fate of northern Syria: Dennis Dean Hammond, "Byzantine Northern Syria, AD 298–610: Integration and Disintegration" (Unpub. Ph.D. diss., UCLA, 1987) 326.

[61] Limits of trade: Patricia Crone, *Meccan Trade and the Rise of Islam* (Princeton: Princeton University Press, 1987).

[62] Abd al-Ḥamīd ibn Yaḥyā, *Risāla* 4: 512 = Schönig, *Sendschreiben* 53.

cool decision-making very difficult, if not impossible. Heraclonas and Martina reigned from 24 May until November 641, when they were removed in favor of the nominal rule of the eleven-year-old grandson of Heraclius and son of Heraclius Constantine, Constans II. These internal struggles, plus other ecclesiastical ones, diverted leading officials' attention from the critical military situation on various exposed borders. The government could not concentrate either its attention or its best soldiers to check the Muslims at that decisive time.[63] The internal crisis drained much attention from the Muslim threat during the years from 637 to the end of 641, and its negative effects lingered even beyond the government's suppression of another rebellion by General Valentinus in early 642.

As harmful as it was, the succession crisis could have been worse, for Heraclius' death two or three or four years earlier than it actually occurred would have deprived the empire of the positive contributions of his desperate efforts to halt the Muslim expansion and to establish some viable defensive strategy and tactics and to restore the shattered morale of his soldiers and commanders. There was only a brief period of time remaining to him in his life after the battle of the Yarmūk, which was essential for the survival of the Byzantine state. Heraclius' direct heirs, given their youth and dissensions, would not have been able at that time to provide that leadership.

BYZANTINE COMBAT INEFFECTIVENESS

Most striking is the Byzantine armies' inability to gain the initiative, move readily, and project their power during the course of military operations from the very start of the Muslim invasions. Too often the Byzantines merely reacted to Muslim initiatives or, even more frequently, just remained passive. This conscious or unconscious ceding of the initiative to the Muslims contributed significantly to the ultimate outcome. The Muslims themselves had expected more Byzantine initiatives than ever materialized. It is here, quite possibly, that the failure of the Byzantine policies among the Arabs revealed its greatest limitations and negative effects.

The nonexistence or scarcity or inadequacy of extant primary sources makes it difficult to attempt to assess the combat effectiveness, that is, ineffectiveness, of the Byzantine soldiers in those military operations in Syria, Palestine, and Mesopotamia, including primary group cohesion and the

[63] W. E. Kaegi, Jr., *BMU* 134–85, and, in more detail, Dionysia Misiu, ʽΗ διαθήκη του ʽΗρακλείου Α᾽ καὶ ἡ κρίση του 641 (Thessaloniki 1984). Critical observations on the Greek sources: P. Speck, *Das geteilte Dossier* 44–50, 414–97; A. Stratos, Βυζάντιον (Athens 1969) 3: 144–220. Note: Michael the Syrian, *Chron.* 11.8 (2: 426 Chabot); Georgius Elmacinus (al-Makīn), *Historia Saracenia qua Res Gestae Muslimorum inde a Muhammade* ..., trans. by Thomas Erpenius (Leiden: Typographia Erpeniana, 1625) 36.

quality and commitment of officers. Even in well-documented modern campaigns it has been difficult to achieve a generally satisfactory methodology for evaluating combat effectiveness.[64] Muslim sources do not imply that there was a rout from the beginning. Instead they indicate that there were sharp and tough clashes in some of the early battles such as Ajnādayn. Muslim victories, however, contributed to a favorable momentum for Muslims themselves and to Byzantine defeatism.

No specific Byzantine heroes and no outstanding new military commanders emerged from the Byzantine efforts to defend Syria and Mesopotamia. No one great strategic mind conceptualized the Muslim victories – unless one wishes to ascribe something to Muḥammad himself. Moreover, Byzantine writers did not ascribe their losses to any one great Muslim military mind and commander. Also, there was no great new tactical treatise written, which provided the military doctrine for the successful implementation of the conquest.

Most of the narrative sources, both Christian and Muslim, describe events of the conquest in terms of personalities: personal confrontations, decisions, overcoming of challenges, displays of bravery and wit and piety. These are all individual acts of valor and virtue. Beyond concession of power to a deity, the key role is conceded to the virtuous decisions and actions of specific leaders or military commanders. This unsophisticated and incomplete view of historical reality places most of the responsibility for outcomes on leadership. It gives insufficient attention and respect to the other ranges of causes. It implicitly assumes a great freedom of action and responsibility on the part of great men – that is, particular military commanders and heads of state. It naturally leaves others, especially long-term causal explanations, ignored or undervalued. The quality of Byzantine leadership in the field was not exemplary, but Vahān and Heraclius appear to have devoted their utmost efforts to achieving victory and certainly to retaining the empire's recent gains. The capture of Byzantine cities involved no apparent innovations in military technique.

ILLUSIONS OF CLEVERNESS AND THE FAILURE OF BYZANTINE CUNNING

The Byzantine effort to negotiate with the Muslims during the course of warfare was not unique. They had done so, sometimes successfully and sometimes unsuccessfully, in wars with the Persians in the sixth and early seventh century. Such negotiations had, however, sometimes involved more

[64] On problems in the subsequent eighth and ninth centuries: Friedhelm Winkelmann, *Quellenstudien zur herrschenden Klasse von Byzanz im 8. und 9. Jahrhundert* (Berlin: Akademie-Verlag, 1987).

formal protocol and more eminent envoys. What happened in the 630s was a modified form of what the Byzantines had frequently attempted to do: negotiate during the course of fighting.

The Muslim conquests did not drastically alter Byzantine mental outlooks that had developed and settled into permanent form long earlier. Disastrous Byzantine defeats at the hands of the Muslims reinforced existing Byzantine inclinations to wage warfare of cleverness and ruses with an effort to hold casualties to a minimum – although this is virtually always a desirable military goal. The Byzantines turned to one aspect of their Graeco-Roman military heritage and emphasized it: cleverness. They no longer resorted to the major expeditionary campaigns that had occasionally characterized Byzantine warfare in the previous reigns of Leo I, Justinian I, and Heraclius.

If one can trust such military treatises as the letter of ʿAbd al-Ḥamīd bin Yaḥyā, Muslims similarly strove to use cunning and cleverness more than the shock of battle to accomplish military victories. It seems likely that craft and cunning, including the use of promises to encourage desertion and dissension within the ranks of the Byzantines and their Arab allies, were important Muslim techniques for the achievement of victory in the Muslim conquests. In any case, as the letter illustrates, they unquestionably became important features of waging war within the century that followed the early conquests.[65] Resort to these tactics increased volatility in warfare and offered potentially great rewards – together with minimal casualties – for those who could master this combination of craft, diplomacy, and war. Both sides competed to succeed at waging war through craft rather than open and risky battle whenever possible. Here was another convergence or symmetry between the two competitors.

Among the reasons for the Byzantines' defeat may have been their underestimation of the Muslims' ability to resort to and use effectively techniques of craft and cunning that the Byzantines assumed that they themselves knew best how to master. It is possible that the Muslims had learned some of such attitudes and techniques from the Byzantines, but it is unnecessary to assume that they depended on Byzantine examples alone for their development and exploitation of these kinds of skills. Conversion to Islam did not in itself create a new propensity of Arabs to resort to cunning, craft, and the encouragement of one's opponents to desert or switch sides.[66] But Byzantine military planners may well have ignored the logical consequences of such a tendency: that such opponents might be expert in enticing elements of the Byzantine forces to switch, desert, or to dissolve. Muslim cultivation of such techniques significantly contributed to the

[65] ʿAbd al-Ḥamīd bin Yaḥyā, *Risāla* 4: 473–533, esp. 495–533 = Schönig, *Sendschreiben* 38–73.
[66] Theophylact Simocatta, *Hist.* 3.17.7 (De Boor 151).

disintegration and dissolution of Byzantine armies as effective fighting forces in Syria and Mesopotamia, in particular, to the desertion of Byzantine Arab allies and the intensification of dissension and rivalries among the other heterogeneous Byzantine forces and their leaders. The Byzantines concluded that cleverness was a key to Muslim victories and lack of cleverness a key to Byzantine defeats. This simply reinforced existing Byzantine proclivities and was consistent with the lack of Byzantine resources that could have permitted other forms of military action anyway.

CHRISTIAN MOTIVATION AND SOCIAL CONDITIONS

The absence of a Christian religious motivation comparable to that of the Muslim invaders probably was a factor in the Byzantine loss of those key provinces in the Levant. Many of the Christian clergy did not regard the invasion as the final test of Christian truth or Christian survival. There were religiously charged military rituals in Byzantium. But the clergy did not rise to stir the laymen to violent resistance to the death against the Muslims. The absence of such involvement probably contributed to the failure of the resistance of walled towns, in contrast to the role of the clergy in stiffening the resistance of Constantinople against the Avars and Persians, and later against the Muslims. There are no significant episodes reported about efforts to use Christian relics to save various towns from the Muslims, perhaps because no one wanted to demonstrate the weakness of Christian relics.

No St. Demetrius (patron saint of Thessalonica, and its reputed savior from besieging Slavs and Avars)[67] saved the towns of the Levant from the Muslims, even though the inhabitants of those Levantine towns were known for their piety, both public and private. Only Sophronius is prominently identified as an ecclesiastic in Syria and Palestine, and he, of course, does not perish fighting the Muslims. His sermons and other writings do give some impression of vocal lament for what was happening. Cyrus in Alexandria was prominently identified with and criticized for seeking terms with the Muslims. The Chalcedonian or Monothelite clergy were not diehard resisters of the Muslim armies, and they obviously did not succeed in creating the will and morale within the Christian populations even of walled towns to resist for a protracted period.

Whether or not Monophysite and other Christian dissident clergy actively assisted the Muslims in their invasion of Syria and other provinces, they did not strenuously encourage their communicants to resist the Muslims to the death. They did not stir any fanatical, zealous resistance in towns and

[67] Paul Emile Lemerle, *Les Plus Anciens Recueils des miracles de Saint Démétrius et la pénétration des Slaves dans les Balkans*, I, II (Paris: Editions du C.N.R.S., 1979, 1981).

countryside. There may have been isolated instances of clergy successfully encouraging hard resistance, but there does not appear to have been any last-ditch violent resistance that they created.

There are reports of at least sporadic local resistance to the Muslims east of the Dead Sea as early as 629, but there and elsewhere it failed to coalesce into any coherent and effective movement. One tradition of unyielding local resistance did survive in the memorialization of Christian martyrs, who left their imprint on Latin, not Greek, hagiography. The martyrdom of the Byzantine garrison at Gaza in 637 may have resulted from the anger of ʻAmr at the Byzantine commander's earlier efforts to capture and kill him during negotiations. The preservation of the memory of this martyrdom may have originated with surviving clergy at or from Gaza. Yet it was not local Christian clergy at Gaza or Eleutheropolis who convinced the garrison to refuse to convert to Islam. Their refusal may well have been an independent decision. The local inhabitants do not appear to have been forced to convert or to undergo other severe trials. The author of the account of the Martyrs of Gaza would naturally not have mentioned the attempted treacherous murder of ʻAmr and other Muslim commanders by the Byzantine commander at Gaza – even if the report were true.[68]

In the sixth century and early in the seventh century, a number of Byzantine towns in Mesopotamia, Syria, Palestine, and Egypt had negotiated terms with the commanders of invading Zoroastrian Sassanian armies. There is no reason to be surprised that the leaders of a number of towns again negotiated terms for the surrender of their towns to the invading Muslims in the 630s and later. They were, in a very real sense, following earlier precedents in the region. It is presumptuous for modern critics to have expected the leaders of those Byzantine towns to have resisted to the death. Their degree of zeal in resistance was neither greater nor lesser in the 630s and 640s than it had been previously against the Persians. This lack of zealous resistance is not necessarily attributable to Monophysite leanings of the populace, but to earlier precedents including even the local troops' preference to avoid, when possible, sharp open combat against the Persians.[69] The precedents anticipated the passivity of the population and even Byzantine soldiery in the 630s and 640s. There had previously been a preference to find some negotiated settlement to avoid the risks of battle and ravages of the storming of towns. It was not surprising to find it recur at this time.

68 Hippolyte Delehaye, "Passio sanctorum sexaginta martyrum," *AB* 28 (1904) 289–307; J. Pargoire, "Les LX soldats martyrs de Gaza," *EO* 8 (1905) 40–3.

69 Destructiveness: Benjamin Z. Kedar, "The Arab Conquests and Agriculture: A Seventh-Century Apocalypse, Satellite Imagery, and Palynology," *Asian and African Studies, Journal of the Israel Oriental Society* 19 (1985) 1–15.

The moral and the psychological dimensions were more important than the military for the Muslim victories, and probably also for the Byzantine defeats. Measurement of the moral and psychological dimensions, however, is not easy. The Muslims gained from the psychological impact of victories even in small clashes. These contributed to the creation of psychological momentum, while the Byzantines suffered from the reverse phenomenon, negative momentum as defeats, even small ones, worsened morale and contributed to the creation of a momentum of inevitability and defeatism and, for some, of divine favor for the Muslims.

Resort to truces, blockades of cities to induce negotiations under pressure of famines and strangulation of commerce were not a creation of the era of the conquest of Syria. Muslims, including the prophet Muḥammad himself, had already used and refined them in their ultimately victorious struggle to extend dominion over the recalcitrant Arab and Jewish tribes and clans within the Arabian peninsula.

There are instances of alleged friction between Monophysite clergy and the Byzantine military commanders, especially in northern Syria and the upper Tigris, as reported, however, by very late sources.[70] Yet they may have drawn on sources that were contemporary with the events that they describe. The Monophysite Mārūtha and the Nestorian Mār Emmeh respectively betrayed Takrīt and Mosul to the Muslims, yet these were located in regions where Byzantine rule was exceptionally brief and unstable, and furthermore, where there was a long tradition of alleged betrayals of secrets by Christian clergy to Byzantium's enemies long before Chalcedon and the outbreak of the Christological controversy, namely, in the fourth century. The evidence for the hostility of Monophysites against Byzantines as a cause for the Byzantine failure to resist the Muslims – with the important exception of Armenia, where its local history and situation did reinforce the role of religious strife – is tenuous. Friction between Monophysites, the officially recognized Monothelites, and the Chalcedonians cannot have helped the development of a coordinated and effective resistance against the Muslims, but it was not the decisive element in causing the Byzantine failure and the Muslim successes.[71]

Later Christian writers do not criticize those Christian laymen and clergy of the period of the Muslim conquests for their failure to stir such diehard resistance to the Muslims. In no sense is the Byzantine debacle perceived as attributable to any actions or lack of actions on the part of the clergy –

[70] Michael the Syrian, *Chron.* 11.5 (2: 418 Chabot). Ammianus 20. 7. 9.

[71] John W. Jandora, "Developments in Islamic Warfare: The Early Conquests," *Studia Islamica* 64 (1986) 101–13, who argues with excessive enthusiasm for the positive role of Muslim military science in the accomplishment of the various conquests. On Monotheletism and Monophysitism, Friedhelm Winkelmann, "Die Quellen zur Erforschung des monoenergetisch-monotheletischen Streites," *Klio* 69 (1987) 515–9.

although some dissident Christian groups understandably sought to attribute the disaster more broadly to sins of the empire and especially its leaders at the time of the conquests.

The role of the Byzantine clergy in arousing resistance is possible but not proven in extant sources. Yet Muslim sources do claim that Byzantine clergy and monks did accompany Byzantine troops and commanders at some battles, including that of the Yarmūk. So they were not entirely absent. Their efforts led to no great successes. But the clergy do not appear to have recruited large numbers, or any persons at all, for the Byzantine defense of the region.

The question of the degree to which the local inhabitants of Palestine, Syria, Mesopotamia, and Egypt did or did not make efforts to rely on self-help to resist the Muslims is a crucial point. Long-term trends encouraged placing some of the burden of local defense on local persons of substantial private means in parts of Syria and mainland Greece. The policy shifted away from reliance on local armed inhabitants to professional and highly paid soldiers.[72]

The role of Christian clergy in the sixth century in directing the control of cities in the wake of the Persian invasions had been complex. Sometimes clergy, that is, bishops, had involved themselves in negotiations, and at other times they had paraded relics and participated in various prophylactic rituals to save their cities from the Persians.[73] Their role is not so prominent or clear-cut in the 630s. Their failure to perceive the seriousness of Islam may help to explain their conduct.

Historians often invoke social structure and social conditions in an attempt to explain major events and changes. However tempting, it is not satisfactory, however, to attribute the failure of Byzantine resistance to the social structure that prevailed in early seventh-century Byzantine Syria, Palestine, and Mesopotamia. If anything, the social structure appears to have contributed to creating the conditions in which Armenian resistance faltered. It is true that the prevailing social structure helped to determine the conditions and the mental outlook that existed among Byzantines at the moment of the Muslim penetrations. Social causes are insufficient to explain the Byzantine collapse and the Muslim successes, even though they may help to explain what features within Syria helped the Muslims to consolidate their authority there on a long-term basis. No simple factor can be invoked to explain fully the shape and fortunes of the Byzantine military response to the Muslim invasions. Yet the social conditions in Syria, Palestine, and Mesopotamia did help to create the environment in which the Byzantine

[72] Procopius, *Anecd.* 26.31–3.
[73] Glanville Downey, "The Persian Campaign in Syria in AD 540," *Speculum* 28 (1953) 342–5, cf. also 348.

armies and their commanders had to try to function and cope. It would be foolish to deny any role to social factors, but it is easy to exaggerate them. One could not have easily predicted the success of the Muslims from an examination of social conditions in Syria at the end of the sixth century.

THE ROLE OF ISLAM

Islamicists have pointed persuasively to Islam as a unifying factor that held the Arab tribes together and thereby contributed much to the achievement and the consolidation and permanence of the Islamic conquests, and the role of religion in bolstering "the practical resolve of the elite to embark on an expansion,"[74] and "as an important factor contributing to the successful integration of the Islamic state,"[75] one that integrated tribal groups with the Islamic elite during the conquests.[76] There were no major rebellions against the Islamic leadership during the conquests. These observations have significance not only for Islamic studies, but also for the study of the failure of the Byzantine military leadership and its military operations in those campaigns. Byzantine leaders often attempted to pursue a policy of divide and conquer, sowing dissension within the ranks and leadership of their enemies. The religious impulse to cohesion within the Muslim ranks, although certainly not a universal one, made it more difficult for the Byzantines to use traditional methods of causing desertion, side switching, and betrayal within the ranks of the Muslims. In fact, it was the Byzantines who suffered more losses due to desertion than did the Muslims, it would appear from the sources. It is true, however, that a number of Christian Arab tribesmen, and most notably Jabala b. al-Ayham, who was the last king of the Ghassānid Arabs, in addition to Niketas, the son of Shahrbaraz, did desert to the Muslims. Some of these switched sides, or attempted to do so, several times, and some who had initially deserted to the Muslims ultimately fled to the Byzantines. The role of Islam therefore had many indirect effects on the course of the warfare and the eventual outcome. It forced the Byzantine leadership to attempt to give battle, because it was impossible to use bribery, guile, and emissaries to break up the cohesion of the Muslims.

However reluctantly, the Byzantines joined battle. This is what the Muslim leadership wanted them to do, if one trusts the testimony of al-Azdī al-Baṣrī's *Ta'rīkh futūḥ al-Shām*.[77] In fact, most battles occurred at places of the Muslim leadership's choosing. The Byzantines had not previously encountered such difficulties in undermining the cohesion of their opponents through deceit, money, promises, and false information. The contribution of

[74] Donner, *EIC* 270. [75] Donner, *EIC* 256. [76] Donner, *EIC*, 255.
[77] Azdī 15.

Islam to the cohesion of the Muslims created a new and unprecedented element that made the task of the Byzantine leadership, with its conservative outlook and tendency to look to earlier examples for guidance, much more difficult and uncertain. These observations do not presuppose any religious "fanaticism" on the part of the Muslim combatants or indeed any profound understanding of Islam on their part. What was important was their leaders' religious motivation, however mixed with other impulses and desires.

Islam unified and motivated the hitherto disunited elements of Arabian society and created a state where none had existed before. Hence Byzantines were unprepared for attacks by armies of the new Islamic society when they occurred, and tended at first to underestimate them, assuming them to be merely more beduin raids, the likes of which they had experienced for centuries. The lack of a Byzantine fallback position is partly explained by the simple fact that the Byzantines never expected a serious onslaught from this quarter. It blunted and negated the possible Byzantine efforts to corrupt and split the enemy. It made it difficult to corrupt the Muslim leadership, through the normal Byzantine approach. It is unclear whether the difficulty with corrupting Muslim Arabs also affected Byzantine techniques and approaches and efforts to try to corrupt their enemies on the eastern frontier in the years that immediately followed the initial Muslim conquests. The new religious dimension may have created even more reason for the Byzantines to try to rethink how they waged war and diplomacy and secret contacts, and how they used ruses and craft. Some techniques would no longer work very effectively with a religiously motivated leadership of the Muslims, including local commanders who shared such religious dedication.

There are no records of later reminiscences or stories about Christian veterans of the conquests long after the conclusion of hostilities. On the Muslim side, there are many traditions of participants, alleged or real, in those events of the conquests, but not on the Byzantine side.

EFFECTS

The effects of the Byzantine defense and Muslim invasions did not wreak much immediate permanent physical damage in the course of the actual fighting, even at Caesarea in Palestine, where the city fell by storm. The most serious effects were the willful creation of a devastated no man's land in northern Syria, which was to become the *Thughūr*, a kind of border fortress zone.[78] The reasons for the gradual decline of agriculture and habitation in the Negev Desert areas are complex and do not appear to have

[78] Michael Bonner, "The Emergence of the Thughūr: The Arab–Byzantine Frontier in the Early 'Abbāsid Age" (unpub. Ph.D. diss., Princeton University, 1987).

taken place precisely at the time of the Muslim conquests, even though these invasions surely increased local insecurity.[79] Other areas of agriculture and towns recovered, although some Syrian Christian authors do claim that the Muslims inflicted considerable damage and loss of life.[80]

Long-term social changes included the altered layout of cities and the gradual shift, in part for reasons of security, of substantial population and commercial activity, away from the Mediterranean coastal areas to the interior. The relatively short period of actual hostilities itself did not cause that much permanent destruction, even though commerce was interrupted and some agriculturists were harmed. But in general, traditions about the conquest, even on the part of Christian writers, do not emphasize physical destruction of buildings, civilians or livestock, even though some were caught and destroyed in the course of hostilities.[81]

Even though the amount of physical destruction was modest, the fear of great devastation very probably was a major factor in the decision of inhabitants of towns and countryside to negotiate terms with the Muslims. In this sense, the role of destruction was important. Perceptions were as important as reality – indeed, perceptions created some realities. Presumably destruction would have been greater if they had not readily negotiated terms.

ROLE OF CHRISTIAN ARABS

The Byzantines did not make the best use of Christian Arabs when they decided upon a strategy of relying on walled towns. Christian Arabs could and did serve as guards. Christian guards were recruited from their *ḥāḍir* or camp near towns. But their best use by the Byzantines would have been in mobile warfare against other Arabs, not manning fixed defenses. These Arabs potentially could become as much or more a drain on resources, especially provisions, in the towns instead of being an aid against the Muslim Arabs and their other Arab allies. It is even possible that members of the Arab tribe of Iyād had migrated to Anatolian Ancyra in the pre-conquest period

[79] Balādhurī 163–72; Haase, *Untersuchungen* 33ff. Kenneth Holum and Professor Yoram Tsafrir believe, however, that there is evidence for destructiveness at the site Rehovot ba-Negev.

[80] On the Negev, esp. Philip Mayerson, "The Agricultural Regime," *Excavations at Nessana*, vol. 1, ed. by H. Dunscombe Colt (London: British School of Archaeology in Jerusalem, 1962); A. Negev, "Eboda," in: *Encyclopaedia of Archaeological Excavations in the Holy Land* (New York, Jerusalem: Prentice Hall, Massada) 2: 343–55.

[81] The Pirenne Thesis is now obsolete: Dietrich Claude, *Untersuchungen zur Handel und Verkehr der vor- und frühgeschichtlichen Zeit in Mittel- und Nord-Europa*, II (Göttingen: Vandenhoek und Ruprecht, 1984) and, R. Hodges, D. Whitehouse, *Mohammed, Charlemagne and the Origins of Europe* (Ithaca, NY: Cornell University Press, 1983). See Fred M. Donner, s.v., "Islam, Conquests of," *DMA* 6 (1985) 566–74.

and that other Arabs had inhabited the Cappadocian town of Arabissos.[82] The memory of the presence of such tribesmen in Anatolia, even in modest numbers, could have facilitated the flight of various Christian Arab tribes in the seventh century to Anatolia in the wake of the Muslim conquests.

Although there are reports of fluctuating loyalties among some Christian Arabs, who reportedly switched from Byzantine to Muslim allegiance in battle, there is relatively little evidence of conversion of Byzantine troops, especially non-Arab ones. Even at the battle of the Yarmūk, in which the Byzantines suffered grievously from desertions of Arabs and apparently from military revolt on the part of some Armenians, not all desertions hit the Byzantines. The tribes of Lakhm and Judhām, as Arabic poetry relates, deserted from the Muslim side during the earlier more uncertain stages of that battle.

The leadership of both sides sought to exploit volatility and its threat to cohesion. They were familiar with such practices. Yet Ibn ʿAbd al-Ḥakam and Ibn Duqmāq (who is admittedly a late and therefore somewhat questionable authority, who does not explain the source of his information) report that ʿAmr b. al-ʿĀṣ brought some Byzantine (*Rūm*) troops who had converted to Islam "before Yarmūk" to Egypt, where they settled.[83] This is a rare report. These former Byzantine troops accompanied ʿAmr in his conquest of Egypt. Their permanent resettlement in Egypt, of course, removed a potential security hazard from newly conquered Syria and Palestine, where their superior proximity to the Byzantine Empire might have created temptations for them and embarrassment for the Muslim authorities. Yet the unreliability of troops in Egypt persisted, for in the year CE 661 15,000 Egyptian soldiers reportedly negotiated with the Byzantine emperor, Constans II, and deserted to his side. Many converted to Christianity.[84]

Christian Arabs in Iraq at the time of the Muslim conquest potentially could have been of much assistance in defending northern Iraq against Muslim Arabs. In Sassanian Iraq, Christian Arabs did oppose but they did not succeed in halting, let alone in driving out, the Muslims. If some of them

[82] Shahid, *BAFIC* 274–6, 327–8.

[83] Ibn ʿAbd al-Ḥakam, *Futūḥ miṣr* (129 Torrey). Ibn Duqmāq, *al-Intiṣār li-Wāsiṭat ʿIqd al-Amṣār*, ed. by Karl Vollers (Beirut: al-Maktab al-Tijārī li Ṭibāʿa wa al-Nashr wa al-Tawzīʿ, 1966) 5; Wladyslaw Kubiak, *Al Fusṭāṭ. Its Foundation and Early Urban Development* (Warsaw: Wydawnictwa Uniwersytetu Warsawskiego, 1982) 95.

[84] Sebēos, *Hist.* c. 38 (182 Bedrosian, 149 Macler). The case underscores continuing volatility in military loyalties. In the siege of Constantinople in 717–18, there are reports of the unreliability and desertion of Christian sailors from the Muslim fleet that was blockading and besieging Constantinople: Theoph., *Chron.*, AM 6209 (397 De Boor). Rejection of allegations that Christian troops from the Banū Taghlib participated in the campaign for Marwān: Gernot Rotter, *Die Umayyaden und der zweite Bürgerkrieg* (680–692) (Abhandlungen für die Kunde des Morgenlandes [Wiesbaden: Deutsche Morgenländische Gesellschaft, Kommissionsverlag Franz Steiner, 1982]) 150 n. 261.

were serving as a garrison friendly to Byzantium in Sassanian Iraq, this would have stretched their strength thin and made fewer of them available for service in combating the Muslims in Syria.

OPERATIONAL PLANNING AND EFFECTIVENESS

The histories of the conquests, irrespective of the language in which they are written, do not provide a very good understanding of the nature of warfare and the realities of warfare in that period. The resulting condition of the sources permits many inferences to be drawn, and the information provided is better than having nothing, but many questions are left inadequately understood and explained. Why these wars failed to produce a great historian or at least a reporter of the caliber of some of those of the sixth century is not easy to explain, but the fact is that none emerged. Whether Heraclius and his court ever hoped to find such an official historian or panegyrist is uncertain, but the disastrous trend and turn of events would have quickly discouraged any such enterprise in the middle of the 630s.[85]

Heraclius' decision to direct or follow the military operations from Ḥimṣ and Antioch is not surprising. Although he saw no combat in person, he was reasonably close to the scenes of combat. His actions in the 630s were consistent with his efforts to be close to military operations ever since 612. His relative proximity or distance from battle was not the Byzantine problem in the 630s. Of course, on the Muslim side, Abū Bakr and 'Umar also were not personally present at the scene of battle. They were located further from it than was Heraclius, so the proximity of the head of government was not a decisive factor.

Given the lack of a staff college, oral reports to military superiors were very important. Many of the Byzantine leaders perished or in some fashion were eliminated in the course of the fighting: Sergios, Vahān, Niketas (or the other son of Shahrbaraz). They were obviously not capable of transmitting detailed reports or advice about their experiences to Heraclius and his circle, where most military strategy and tactics were developed and critically evaluated and changed, where necessary. The recriminations and purges after Yarmūk probably contributed to the difficulty of drawing sensible conclusions from experiences. It is impossible to know just how accurate the reporting was that Heraclius and his circle were receiving at Emesa and Antioch about conditions at the front. The best estimate is, however, that critical strategic decisions and responsibility for making changes were made at the level of Heraclius and his immediate advisers.

[85] W. E. Kaegi, "Initial Byzantine Reactions to the Arab Conquest," *Church History* 38 (1969) 11, reprinted with corrections in *ASRB*, Also, Telemachos Lounghis, "'Η πρώιμη βυζαντινὴ ἱστοριογραφία καὶ τὸ λεγόμενο 'μεγάλο χάσμα'," Σύμμεικτα 4 (Athens 1981) 49–85.

Part of Byzantium's difficulties was generally poor intelligence on the Muslims and failure to act rapidly, properly, and decisively on what intelligence they did acquire about the Muslims. Although some Byzantines were immediately aware of the Islamic component in the motivation of Arabs, Byzantines generally underestimated the religious motivation of Arabs as Muslims and understood very little about this new religion. It is unclear how much Byzantine and Muslim decisionmakers knew about their own forces and commanders, their weaknesses and strengths, including potential rivalries and fissures within their ranks, and exact numbers, in comparison with their knowledge of their foes.

The Byzantines may never have possessed a good idea of what had happened in the course of the Muslim conquests. All that was coming back from Syria was rumor, speculation, and devoid of a coherent picture or understanding of the specific sequence and timing of events or the numbers of combatants. The information that the Byzantines at Constantinople received may have been little more than a jumble of undigested data.

Once the Byzantine–Muslim frontier became somewhat solidified near the Taurus Mountains, walled towns apparently ceased to be as important in Byzantine strategy as they had been in Syria. Walled towns and citadels still existed as important places of refuge, but the mountainous topography of Anatolia did not require so much reliance on walled towns or so much flight of the civilian population in the countryside to the protection of walled towns.[86]

OLD MILITARY DEFICIENCIES REAPPEAR

What is so striking about the failure of Byzantine defenses of Palestine, Syria, and Mesopotamia is the similarity of many of its features to the weaknesses of Roman frontier defenses in earlier centuries.[87] The soldiers' refusal to venture forth aggressively from fortified points to fight the invader, their inclination to stay behind the more comfortable fixed walls of towns, and the numerous gaps in defenses were dangerous features of Byzantine vulnerability that had revealed themselves in the east and the west in the fourth, fifth, and sixth centuries, long before the appearance of Islam. Those earlier weaknesses at that time did not result in major permanent territorial losses. Yet the weaknesses had been exposed and had not been repaired. The preservation of the Byzantine borders up to the reign of Emperor Phocas deceptively obscured many military vulnerabilities.

[86] Role of towns, villages, and topography in the tenth century: *Le Traité sur la guérilla (De velitatione) de l'empereur Nicéphore Phocas*, ed. by G. Dagron, H. Mihaescu (Paris: Editions du C.N.R.S., 1986).

[87] Ramsay MacMullen, *Corruption and the Decline of Rome* 177–97.

Some of the same kinds of Byzantine weaknesses appeared again in the seventh century and this time the Byzantine Empire was not to escape catastrophic territorial losses. A lot of the very old and familiar problems reemerged in the seventh century. The new elements this time – greater fiscal strains, the new directions from which the threat came, the great role of Islam in motivating Arab leadership and some, if not all, Arab combatants, and the greater number of Arab invaders – were, of course, very important in determining the favorable outcome for the Muslim invaders. But the feebleness of Byzantine defenses had been there all along. The wonder is that there had not been some major debacle earlier. In fact, a more serious earlier reverse might have stimulated the Byzantine government to eliminate some of the more glaring weaknesses in its defenses. It is unnecessary to ascribe the Byzantine collapse to a failure to wage or understand holy war.[88]

Many of the Byzantine army's problems in defending territory antedated the 630s. These weaknesses had existed on the eastern frontier for a long time, and were not necessarily a consequence of Muslims waging holy war. There were marked religious dimensions to Heraclius' wars against the Persians. The recovery of the cross was an important feature of the termination of those campaigns and the final settlement. Yet whatever religious dimensions Byzantine warfare against the Persians assumed, it did not become transferable to Byzantine resistance against the Muslims only a few years later. The Maurice *Strategikon* shows that Christianity and its liturgy had penetrated the Byzantine army to a profound degree by AD 600. The Byzantine army did expect divine assistance because it was fighting for a God-protected empire and its people. There is no evidence, however, that the empire was anticipating any new religious war after having defeated the Persians in a war in which religious imperatives and causes had become prominent.

The Byzantines showed no signs of developing any immediate emotional reaction to the Muslim successes that could have resulted in a massive collective resistance to the Muslims. Byzantium was becoming a weaker state, yet psychologically it still thought like a great power and it was still a great power, only it was less of one than it had been. On the other hand, there could have been dangers of a dramatic psychological letdown if such a momentary collective movement had failed. There were, however, some

[88] Judith Herrin, *The Formation of Christendom* (Princeton: Princeton University Press, 1987) 211, probably exaggerates the consciousness of "holy war" in most tribesmen. Albrecht Noth argues that "holy war" was not characteristic of Islam at the earliest period of the conquests, *Heiliger Krieg und Heiliger Kampf* (Bonner historische Forschungen, 28 [Bonn: Röhrscheid, 1966]) 41–2, 87–8, and esp. 139–48, although at that era the foundation was being laid for such a latter concept of "Heiliger Kampf." Wilferd Madelung, s.v. "Jihad," *DMA* 7: 110–11.

features of the Byzantines that made possible long-term resistance, and a psychological disposition that was favorable to such a development. There was no mass reaction of Byzantines against the Muslims at the time of the earliest conquests. The Byzantines ultimately demonstrated that they had the resilience to endure, albeit in truncated form.

INTERRELATIONSHIP WITH OTHER EVENTS

The interrelationship of the mopping-up on the Palestinian coast with the conquest of Egypt is significant. As long as the Byzantines held Caesarea and possibly also Ascalon, it was risky for the Muslims to invade Egypt. There was, however unrealistic it may seem, the chance of a Byzantine sally from Caesarea as long as the Byzantines controlled the eastern Mediterranean, including islands such as Cyprus. Yet they had not used such measures against the Sassanians. The account in Balādhurī, *Kitāb Futūḥ al-Buldān*, indicates that only after the completion of the capture of Caesarea did ʿAmr receive permission to invade Egypt. ʿAmr knew more about the opportunities and hazards associated with the undertaking of military operations in Egypt than any other Muslim commander. His seizure of Eleutheropolis (Bayt Jibrīn) and then Gaza in 637 gave him admirable staging points for actual operations against Egypt or, by virtue of his strategic position, for squeezing tribute payments out of the frightened Byzantine authorities in Egypt. ʿAmr had long wished to invade Egypt, but he was unable to win over approval for this expedition until the fall of Caesarea.[89] This was a prudent and rational military and political decision to avoid a precipitous attack.

There is no evidence that the Byzantine defense of Egypt benefited much from experience that the Byzantines gained in fighting the Muslims in Palestine and Syria. If anything, the negative effects of repeated decisive defeats probably greatly affected morale, far offsetting any experience that they gained in knowing how to fight the Muslims. Obviously the ultimate outcome was not changed in Egypt. The Byzantine soldiers and commanders in Egypt did little to defend Syria and Palestine. Coordination of efforts was appallingly poor. To some extent, Byzantine efforts to maintain communications with Egypt may have resulted in competition for limited supplies and ships with the beleaguered coastal towns of Syria and Palestine. Byzantine Egypt fell to the Muslims after the invasion of ʿAmr in December, 639. His was a military conquest, which took advantage of Cyrus' inept governance of Egypt, not a result of blue and green factional strife.[90]

[89] Balādhurī (212–13 De Goeje).

[90] Jacques Jarry, "L'Egypte et l'invasion musulmane," *Annales Islamologiques* 6 (1966) 1–29, is hopelessly confused in ascribing social, political, and religious significance to the circus factions in Egypt and interpreting the entire Byzantine defense of Egypt and its fall to the

Peace, however temporary, with Byzantine Egypt and with Byzantine forces at Qinnasrīn permitted the Muslims to concentrate their maximum strength elsewhere.[91] The Muslim temporary peace with Egypt permitted Muslim concentration on Iraq and the conquest of northern Syria, as well as efforts to mop up any towns that had been trying to hold out. It had some advantages for the Muslims: it was not a stupid agreement for them to make for a temporary period. There was no reason for the Muslims to endanger everything that they had won by committing themselves to a possibly premature invasion of Egypt. It was better to consolidate somewhat more slowly but surely. This avoided possible overextension and excessive risk. As it turned out, the Byzantines lacked a bold commander who could exploit the Byzantine retention of important footholds on the Syro-Palestinian coast.

Byzantium never used her naval power effectively in the course of the campaigns of the 630s and early 640s. The reasons for this are unclear, especially since Heraclius and his family had profitably used naval power to seize the throne in 610.

THE REPUTATION OF THE BYZANTINES

The Byzantines left a poor reputation in their last moments in Syria, Mesopotamia, and Egypt, if one trusts the admittedly biased histories and chronicles of dissident Christians and Muslims. The Byzantines were principally remembered for poor judgments, but above all for plundering the regions before they left them, for abusing the civilian population – in contrast to the exemplary conduct of the Muslims who were under strict orders from Abū Bakr to spare the population and their livestock. The Byzantines were also remembered for some scorched-earth policies, especially in northern Syria. In other words, much of that physical damage that occurred in the wake of the Muslim conquests was blamed on the Byzantines' willful acts, not on accidental occurrences or side effects and not on the Muslims.

Such actions and memories cannot have endeared the Byzantines to the local population in much of northern Syria and Mesopotamia. They made it even more difficult and unrealistic to expect any real local support for a return of Byzantine armies and any restoration of Byzantine authority. It may never have been practicable to expect a return of the Byzantines, but these memories helped to prevent any possibility of it.

Muslims in the light of these false theories; cf. Alan Cameron, *Circus Factions: Blues and Greens at Rome and Byzantium* (Oxford: Clarendon Press, 1976).

[91] Muslim conquest of Iraq: Donner, *EIC*; Morony, *Iraq after the Muslim Conquest* (Princeton: Princeton University Press, 1984).

The events in the Levant in the 630s did not provide solutions to many old Byzantine military dilemmas. If anything, the ability of the imperial armies to wage mobile warfare became seriously eroded because of heavy casualties and the dispersion of many of the surviving soldiers to various far-flung duties in a diminished empire that now faced danger in almost every zone. The empire was still groping for a viable strategy that it had not yet developed. It was temporarily improvising a passive and relatively immobile and static strategy that was conceding the initiative to the Muslims. These improvisations developed out of Byzantine experiences in Syria in the 630s.[92]

THE VIABILITY OF THE HERACLIAN DYNASTY

However serious the Byzantine losses were, they did not result in the overthrow of the Heraclian dynasty, which lasted to the end of the century and slightly beyond, to 711. Somehow loyalty to the dynasty, and the success of the deflection of the responsibility for the disaster to other causes and persons, helped to spare the dynasty and permit its survival.

It is less clear whether there were purges of the Byzantine officers after the debacle. Vahān either died at the battle of the Yarmūk or retired in disgrace, as Eutychius claimed, to a monastery at Sinai.[93] Theodore the Sakellarios, who was a second important commander, perished in that battle. Another important commander, Theodore, the brother of Heraclius, also allegedly died at the Yarmūk, although he probably died later, after his recall to Constantinople. Theodore's presence and role in some fashion did involve the dynasty, but the popular reports that he ignored the advice of his brother the emperor helped to save the latter's and the dynasty's prestige and reputation. The Ghassānid commander Jabala b. al-Ayham did survive at Byzantium and received a privileged position, but his circumstances were special. Niketas the son of Shahrbaraz, who had some responsibility, fled to the Muslims at Ḥimṣ and was slain by them. It is unknown how other surviving officers and soldiers were treated, how they acted, or what they said or thought about their experiences of defeat. Their military services may have been so necessary at that critical time that it was impractical to purge many of them, especially in light of the contemporary shortage of military manpower and of funds for hiring mercenaries.[94]

[92] Gilbert Dagron, "Byzance et le modèle islamique au Xe siècle. A propos des *Constitutions tactiques* de l'empereur Léon VI," *Comptes rendus, Académie des inscriptions et belles-lettres* (1983) 2319–43; Dagron, "'Ceux d'en face': les peuples étrangers dans les traités militaires byzantins," *TM* 10 (1986) 222–8; *Le Traité sur la guérilla* (*De velitatione*) *de l'empereur Nicéphore Phocas*, ed. by G. Dagron, H. Mihaescu (Paris: Editions du C.N.R.S., 1986).

[93] Eutychius, *Ann.* 279 (136–7 Breydy). Kūfī 1: 269–70.

[94] Eutychius, *Ann.* 279 (136–7 Breydy text, 116 Breydy trans.); Michael the Syrian, *Chron.* 11.6 (2: 421 Chabot).

RELEVANCE FOR THE CONTROVERSIAL EMERGENCE OF THE BYZANTINE THEMES

No Greek or Arabic or Armenian source attributes the outcome of the Muslim invasions to the condition of Byzantine institutions. The nature of the late Roman institutions that existed on the eve of the Muslim conquests did not make the Byzantine losses inevitable. This proposition assumes that the so-called Byzantine "theme system" – Byzantine army corps and their military districts – was not in existence at the time of the Muslim invasions. If it had been in existence at that time, however, it certainly did not prevent the Muslim conquests.[95]

The implications of this material for the development of Byzantine institutions of the middle period are quite significant. Detailed rereading of the primary sources and modern scholarship on the themes and the question of the soldiers' properties leads to the conclusion that Heraclius probably was improvising (experimenting may be too strong a word) on an *ad hoc* basis with emergency military commands that included political responsibilities as part of his desperate effort to find some means for checking the Muslims and increasing the efficiency of his defenses.[96]

Most relevant are the sources who speak of Heraclius' appointment of commanders over cities, demonstrating that Heraclius was implementing some kind of militarization of governmental authority. Azdī reported that Heraclius "appointed as his deputies over the cities of Syria commanders from his army" (*khallafa umarā' min jundihi 'alā madā'in al-Shām*).[97] The

[95] Ralph-Johannes Lilie, "Die zweihundertjährige Reform. Zu den Anfängen der Themenorganisation im 7. und 8. Jahrhundert," *Byzsl* 45 (1984) 27–39, 190–201.

[96] The maximalist case for evidence from Arabic sources on the existence of districts with "theme-like" characteristics in Syria before the Muslim conquest: Irfan Shahid, "Heraclius and the Theme System: New Light from the Arabic," *Byzantion* 57 (1987) 391–403; and Shahid, "Heraclius and the Theme System: Further Observations," *Byzantion* 59 (1989) 208–43. These are important and welcome contributions to the debate on the emergence and nature of the themes. I shall avoid discussion until I have the opportunity to discuss these papers in detail elsewhere. It is important for any connections between Byzantine and Muslim military institutions to receive scholarly examination, including comparative study, and there is some evidence that Heraclius was engaged in some kind of creation of emergency military government jurisdictions to cope with the critical situation that existed in the face of the Muslim invasions. The question is, What was the precise character and aim of that improvisation? I likewise suspend judgment on the Ph.D. dissertation of Alan G. Walmsley, "Administrative Structure and Urban Settlement in Filasṭīn and Urdunn" (unpub. Ph.D. diss., University of Sydney, Australia, 1987). In contrast to Shahid, he asserts that the *ajnād* originated in the caliphate of 'Umar, without any direct Byzantine origins. I must also suspend judgment on his thesis until I can study the details of his logic and documentation. As I understand it, he has attempted to use extensive archaeological and numismatic evidence to support his conclusions, and if well done it will be an important contribution to our knowledge.

[97] Azdī 31; Ibn al-Athīr 2: 311, 317–18; al-Ṭabarī i 2104.

word θέμα (Byzantine military corps and its later military district) is not used in connection with these appointments, at least not in these sources. These offices are not even given a common term, as far as is known. But it is a form of militarization. It has no connection with any social or economic reform, even though it might well have had implications for the economy, fisc, and society. Heraclius did not make all of these appointments at once. He made these *ad hoc*, in the face of and under the pressure of specific threats to specific regions. There was no overall plan to this on his part, at least nothing that can be gleaned from known sources.

It is impossible to determine the number or exact official names of these institutional improvisations. It was a gradual process that accelerated under the pressure of events, namely, the growing Muslim threat and the weakening Byzantine military position. The exact nature of these *ad hoc* appointments is not clear, including whether these military commanders with special powers had identical bureaucracies beneath them. Sources allow glimpses at these improvisations as they were made in the midst of the military crisis of the Muslim invasions. They do, to some degree, give some precise documentation, with important modifications, for some scholarly reflections on administrative actions of Emperor Heraclius. Earlier precedents for unifying civilian and military powers in the hands of one official are numerous, most notably from the reign of Justinian I. All of this reinforces the previously made scholarly arguments for the Muslim invasions as the external cause for a major leap toward the creation of what would eventually become "themes," but there is no accompanying social and economic reform of the kind that some scholars have argued was an essential ingredient of those "themes." The commanders were probably *vicarii*.

Heraclius' energetic actions even at the end of his reign contributed to the creation of military "themes," but in a way very different from what some scholars had assumed. They were emergency creations of administrative authority in the face of a military crisis as the situation on the military front demands it. They are created because of fear of incompetent civilian handling of affairs, especially weakness and the propensity to surrender or negotiate too easily with the invader. These emergency administrative creations did not explain or cause Heraclius' victories against the Persians. They were so weak that they were easily swept away in the wake of the Muslim conquests. They did not halt those conquests at that time, although they were intended to stiffen resistance and to insure absolute implementation of the emperor's will in waging war against and generally resisting the Muslims. Byzantine historical traditions do not recognize these improvisations as the origins of the later military theme system, and in fact tend to criticize Heraclius for encouraging military resistance that was doomed to fail against the Muslims, as they criticize the foolhardiness of those commanders who zealously followed Heraclius' orders to resist the Muslims instead of attempting to reach some compromise with them.[98]

On the other hand, it does not require brilliance to create such emergency administrative jurisdictions. The critical situation might well have stimulated any emperor to attempt to consolidate civilian and military authority in a single person in endangered regions. A similar response is not unknown in other areas in other times: creation of emergency military districts or powers, with military commanders given discretionary powers for the duration of the present emergency or until further notice, is a reasonably common historical phenomenon.

The emergence of the Arab *ajnād* (armies and affiliated military districts) and any possible connection with Byzantine military institutions are problems. The *ajnād* have some relationship to Byzantium, because they do not exist in former Sassanian Persian territories. A principal problem with assuming that they existed under Heraclius is their absence in Byzantine and Arabic texts concerning actual military operations during the Muslim conquests. There is likewise no supporting epigraphic or sigillographic evidence that has thus far been discovered. The sources continue to use traditional late Roman nomenclature, such as *sacellarius*, *cubicularius*, *drungarius*, *curator*, and names of old *numeri* in descriptions of commands and units. Heraclius did experiment with some kind of emergency military powers, which Azdī mentions, but he does not give the specific names of such institutions.[99] The experimentation took place not so much under pressure of the Persians earlier in the 620s, but under the pressure of the actual Muslim conquests. Furthermore, it is obvious from the catastrophic Byzantine defeats in Syria that whatever experimentation was happening Heraclius had not discovered any formula for institutionalizing military success. This early unsuccessful experimentation may, however, have ultimately reaped rewards in the development of successful military institutions and defenses north of the Taurus Mountains. It is impossible to determine how many such emergency commands Heraclius temporarily created and what was the administrative hierarchy connected with them. It is likewise impossible to know what these military commands were called (and certainly no evidence whether the term θέμα, plural θέματα, was used) or whether they all had the same terminology.

There is no evidence that such experimentation delayed the Muslim

98 Niceph., *Hist.* 23 (70–3 Mango); Theoph., *Chron.*, AM 6128 (De Boor 340).

99 Azdī's information, on pp. 28–31 of the Āmir edition of al-Azdī al-Baṣrī's *Ta'rīkh futūḥ al-Shām*, coupled with that of Kūfī 1: 101, and al-Ṭabarī/Sayf i 2104, and Ibn al-Athīr (2: 311 Tornberg), is the most complete.

conquests of Syria and Egypt and Mesopotamia, but the experiences may have helped Heraclius' successors to develop a better defense of what was left, Anatolia. There is, however, no explicit testimony on any of this in the extant sources in Greek, Armenian, or Arabic.

The Byzantine military units that opposed the Muslims in Syria, Palestine, Mesopotamia, and Egypt are not readily recognizable as "thematic" units. They may have ultimately evolved into "thematic" units, especially after their withdrawal from Syria and Mesopotamia and their regrouping in Anatolia, but Arabic, Armenian, and Greek sources do not clearly designate any of them as "themes" in the 630s.[100] The Arabic historian al-Ṭabarī reports a tradition that in AH 18 (AD 638/9) "The Byzantines are busily regrouping themselves. Let us therefore attack them..."[101] It is tantalizing to speculate precisely what "regrouping" meant in that Arabic tradition, but it is impossible to reach any secure conclusion. Some kind of Byzantine military regrouping was happening in Anatolia at the end of the reign of Heraclius. That is logical. It is possible that an embryonic form of the Armeniak Theme was appearing in the 640s but even that identification has been contested.[102]

Whatever Byzantine military institutions existed in the 630s and early 640s were insufficiently strong in themselves to check, let alone roll back the Muslims. Even if some embryonic Byzantine theme system was in the process of formation at that time, it was, as the record shows, too weak to halt the Muslims at that time. Other evidence may eventually modify these conclusions, but this is the best judgment that can be made on the basis of presently available sources. The principal change in the financing of

[100] M. De Goeje, *Mémoire*² 73, citing al-Ṭabarī i 2087 (Sayf), believed that the "Daraqis" mentioned at Faḥl, in 635, was possibly the "Thrakesios" or commander of the Thrakesian Theme, but he was not certain. It is not possible to be more certain about his identification even today. But the reading in al-Ṭabarī i 2087 in De Goeje's own edition is "Durāqiṣ." It probably refers to the Thrakesios not as thematic commander, but in the traditional sense of *magister militum per Thraciam* or commander of Thracian forces, whose troops unsuccessfully defended Egypt a few years later. It may even be an inaccurate rendering of *drungarios* (δρουγγάριος), not "Thrakesios" (Θρᾳκήσιος). The *drungarios* is mentioned in other Arabic texts. The scribe may have made an error in copying or transcribing *drungarios*. But even if it is "Thrakesios," there is no evidence that it is a thematic unit already at that time instead of some military unit before it became a "theme." De Goeje wrote his conjecture before much research had taken place on the Byzantine "themes." At best, De Goeje's hypothesis is a possible explanation, but no more than that. No additional confirmation of his surmise has been found. No other scholars have even commented on De Goeje's hypothesis. Kaegi, "al-Baladhuri and the Armeniak Theme," *ASRB*, for possible Arabic source on the problem of thematic origins.

[101] al-Ṭabarī, i 2572–3; the English translation is from *The History of al-Ṭabarī*, 13: *The Conquest of Iraq, Southwestern Persia, and Egypt*, trans. by Gautier H. A. Juynboll (Albany: State University of New York Press, 1989) 154.

[102] Walter E. Kaegi, Jr., "al-Baladhuri and the Armeniak Theme," *Byzantion* 38 (1969) 273–7; but see Ralph-Johannes Lilie, "Die zweihundertjährige Reform. Zu den Anfängen der Themenorganisation im 7. und 8. Jahrhundert," *Byzsl* 45 (1984) 27–39, 190–201.

Byzantine armies at that time was the emergence, at the end of a long process, of the *sakellarios*, but his assumption of control over general tax assessments between 636 and 640 did not affect the outcome of the fighting with the Muslims in Syria, Mesopotamia, and Egypt. It is conceivable that if what were later known as "soldiers' properties" had existed in the 630s, the soldiers who possessed them in Syria and Mesopotamia might have fought harder than they did to preserve them, but this is so speculative and counterfactual that it does not deserve further discussion.

Problems in equitably distributing payments in kind exacerbated Byzantine military unrest during the Byzantine effort to create a viable defense against the Muslims, but cease to receive mention in the truncated Byzantine Empire after the loss of Palestine, Syria, Byzantine Mesopotamia, and Egypt.[103] The logistical and military system of compensation that depended on payments in kind was modified or transformed somehow in the later part of the seventh century. That process appears to have accelerated because reduction in the distances that the Byzantine troops needed to travel after those major territorial losses made provisioning less dependent on distribution of payments in kind. The change had consequences for imperial taxpayers and for imperial finances.

If anything, the study of the Byzantine defenses against the Muslim conquests of Syria and Mesopotamia refines the issues in the investigation of the emergence and development of Byzantine institutions, and leads the researcher to posit the greatest likelihood of major and permanent institutional change to the end of the 630s and the immediately following years. Substantial Byzantine institutional change resulted from the shattering effects of the early Islamic conquests; it had not taken place before these invasions. The reign of Constans II (641–68) was critical. The investigation of this conundrum is far from complete. In the late 630s and early 640s the growing pressure of the external military and political crisis accelerated Byzantine institutional change that had previously been very slow. Suddenly much was in flux. But the institutional situation in itself cannot explain the fate of Byzantine resistance to the Muslims, whether one thinks of that in 634, 641, or some later date. A complex of other considerations, including human decisions, contributed to the outcome.

There is no simple relationship of the Byzantine "themes" to the Byzantine loss of critical provinces in Syria and Mesopotamia. There is no conclusive evidence that the theme system was so excellent that it could have saved those regions for Byzantium if it had existed at the time of the Muslim conquests. There was no simple institutional key to Byzantine retention of those

[103] Kaegi, *BMU* 148–53. Eutychius, *Ann.* c. 278 (135–6 Breydy text); Azdī 151–2, 175–7.

regions. The Byzantine institutional structure is only one element among many that must be evaluated. The early record of thematic resistance to the Muslims in Anatolia was not an outstanding one, especially with respect to pitched battles – which were a necessary element in any effective defense of Syria proper.

One of the reasons for the emergence of the Byzantine themes was probably the imperial government's negative experiences with the perils of local civilian officials attempting to negotiate settlements with the Muslim invaders in Palestine, Syria, Egypt, and Mesopotamia. The government experimented with appointing what it hoped would be more reliable and more resolute leaders of resistance in the persons of military commanders who ought to obey the will of their emperor and not negotiate with the Muslims without explicit permission. The related process of making such appointments on an *ad hoc* basis, like the creation of emergency prefects of the army for logistical and internal security reasons, was part of the process of the creation of the themes during and as a result of and as a reaction to the Muslim conquests. Again, there were problems with the same local officials who threatened the empire by negotiating on their own with Muslims. These same officials, as the disastrous case of Manṣūr demonstrates at Damascus in 636, were withholding or in various ways not collecting and disbursing necessary amounts of supplies and support for soldiers. Glimpses of logistical failures and local collaboration with Muslims indicate that the government saw that it was necessary to change a broken system, that part of the problem lay in the local civilian officials who collected and disbursed, and often withheld for their profit, taxes and provisions that the remnant of the praetorian prefecture was trying to raise. The campaigns of the 630s show that the system was ripe for change, and not merely because the government lacked monetary funds. The problem was not merely a lack of money. The system of dependence on local officials for loyalty and supplies was very unreliable and prone to sabotage. These conditions created prerequisites for concentration of new powers in what the government might hope were reliable military commanders. Yet it took time: the gradual disappearance of the older late Roman provincial institutions and the emergence of the Byzantine themes was incomplete at the end of the seventh century.[104]

In addition to issues of providing manpower and reducing the financial drain of monetary payments to troops there was a need to stiffen central Byzantine controls to prevent more erosion of resistance, such as had already

[104] Survival of the old provinces: Heinrich Gelzer, *Die Genesis der byzantinischen Themenrverfassung* (Leipzig 1899; repr. Amsterdam: Hakkert, 1966) 64–72; J. Karayannopoulos, *Die Entstehung der byzantinischen Themenordnung* (Munich: Beck, 1959) 35, 57–8, 70; Haldon, *Byzantium* 196–200, 212.

happened in Syria and Palestine. The themes never provided a perfect solution to the external military challenges. They were imperfect. The case of Cyrus in Egypt indicated that a combination of civil and military authority in itself did not guarantee reliability of local authorities and their strict adherence to conduct laid down by the emperor and his advisers. And it certainly did not bring or guarantee successful resistance against the Muslims. Local efforts to preserve the continuity of daily life and earlier norms resulted in pressures at the highest governmental level, namely that of the emperors and their advisers, to prevent more unauthorized local arrangements by evacuating or deporting the local populations and establishing much tighter military administrative control, including stricter control of the border. Efforts to avoid change perversely intensified change and accelerated the disappearance of late Roman administrative structures and the emergence of new Byzantine bureaucratic controls.[105] But later Byzantine historians and antiquarians never identified the improvisation of the period of the initial Islamic conquests as the foundation of the classic theme structure of the ninth and tenth centuries. The conditions of the breakdown of local provisioning and the propensity of local officials to negotiate with the Muslim were not the start of the long process of the creation of the themes, which had already slowly begun, but they created incentives, indeed imperatives, to accelerate the process of change.

COMPARATIVE PERSPECTIVES

The Muslim conquests in Syria contrast with those of the Slavs and Avars in the Balkans, which were almost contemporary. The Slavic invasions were slower, less well organized, and without so many well-known battles. The Slavic and Avaric invasions probably resulted in greater physical destruction of towns and agriculture and more population loss and displacement. But the character of the physical geography of the Adriatic, the Greek and Black Sea coasts, with its many inlets, peninsulas, and islands, permitted the survival of Graeco-Byzantine pockets more easily and more effectively than along the smoother Syrian littoral. There was no Monemvasia, Nin, or Mesembria on the Mediterranean coast of Syria and Palestine. Likewise the Slavic invasions did not result in the creation of a unified empire as quickly as did those of the Muslim caliphate. These realities contributed to the failure of any Byzantine strongholds to hold out indefinitely against the Muslims. They all eventually

[105] Kaegi, "Observations on Warfare Between Byzantium and Umayyad Syria," 1987 *Bilād al-Shām Proceedings* 2: 49–70; Kaegi, "Changes in Military Organization and Daily Life on the Eastern Frontier," Ἡ Καθημερινὴ Ζωὴ στὸ Βυζάντιο, ed. by Chrysa Maltezou (Athens: Hellenic Center for Byzantine Studies, 1989) 507–21.

succumbed, in contrast to what happened in the Balkans, where the possibility existed and ultimately permitted recovery of much territory from the invader.[106]

The experiences of the later Roman Empire between AD 395 and 410 show how a series of contingent events, which were for the most part political and military, as well as human decisions resulted in a fundamental change in the condition of the empire in the west to an extent that was not foreseeable in 395. A synergism of momentary decisions and contingent military events within fifteen years transformed a situation and its related institutional conditions.[107] Something similar happened between 634 and 641 in Palestine, Syria, Egypt, and Mesopotamia.

THE NONINEVITABILITY OF THE CONQUESTS

The Muslim conquests were not inevitable, nor was the Byzantine loss. There was vitality in religious, social, and economic life in Byzantine Syria and Palestine in the wake of the Persian evacuation of the Levant after they made peace with Byzantium in 628. No inexorable process was developing at that time. From the perspective of Islam, religious events and change understandably provided the decisive catalyst. From the perspective of Byzantine history, it was exogenous events, that is, the military events, that were decisive, because they unleashed a cumulative series of changes, a cumulative synergism that transformed an admittedly unstable and precarious situation, thereby creating a turning point. For the Byzantines, these were Arab (i.e., "Saracen"), not Muslim, conquests. For them there was no implicit concession that the religion of Islam was responsible for the success of these conquests, let alone any desire to leave open the related possibility that such events indicated the possibility that there was any truth or power in Islam. In the final analysis, causation and consequences were complex. The situation of the Byzantine Empire in the middle of the 640s had not been foreseeable in 628 or 629.

The initial Byzantine clashes with Muslims east of the Jordan and of the Dead Sea caught the empire's military forces at a moment of great vulnerability in 629/30. Byzantine authority was in the process of being restored when Byzantine forces initially encountered Muslim units. Even these initial engagements, in which the Byzantines won some victories, could not eliminate the military volatility. There was no secure respite. The

106 Maria Nystazopoulou-Pelekidou, "Les Slaves dans l'empire byzantin," *Major Papers, The 17th International Byzantine Congress* (New Rochelle, NY: Caratzas, 1986) 345–67.

107 Emilienne Demougeot, *De l'unité à la division de l'empire romain (395–410)* (Paris: Geuthner, 1951). Cf. Walter E. Kaegi, *Byzantium and the Decline of Rome* (Princeton: Princeton University Press, 1968).

Byzantine forces were off balance from the initial moments of their efforts to restore Byzantine authority in the vacuum left by the evacuation of the Persians. The dynamics of the situation were militarily unstable.

No narrowly military explanation can be satisfactory. Yet both sides – Muslim and Byzantine – pointed to specific battles respectively as victories or catastrophes. But they resorted to religious causation to explain the outcomes of those battles. Military judgments were important in the outcome of events, as were military institutions. Probably some of those battles could have had different outcomes. Erroneous judgments, miscalculations, and human rivalries contributed to explain what happened. Although it is possible to conceive of *la longue durée* in Mediterranean history, these years of the seventh century experienced an acceleration of a process, the understanding of which requires both an appreciation of elements of the long term and the critical moment. The initiation of a general tax reassessment by *sakellarios* Philagrios on the instructions of Heraclius was a symptom of resilience, for it marked the beginning of institutional revival while the empire was still reeling from its military reverses.

BIBLIOGRAPHY

SELECTIVE BIBLIOGRAPHY OF PRIMARY SOURCES: GREEK

ANONYMOUS WORKS

Doctrina Iacobi nuper baptizati, ed. by N. Bonwetsch. *Abhandlungen der Königl. Gesellschaft der Wissenschaften zu Göttingen.* Philologisch-Historische Klasse, n.s. vol. 12, n. 3. Berlin 1910.

La narratio de rebus Armeniae, ed. and comment. by Gérard Garitte. CSCO, Subsidia, T. 4. Louvain 1952.

Vie de Théodore Saint de Sykéôn, ed. by A. J. Festugière. Subsidia Hagiographica, 48. 2 vols. Brussels 1970.

Three Byzantine Military Treatises, ed. and trans. by G. T. Dennis. Washington: Dumbarton Oaks, 1985.

Trophées de Damas, ed. by G. Bardy. *PO* 15 (1927) 189–275.

Die griechische Daniel Diegese: Eine altkirchliche Apokalypse, ed. by Klaus Berger. Studia Post-Biblica, vol. 27. Leiden: Brill, 1976.

Pseudo-Methodius, *Die Apokalypse des Ps.-Methodios*, ed. and trans. by A. Lolos. Beiträge zur Klassischen Philologie, part 83. Meisenheim am Glan: Verlag Anton Hain, 1976.

Die dritte und vierte Redaktion des Ps.-Methodios, ed. and trans. by A. Lolos. Beiträge zur Klassischen Philologie, part 94. Meisenheim am Glan: Verlag Anton Hain, 1978.

Παραστάσεις Σύντομοι Χρονικαί. *Constantinople in the Eighth Century*, ed. and trans. by Av. Cameron, Judith Herrin, *et al.* Leiden: Brill, 1984.

"Sancti Georgii Chozebitae Confessoris et Monachi Vita Auctore Antonio ejus discipulo." *AB* 7 (1888) 95–144.

OTHER WORKS

Agathias, *Historia*, ed. by R. Keydell. CFHB. Berlin: De Gruyter, 1969.

Anastasius the Persian, *Acta M. Anastasii Persae*, by H. Usener. Program, Bonn 1894.

Anastasius the Sinaite, *Adversus Judaeos Disputatio*. *PG* 89: 1203–72.

Anastasii Sinaitae Opera. Sermones due in constitutionem hominis secundum imaginem Dei necnon Opuscula adversus Monotheletas, ed. by Karl-Heinz

Uthemann. CC, Series Graeca, 12. Brepols-Turnhout: Leuven University Press, 1985.

"Le Texte grec des récits inédits du moine Anastase sur les saints Pères du Sinai," ed. by F. Nau. *Oriens Christianus* 2 (1902) 58–89.

"Le Texte grec des récits utiles à l'âme d'Anastase (le Sinaïte)," ed. by F. Nau. *Oriens Christianus* 3 (1903) 56–90.

Constantine VII Porphyrogenitus, *De administrando imperio*, ed. and trans. by G. Moravcsik, R. Jenkins. 2nd edn. Washington: Dumbarton Oaks, 1967.

De thematibus, ed. by A. Pertusi. Studi e Testi. Rome 1952.

Evagrius Scholasticus, *HE* = *Ecclesiastical History*, ed. by J. Bidez, L. Parmentier. London: Methuen, 1898; repr., Amsterdam: Hakkert, 1966.

Georgius Cedrenus, *Historiarum compendium*, ed. by I. Bekker. CSHB. 2 vols. Bonn 1838.

Georgius Cyprius, *Le Synekdèmos d'Hieroklès et l'opuscule géographique de Georges de Chypre,* ed., trans. and comment. by Ernst Honigmann. CBHB, Forma Imperii Byzantini, fasc. 1. Brussels: Editions de l'Institut de Philologie et d'Histoire Orientales et Slaves, 1939.

Georgius Monachus, *Chronicon*, ed. by C. De Boor. 2 vols. Leipzig: Teubner, 1904.

Jalabert, Louise and René Mouterde, eds., *Inscriptions grecques et latines de la Syrie*, Bibliothèque archéologique et historique, T. 12, 32, 46, 51, 61, 66, 78, 89, 104. Paris: Geuthner, 1929–80.

Johannes of Antioch. *FHG* 4: 535–622; 5: 27–39.

Johannes Malalas, *The Chronicle of John Malalas*, trans. by Elizabeth Jeffreys, Michael Jeffreys, Roger Scott. Byzantina Australiensia, 4. Melbourne: Australian Association for Byzantine Studies, Sydney: University of Sydney, 1986.

Chronographia, ed. by L. Dindorf. CSHB. Bonn 1831.

Johannes Zonaras, *Epitome historiarum*, ed. by L. Dindorf. 6 vols. Leipzig 1868–75.

Leo III, *Ecloga. Das Gesetzbuch Leons III. und Konstantinos' V*, ed. by Ludwig Burgmann. Forschungen zur byzantinischen Rechtsgeschichte, vol. 10. Frankfurt: Löwenklau, 1983.

Leo VI, *Tactica*, ed. by R. Vári. 2 vols. Budapest 1917–22.

Tactica. PG 107: 669–1120.

Leontios of Neapolis, *Vie de Syméon le Fou et Vie de Jean de Chypre*, ed. and comment. by A. J. Festugière, Lennart Rydén. Institut Français d'Archéologie de Beyrouth, Bibliothèque Archéologique et Historique, T. 95. Paris: P. Geuthner, 1974.

Mansi, Joannes Dominicus, *Sacrorum conciliorum nova et amplissima collectio*, repr. Graz: Akademische Drück- und Verlagsanstalt, 1960.

Mauricius, *Strategikon*, ed. by G. T. Dennis, trans. by E. Gamillscheg. CFHB. Vienna: Akademie, 1981.

Maurice's Strategikon: Handbook of Byzantine Military Strategy, trans. by George T. Dennis. Philadelphia: University of Pennsylvania Press, 1984.

Maximus the Confessor, *Opera. PG* 90–1.

Menander Protector, *The History of Menander the Guardsman*, ed. and trans. by R. C. Blockley. ARCA, 17. Liverpool: Francis Cairns, 1985.

Nicephorus, *Hist.* = Nicephorus, *Short History*, ed. by C. Mango. Washington: Dumbarton Oaks, 1990.

Nicephorus Phocas, *Le Traité sur la guérilla (De velitatione) de l'empereur Nicéphore Phocas*, ed., trans., and comment. by Gilbert Dagron, Haralambie Mihaescu. Le Monde Byzantin. Paris: editions du Centre National de la Recherche Scientifique, 1986.

Pantaleon, "Un discours inédit du moine Pantaléon sur l'élévation de la Croix *BHG* 427 p.," ed. by F. Halkin. *OCP* 52 (1986) 257–270.

Procopius of Caesarea, *Opera omnia*, ed. by J. Haury, G. Wirth. 4 vols. Leipzig; Teubner, 1905–13; repr., 1962–4.

Sargis d'Aberga, *Controverse Judéo-Chrétienne*, ed. and trans. by Sylvain Grébaut. *PO* 3: 551–643; 13: 5–109.

Sophronius, *Sermones. PG* 87.3: 3201–364.

"Weihnachtspredigt des Sophronios," ed. by H. Usener. *Rheinisches Museum für Philologie*. n.s. 41 (1886) 500–16.

Theodore Skutariotes, Σύνοψις Χρονική, ed. by Constantine Sathas. Μεσαιωνική Βιβλιοθήκη, vol. 7. repr., Venice 1894.

Theophanes, *Chronographia*, ed. by C. De Boor. 2 vols. Leipzig 1883.

Theophylact Simocatta, *Historiae*, ed. by C. De Boor. Leipzig: Teubner, 1887; repr., 1972.

The History of Theophylact Simocatta, trans. by Michael Whitby and Mary Whitby. Oxford: Clarendon Press, 1986.

Theophylactos Simokates, Geschichte, trans. and comment. by Peter Schreiner. Bibliothek der griechischen Literatur, 20. Stuttgart: Anton Hiersemann, 1985.

Zosimus, *Historia nova*, ed. by L. Mendelssohn. Leipzig: Teubner, 1887.

SELECTIVE BIBLIOGRAPHY OF PRIMARY SOURCES: LATIN

ANONYMOUS WORKS

Codex Theodosianus, ed. by Th. Mommsen, Paul M. Meyer. Berlin: Weidmann, 1905.

Continuationes Isidorianae Byzantia Arabica et Hispana, ed. by T. Mommsen. MGH, AA, T. 11, CM, 2: 334–69.

Corpus Juris Civilis, ed. by T. Mommsen, P. Krueger, R. Schoell, W. Kroll. 3 vols. Berlin: Weidmann, 1928.

Crónica mozárabe de 754. Edición crítica y traducción, ed. by Jose Eduardo López Pereira. Textos Medievales, 58. Zaragoza 1980.

De rebus bellicis, ed. by R. I. Ireland. Leipzig: B. G. Teubner, 1984.

Notitia Dignitatum, ed. by O. Seeck. Berlin 1876; repr., Frankfurt: Minerva, 1962.

Sibyllinische Texte und Forschungen, ed. by Ernst Sackur. Halle 1898.

OTHER WORKS

Fredegarius, *Chronicles*, ed. by Bruno Krusch. MGH Scriptores Rerum Merovingicarum, T. 2. Hanover 1888; repr., 1984.

The Fourth Book of the Chronicle of Fredegar with Its Continuations, trans. by J. M. Wallace-Hadrill. London: Thos. Nelson and Sons, 1960.

Johannes Monachus, *Liber de miraculis. Ein neuer Beitrag zur mittelalterlichen Mönchsliteratur*, ed. by Michael Huber. Sammlung Mittellateinischer Texte, 7. Heidelberg: Carl Winters Universitätsbibliothek, 1913.

Vegetius, *Epitoma rei militaris*, ed. by C. Lang. Leipzig: Teubner, 1885; repr., 1967.

SELECTIVE BIBLIOGRAPHY OF PRIMARY SOURCES: ARABIC

ANONYMOUS WORKS

Muslim Military Manual [thirteenth century AD], ed. by Heinrich Ferdinand Wüstenfeld, "Das Heerwesen der Muhammadaner," *Abhandlungen d. Königl. Gesell. d. Wiss. zu Göttingen.* Hist.-Philol. Classe 26 (1880) = *Das Heerwesen der Muhammadener und die arabische übersetzung der Taktik des Aelianus.* Göttingen: Dieterich, 1880.

Pseudo-Wāqidī, *Futūḥ al-Shām*. Beirut 1972.

Libri Wakedii De Mesopotamiae expugnatae historia, ed. by G. H. A. Ewald. Göttingen: Dieterich, 1827.

OTHER WORKS

'Abd al-Ḥamīd bin Yaḥyā, *Risāla* = 'Abd al-Ḥamīd bin Yaḥyā, *Risāla ... 'an Marwān ilā ibnihi 'Abd Allāh ibn Marwān, Jamharat rasā'il al-'arab*, ed. by Aḥmad Zakī Ṣafwat, 4: 473–533. Cairo 1937.

'Abd al-Ḥamīd bin Yaḥyā/Schönig, *Sendschreiben* = *Das Sendschreiben des 'Abd al-Ḥamīd bin Yaḥyā (gest 132/750) an den Kronprinzen 'Abdallāh b. Marwān II.*, trans. and comment. by Hannelore Schönig. Akademie der Wissenschaften und der Literatur, Mainz, Veröffentlichungen der orientalischen Kommission, 38. Stuttgart: Franz Steiner Verlag, 1985.

Abū al-Fidā', *al-Mukhtaṣar fī akhbār al-bashar*. Beirut: Dār al-Fikr, 1956.

Abū 'Ubayd al-Qāsim b. Sallām, *Kitāb al-amwāl*, ed. by Muḥammad Khalīl Harās. Cairo: Maktabat al-Kullīyāt al-Azhariyya, 1968; Beirut: Dār al-Kuttub al-'Almiyya, 1986.

Abū Yūsuf, Ya'qūb b. Ibrāhīm, *Kitāb al-kharāj*. Cairo: Maktabat al-Salafiyya, 1933/4.

Kitāb al-kharāj, ed. by Iḥsān 'Abbās. Beirut: Dār al-Shirūk, 1985.

Agapius, *Kitāb al-'Unvān*, ed. by A. A. Vasiliev. *PO* 5.4 (1910) 557–692; 7.4 (1911) 457–91; 8.3 (1912) 399–547.

Antiochus, *Expugnationis Hierosolymae AD 614 Recensiones Arabicae*, ed. by Gérard Garitte. CSCO, SA, T. 26–9. Louvain 1973–4.

al-Aṣma'ī [attributed], *Ta'rīkh al 'arab qabl'al-Islam*, ed. by Muḥammad Ḥasan Āl-Yāsīn. Baghdad 1959.

Azdī = Muḥammad b. 'Abdullāh Abū Isma'īl al-Azdī al-Baṣrī, *Ta'rīkh futūḥ al-Shām*, ed. by 'Abd al-Mun'im 'Abdullāh 'Āmir. Cairo: Mu'assasat Sijill al-'Arab, 1970; ed. by William Nassau Lees. Bibliotheca Indica. Calcutta 1857.

al-Balādhurī, Aḥmad b. Yaḥyā, *Ansāb al-Ashrāf* I, ed. by Muḥammad Hamīdullāh. Cairo: Dār al-Ma'ārif, 1959.

Ansāb al-Ashrāf IVA, ed. by Max Schloessinger and M. J. Kister. Jerusalem: Magnes, 1971.

Ansāb al-Ashrāf V, ed. by Shlomo D. F. Goitein. Jerusalem: Hebrew University Press, 1936.

Balādhurī [= al-Balādhurī, Aḥmad b. Yaḥyā], *Futūḥ al-Buldān*, ed. by Michael Jan De Goeje. Leiden: Brill, 1866; repr.

Balādhurī, Aḥmad b. Yaḥyā, *The Origins of the Islamic State*, trans. by Philip K. Hitti, F. C. Murgotten. New York: Columbia University Press, 1916, 1924.

al-Dīnawarī, Abū Ḥanīfa Aḥmad b. Dā'ūd, *al-Akhbār al-tiwāl*, ed. by 'Abd al-Mun'im 'Abdullāh 'Āmir. Jamal al-Dīn al-Shayyāl. Cairo: Dār Ihyā al-Kutub al-'Arabīyya, 1960.

Kitāb al-Akhbār al-tiwāl, ed. by Vladimir Guirgass. Leiden: Brill, 1888.

al-Diyārbakrī, Ḥusayn ibn Muḥammad, *Ta'rīkh al-khāmis fī aḥwāl anfas nafīs*. 2 vols. in 1. repr., Beirut 1970, of 1866 original.

Eutychius, *Das Annalenwerk des Eutychios von Alexandrien*, ed. and trans. by Michael Breydy. CSCO, vol. 471–2. Scriptores Arabici, T. 44–5. Louvain: E. Peeters, 1985. Now standard.

Annales, ed. by L. Cheikho, B. Carra de Vaux, H. Zayyat. 2 vols. CSCO, Scriptores Arabici, ser. 3, vol. 7.

Ibn 'Abd al-Ḥakam, *Futūḥ miṣr*, ed. by Charles C. Torrey. New Haven: Yale University Press, 1922.

Ibn al-'Adīm, Kamāl al-Dīn 'Umar b. Aḥmad, *Zubdat al-Ḥalab min Ta'rīkh Ḥalab*, ed. by Samā al-Dahhān. 2 vols. Damascus: Institut français de Damas, 1951–68.

Ibn 'Asākir, *Mukhtaṣar Ta'rīkh madīnat Dimashq*, ed. by Ruḥiya al-Naḥḥas, Riyāḍ 'Abd al-Ḥamīd Murād, Muḥammad Muṭī' al-Ḥāfiz, *et al.* Damascus: Dār al-Fikr, 1984.

Ibn 'Asākir, *TMD* = Ibn 'Asākir, 'Alī b. al-Ḥasan, *Ta'rīkh madīnat Dimashq* I, ed. by Salah al-Din al-Munajjid. Damascus: al-Majma 'al-'Ilmī al-'Arabī, 1951.

Ibn al-Athīr, 'Izz al-Dīn, *al-Kāmil fī-l Ta'rīkh*, ed. by C. J. Tornberg. 13 vols. repr., Beirut: Dār Sadir, 1965.

Ibn Ḥajar al-'Asqalānī, Aḥmad b. 'Alī, *al-Iṣāba fī tamyīz al-ṣaḥaba*. 4 vols. Cairo: Matba'at al-Sa'ada, 1910; repr., Beirut: Dār Ṣādir, n.d., but probably *c.* 1960.

Ibn Hishām, 'Abd al-Malik, *al-Sīra al-nabawīyya*, ed. by Heinrich Ferdinand Wüstenfeld. *Sīrat Rasūl Allāh = Das Leben Muhammeds*... 2 vols. Göttingen: Dieterischen Buchhandlung, 1858–60.

Ibn Ḥubaysh, *Ta'rīkh*. Mss. Berlin, Leiden. Microfilm. No complete printed text.

Ibn Kathīr, *Tafsīr al-Qur'ān*. 7 vols. Beirut: Dār al-Andalus, 1983.

Ibn Khaldūn, *Ta'rīkh*. 2 vols. in 3. Cairo 1936.

Ibn Khayyāṭ al-'Uṣfurī, Khalīfa, *Ta'rīkh*, ed. by Akram Ḍiyā' al-'Umarī. 2 vols. Baghdad: al-Najaf, 1967.

Ibn Qutayba, *Kitāb al-'Uyūn al-Akhbār*. Cairo 1925.

Ibn Sa'd, Muḥammad, *Kitāb al-Ṭabaqāt al-kabīr*, ed. by Eduard Sachau, *et al.* 9 vols. Leiden: Brill, 1904–40.

al-Iṣṭakhrī, *Viae regnorum. BGA*, ed. by M. J. De Goeje. repr., Leiden: Brill, 1961.

Kūfī = Ibn A'tham al-Kūfī, Abū Muḥammad Aḥmad, *Kitāb al-futūḥ*, ed. by Muḥammad 'Alī al-'Abbasī and Sayyid 'Abd al-Wahhāb Bukhari. 8 vols. Hyderabad: Da'irat al-Ma'arif al-'Uthmānīyya, 1968–75.

al-Nuwayrī, Aḥmad ibn 'Abd al-Wahhāb, *Nihāyāt al-'arab fī funūn al-adab*, ed. by Muḥammad Abū'l Faḍl Ibrāhīm. 27 vols. Cairo 1964– .

Ṭabarī = al-Ṭabarī, Abū Ja'far Muḥammad b. Jarīr, *Ta'rīkh al-rusūl wa'l-mulūk* (*Annales*), ed. by M. J. De Goeje, *et al.* 15 vols. Leiden: Brill, 1879–1901. Cited by De Goeje pagination.

Ṭabarī, *History* = *al-Ṭabarī, Abū Ja'far Muḥammad b. Jarīr, The History of al-Ṭabarī*, ed. by Ihsan Abbas, C. E. Bosworth, *et al.* Bibliotheca Persica. SUNY Series in Near Eastern Studies. Albany, NY: State University of New York Press, 1985– . Publication in progress.

Wāqidī = al-Wāqidī, Muḥammad b. 'Umar, *Kitāb al-maghāzī*, ed. by Marsden Jones. 3 vols. Oxford: Oxford University Press, 1966.

al-Ya'qūbī, Aḥmad b. Abī Ya'qūb, *Ta'rīkh*, ed. by M. Th. Houtsma. 2 vols. Leiden: Brill, 1883.

Yāqūt, *Jacut's Geographisches Wörterbuch*, ed. by Heinrich Ferdinand Wüstenfeld. 6 vols. Leipzig 1866–73.

SELECTIVE BIBLIOGRAPHY: OTHER ORIENTAL SOURCES

ANONYMOUS WORKS

Chronica Minora, ed. by Ignatius Guidi. CSCO, SS, ser. 3, T. 4, parts 1–3. Paris, Leipzig 1903–5.

Chronicon ad A.D. 819 pertinens, ed. by J. B. Chabot. CSCO, SS, ser. 3, vol. 14, 1937; repr., 1952.

Incerti auctoris, *Chronicon anonymum Pseudo-Dionysianum vulgo dictum*, ed. by J.-B. Chabot, E. W. Brooks. CSCO, SS, ser. 3, T. 1–2. Paris 1927–49.

The Gospel of the Twelve Apostles together with the Apocalypses of Each One of Them, ed. and trans. by James Rendall Harris. Cambridge: Cambridge University Press, 1900.

Pseudo-Methodius, "Eastern Christian Apocalyptic in the Early Muslim Period," by Francisco Javier Martinez, incl. ed. Ph.D. diss., Catholic University, 1985, for Syriac text, trans., and comment. pp. 58–205.

Antiochus Strategius, *La Prise de Jérusalem par les Perses en 614*, ed. and trans. by Gérard Garitte. CSCO, vol. 202–3, Scriptores Iberici, T. 11–12. Louvain 1960.

OTHER WORKS

Bar Hebraeus, *The Chronography of Bar Hebraeus*, trans. by E. A. Wallis Budge. 2 vols. Oxford: Oxford University Press, 1932; repr., Amsterdam: Philo Press, 1976.

Ghevond/Lewond, *History of Lewond The Eminent Vardapet of the Armenians*, trans. by Zaven Arzoumanian. Philadelphia 1982.

Johannes, Bishop of Ephesus, *Historiae ecclesiasticae pars tertia*, ed. and trans. by E. W. Brooks. CSCO, SS, ser. 3, T. 3, vols. 105–6. Louvain 1935, 1936; repr., 1952.

John, Bishop of Nikiu, *Chronicle*, trans. by R. M. Charles. Oxford: Oxford University Press, 1916.

Joshua the Stylite, *Chronicle*, ed. and trans. by W. Wright. Cambridge: Cambridge University Press, 1882.

Michael the Syrian, *Chronique*, ed. and trans. by J.-B. Chabot. 4 vols. Paris: E. Leroux, 1899–1910.

Moses of Chorene, *Géographie de Moïse de Corène*, ed. and trans. by P. Arsène Soukry. Venice: Imprimerie Arménienne, 1881.

Movses Dasxuranci, *A History of the Caucasian Albanians, by Movses Dasxuranci*, trans. by Charles J. Dowsett. London Oriental Series, 8. London: Oxford University Press, 1961.

Palmer, *Chronicles* = Palmer, Andrew, Andrew, ed. trans. *The Seventh Century in the West-Syrian Chronicles*, Liverpool, Philadelphia: Liverpool University Press, University of Pennsylvania Press, 1993.

Samuel of Ani, *Tables chronologiques*, in: Marii Ivanovich Brosse [Brosset], ed. and trans., *Collection d'historiens arméniens*, vol. 2, pp. 339–483. St. Petersburg: Imprimerie de l'Académie Impériale des Sciences, 1876.

Sebēos, *Histoire d'Héraclius*, trans. by F. Macler. Paris 1904.

Pamut'iwn Sebeosi, ed. by G. V. Abgarian. Yerevan: Acad. Arm. SSR, 1979.

Sebēos' History, trans. by Robert Bedrosian. New York: Sources of the Armenian Tradition, 1985.

Sebēos, *Zur Geschichte Armeniens und der ersten Kriege der Araber Aus dem Armenischen des Sebeos*, trans. and comment. by Heinrich Hübschmann. Habilitationsschrift, Universitāt Leipzig, 1875.

Thomas Artsruni, *History of the House of the Artsrunik'*, trans. and comment. by Robert W. Thomson. Detroit: Wayne State University Press, 1985.

SELECTIVE BIBLIOGRAPHY: SECONDARY SOURCES

(Includes frequently cited titles only, including shortened references)

Abel, F.-M., *Géographie de la Palestine*. 2 vols. Paris: Librairie Lecoffre, J. Gabalda, 1933–8.

Histoire de la Palestine depuis la conquête d'Alexandre jusqu'à l'invasion arabe. 2 vols. Paris: J. Gabalda, 1952.

"Inscription grecque de Gaza." *Revue Biblique* 40 (1931) 94–6.

Alexander, Paul J., *The Byzantine Apocalyptic Tradition*, ed. by Dorothy de Ferrante Abrahamse. Berkeley: University of California Press, 1985.

Religious and Political History and Thought in the Byzantine Empire, London: Variorum, 1978.

Alt, Albrecht, "Die letzte Grenzverschiebung zwischen den römischen Provinzen Arabia und Palästina." *ZDPV* 65 (1942) 68–76.

"Der limes Palästinae im sechsten und siebenten Jahrhundert nach Chr." *ZDPV* 63 (1940) 129–42.

Armées et fiscalité dans le monde antique. Paris 14–16 octobre 1976. Colloques nationaux du Centre National de la Recherche Scientifique, 936. Paris: Editions du Centre National de la Recherche Scientifique, 1977.

Bakhit, Muḥammad and Iḥsān 'Abbās, eds., *Proceedings of the Second Symposium on the History of Bilād al-Shām during the Early Islamic Period up to 40 A.H./640 A.D.* 5 vols. Amman: University of Jordan and Yarmouk University, 1987.

Bakhit, Muḥammad Adnan and Muḥammad Asfour, eds., *Proceedings of the Symposium on Bilād-al-Shām During the Byzantine Period.* 2 vols. Amman: University of Jordan and Yarmouk University, 1986, 1987.

Bartikian, Chr. [Hratz] M., Τὸ Βυζάντιον εἰς τὰς 'Αρμενικὰς Πηγάς. Byzantina Keimena kai Meletai, 18. Thessaloniki: Center for Byzantine Studies, 1981.

Basnage, J., *Thesaurus Monumentorum Ecclesiasticorum et Historicorum sive Henrici Canissi Lectiones Antiquae.* 2 vols. Antwerp: apud... Wetstenios, 1725.

Bates, Michael L., "History, Geography and Numismatics in the First Century of Islamic Coinage." *Revue Suisse de Numismatique* 65 (1986) 231–62.

Baynes, N. H., "The Military Operations of Emperor Heraclius," *United Services Magazine* n.s. 46 (1913) 526–33, 659–66; 47 (1913) 30–8, 195–201, 318–24, 401–12, 532–41, 665–79.

"The Successors of Justinian," *Cambridge Medieval History* 2: 263–301. Cambridge 1913; repr., 1926.

Beck, Hans-Georg, *Kirche und Theologische Literatur im byzantinischen Reich.* Munich: Beck, 1959.

Bowersock, Glen W., *Roman Arabia.* Cambridge, MA: Harvard, 1983.

Brandes, Wolfram, *Die Städte Kleinasiens im 7. und 8. Jahrhundert.* Berliner Byzantinische Arbeiten, 56. Berlin: Akademie-Verlag, 1989.

Brock, S. P., "North Mesopotamia in the Late Seventh Century. Book XV of John Bar Penkāyē's *Rīš Mellē.*" *JSAI* 9 (1987) 51–75.

"Syriac Sources for Seventh-Century History." *BMGS* 2 (1976) 17–36.

"Syriac Views of Emergent Islam." *Studies on the First Century of Islamic Society.* Papers on Islamic History, vol. 5, pp. 9–22, ed. by G. H. A. Juynboll. Carbondale: Southern Illinois University Press, 1982.

Brockelmann, Carl, *Geschichte der arabischen Litteratur. Supplementbände.* 2 vols. and 3 suppl. vols. Leiden: Brill, 1936–49.

Brooks, E. W., "The Arabs in Asia Minor (641–750), from Arabic Sources." *JHS* 18 (1898) 182–208.

"The Successors of Heraclius." *CMH* 4: 119–38. Cambridge 1923.

Brünnow, R. and A. von Domaszewski, *Die Provincia Arabia.* 3 vols. Strasburg: Trübner, 1904–9.

Buchwald, Wolfgang, Armin Hohlweg, and Otto Prinz, eds., *Tusculum-Lexikon griechischer und lateinischer Autoren des Altertums und Mittelalters.* 3rd edn. Munich, Zurich: Artemis, 1982.

Bury, *LRE*[1] = Bury, John B., *History of the Later Roman Empire from Arcadius to Irene (395 A.D. to 800 A.D.).* 2 vols. London: Macmillan, 1889; repr. Amsterdam: Hakkert, 1966.

Butler, Alfred, *The Arab Conquest of Egypt*, revised by P. M. Fraser. Oxford: Oxford University Press, 1978.

Caetani, *AI* = Caetani, Leone, *Annali dell'Islam*. 10 vols. in 12. Milan: U. Hoepli, 1905–26; repr., Hildesheim: G. Olms, 1972.

Cameron, Averil, "Images of Authority: Elites and Icons in Late Sixth-Century Byzantium." *Past and Present* 84 (1979) 3–35.

Canard, Marius, *Byzance et les musulmans du Proche Orient*. London: Variorum, 1973.

Miscellanea Orientalia. London: Variorum, 1973.

Chapot, Victor, *La Frontière de l'Euphrate de Pompée à la conquête arabe*. Bibliothéque des Ecoles françaises d'Athènes et de Rome, fasc. 99. Paris: Albert Fontemoing, ed., 1907.

Charanis, Peter, "The Armenians in the Byzantine Empire." *Byzsl* 22 (1961) 196–240.

Charles, Henri, *Le Christianisme des arabes nomades sur le limes et dans le désert syro-mésopotamien aux alentours de l'Hégire*. Paris: Librairie Ernest Leroux, 1936.

Christensen, Arthur, *L'Iran sous les Sassanides*. 2nd edn. Copenhagen, 1944; repr., Osnabrück: O. Zeller, 1971.

Clausewitz, Carl von, *On War*, trans. by P. Paret and M. Howard. Princeton: Princeton University Press, 1976.

Vom Kriege, ed. by Werner Hahlweg. 18th edn. Bonn: Ferd. Dümmlers Verlag, 1973.

Clover, Frank M. and R. S. Humphreys, eds., *Tradition and Innovation in Late Antiquity*. Madison: University of Wisconsin Press, 1989.

Conrad, Lawrence I., "al-Azdī's History of the Arab Conquests in Bilād al-Shām: Some Historiographical Observations." *1985 Bilād al-Shām Proceedings* 1: 28–62. (1985 papers publ. in) Amman: University of Jordan and Yarmouk University, 1987.

"The Plague in the Early Medieval Near East." unpub. Ph.D. diss., Princeton, 1981.

"Theophanes and the Arabic Historical Transmission: Some Indications of Intercultural Transmission." *ByzF* 15 (1990) 1–45.

Constantelos, Demetrios J., "The Moslem Conquests of the Near East as Revealed in the Greek Sources of the Seventh and Eighth Centuries." *Byzantion* 42 (1972) 325–57.

Cook, M. A., *Muhammad*. Oxford: Oxford University Press, 1983.

Couret, Alphonse, *La Palestine sous les empereurs grecs. 326–636*. Grenoble: F. Allier, 1869.

"La Prise de Jérusalem par les Perses en 614." *ROC* 2 (1897) 125–64.

Crone, Patricia, "Islam, Judaeo-Christianity, and Byzantine Iconoclasm." *JSAI* 2 (1980) 59–95.

Crone, Patricia and Michael A. Cook, *Hagarism: The Making of the Islamic World*. Cambridge: Cambridge University Press, 1977.

Dagron, Gilbert, "Byzance et le modèle islamique au Xe siècle. À propos des *Constitutions tactiques* de l'empereur Léon VI." *Comptes rendus, Académie des inscriptions et belles-lettres* (1983) 219–43.

"'Ceux d'en face': Les peuples étrangers dans les traités militaires byzantins." *TM* 10 (1986) 207–32.

Dédéyan, Gérard, *et al.*, eds., *Histoire des Arméniens*. Toulouse: Privat, 1982.

De Goeje, *Mémoire*[1] = De Goeje, M. J., *Mémoire sur le Fotouh's-Scham attribué à Abou Ismail al-Baçri. Mémoire d'histoire et de géographie orientales*. no. 2. 1st edn. Leiden: Brill, 1864.

De Goeje, *Mémoire*[2] = De Goeje, M. J., *Mémoire sur la conquête de la Syrie*. 2nd edn. Leiden: Brill, 1900.

Delehaye, Hippolyte, "Passio sanctorum sexaginta martyrum." *AB* 28 (1904) 289–307.

Déroche, Vincent, "L'Autenticité de l''Apologie contre les Juifs' de Léontios de Néapolis." *BCH* 110 (1986) 655–69.

Dillemann, Louis, *Haute Mésopotamie orientale et pays adjacents. Contribution à la géographie historique de la région, du Ve s. avant l'ère chrétienne au VIe de cette ère*. Institut français d'archéologie de Beyrouth, Bibliothèque archéologique et historique, T. 72. Paris: P. Geuthner, 1962.

Dölger, F., *Regesten der Kaiserurkunden des oströmischen Reiches von 565–1025*, facs. 1–5. Munich, Berlin: Verlag R. Oldenburg, 1924–65.

Donner, *EIC* = Donner, Fred M., *The Early Islamic Conquests*. Princeton: Princeton University Press, 1981.

"The Problem of Early Arabic Historiography in Syria," *1985 Bilād al-Shām Proceedings* 1: 1–27.

Downey, Glanville, *A History of Antioch in Syria*. Princeton University Press, 1961.

"The Persian Campaign in Syria in AD 540." *Speculum* 28 (1953) 340–8.

Duri, Abd al-Aziz, *The Rise of Historical Writing Among the Arabs*, ed. and trans. by Lawrance I. Conrad. Princeton: Princeton University Press, 1983.

Durliat, Jean, "Le Salaire de la paix sociale dans les royaumes barbares (Ve–VIe siècles)," in: Herwig Wolfram and Andreas Schwarcz, eds., *Anerkennung und Integration* 21–72.

Dussaud, René, *La Pénétration des arabes en Syrie avant l'Islam*. Paris: Geuthner, 1955.

Topographie historique de la Syrie antique et mediévale. Paris: Geuthner, 1927.

Excavations at Nessana. 3 vols. Colt Archaeological Institute. Princeton: Princeton University Press, 1950–62.

Fahd, Toufic, ed., *L'Arabie préislamique et son environnement historique et culturel*. Université des Sciences Humaines de Strasbourg. Travaux du Centre de Recherche sur le Proche-Orient et la Grèce Antiques, 10. Leiden: Brill, 1989.

Fiey, J. M., *Communautés syriaques en Iran et Irak des origines à 1552*. London: Variorum, 1979.

"The Last Byzantine Campaign into Persia and its Influence on the Attitude of the Local Populations Towards the Muslim Conquerors," *1985 Bilād al-Shām Proceedings* 1: 96–103. 1985 papers publ. in Amman: University of Jordan and Yarmouk University, 1987.

Foss, Clive, "The Persians in Asia Minor and the End of Antiquity." *EHR* 90 (1975) 721–47.

Freeman, Philip and David Kennedy, eds., *The Defence of the Roman and Byzantine East*, British Institute of Archaeology at Ankara, Monograph No. 8. Oxford: BAR International Series 297 (i and ii), 1986.

Fries, Nikolaus, *Das Heerwesen der Araber zur Zeit der Omaijiden nach Tabari.* Tübingen 1921.

Frolow, A., "La Vraie Croix et les expéditions d'Héraclius en Perse." *REB* 11 (1953) 88–105.

Garsoïan, Nina, *Armenia between Byzantium and the Sasanians.* London: Variorum, 1985.

La Géographie administrative et politique d'Alexandre à Mahomet. Actes du Colloque de Strasbourg, 14–16 juin 1979. Strasburg: Brill, 1981.

Gerö, Stephen, *Byzantine Iconoclasm during the Reign of Leo III with Particular Attention to the Oriental Sources.* Louvain 1973.

Ghawanmā, Yūsuf, *Ma'rakat al-Yarmūk.* Irbid 1985.

Giardina, Andrea, ed., *Società romana e impero tardoantico.* 4 vols. Rome, Bari: Edizioni Laterza, 1986.

Gibb, H. A. R., "Arab–Byzantine Relations under the Umayyad Caliphate." *DOP* 12 (1958) 219–33.

Gichon, M., "The Negev Frontier," in: *Israel and Her Vicinity in the Roman and Byzantine Periods.* Tel Aviv: Tel Aviv University, 1967.

Glubb, John Bagot, *The Great Arab Conquests.* London: Hodder and Stoughton, 1963.

Glucker, Carol A. M., *The City of Gaza in the Roman and Byzantine Periods.* Oxford: BAR International Series 325, 1987.

Goffart, Walter, "After the Zwettl Conference: Comments on the 'Techniques of Accommodation'," in: Herwig Wolfram and Andreas Schwarcz, eds., *Anerkennung und Integration* 73–85. Vienna: Verlag der Österreichischen Akademie der Wissenschaften, 1988.

Barbarians and Romans A.D. 418–584. Princeton: Princeton University Press, 1980.

Goubert, Paul, *Byzance avant l'Islam.* 2 vols. in 3. Paris: Geuthner, 1951–65.

Graf, David F., "The Saracens and the Defense of the Arabian Frontier." *BASOR* 229 (1978) 1–26.

Graf, Georg, *Geschichte der christlichen arabischen Literatur.* 5 vols. Studi e Testi, 118, 133, 146, 147, 172. Vatican City: Biblioteca Apostolica Vaticana, 1944–53.

Grierson, Philip, *Catalogue of the Byzantine Coins in the Dumbarton Oaks Collections and in the Whittemore Collection*, vol. 2, parts 1 and 2. Washington: Dumbarton Oaks, 1968.

Gutwein, Kenneth, *Third Palestine.* Washington: University Press of America, 1981.

Haase, C.-P., *Untersuchungen zur Landschaftsgeschichte Nordsyriens in der Umayyadenzeit.* Diss. Hamburg, pub. Kiel 1975.

Hage, Wolfgang, *Die syrisch-jakobitische Kirche in frühislamischer Zeit.* Wiesbaden: Otto Harrassowitz, 1966.

Hahn, Wolfgang, *Moneta Imperii Byzantini.* 3 vols. Österreichische Akademie der Wissenschaften, Denkschriften, Philosophische-Historische Klasse, 109, 148. Vienna: Verlag der Akademie, 1973–81.

Haldon, John, *Byzantine Praetorians: An Administrative, Institutional, Social Survey of the Opsikion and the Tagmata, c. 500–900.* Ποικίλα Βυζαντινά, 3. Bonn: R. Habelt, 1984.

Byzantium in the Seventh Century. Cambridge: Cambridge University Press, 1990.

"Recruitment and Conscription in the Byzantine Army *c.* 550–950," *Sitzungsberichte*. Österreichische Akademie der Wissenschaften, Philosophische-Historische Klasse, 357. Vienna: Verlag der Akademie, 1979.

Haldon, John and Hugh Kennedy, "The Arab–Byzantine Frontier in the Eighth and Ninth Centuries: Military Organisation and Society in the Borderlands." *ZRVI* 19 (1980) 79–116.

Hendy, Michael, *Studies in the Byzantine Monetary Economy, c. 300–1450*. Cambridge: Cambridge University Press, 1985.

Herrin, Judith, *The Formation of Christendom*. Princeton University Press, 1987.

Hild, Friedrich, *Das byzantinische Strassensystem in Kappadokien*. Vienna: Verlag der Akademie, 1977.

Hild, Friedrich and Marcell Restle, *Kappadokien* (*Kappadokia, Charsianon, Sebasteia und Lykandos*). Tabula Imperii Byzantini 2. Vienna: Verlag der Akademie, 1981.

Hill, D. R., "The Role of the Camel and the Horse in the Early Arab Conquest," in: V. J. Parry and M. E. Yapp, eds., *War, Technology and Society in the Middle East*, pp. 32–43. New York: Oxford University Press, 1977.

The Termination of Hostilities in the Early Arab Conquests A.D. 634–656. London: Luzac, 1971.

Honigmann, Ernst, *Die Ostgrenze des byzantinischen Reiches von 363 bis 1071*. Brussels: Editions de l'Institut de Philologie et d'Histoire Orientales, 1935; repr., 1961.

Isaac, Benjamin, *Limits of Empire*. Oxford: Clarendon, 1990.

Jandora, John W., "Developments in Islamic Warfare: The Early Conquests." *Studia Islamica* 64 (1986) 101–13.

Jones, *LRE* = Jones, A. H. M., *Later Roman Empire*. Oxford: Blackwell, 1964.

Jones, Marsden, "The *Maghāzī* Literature," in: *Arabic Literature to the End of the Umayyad Period*, ed. by A. F. L. Beeston, T. M. Johnstone, *et al.*, pp. 344–52. Cambridge: Cambridge University Press, 1983.

Juynboll, G. H. A., ed., *Studies on the First Century of Islamic Society*. Papers on Islamic History, 5. Carbondale: Southern Illinois University Press, 1982.

Kaegi, Walter, "The Annona Militaris in the Early Seventh Century," *Byzantina* 13 (1985) 591–6.

Kaegi, *ASRB* = Kaegi, Walter, *Army, Society and Religion in Byzantium*. London: Variorum, 1982.

Kaegi, *BMU* = Kaegi, Walter, *Byzantine Military Unrest, 471–843: An Interpretation*. Amsterdam and Las Palmas: Hakkert, 1981.

Kaegi, Walter, *Byzantium and the Decline of Rome*. Princeton: Princeton University Press, 1968.

"Changes in Military Organization and Daily Life on the Eastern Frontier," in: Ἡ Καθημερινὴ Ζωὴ στὸ Βυζάντιο. Τομὲς καὶ συνέχειες στὴν ἑλληνιστικὴ καὶ ρωμαϊκὴ παράδοση. Πρακτικὰ τοῦ Α΄ Συμποσίου. 15–17 Σεπτεμβρίου 1988 [*Daily Life in Byzantium*], ed. by Chrysa Maltezou, pp. 507–21. Athens: Hellenic Center for Byzantine Studies, 1989.

"The Frontier: Barrier or Bridge?," in: *Major Papers, The 17th International Byzantine Congress*, pp. 279–303. (New Rochelle, NY: A. D. Caratzas, 1986).

"Heraklios and the Arabs." *Greek Orthodox Theological Review* 27 (1982) 109–33.

"Late Roman Continuity in the Financing of Heraclius' Army." *XVI. Internationaler Byzantinisten-Kongress, Akten = JÖB* 32/2 (1982) 53–61.

"Observations on Warfare Between Byzantium and Umayyad Syria." *1987 Bilād al-Shām Proceedings* (English section) 2: 49–70.

Some Thoughts on Byzantine Military Strategy. Ball State University Hellenic Studies Lecture. Brookline, MA: Hellenic College Press, 1983.

"The Strategy of Heraclius." *1985 Bilād al-Shām Proceedings* 1: 104–15.

"Two Studies in the Continuity of Late Roman and Byzantine Military Institutions." *ByzF* 8 (1982) 87–113.

"Variable Rates of Change in the Seventh Century," in: *Tradition and Innovation in Late Antiquity*, ed. by Frank M. Clover, R. S. Humphreys, pp. 191–208. Madison: University of Wisconsin Press, 1989.

Καθηγητρία: *Essays Presented to Joan Hussey for Her 80th Birthday*. Camberley, Surrey: Porphyrogenitus, 1988.

Kamāl, Aḥmad 'Adl, *Ṭarīq ilā Dimashq. Futūḥ bilād al-Shām*. Beirut: Dār al-Nifash, 1982.

Karayannopulos, Johannes, *Dar Finanzwesen des frühbyzantinischen Staates*. Munich: R. Oldenbourg, 1958.

Karayannopulos-Weiss, *Quellenkunde* = Karayannopulos, Johannes and Günter Weiss, *Quellenkunde zur Geschichte von Byzanz (324–1453)*. 2 vols. Wiesbaden: Otto Harrassowitz, 1982.

Kawar, I. *See* Shahid.

Kennedy, D. L., *Archaeological Explorations on the Roman Frontier in North-East Jordan. The Roman and Byzantine Military Installations and Road Network on the Ground and From the Air*. Oxford: BAR International Series 134, 1982.

Kennedy, Hugh, "From *Polis* to *Madina*: Urban Change in Late Antique and Early Islamic Syria." *Past and Present* 106 (1985) 3–27.

"The Last Century of Byzantine Syria: A Reinterpretation." *ByzF* 10 (1985) 141–85.

Kmosko, M., "Das Rätsel des Pseudomethodius." *Byzantion* 6 (1931) 273–96.

Kolias, Taxiarchis G., *Byzantinische Waffen*. Vienna: Verlag der Österreichischen Akademie der Wissenschaften, 1988.

Köpstein, Helga and Friedhelm Winkelmann, eds., *Studien zum 7. Jahrhundert in Byzanz. Probleme der Herausbildung des Feudalismus*. Berliner Byzantinische Arbeiten, 47. Berlin: Akademie-Verlag, 1976.

Kremmydas, Vasiles, Chrysa Maltezou and Nikolaos Panayiotakis, eds., Ἀφιέρωμα στὸν Νίκο Σβορῶνο. 2 vols. Rethymnon: University of Crete, 1986.

Krivov, M. V., "Nekotor'ie vopros'i arabskogo zavoevaniya Sirii i Palestin'i." *VizVrem* 46 (1986) 88–89.

Krumbacher, Karl, *Geschichte der byzantinischen Litteratur*. 2nd edn. Munich 1897.

Kumpfmüller, J., *De Anastasio Sinaita*. Diss., Würzburg, 1865.

Kyrris, Costas P., *History of Cyprus*. Nicosia 1985.

Lapidus, Ira, "The Arab Conquests and the Formation of Islamic Society." in: *Studies on the First Century of Islamic Society*, ed. by G. H. A. Juynboll, pp. 49–72. Carbondale: Southern Illinois University Press. 1982.

Laurent, *Arménie*[2] = Laurent, Joseph, *L'Arménie entre Byzance et l'Islam depuis la conquête arabe jusqu'en 886*. 2nd edn., rev., enlarged by Marius Canard. Armenian Library of the Calouste Gulbenkian Foundation. Lisbon: Librairie Bertrand, 1980.

Liebeschuetz, J. H. W. G., *Antioch. City and Imperial Administration in the Later Roman Empire*. Oxford: Clarendon, 1972.

"The Defenses of Syria in the Sixth Century." *Beihefte der Bonner Jahrbücher* 38 = *Studien zu den Militärgrenzen Roms II* (1977) 461–71.

Lilie, Ralph-Johannes, *Die byzantinische Reaktion auf die Ausbreitung der Araber*. Miscellanea Byzantina Monacensia, 22. Munich 1976.

"Die zweihundertährige Reform. Zu den Anfängen der Themenorganisation im 7. und 8. Jahrhundert." *Byzsl* 45 (1984) 27–39, 190–201.

McEvedy, Colin and Richard Jones, *Atlas of World Population History*. London: Allen Lane, 1978.

MacMullen, Ramsay, *Corruption and the Decline of Rome*. New Haven: Yale, 1988.

Manandian, H. A., "Les Invasions arabes en Arménie." *Byzantion* 18 (1948) 163–92.

Mango, Cyril, *Byzantium: The Empire of New Rome*. New York 1980.

"Deux études sur Byzance et la Perse Sassanide." *TM* 9 (1985) 91–118.

"Who Wrote the Chronicle of Theophanes?" *ZRVI* 18 (1978) 9–18.

Martinez, Francisco Javier, "Eastern Christian Apocalyptic in the Early Muslim Period." Unpub. Ph.D. diss., Catholic University, 1985.

Mayerson, Philip, "The Desert of Southern Palestine According to Byzantine Sources." *Proc. Am. Philos. Soc.* 107.2 (1963) 160–72.

"The First Muslim Attacks on Southern Palestine." *TAPA* 95 (1964) 155–99.

"Saracens and Romans: Micro-Macro Relationships." *BASOR* 274 (1989) 71–81.

Miednikov, Nikolai A., *Palestina ot zavoevaniia eia arabami do krestov'ich pochodov po arabskim istochnikam*. 2 vols. in 4. St. Petersburg: V. Kirshbaum, 1902, 1897.

Miller, Karl, *Die peutingersche Tafel oder Weltkarte des Castorius*. Stuttgart 1916.

Miller, Konrad, *Itineraria Romana. Römische Reisewege an der Hand der Tabula Peutingeriana*. Stuttgart: Strecker and Strecker, 1916.

Mitchell, Stephen, ed., *Armies and Frontiers in Roman and Byzantine Anatolia*. British Institute of Archaeology at Ankara Monograph no. 5. Oxford: BAR International Series 156, 1983.

Moravcsik, G., *Byzantinoturcica*. 2 vols. 2nd edn. Berlin: Akademie Verlag, 1958.

Morony, Michael, *Iraq after the Muslim Conquest*. Princeton: Princeton University Press, 1984.

Morrisson, Cécile, "Le Trésor byzantin de Nikertai," *Revue belge de Numismatique* 118 (1972) 29–91.

Mouterde, R. and A. Poidebard, *Le Limes de Chalcis. Organisation de la steppe en Haute Syrie Romaine*. Paris: Geuthner, 1945.

Musil, A., *Arabia Petraea*. 3 vols. Vienna: Holder, 1907.

The Northern Hegaz. New York: American Geographical Society, 1926.

Nicolle, David C., *Early Medieval Islamic Arms and Armour*. Madrid 1976.

"The Military Technology of Classical Islam." Unpub. Ph.D. diss., University of Edinburgh, 1982.

Nöldeke, Theodor, "Die Ghassanidischen Fürsten aus dem Hause Gafna's." *Abhandlungen der königl. Preuss. Akad. d. Wiss. zu Berlin*, Philosophische-Historische Klasse 2: 1–63. 1887.

"Zur Geschichte der Araber im 1. Jahrhundert d. H. aus syrischen Quellen." *ZDMG* 29 (1875) 76–85.

Noth, Albrecht, "Abgrenzungsprobleme zwischen Muslimen und Nicht-Muslimen. Die 'Bedingungen 'Umars (*aš-šurūt al-'umariyya*)' unter einem anderen Aspekt gelesen." *JSAI* 9 (1987) 290–315.

"Die literarisch überlieferten Verträge der Eroberungszeit als historische Quellen für die Behandlung der unterworfenen Nicht-Muslime durch ihre neuen muslimischen Oberherren." *Studien zum Minderheitenproblem im Islam*, 1: *Bonner Orientalische Studien* n.s. 27/1 (1973) 282–314.

Quellenkritische Studien zu Themen, Formen, und Tendenzen Frühislamischer Geschichtsüberlieferung. Bonn: Selbstverlag der Orientalischen Seminars der Universität Bonn, 1973.

Oikonomides, Nicholas, *Les Listes de préséance byzantines des IXe et Xe siècles*. Paris 1972.

"Middle-Byzantine Provincial Recruits: Salary and Recruits," in: *Gonimos. Neoplatonic and Byzantine Studies Presented to Leendert G. Westerink at 75*, ed. by John Duffy and John Peradutto, pp. 121–36. Buffalo, NY: Arethusa, 1988.

"Les Premiers Mentions des thèmes dans la Chronique de Théophane." *ZRVI* 19 (1975) 1–8.

Olster, David, *The Politics of Usurpation in the Seventh Century: Rhetoric and Revolution in Byzantium*. Amsterdam, Las Palmas: Hakkert, 1993.

***Roman Defeat, Christian Response, and the Literary Construction of the Jew*. Philadelphia: University of Pennsylvania Press, 1994.**

Ostrogorsky, George, *History of the Byzantine State*. New Brunswick: Rutgers, 1969.

Oudin, Casimir, *Trias dissertationum criticarum*... Leiden: Luchtmans, 1717.

Papadopoulos-Kerameus, A., Ἀνάλεκτα Ἱεροσολυμιτικῆς Σταχυολογίας. 5 vols. St. Petersburg 1898.

Pargoire, J., "Les LX Soldats Martyrs de Gaza." *EO* 8 (1905) 40–3.

Parker, S. Thomas, "Peasants, Pastoralists, and *Pax Romana*: A Different View." *BASOR* 265 (1987) 35–51.

The Roman Frontier in Central Jordan. Oxford: BAR International Series 340, 1987.

Romans and Saracens: A History of the Arabian Frontier. Dissertation Series 6, ASOR. Winona Lake, IN, 1986.

Parry, V. J. and M. E. Yapp, eds., *War, Technology and Society in the Middle East*. New York: Oxford, 1977.

Pernice, Angelo, *L'Imperatore Eraclio. Saggio di storia bizantina*. Florence: Galletti and Cocci, 1905.

Pertusi, Agostino, "Ordinamenti militari, guerre in Occidente e teorie di guerre dei Bizantini (secc. VI–X)." *Settimane di Studio del Centro Italiano di Studio sull'*

Alto Medioevo. 15: Ordinamenti Militari in Occidente nell'Alto Medioevo, pp. 631–700. Spoleto 1968.

"La Persia nelle fonti bizantini del secolo VII." *Atti del convegno internazionale sul tema: La Persia nel Medioevo. Problemi attuali di Scienze e di Cultura, Quaderno* 160: 605–28. Rome: Accademia Nazionale dei Lincei, 1971.

Piccirillo, Michele, "Le iscrizioni di Um er-Rasas-Kastron Mefaa in Giordania I (1986–1987)." *Liber Annuus Studium Biblicum Franciscanum* 37 (1987) 177–239.

Chiese e mosaici della Giordania settentrionale. Studium Biblicum Franciscanum. Collectio Minor, 30. Jerusalem: Franciscan Printing House, 1981.

Pohl, Walter, *Die Awaren*. Munich: C. H. Beck, 1988.

Poidebard, A., *Le Trace de Rom dans le désert de Syrie*. 2 vols. Paris: Geuthner, 1934.

Posner, Nadine F., "The Muslim Conquest of Northern Mesopotamia: An Introductory Essay into its Historical Background and Historiography." Unpub. Ph.D. diss., New York University, 1985.

"Whence the Muslim Conquest of Northern Mesopotamia?," in: *A Way Prepared. Essays on Islamic Culture in Honor of Richard Bayly Winder*, ed. by Farhad Kazemi and R. D. McChesney, pp. 27–52. New York: New York University Press, 1988.

Proudfoot, Ann S., "The Sources of Theophanes for the Heraclian Dynasty." *Byzantion* 44 (1974) 367–439.

Rosenthal, Franz, *A History of Muslim Historiography*. 2nd edn. Leiden: Brill, 1968.

Rothstein, Gustav, *Die Dynastie der Lakhmiden in al-Ḥira: ein Versuch zur arabisch–persischen Geschichte zur Zeit der Sasaniden*. Berlin 1899; repr., Hildesheim: Olms, 1968.

Rotter, Ekkehart, *Abendland und Sarazenen. Das Okzidentale Araberbild und seine Entstehung im Frühmittelalter*. Studien zur Sprache, Geschichte und Kultur des islamischen Orients n.s. vol. 11. Berlin, New York: Walter de Gruyter, 1986.

Sartre, Maurice, *Bostra des origines à l'Islam*. Paris 1985.

Trois études sur l'Arabie romaine et byzantine. Collection Latomus, vol. 178. Brussels: Latomus, 1982.

Schick, Robert, *The Christian Communities of Palestine from Byzantine to Islamic Rule: A Historical and Archaeological Study*. Princeton: Darwin, 1995.

Schwarzlose, F. W., *Die Waffen der alten Araber aus ihren Dichtern dargestellt*. Leipzig 1886.

Segal, J. B., "Syriac Chronicles as Source Material for the History of Islamic Peoples," in: *Historians of the Middle East*, ed. by Bernard Lewis and P. M. Holt, pp. 246–58. London: Oxford University Press, 1962.

Sezgin, Fuat, *Geschichte des arabischen Schrifttums*. 9 vols. Leiden: Brill, 1967–84.

Shaban, Muhammad Abdulhayy, *Islamic History, A.D. 600–750 (A.H. 132). A New Interpretation*. Cambridge: Cambridge University Press, 1971

Shahid, *BAFIC* = Shahid, Irfan, *Byzantium and the Arabs in the Fifth Century*. Washington: Dumbarton Oaks, 1989.

Shahid, *BAFOC* = Shahid, Irfan, *Byzantium and the Arabs in the Fourth Century*. Washington: Dumbarton Oaks, 1984.

Shahid, *BSOBRI* = Shahid, Irfan, *Byzantium and the Semitic Orient Before the Rise of Islam*. London: Variorum, 1988.

Shahid, Irfan, "Heraclius and the Theme System: New Light from the Arabic." *Byzantion* 57 (1987) 391–403.

"Heraclius and the Theme System: Further Observations." *Byzantion* 59 (1989) 208–43.

Rome and the Arabs. Washington: Dumbarton Oaks, 1984.

Shboul, Ahmad, "Arab Attitudes Towards Byzantium: Official, Learned, Popular," in: Καθηγητρία: *Essay Presented to Joan Hussey for Her 80th Birthday*, pp. 111–28. Camberley, Surrey: Porphyrogenitus, 1988.

Shoufani, Elias S., *Al-Riddah and the Muslim Conquest of Arabia.* Toronto: University of Toronto Press, 1972.

Speck, Paul, *Das geteilte Dossier. Beobachtungen zu den Nachrichten über die Regierung des Kaisers Herakleios und die seiner Söhne bei Thophanes und Nikephoros.* Ποικίλα Βυζαντινά, 9. Bonn: Habelt, 1988.

Starr, Joshua, "Byzantine Jewry on the Eve of the Arab Conquest." *Journal of the Palestine Oriental Society* 15 (1935) 280–93.

Stein, Ernest, *Histoire du Bas-Empire.* 2 vols. Paris: Desclée de Brouwer, 1949–59.

Sternbach, Leo, *Analecta Avarica. Rozprawy, Polska Akademii Umieketnosci, Wydzial Filologiczny*, ser. 2, vol. 15, pp. 297–365. Cracow, 1900.

Stratos, Βυζάντιον = Stratos, Andreas, Τὸ Βυζάντιον στὸν Ζ' αἰῶνα. 6 vols. Athens: Estia, 1965–78.

Stratos, Zia, ed., Βυζάντιον. 'Αφιέρωμα στὸν 'Ανδρέα Στράτο. *Byzance. Hommage à Andreas Stratos. Byzantium. Tribute to Andreas Stratos.* 2 vols. Athens 1986.

Suermann, Harald, *Die geschichtstheologische Reaktion auf die einfallenden Muslime in der edessenischen Apokalyptik des 7. Jahrhunderts.* Europäische Hochschulschriften, ser. XXIII, Theology, vol. 256. Frankfurt, Bern, New York: Peter Lang, 1985.

Ṭalās, Muṣṭafa, *Sayf Allāh, Khālid ibn al-Walīd.* Damascus 1978.

Tchalenko, Georges, *Villages antiques de la Syrie du Nord: le massif du Belus à l'époque romaine.* 3 vols. Bibliothèque Archéologique et Historique, Institut Français d'Archéologie de Beyrouth, T. 50. 1953–8.

Ter-Ghewondyan, Aram, *The Arab Emirates in Bagratid Armenia*, trans. by Nina Garsoïan. Lisbon: Livraria Bertrand, 1976.

[Ter-Gevondian] *Armeniya i arabskii Khalafat.* Yerevan 1977.

[Ter-Ghévondian] "L'Arménie et la conquête arabe," in: *Armenian Studies/ Etudes Arméniennes in Memoriam Haïg Berbérian*, ed. by Dickran Kouymjian, pp. 773–92. Lisbon: Calouste Gulbernkian Foundation, 1986.

Thomson, R. W., "Muhammad and the Origin of Islam in Armenian Literary Tradition," in: *Armenian Studies/Etudes Arméniennes in Memoriam Haïg Berbérian*, ed. by Dickran Kouymjian, pp. 829–58. Lisbon: Calouste Gulbenkian Foundation, 1986.

Toumanoff, Cyril, *Studies in Christian Caucasian History.* Washington: Georgetown University Press, 1963.

Treadgold, Warren, *Byzantine State Finances in the Eighth and Ninth Centuries.* Boulder: East European Monographs, 121. Byzantine Series, 2. New York: Distributed by Columbia University Press, 1982.

"The Military Lands and the Imperial Estates in the Middle Byzantine Period." *Harvard Ukrainian Studies* [*OKEANOS*] 7 (1983) 619–31.

Trimingham, J. S., *Christianity Among the Arabs in Pre-Islamic Times*. London, New York, Beirut: Longman, Librairie du Liban, 1979.

Turtledove, Harry, "The Immediate Successors of Justinian: A Study of the Persian Problem..." Unpub. Ph.D. diss., UCLA, 1977.

Urman, Dan, *The Golan: A Profile of a Region During the Roman and Byzantine Periods*. Oxford: BAR International Series 269, 1985.

Vasiliev, A. A., *Byzance et les arabes*, trans. by H. Grégoire, M. Canard, *et al.* Corpus Bruxellense Historiae Byzantinae, 1, 2. 2 vols. in 3. Brussels 1935–50.

Walmsley, Alan G., "Administrative Structure and Urban Settlement in Filasṭīn and Urdunn." Unpub. Ph.D. diss., University of Sydney, Australia, 1987.

Wellhausen, Julius, "Die Kämpfe der Araber mit den Romäern in der Zeit der Umaijiden." *Nachrichten der Königl. Gesellschaft der Wissenschaften in Göttingen*, Philol.-Hist. Klasse, pp. 414–47.

Skizzen und Vorarbeiten. 6 vols. Berlin: Reimer, 1884–99.

Whitby, Michael, *The Emperor Maurice and His Historian*. Oxford: Clarendon Press, 1988.

Williams, Arthur Lukyn, *Adversus Judaeos: A Bird's Eye View of Christian Apologiae until the Renaissance*. Cambridge: Cambridge University Press, 1935.

Winkelmann, Friedhelm, "Ägypten und Byzanz vor der arabischen Eroberung." *Byzsl* 40 (1979) 161–82.

ed., *Byzanz im 7. Jahrhundert. Untersuchungen zur Herausbildung des Feudalismus*. Berliner Byzantinische Arbeiten, 48. Berlin: Akademie-Verlag, 1978.

Quellenstudien zur herrschenden Klasse von Byzanz im 8. und 9. Jahrhundert. Berlin: Akademie-Verlag, 1987.

"Die Quellen zur Erforschung des monoenergetisch-monotheletischen Streites." *Klio* 69 (1987) 515–59.

Wirth, Eugen, *Syrien. Eine geographische Landeskunde*. Darmstadt: Wissenschaftliche Buchgesellschaft, 1971.

Wolfram, Herwig and Andreas Schwarcz, eds., *Anerkennung und Integration. Zu den wirtschaftlichen Grundlagen der Völkerwanderungszeit 400–600*. Vienna: Verlag der Österreichischen Akademie der Wissenschaften, 1988.

Wroth, W., *Catalogue of the Imperial Byzantine Coins in the British Museum*. London 1908.

Zakos, Veglery, *BLS* = Zacos, G., A. Veglery, and J. Nesbitt, *Byzantine Lead Seals*. Basel, 1972–85.

MAPS

Syrian Topographic Map Series 1:200,000, "Fīq-Haifa," produced at Damascus between 1945 and 1984.

PEF Palestine

Survey of Palestine 1935. Scale 1:100,000.

Israel Series 1:100,000. Scale 1:100,000. Tel Aviv: Survey of Israel, 1981.

INDEX

Ramla, 98
Raqqa (Callinicum), 42, 147–8, 160, 171, 172, 193, 240
recruitment, 34–9, 43, 52–5, 79–80, 86, 102, 110, 131, 150–1, 154, 157–8, 175, 181–3, 268, 271
Red Sea, 44, 81
Reshtuni, Theodore, 182, 185, 189, 190, 191, 193–7, 202–4
resistance against Muslims, 12–14, 50, 51, 71, 77, 85, 199, 268, 280
Rhodes, 248
Ridda wars, 62, 83
Romania, 205, 211, 228
Rūbīl al-Armanī, 187

Saborios, 203, 227, 228, 229
sakellarios, 34–6, 38, 59, 100, 112, 119, 217, 256–8, 281, 283, 287
Salīḥ, 79
Salmān b. Rabī'a b. Yazīd b. 'Umar, 196
Sama, 240
Samaritan communities, 16, 30, 63
Samosata, 148, 149n., 179, 183, 191
Samuel of Ani, 89
Sayf b. 'Umar, 10, 22, 78, 127, 130, 132, 148, 152, 154, 155, 250
Scythopolis, 67, 110, 114
Sebēos, 2, 11, 21, 66, 85, 86, 95, 126, 187, 195, 199, 213–14
Sergios, commander at Dāthin, 63, 88–90, 93–4, 98n., 211, 273
Sergios, general of rebel Saborios, 227–8
Shahīd, I., 20
Shahrbaraz, 66, 72–3, 75n., 117, 129, 137, 152, 153, 156
Shahryāḏ b. Farūn, 172, 187
Sinai, 90, 91, 96, 139, 186, 278
Siroes (Kawadh), 27, 66, 118, 259
Sision, 240
Sixth Ecumenical Council, 218–20, 229
Skutariotes, Theodore, 256, 257
Slavs, 30, 42, 285
Smbat, 194
soldiers' properties, land grants, 35, 37, 283
Sophronius, 5, 21, 75, 76, 94, 101, 109, 210–11, 265
sparapet, 190
statistics, 12, 16, 27, 30, 40, 131, 176, 182
stipends, 92, 256
stratagems, 94, 130
Strategikon, 5, 58, 123, 124, 126, 127, 275
strategy, 2, 13, 14, 25, 30, 56, 58, 59, 60, 61, 77, 88, 101–10, 128–30, 136, 146, 157–8, 165, 178–9, 206, 236, 239, 243, 247, 248, 258–60, 273–4, 278
Stratos, A., 192, 253n.
succession crisis, Heraclian, 16, 65, 68, 182, 190, 261–2
ṣulḥ, 159–60, 163
Sycamina, 94
Syria, 1, 4, 12–19, 25–7, 31–153, 156–69, 172, 173, 176–83, 185–90, 192–200, 205, 206, 213, 236, 238–40, 243, 244, 246–8, 253, 255, 257, 258, 259, 260, 262, 265–70, 272, 273, 274, 276–9, 282–6

al-Ṭabarī, 8, 11, 20, 78, 126, 135, 140, 152, 172–3, 249, 250
Tabūk, 67, 80, 82
tactics, 2, 13, 56, 59, 61, 81, 100, 130, 143, 175, 179, 199, 200, 201, 206, 236, 262, 264, 273
Takrīt, 42, 154, 155n., 267
Tall al-Jumū'a, 142–3
Tanūkh, 11, 79, 178
Taron, 193
Taurus, 47, 60, 61, 63, 148, 149, 179, 180, 237, 238, 239, 240, 243, 252, 274, 281
taxation, taxes, 18, 19, 36–8, 51, 90, 107, 124, 140, 144, 167, 173, 177, 256–8, 283, 284, 287
Tella, 160
themes, thematic institutions, Byzantine, 77, 105, 176–7, 227–9, 279–85
Theodore, brother of Heraclius, 67, 81, 85–6, 98, 99–100, 110–11, 129, 133, 156, 158, 160, 278
Theodore, commander for Constans II, 194
Theodore of Sykeon, 212
Theodore Trithurios, 35, 100, 112, 118, 119, 120, 131–2, 137, 161, 257, 278
Theodore, *vicarius*, 34, 71, 72, 79, 86
Theodosiopolis (Erzurum), 76, 159, 181, 185, 191, 195, 197, 227
Theodosiopolis (Rās al-'Ayn), 150, 153, 160, 172, 187
Theodosius I, 1, 26, 63
Theophanes, 3, 21, 72, 90, 92, 96, 107, 133, 138, 159, 160, 162, 167, 169, 173, 174, 195, 227, 228, 258
Theophylact Simocatta, 32, 53, 57, 116, 212, 258n.
Thessalonica, 230, 265
Thracesians, Thracesian Theme, 42, 282n.
thughūr, 242
Thuma, 194
Tiberias, Lake, 114
Tiflis, 166
Tigris, River, 42, 147, 154, 191, 267
Trajan, 166
travelers, 30, 101, 186n.
Trophies of Damascus, 220